The Hidden History of the Vietnam War

*Combined Fleet Decoded: The Secret History of American
Intelligence and the Japanese Navy in World War II*
*Keepers of the Keys: A History of the National Security Council
from Truman to Bush*
Valley of Decision: The Siege of Khe Sanh (with Ray W. Stubbe)
*Presidents' Secret Wars: CIA and Pentagon Covert
Operations from World War II to Iranscam*
Pentagon Games
The Soviet Estimate: U.S. Intelligence and Soviet Strategic Forces
*The Sky Would Fall: The Secret U.S. Bombing Mission to Vietnam,
1954*

JOHN
PRADOS

The Hidden History of the Vietnam War

CHICAGO
Ivan R. Dee
1995

Maps by Victor Thompson

Library of Congress Cataloging-in-Publication Data:
Prados, John.
    The hidden history of the Vietnam War / John Prados.
        p.   cm.
    Includes bibliographical references and index.
    ISBN 1-56663-079-7
    1. Vietnamese Conflict, 1961–1975—United States. I. Title.
DS558.P73   1995
959.704'3373—dc20   94-46662

For Danielle

THAT HER GENERATION MAY SEE EVEN MORE SHARPLY

Contents

Preface

Accounts of the Persian Gulf War of 1991, where they discuss President George Bush's initial commitment and the rationales of his military leaders, frequently refer to a need for intervention to be "decisive," to occur instantly and in overwhelming force. Usually the sentence that follows makes the point that this requirement for "decisive" military action is a lesson of the Vietnam War. Proposed, accepted— and the reader moves on to other things. But like much conventional wisdom, the notion of "decisive" warfare in Vietnam is a latter-day construct. In fact, *many* of the conventional "lessons" of Vietnam are not that at all. They are someone's retrospective view of what should have been the strategy pursued in the Vietnam War.

This book is about the lessons of Vietnam, about hindsight and foresight and strategies lost and won. It is also about history—what happened in Vietnam and the forces that operated on certain events. Along the way we try to tell some stories as well, stories of brave mountaineers in South Vietnam and Laos, of Americans facing fierce battles and hardships, of presidents facing stark decisions and of their thinking, and why things turned out the way they did. We try to shed new light on neglected corners of the Vietnam experience, such as the actions of intelligence agencies and operators, but we do not neglect the main historical events of the war. Yet this is not an overview history of Vietnam; no attempt is made here to present an exhaustive panorama of the conflict. Rather, the focus is on specific microcosms of the war, special subjects relevant to the "lessons" of Vietnam. We try to show that some supposed lessons of the war, based on preferred winning strategies, flow from historical assertions whose truth is not so self-evident. Finally, we postulate some tests that a proposed winning strategy should have to meet.

This examination of hidden facets of the Vietnam War covers some ground that is completely fresh, some that is relatively familiar, and some that is well trodden. General outlines of the war have been recounted as necessary to provide a framework for particular aspects. In some well-known areas, such as the incidents in the Gulf of Tonkin, we have tried to add perspective by approaching the subject in novel ways, in this case the notion of "mysteries" surrounding the incidents. Some chapters originated as essays illuminating given strategic claims, others as narratives of events or profiles of people affected by the Vietnam experience. A number of these chapters first appeared in slightly different form in *The VVA Veteran,* the monthly magazine of the Vietnam Veterans of America, Inc. These have been updated where necessary with recent research results. Several portions of the book are published here for the first time, and a few are collected from other places.

Regardless of provenance, the issues raised here are of enduring and legitimate concern. The "lessons" of Vietnam are frequently invoked everywhere America is engaged abroad. In United States interventions in Grenada, Nicaragua, Panama, the Persian Gulf, Somalia, and Haiti in the 1980s and 1990s, as well as in would-be interventions like that in Bosnia and the former Yugoslavia, we are constantly reminded that the lessons of Vietnam require America to act a certain way. What if the "lessons" are wrong, or misunderstood? Can lessons of Vietnam be valid for another place and time? There has been too much assertion of purported lessons, and not enough focused analysis of the basis of those claims. Here we try to use history to reveal some of the flaws in conventional wisdom, and make a start at reining in the more extravagant claims. The beginning of wisdom is to double-check the conventions.

Both individually and collectively, many persons are responsible for the good things in this book. I particularly want to thank the wonderful archivists and staff of the National Archives and the Lyndon Johnson and Dwight Eisenhower libraries as well as the Nixon Library Project. David Humphrey and Regina Greenwell deserve special commendation, as do all those who contributed their insight in interviews. This book would not exist but for the vision of editors Mark Perry, Mokie Pratt Porter, Gayle Garmise, and Ivan R. Dee. David Marr and William R. Roff sparked my interest in Southeast Asia at a relatively tender age; to them an extra thanks. All the mistakes and errors in this book are my own.

J. P.

Washington, D.C.
January 1995

AID   Agency for International Development
ARVN   Army of the Republic of Vietnam
BLT   Battalion Landing Team
BOQ   Bachelor Officers' Quarters
CDEC   Combined Documents Exploitation Center
CDNI   Committee for the Defense of National Interests
CI   Counterinsurgency
CIA   Central Intelligence Agency
CICV   Combined Intelligence Center Vietnam
CIDG   Civilian Irregular Defense Group
CINCPAC   Commander-in-Chief Pacific
CIO   Central Intelligence Organization (South Vietnamese
    CIA)
CNO   Chief of Naval Operations
COMINT   Communications Intelligence
COMSEC   Communications Security
CORDS   Civil Operations and Revolutionary Development
    Support
CTT   Counter-Terror Team
DRV   Democratic Republic of Vietnam (North Vietnam)
DZ   Drop Zone
FAR   *Forces Armées du Royaume* (Royal Laotian Armed
    Forces)
FOB   Forward Operating Base
GI   Government Issue (American soldier or his
    equipment)
GVN   Government of Vietnam (South Vietnam)
HES   Hamlet Evaluation Survey
ICEX   Intelligence Coordination and Exploitation
JCS   Joint Chiefs of Staff (U.S. high command)
JGS   Joint General Staff (South Vietnamese high command)
KIA   Killed in Action
LAAW   Light Antitank Assault Weapon
LLDB   *Luc Luong Dac Biet* (South Vietnamese Special
    Forces)

xi

LS	Lima Site
LZ	Landing Zone
MACSOG	Military Assistance Command Studies and Observation Group
MACV	Military Assistance Command Vietnam
MAF	Marine Amphibious Force
MAROP	Maritime Operation
MIA	Missing in Action
MP	Military Police
MR	Military Region
MRTTH	Military Region Tri-Thien-Hue (one North Vietnamese military region)
NIE	National Intelligence Estimate
NLF	National Liberation Front
NSA	National Security Agency
NSAM	National Security Action Memorandum
NSSM	National Security Study Memorandum
NVA	North Vietnamese Army
OB	Order of Battle
OCO	Office of Civil Operations
OPCON	Operational Control
PAT	People's Action Team
PEO	Program Evaluation Office
PIRAZ	Positive Identification Radar Advisory Zone
POL	Petroleum, Oil, Lubricants
PT	Patrol Torpedo (boat)
RD	Revolutionary Development (or Rural Development)
RDF	Radio Direction Finder
REMF	Rear-Echelon Mother-fuckers (colloquial acronym of American GIs in South Vietnam)
SEAL	Sea-Air-Land (U.S. Navy Special Forces)
SF	Special Forces (Green Berets)
SGU	Special Guerrilla Unit
SNIE	Special National Intelligence Estimate
USAF	United States Air Force
USASA	United States Army Security Agency
USN	United States Navy
VC	Viet Cong
VNAF	(South) Vietnamese Air Force
VVA	Vietnam Veterans of America
VVAW	Vietnam Veterans Against the War

A NOTE ON MILITARY UNIT NAMES

In some places this book provides fairly detailed accounts of battles and military actions. In these cases we follow a standard format in identifying military units: first a subordinate designation, if any (such as "Second Battalion"), then the parent formation (e.g., "Thirty-fourth Armored Regiment"), so that a full title might read, "Second Battalion, Thirty-fourth Armored Regiment." Except for numbered "corps" or "military regions," which are always South Vietnamese, a South Vietnamese (ARVN) or North Vietnamese (NVA) unit is also identified by nationality.

Victory is no longer a truth. It is only a word
to describe who is left alive in the ruins.
—Lyndon Johnson, 1964

The Hidden History of the Vietnam War

NORTH
VIETNAM

*South
Vietnam
&
Cambodia*

Tchepone
Quang Tri
Khe Sanh
Hue

Da Nang

I CORPS
Kham Duc

LAOS
Quang
Ngai
Ngok Tavak
Duc
Pho

Kontum

Pleiku

Qui Nhon

SOUTH
VIETNAM

II CORPS

CAMBODIA
Ban Me Thuest

Kratie

Nha Trang

Pnom Penh
Snoul
Cam Ranh
Prey Veng
"The Fishhook"

III CORPS
Hau Nghia

Sihanoukville
(Kompong Som)
"Parrot's
Beak"
Long
An
Vung Tau

Can Tho

**IV
CORPS**

1   The First American Prisoners

When does a war begin? When did the Vietnam War begin for the United States? Perhaps it was toward the end of World War II, when an ailing President Franklin D. Roosevelt failed in his intention to place Indochina under a United Nations trust. Perhaps Harry Truman was the president at the creation, for it was he who permitted France to return to the former French Indochina, and who later extended U.S. diplomatic recognition and military aid to the states of Indochina "associated" with France. A common answer to the origins question is that President John F. Kennedy got the United States into the Vietnam War by aggressively pursuing so-called counterinsurgency, a fight against Vietnamese Communist guerrillas, and by expanding the U.S. military presence and level of commitment in Vietnam. Some people date the beginning of the war from the moment the United States sent ground combat forces to South Vietnam, and that happened under President Lyndon B. Johnson.

While there are many possible answers to the question of origins of the American involvement, and myriad explanations for why presidents made the decisions they did, in terms of dates it is undeniable that Harry Truman, by initiating U.S. military aid to Indochina in May 1950, took a giant step toward an American war in Vietnam. Still, dates can be misleading; if we wished to measure involvement by extension of military aid pure and simple, for example, one could easily go back to 1945. The French troops who returned to Vietnam at that time had much American equipment, as did British troops who preceded them and left their surplus stocks for the French, with American approval. American equipment that had been stockpiled on Okinawa for a planned but finally unnecessary invasion of Japan in 1945–1946

3

is also said to have gotten to Vietnam. And then there are the five thousand rifles provided to the Vietnamese Communists (then called Viet
Minh) by the Office of Strategic Services (OSS), the World War II forerunner of the Central Intelligence Agency. Certain U.S. parachute
equipment was suddenly declared surplus and sent to Vietnam for the
French in 1947, despite an official embargo on assistance to France in
Indochina imposed at that time. The embargo was ignored again in
1949 when the U.S. sold France several naval craft which French
sailors picked up on the West Coast and sailed directly across the Pacific, eventually reaching Vietnam.

By then France and Vietnam had been at war since December 1946.
The conflict had grown out of France's attempt to reestablish her colonial relationship with Indochina (which had been terminated by Japanese action during World War II), opposing Vietnam's determination to
be free. Vietnamese nationalism had embodied itself in a government
with which the French negotiated their return in 1945 and 1946, but
France had proved unable or unwilling to accord Vietnam much more
than the cosmetic appearance of independence, with French officials still
exercising the real power in the country. This formula was unacceptable
to Vietnamese nationalists, among whom the leading faction were the
Communists of Ho Chi Minh. In November 1946 uneasy cooperation
degenerated into a bloody incident in which many Vietnamese were
killed at Haiphong. A month later full-scale war broke out.

One way to measure military involvement is by dispatch of forces,
and by that standard the United States again can be said to have entered the Vietnam War under Harry Truman, who sent two hundred
air force specialists to Vietnam on temporary duty in January 1953.
This project involved helping the French air force improve its maintenance of aircraft used in the war the French were fighting at the time.
This first step was a tentative one, however, and Dwight Eisenhower
soon recalled the airmen to their regular assignments.

It was President Eisenhower who broadened and deepened the
American involvement in the Vietnam conflict, and took a series of
steps that conditioned future U.S. policies in Southeast Asia in a way
that made war in the future much less avoidable. In fact, the first
American prisoners of war were seized not under John Kennedy or
even Lyndon Johnson but during the Eisenhower administration. This
is their story, the beginning of a commitment that became an American
quagmire.

■ American technicians who came to help the French with their airplanes were separate and distinct from the Military Assistance Advisory Group (MAAG) established in Indochina August 2, 1950, when the first 10 U.S. officers arrived. There were 70 before the end of that year, and a table of organization in 1951 provided for 128 positions. The MAAG force remained constant, even during 1953, when President Eisenhower agreed to furnish additional support for the "Navarre Plan," a new military strategy developed by the French commander-in-chief designed to restore the military situation and create favorable conditions for negotiations with the Viet Minh. In early 1954 when, as a result of operations conducted under his plan, General Navarre became embroiled in a bitter siege of a large French post at Dien Bien Phu, there were 117 Americans with MAAG and 26 more with the attaché office at the United States legation.

The battle of Dien Bien Phu posed special problems for the French air force because that position was situated in a mountain valley near the Laotian border. The road to Dien Bien Phu had not been maintained for years and traversed miles of Viet Minh–held territory. Thus all supplies for Dien Bien Phu had to go by air, and once the battle began in March 1954, had to be delivered by parachute as well. Moreover, the only possible source of reinforcement for the French garrison was paratroops by air transport, and the only potential augmentation for the firepower of French forces were combat aircraft flying from bases in the Red River Delta of northern Vietnam or from Da Nang (then called Tourane) on the central Vietnamese coast. The strain upon French air assets quickly became unbearable. When General Paul Ely, French armed forces chief of staff, visited Washington a week after the battle began, he hoped to persuade Eisenhower to send more airplanes to the French, transports as well as fighters and bombers.

By then the die had already been cast for American servicemen. Even before Dien Bien Phu the French had been pestering Washington with claims that they were unable to provide sufficient ground crews for their planes in Indochina, along with complaints that having to service all those older piston-engine aircraft in Vietnam was hindering their transition to a modern, jet-powered air force—the type needed to help defend Western Europe against a putative Russian military threat. Washington had gone along with the French appeals and, in a highly classified operation code-named Paul Revere, moved special detachments of airmen to Vietnam beginning in February 1954. Eighteen C-119 "Flying Boxcar" transports and three huge C-124 "Globemasters" transferred the American airmen from Clark Air Base in the Philippines to Vietnam. The deployment was supported thereafter by scheduled air service—three flights a week (later four) to Da Nang, and three to Cat Bi, a French airfield near Hanoi. By May the flights had moved 10,354 passengers and 7,489 tons of freight.

Tom Julian was a young C-119 pilot with the 483rd Troop Carrier Wing at that time, based at Ashiya in Japan. For months, since the fall of 1953, he had been aware that buddies would quietly disappear for a few weeks at a time. They had in fact been sent to Clark to fly Indochina transport missions code-named Iron Age. One day the squadron operations officer, a big Texan named Yarbrough, told Julian his turn had come. Lieutenant Julian spent the next few months successively at Clark, at Cat Bi, at Clark again for more of the Iron Age flights, and then at Da Nang, dividing his time between helping maintain C-119s to be flown by French or Central Intelligence Agency (Civil Air Transport) crews, and flying the Clark-to-Vietnam run himself. Beginning in April 1954 the Iron Age pilots at Clark were grouped into an ad hoc 816th Troop Carrier Squadron. So numerous were they that 816th people took over the local bars and blemished Clark's base safety record, disrupting normal activities by driving their Vietnam-produced Vespa motorbikes all over. An apocryphal story, which may be true, is that Clark's commander told his morning staff meeting that the worst thing that had ever happened there was the Japanese surprise attack of December 1941, and the second worst the advent of the 816th Squadron.

At Clark Air Base the Vietnam support mission involved inconvenience but little more than administrative headaches. For Americans sent to Vietnam there were more palpable dangers. Detachments of Americans were posted to three airfields in northern Vietnam, including Cat Bi, Do Son, and Kien An, and to Da Nang in central Vietnam. The first significant incident occurred at Gia Lam, outside Hanoi, where, at about 2:30 in the morning on March 4, Viet Minh commandos put gasoline cans with explosives attached under the engines of a number of aircraft. Ten C-47 planes, military versions of the venerable Douglas DC-3, were wrecked. A strike at Haiphong followed three days later, when the Viet Minh staged a spectacular raid at Cat Bi. It happened that U.S. air force officers, staying at Haiphong's Hotel de Paris, staged a party that night for their forty-four enlisted men who had much poorer quarters. A huge amount of champagne flowed at the party held in the hotel's inner court, surrounded by several floors of veranda, cream-colored masonry, and green window shutters. Thus the Americans were away when Viet Minh infantry struck Cat Bi two hours before dawn. The attack led to a pitched battle with the vaunted French Sixth Colonial Paratroop Battalion of Major Marcel Bigeard, a unit that would soon be thrown into the maelstrom of Dien Bien Phu.

Even worse nightmares awaited the 4 officers and 103 airmen at Do Son, Haiphong's other satellite airfield. French commanders responded to the Gia Lam and Cat Bi raids by establishing prohibited zones around both Cat Bi and Do Son, but a Viet Minh battalion ignored such administrative decrees on the night of March 16 to cross a branch of the Red River and cut the Do Son–Haiphong road. With the battle of Dien Bien Phu at an early crescendo that night, Do Son quaked in fear of immediate Viet Minh assault. The American detachment leader armed his airmen and posted them along the beach and part of the Do Son perimeter. Men unable to handle weapons took cover in an airfield drainage ditch. Fortunately the Viet Minh made no direct attack, and the next day the French sent three rifle companies to strengthen Do Son's defenses.

American technicians had first been sent to help the French on the explicit understanding that they would be protected and not have to fight, not to mention that they were to be only a temporary expedient pending French government dispatch of sufficient mechanics to replace them. When the Eisenhower administration announced its initiative to reporters during February it emphasized the noncombat role and the date of June 15, by which all the airmen were to be out of Vietnam. The attacks on Red River delta airfields called into question the safety of the Americans, while the French also began to talk about their inability to produce aircraft mechanics of their own. By the time of General Ely's late March visit to Washington, it was clear that both American safety and the June 15 termination date were no longer firm. With Ely's requests for even more aircraft, it was becoming apparent that more American airmen would also be required. President Eisenhower showed some interest in hiring civilian mechanics under the U.S. aid program to replace air force personnel, but this would not be the path actually taken. Instead the decision was to further increase the U.S. air force contingent (as well as the 8081st Service Unit, which comprised army specialists in parachute delivery and packing) while regrouping the Americans at the safer base of Da Nang.

All these decisions were taken separately from another track of U.S. policy, the planning for possible bombing, including use of atomic weapons, and large-scale military intervention in support of the French. Eisenhower considered, and came close to ordering, that intervention, but ultimately he shied away. The agreement to send American military personnel to help the French was, to a degree, intended as a demonstration that the U.S. stood at France's side even though Washington was refusing the larger intervention. Thus by April 1954 the number of U.S. personnel in assistance detachments had grown to 399, almost precisely double the original number agreed, and by the end of May there were 462 American technicians, counting two civilians, in Vietnam.

The regrouping of the American personnel to Da Nang proceeded apace throughout this period. French base commander Lieutenant Colonel François Grogshillier accepted the Americans with more or less good grace and assigned them their own section of the facility. The initial U.S. Indochina air commander was Lieutenant Colonel Walter A. Miller of Waynesburg, Ohio, who brought airmen selected from the Far East Air Force bases at Tachikawa and Iwakuni in Japan as well as Clark in the Philippines. Miller started with nothing, or at least very little, and had his men working sixteen-hour days repairing hangars in addition to planes, and constructing wooden barracks buildings where the men could live under conditions slightly better than primitive. The Da Nang facility quickly acquired the nickname "Little America."

Possibilities at Da Nang in those days were strictly limited. Not only were there no living quarters, recreation was another problem. Americans of the 1950s were not enthusiastic about soccer, a popular sport in France, and Frenchmen had little interest in, and had made no provision for, sports like basketball or baseball. Colonel Miller had to make appeals to the U.S. Far East Command for sports equipment to be furnished at Da Nang. Not much came by the regular air flights, whose pilots used to joke they mostly carried bales of barbed wire. At length a special collection within the Far East Air Force yielded a modicum of recreational equipment, which was carried aboard Captain Doyle G. Donaho's light carrier *USS Saipan,* in addition to a load of helicopters and fighter-bombers for delivery to the French navy and air force. Originally slated to deliver the aircraft to Cat Bi, following a port call at Hong Kong the *Saipan* was rerouted to Da Nang, where she arrived on April 18, escorted by an American destroyer and a French corvette. At Da Nang the French aircraft carrier *Arronmanches* lay ready to take the Corsair fighters from the *Saipan,* while helicopters (and material for "Little America") were landed directly at Da Nang. The *Arromanches* sailed off to war, her Corsairs flying through the last desperate days of the siege of Dien Bien Phu.

On the surface at least, Da Nang lay relatively serene amid the con-

flict. But, as the French would soon be obliged to admit, the only secure area in the region lay within the perimeter of the base itself. Even
the nearby town was not protected or defended in any way, and the
Vietnamese there could all be Viet Minh for all anybody knew. Now as
Americans regrouped to Da Nang they were lectured on appropriate
security measures by the Texan from Ashiya, Major Yarbrough, an
early leader of the U.S. detachment. But the French gate guards had orders not to halt any vehicle bearing Americans, the Americans had
myriad small needs that had to be met in town, and after awhile what
caution they had dulled with the seeming calm of the place. It was just
a matter of time before problems arose.

Da Nang hopped for a few days immediately following the fall of
Dien Bien Phu on May 7. Then an emergency airlift ordered by Washington brought a new battalion of French paratroops from Europe directly to Da Nang, where they were supplemented by Vietnamese
recruits and put into the field. The U.S. planes left bearing wounded
soldiers from Dien Bien Phu whom the Viet Minh had permitted to be
evacuated. Then Da Nang settled down, and "Little America" with it.
A new commander arrived for the Da Nang detachment, Major J. C.
Mitchell. Walter Miller also came to the end of his temporary duty as
chief of all the American airmen in Vietnam and was replaced by Lieutenant Colonel Donald E. Pricer, seconded from the 483rd Troop Carrier Wing.

It was just a few days after the arrival of Major Mitchell that trouble came to Da Nang. It happened at China Beach, so well known to
Americans a decade later and where some of the first American combat troops landed in Vietnam. Cooped up in "Little America," with
strictly limited possibilities for relaxation, some of the servicemen decided to take matters into their own hands. On the afternoon of June
14 five Americans, three from the air force detachment and two army
specialists from the 8081st unit, took off for China Beach in a three-
quarter truck the French had loaned to the U.S. army. It was a typical
swimming outing, something that had been done before, although at
other times there had been security guards on China Beach.

What happened next cannot be reconstructed with certainty due to
the absence of direct testimony. A board of inquiry met a few days
later, presided over by the U.S. air attaché in Indochina, Colonel
Harold E. Kofahl, and observed by the senior U.S. officer in Vietnam,
Lieutenant General John W. O'Daniel. But the investigation had to
make do with the accounts of the French gate guards and a few Vietnamese villagers, of whom only one, a teenage boy, had even seen the

Americans. Everyone else was merely reporting things heard from others. Pieced together from these sources the story went like this: The Americans had sped through the air base gate in their truck. French guards did not stop them and asked no questions. The Americans had gone to the beach near My Khe village. Viet Minh soldiers had possibly been attracted to the scene by the French truck, and they may have thought the Americans wanted to surrender because white T-shirts were seen draped over the hood of the vehicle, where most likely the Americans had put them to dry. The Viet Minh took the Americans' clothes, then marched them off at gunpoint. A My Khe woman reported at least one of the prisoners crying; another villager saw them among a larger group of prisoners.

The Americans were not reported missing until roll call at 8 a.m. the next morning. A search began, starting with My Khe, just a mile and a half south of Da Nang. Major Mitchell got a plane into the air to scout for signs of the men. From Saigon the MAAG chief, General O'Daniel, ordered intensive ground-search efforts. To help he sent Major Edward G. Lansdale, recently arrived chief of MAAG and CIA psychological warfare. Lansdale, a character who would become familiar to further generations of Americans, had no luck on the Da Nang search mission. He rode one of several jeeps which left Da Nang escorted by a tank belonging to the First Foreign Legion Cavalry Regiment. They drove south until one Vietnamese woman they encountered talked about how American prisoners had been paraded through her village and how one of them had been weeping. At that the crusty Foreign Legion tank commander spat, objected to risking his vehicle for such softies, and turned around to head home. Without heavy support, Lansdale too gave up the effort and returned to camp. Later it would be established that the Americans had actually been held at one village, Quan Khai Tay, for several days, until the evening of June 17. A more determined search might have recovered the men.

These five Americans were listed as missing after the morning of June 15, 1954. They became the first American prisoners of the Vietnam War, and their names should be recorded for posterity: army Private Donald E. Morgan of Flint, Michigan; army Private Leonard R. Sroufek of Chicago; air force Airman Third Class Jerry Schuller of Cleveland; Airman Third Class Giacomo Appice of Elizabeth, New Jersey; and Airman Second Class Ciro Salas, Jr., of Los Angeles.

Viet Minh captors gave the Americans black pajamas. After holding them at the village six miles from Da Nang, they were put on a coastal junk and moved under heavy guard to a point near Tam Ky where the Viet Minh had what they called their Camp No. 3. The Viet Minh were curious, not antagonistic, and asked many questions about the United States. The Americans were given a house to share with a Vietnamese woman; three of them slept on a bed of wooden planks supported by a couple of sawhorses, the others on a straw mat on the floor, one blanket to each man and two small bars of soap per month. According to an air force report on their experience, the prisoners were not confined, closely guarded, or made to stand reveille as were French prisoners. They were allowed to play soccer and volleyball. Camp No. 3 had no walls. The prisoners were kept inside by buried mines whose location was known only to the Viet Minh guards. Vietnamese went out of their way to give Americans some of their own food, and on at least one occasion a Viet Minh guard spent his own money to buy candy for the prisoners. But the Viet Minh were not well provisioned and had practically no medicines. One of the Americans lost fifty pounds in captivity, another contracted malaria.

On July 21, 1954, an agreement signed at Geneva, Switzerland, with side agreements directly between France and the Viet Minh, brought an end to the first Indochina war, the Franco-Vietnamese War. The five American prisoners held at Camp No. 3 were repatriated on August 31. The Vietnamese returned these Americans even though the United States had refused to be a party to the Geneva agreements. Meanwhile, the American technical detachments in Vietnam, far from being withdrawn by June 15 as scheduled, remained active in Indochina through the end of September, although their number was cut back to the originally stipulated 200. In fact, the allotment of American advisers to South Vietnam considered legal under the 1954 Geneva agreement, 342, would be based directly on the presence of these "temporary" U.S. technicians: 200 mechanics as of July 21, plus 24 on the U.S. attaché staff, plus another 118 assigned to MAAG.

■ Eisenhower felt greatly conflicted as a result of his failure to assist the French at Dien Bien Phu. Ike, as the president was familiarly known, determined he would not again fail to come to the aid of a more authentically nationalist government in what became known as South Vietnam. Accordingly, when the Vietnamese leader Ngo Dinh Diem threw off the remaining vestiges of French dominance and outmaneuvered Emperor Bao Dai, France's Vietnamese satrap, Eisenhower felt free to send the South Vietnamese assurances of American help. Those same assurances would be cited repeatedly, as if they were treaty commitments, by later U.S. administrations in attempts to justify our burgeoning Vietnam involvement. The conditional nature of the promises in this 1955 Eisenhower letter were ignored. Similarly, the Southeast Asia Treaty Organization (SEATO), created by a treaty signed at Manila in the fall of 1954, was a direct outcome of the failure of Eisenhower's secretary of state to achieve the multinational coalition the president felt necessary to intervene at the time of Dien Bien Phu. While the SEATO Treaty obliged member states to *no* specific action other than consultation, and though South Vietnam was not a member of SEATO, the treaty again would be used repeatedly in efforts to justify the United States role in Vietnam. Not all Americans would do as well as the prisoners of 1954. American leaders who might have made a difference seem to have drawn the wrong lessons from Dien Bien Phu.

2

Profile: Waiting in the Wings

One American leader who has repeatedly been credited with preventing American intervention at Dien Bien Phu is Lyndon Baines Johnson, then the minority leader of the United States Senate, where the Democratic party held just forty-seven seats after Dwight Eisenhower's victory in the 1952 elections. At a key meeting where Eisenhower's secretary of state, John Foster Dulles, and the chairman of the Joint Chiefs of Staff, Admiral Arthur W. Radford, briefed leaders of both houses of Congress about the project to intervene to save Dien Bien Phu, Senator Johnson asked which allies were behind this endeavor. Dulles admitted that as yet he had no international support, and the intervention policy took a hit from which it never recovered.

But what really happened here? Did LBJ save America from entering the Vietnam War in 1954? These are key questions in their own right and Lyndon Johnson's whole experience has obvious importance for his decisions a decade later when he himself would be president. Johnson's precise role in the 1954 Vietnam crisis has never been directly examined; it forms part of the hidden history of America's war.

To begin with, bucking authority was out of character for Lyndon Johnson. Son of a two-time Texas legislator, farmer, and schoolteacher, Johnson had been watching government in action since he was ten years old, when his father used to take him to Austin to watch from the gallery. Sam Ealy Johnson, Jr., also took young Lyndon along with him on campaign swings through their Texas district, a pastime LBJ, if anything, liked even more than the Texas legislature. Graduating early from high school, at age sixteen in 1924, Johnson's small group of classmates predicted he would someday become governor of Texas. He went to a teachers' college in San Marcos, Texas, and taught school in

Houston as well as in a small Texas town, but he went to Washington with a congressman in 1931, became a congressman in his own right in 1937, and stayed in Washington forever after. Johnson's entire approach was to attain power and then exercise it; the logical corollary had to be to respect power in others' hands so they would respect it in his. Recent biographers' charges about LBJ handling envelopes of cash, other favors and kickbacks, and allegations of manipulation in his 1948 election to the United States Senate do nothing to detract from this observation and in some respects lend further substance to it.

There is an alternative, quite plausible interpretation of Senator Johnson's question at the April 3, 1954, meeting with Dulles: that LBJ believed he was asking a pro forma question, doing exactly what the Eisenhower administration expected of him. In the late 1940s and 1950s, Congress and the administration put great stock in "bipartisanship," the idea of support for a given policy from both major political parties. Bipartisanship was thought to apply especially to foreign policy, where two of its very first achievements had been passage of the Marshall Plan for foreign aid and approval of the North Atlantic Treaty, both of which were alliance measures.

To put the matter more squarely in terms of Lyndon Johnson's personal experience, his entire military career in World War II had consisted of one personal mission, undertaken supposedly at the behest of Franklin D. Roosevelt, to New Zealand and Australia, in the command area of General Douglas A. MacArthur. The six-week-long inspection trip cannot but have alerted LBJ to the vital role being played by these U.S. allies (LBJ would also return to visit Australia when president, and remains to this day the only President of the United States ever to make a state visit to that country). It ought not to be thought unusual for Lyndon Johnson to bring up the matter of allies at the time of Dien Bien Phu, in particular given that just a few days before the leadership briefing, Secretary Dulles had himself called in a speech for "united action" to save the French. LBJ was simply asking how well the administration was lining up support for a *bipartisan* initiative. This point is reinforced by the fact that *after* the session with Dulles, Johnson went right on to take soundings among his Democratic colleagues on their support for Vietnam intervention.

Another way to throw light on this question is to examine Johnson's general attitude toward the United States as a military and global power. Even as a New Deal congressman, LBJ had consistently supported greater military spending and defense efforts. He had done the same during World War II as a member of a House subcommittee on naval affairs, and continued to push in this area as a senator and member of the Armed Services Committee. "It is foolish to talk of avoiding war," LBJ declared in a typical formulation. "We are already in a war—a major war. The war in Korea is a war of Soviet Russia." As senator, Lyndon Johnson assumed showdown to be inevitable.

This remained Johnson's thinking when the question of intervention arose at the time of Dien Bien Phu. A survey of Johnson's newsletters to his Texas constituents makes the point crystal clear. The top-secret meeting with Dulles and Radford was reflected in LBJ's newsletter of April 15, 1954, which advised that in Indochina "we are at the crossroads" and talked about the need to make "hard decisions—the kind that will tax all our determination and willpower." Johnson asserted that the fall of Indochina "would be disastrous to all our plans in Asia," warning of the loss of rich tungsten, tin, and rubber sources, and raising the specter of "the loss of all Southeast Asia and probably all of Asia. Ultimately, we might be driven put of the Pacific itself!" Johnson even mentioned the question of allies: "Shall we continue without clear assurances that others will join with us? Or shall we withdraw altogether and fall back upon the concept of fortress America?" These are not the words of a leader opposed to a Vietnam intervention, even a unilateral one.

In fact, Johnson hewed to this view *despite* the opinions of Texas voters and even though he was just then announcing his candidacy for a second term in the Senate. Seventy constituents expressed themselves in letters to Johnson during the Dien Bien Phu crisis; sixty-three of them rejected intervention. In an April 24 newsletter, however, LBJ chose to quote the woman who wrote, *"Christianity and democracy are stronger than communism and atheism"* (italicized in the original) and referred to tin (again) and manganese (not a major product of Vietnam) in arguing that *"Indochina is a rich prize"* (again italicized). According to LBJ's publication, "It is impossible to exaggerate the seriousness of the situation." Johnson's office put out an identical text as a press release for the senator five days later. Not until May 1, with Dien Bien Phu on its last legs and Eisenhower's intervention project obviously derailed, did an LBJ newsletter state that he shared the prayers of Americans who hoped that the crisis "will not end in another war to be fought by our young men." Even then Johnson declared, "Indochina is still the crossroads of American foreign policy!" Two issues later, after the fall of the French fortress, LBJ stated that "with each passing day, it becomes increasingly apparent that the free world suffered a major setback with the fall of Dien Bien Phu." In a dinner speech on May 6, the eve of the demise of Dien Bien Phu, Johnson lamented, "It is apparent only that American foreign policy has never in all its history suffered such a stunning reversal." Again, these are not the words of an opponent of intervention.

Like Dwight Eisenhower, whose guilt over 1954 led to promises taken for more than they meant, Lyndon Johnson's experience conditioned his actions in the 1960s. In 1961, after Johnson had become vice-president, John F. Kennedy sent him on a trip to South Vietnam during which LBJ met Vietnamese leader Ngo Dinh Diem. Several historians date LBJ's determination to support South Vietnam from that visit. From our examination, however, it would appear that Johnson had acquired a stance on Vietnam at the time of Dien Bien Phu.

Consummate legislator that he was, Lyndon Johnson drew the conclusion that President Eisenhower's error lay in not getting Congress to declare itself sooner in the form of a resolution supporting the president's policies. In 1964, at the time of the Gulf of Tonkin incident, that was the first order of business for President Johnson. Like the Eisenhower letter to Diem and the SEATO treaty, the Tonkin Gulf Resolution would be taken for more than it was, as a virtual declaration of war. For a time Johnson got away with it, at least until opposition grew to the American Vietnam War.

Even in 1965, when President Johnson made his crucial decision to commit American ground forces to combat, he remained mindful of the 1954 parallel. At the time, George Ball, one of the State Department's senior advisers, was using the example of Dien Bien Phu and the way opposition to war had grown in France to argue against deepening the U.S. involvement in South Vietnam. The subject resonated with Johnson, whose own constituent newsletters in 1954 had specifically referred to antiwar political feeling in France. LBJ's special assistant for national security affairs, McGeorge Bundy, could see the president being affected by Ball's Dien Bien Phu references. Bundy worked up a study of his own as to whether France in 1954 provided "a useful analogy" for the United States in South Vietnam in 1965. Despite "superficial similarities," Bundy insisted the two situations were not "fundamentally analogous," for France had been a colonial power. Moreover, in Bundy's view French domestic opinion had been deeply divided, "the victim of seven years of warfare," the last four on a large scale. Bundy's paper reads with eerie prescience in the archives, for aside from the matter of colonialism he postulated an almost precise description of the United States in 1968, by which time (counting from 1961) the U.S. war had been going on for seven years.

Lyndon Johnson's decision in 1965 may also be seen as evidence of his real position in 1954. That LBJ let himself be persuaded by Bundy, not by Ball, may indicate his predisposition all along. This may stretch the point too far, but nevertheless it is the case that Johnson in 1954 did less to save the country from war than often supposed, and that he took lessons from the experience that increased the probability of American entry into the Vietnam War a decade later.

Other American leaders waiting in the wings drew their own lessons from Dien Bien Phu, and those lessons too contributed to war later on. Jack Kennedy was there, a senator of Johnson's party in 1954, president from 1961 to 1963. American planners in 1954 were working on the assumption that American dynamism could succeed where the French had failed. Kennedy as president behaved exactly that way, as if dynamism plus a rhetorical flourish or two could substitute for a popular and effective government in Vietnam. Only slowly did Kennedy appreciate how steadily his South Vietnamese ally Ngo Dinh Diem was losing popularity. Kennedy moved the nation toward, not away from, a Vietnam involvement.

Richard Nixon was Eisenhower's vice-president at the time of Dien Bien Phu. Nixon was the only high-ranking U.S. leader who had actually been to Vietnam, having visited there and Cambodia in the fall of 1953. In the heat of the Dien Bien Phu crisis, Eisenhower had used Nixon to float a trial balloon by publicly mentioning military intervention, and Nixon and the president also had privately discussed using atomic bombs to save the French. Ike ultimately took no action, and the war was lost. The lesson Richard Nixon took away from Dien Bien Phu was that action was always preferable. This point of view underlies Nixon's plan to "end" the Vietnam War in 1969 by threatening Hanoi, his "Madman Theory," his decisions to invade Cambodia in 1970 and Laos in 1971, to mine Haiphong harbor in May 1972, and his orders for the Christmas bombing of Hanoi that December. Ironically, Nixon's Vietnam escalations can be related to Eisenhower's refusal to make war in 1954. The Dien Bien Phu experience proved to be fraught with consequence, and not only for the senior senator from Texas.

Confucians and Quagmires

Lyndon Johnson and other American leaders watched, and participated in, a process of entanglement in Vietnam that began under Harry Truman, became a significant policy under Dwight Eisenhower, and grew into a real headache under John Kennedy. Of course these presidents did not act alone. Not only did Richard Nixon second Eisenhower as his vice-president, or Johnson do the same for JFK; all were backed by a many-faceted (and faced) bureaucracy. Among the explanations advanced for how America became enmeshed in the Vietnam War are ones that focus not only on the persons of presidents but also wider theories that condemn the bureaucratic mind-set—with its hubris and simplistic assumptions of American superiority—and even systemic theories that blame United States economic or imperial interests or just the standard operating principles of the American political system, in which presidents strive to avoid major escalation decisions before the next election.

We could easily examine theories of involvement in Vietnam, and the exercise would be a useful one, but it could fill an entire book, and indeed there are many books of this kind. It is not necessary to engage that discussion here, or to build models in order to understand some of the dynamics and events that increasingly preoccupied the United States and consumed Vietnam.

■ The United States did not start the second Indochina war, except perhaps in Laos, where Washington went out of its way to subvert the 1954 Geneva agreement (see Chapter 24). For Vietnam, the new conflict also flowed from the breakdown of the Geneva accords. Among other things, the accords stipulated the temporary division of Vietnam into two "regroupment zones" (north and south), not countries; elections for a national government within two years, before reunification; a consolidation of Viet Minh loyalists in the north and pro-French and others in the south; and certain provisions regarding nonparticipation in foreign alliances, receipt of military aid, and the like. Observers variously attribute the breakdown to North or South Vietnam. Some lay responsibility at the doorstep of Ho Chi Minh and the northerners for never entirely pulling their cadres out of the south. Others blame the emergent South Vietnamese leader Ngo Dinh Diem, who attained complete power in Saigon in a 1955 military coup, for refusing to hold Vietnam-wide elections by 1956 as promised at Geneva. Defenders of Diem maintain he was not bound by Geneva, since South Vietnam was not a signatory to the 1954 agreement, but they usually do not bother noting that North Vietnam was not a Geneva signatory either. Other aspects of this argument over responsibility may never be settled. As with theories of involvement and decision models, we need only note the persistent debate over what happened to the 1954 Geneva accords on our way to summarizing developments along America's road to quagmire in Vietnam.

Bernard Fall, one of our best Vietnam experts until his tragic death in 1967, writes that "Ngo Dinh Diem's finest hour came, beyond a doubt, in the spring of 1955." This was a period of political maneuvering in which Diem first usurped the traditional Vietnamese monarchy of Bao Dai, faced a coup d'état by opposition elements, mounted a countercoup against them, then outfoxed the leaders of his own coup, who expected certain emoluments for their efforts. A leader accustomed to intrigue and acts of force, Diem had no intention of permitting the Geneva-mandated election that might unseat his own government. Having been given full civilian and military powers by Bao Dai in June 1954, while the French war still continued, Diem made sure an article (number 98) existed in the new South Vietnamese constitution, adopted in October 1956, that extended those powers through the spring of 1961; in the fall of 1961 the National Assembly renewed Diem's dictatorial power, invoking the worsening security situation in the south. The only expression of popular will permitted was an October 1955 referendum, pitched as a vote on monarchy versus republic. Emperor Bao Dai had never been very popular, Vietnamese were being offered a chance to vote for democracy, and the electoral campaign and voting were anything but honest. The outcome: 98.2 percent support for a republic.

Ngo Dinh Diem may never have gone so far as to assert that he had

been "elected" by that percentage of Vietnamese, but Diem's philosophy of "personalism" suggests he would have liked to do so. Far from
a government of laws, not of men, democracy was for Diem a state of
mind and a way of living. He said as much to the National Assembly
on the occasion of the promulgation of his constitution in 1956. In
essence, "personalism" was little more than an appeal by Diem for
people to trust him. As distilled by a (sympathetic) Indian observer as
early as 1960, personalism "ennobles all political actions because ben-
efitting from the Divine spark, it gives that permanency which other
factors cannot give." Democracy would be whatever Ngo Dinh Diem
did, or said it was. This was the political basis for the formation of the
Diemist Can Lao party by Ngo Dinh Nhu, Diem's brother. Nhu called
personalism a mixture of sacrifice, humility, and submissiveness, a
recipe for a public willing to let the Saigon leadership do anything it
wanted.

One thing Diem certainly wanted was the best possible political
base. He found this among the Vietnamese diaspora from the north—
a mass of more than 900,000 northerners who fled after Geneva.
Many were Catholics from the provinces of Phat Diem and Bui Chu
who feared that the Viet Minh government being formed by Ho Chi
Minh would limit freedom of worship. Others were encouraged to flee
by Central Intelligence Agency psychological warfare ploys that cast
the Viet Minh victory as the equivalent of an atomic bomb exploding
over Hanoi (as portrayed in one of the "psywar" posters of the time),
or made a variety of other charges, some true, many mixing truth and
falsehood, some entirely fabricated. Ngo Dinh Diem, though priding
himself on being the scion of a Confucian mandarin and adviser to
Vietnamese emperors, was a Roman Catholic (one of his brothers was
even a bishop). Diem naturally gravitated to the northerners, favored
them, and expected their loyalty. Favoritism fed a growing perception
of Diem's government as corrupt and bloated.

Favoritism showed up everywhere; it was the twin brother of personalism. Ngo Dinh Nhu, soon Diem's closest associate, achieved high
office as minister of the interior. Tran Kim Tuyen, the top Can Lao political operative under Nhu, emerged as director of a Vietnamese intelligence organization equivalent to the CIA. Army officers found their
promotions blocked until they joined the Can Lao or otherwise
showed fealty to Diem. Northerners arriving in the south received free
land—the bulk of such land redistribution as the government carried
out. Being seen as opposed to the Saigon regime became positively
dangerous. The syncretistic religious sects Cao Dai and Hoa Hao, as

well as the piratical political-military sect Binh Xuyen, all of whom had opposed Diem in 1955, and some of whom had fought him in the coups of that year, found themselves hunted down by the South Vietnamese army long after reconciliation had been proclaimed by the government. The same was true, of course, for those Viet Minh cadres who remained in the south after Geneva.

Americans started out in full support of Ngo Dinh Diem, a figure who had graced certain seminaries in the United States during his religious retreats, who had influential backers in this country, and who lacked the pro-French attitudes or French associations of other Vietnamese nationalists. These factors were considered major advantages in Washington, which felt that previous governments had been unsuccessful in mobilizing the Vietnamese because of their colonialist taint. Even when Diem resorted to acts of force in 1955 to consolidate his power, there was not much grumbling. At that time President Eisenhower overrode the advice of his good friend General J. Lawton Collins, whom he had made special envoy to South Vietnam, and who had been unwilling to tolerate the extralegality of Diem's actions. Instead Washington backed Edward Lansdale, an air force officer detached to CIA, who advocated "nation building" and attached himself to Diem as the next great hope. General Collins was called home while Lansdale stayed in South Vietnam another year and more.

Later American proconsuls of that era acted in the spirit of Lansdale in the sense that many created their own microcosms of the land and followed their own agendas. General Samuel T. ("Hanging Sam") Williams, who headed the Military Assistance Advisory Group, trained a conventional Vietnamese army even though force was being used by Diem against irregulars—the Cao Dai and Hoa Hao—in unconventional or counterinsurgency operations (the current jargon is "low-intensity conflict"). Foreign aid specialists of the U.S. operations mission tried to build a Vietnam with standard industrial and infrastructure projects, then wondered why the effects of their assistance could not be seen in the hinterland. CIA chieftains, who during this period included not only Lansdale but John Anderton, Nicolas A. Natsios, William E. Colby, and John A. Richardson, floundered between their desire to maintain the closest possible relationship with Diem and Nhu and the intelligence requirement for keeping in touch with the growing anti-Diem opposition. According to John Mecklin, a senior United States Information Agency official then in the American embassy, a standard Saigon joke was that the U.S. mission resembled "a log floating down a stream, covered with ants, each one of whom thinks he is steering."

While the various elements of the American mission may have been pulling in different directions, all remained committed to support for Diem. Ambassador Eibridge Durbrow and his successor, Frederick Nolting, were not Vietnam specialists or even Asian experts, and not always willing to recognize Diem's political difficulties. Durbrow cautioned Diem and Nhu of the need for reforms, Nolting insisted upon full support for the Diem government; even in retrospect Nolting writes that President Kennedy, when he decided to end American support for Diem, "gave way to the pressures of a misinformed public opinion."

Meanwhile, South Vietnam had held new elections for its National Assembly in 1959, and this time results were even more lopsided—only one opposition candidate won, along with one neutralist, in voting that filled 132 assembly seats. The oppositionist, Dr. Phan Quang Dan, won easily despite the last-minute addition to his constituency of eight thousand South Vietnamese soldiers with instructions to vote for the government candidate. Dan was then charged with offering free medical consultations in exchange for votes, and the whole tenor of the affair grew so ugly that Dr. Dan threw in his lot with a cabal of army officers led by then-Colonel Nguyen Chanh Thi, who mounted a coup against Diem in November 1960. A "young Turk" paratroop officer, Thi's coup failed when his troops hesitated in front of the Presidential Palace, as Diem and Nhu, through CIA station chief William Colby, offered negotiations and stalled long enough to permit the arrival of the loyal troops of General Nguyen Van Thieu.

It was typical of the ineptitude of Ngo Dinh Diem's government that though the president reportedly thereafter regarded Thieu like a son, another of Diem's brothers, Ngo Dinh Can, mayor of Hue, threw Thieu's brother in jail on trumped-up charges. It was the kind of gambit a mandarin might make—to remind someone, even a key someone, that others still have power over them.

Similarly, the Diem government retaliated against the CIA, regarding the U.S. embassy's stand during the attempted coup as treacherous. While Ambassador Durbrow insisted the United States stood with Diem, he and CIA station chief Colby both acknowledged a need to be able to deal with *any* South Vietnamese government that emerged, and that required a hands-off attitude during the coup itself. Thus while Colby offered good offices in going between the rebels and the government, CIA officers remained in constant contact with the coup plotters and their political leadership, most importantly Phan Quang Dan. In the wake of the coup, Ngo Dinh Nhu demanded that Dan's CIA case officer be thrown out of the country. Dr. Dan himself was arrested and put on trial, after being tortured, and was sentenced in 1962 to eight years' hard labor at the penal colony on Con Son Island.

During this period, still before the inauguration of John Kennedy, the Eisenhower administration decided to expand its military advisory effort in support of South Vietnam. The Geneva ceiling of 342 on American military personnel was breached and almost precisely doubled. When President Kennedy entered office in January 1961 the number of U.S. advisers stood at 685. Kennedy immediately became interested in injecting more dynamism into the incipient war against the Vietnamese Communists, who were by now being called Viet Cong, in a contraction of the Vietnamese word for that political persuasion. Kennedy, rejecting the advice of former President Eisenhower, who told him it was Laos and not South Vietnam that was the key to Southeast Asia, pressed ahead with further expansions of the U.S. effort. Helicopter units were sent to South Vietnam to provide greater mobility to Diem's army; Special Forces (soon called Green Berets) went to train Vietnamese counterparts as well as to cooperate in CIA covert missions; quietly disguised air force combat units nicknamed "Jungle Jim" and "Farmgate" went to endow the South Vietnamese with a significant air combat capability; naval support increased; and funds were given to the Vietnamese to create a so-called "strategic hamlet" program and to expand local militias. Counterinsurgency meant a huge expansion in the U.S. advisory effort, which was still a secret program, code-named Project Gold and administered by the ultrasecret Special Group (Counterinsurgency) of the National Security Council. For a time, South Vietnam was the *only* program overseen by that body.

Much has been made of the Taylor-Rostow mission in the fall of 1961, which recommended that the United States commit eight thousand troops to South Vietnam, including combat troops sent in the guise of flood-relief units. This mission, led by Kennedy's military special assistant, General Maxwell D. Taylor, and Walt W. Rostow, then deputy national security adviser (soon to begin a sojourn at the State Department before returning to the White House under President Lyndon Johnson), had a hard time getting in to see Ngo Dinh Diem. One of its members, however, did not. Edward Lansdale, whom Taylor had tried to keep off the delegation, was picked up by a senior South Vietnamese officer and whisked off to meet with Diem the moment the

Taylor-Rostow party landed at Saigon's Tan Son Nhut airport. President Kennedy rejected the Taylor-Rostow recommendations, but refusing that particular drink did not steel JFK to avoid others. From the first action program in the spring of 1961, formulated by deputy secretary of defense Roswell Gilpatric, right through to Robert S. McNamara's Honolulu recommendations in the fall of 1963, Kennedy repeatedly approved augmentations of American effort. The U.S. troop level stood at about twenty-two hundred before the end of 1961, at roughly eleven thousand in 1962, and at more than sixteen thousand before Kennedy's death by assassination in November 1963. The Geneva ceilings were honored in the breach.

Since 1992 some historians have argued that John Kennedy's death canceled an American withdrawal from South Vietnam and was doubly tragic for that reason. In its most sophisticated articulation this argument runs like this: U.S. military and other authorities, such as General Paul D. Harkins, who took over the military assistance group, soon to be titled Military Assistance Group Vietnam (MACV), systematically deceived Kennedy on the progress of the growing war in Vietnam, in effect conspiring to conduct a war of their own. JFK finally wised up to the ploy and by 1963 was determined to get America out of Vietnam. In October of that year he approved a decision document, known as National Security Action Memorandum (NSAM) 263, which sanctioned a measure announced by Secretary of Defense Robert McNamara—an immediate withdrawal of one thousand men from South Vietnam as a start toward the full withdrawal that JFK intended. But that November, at the very moment of the Kennedy assassination, NSAM-273 was in draft. The document, calling for greater U.S. participation in covert operations, was revised immediately after the president's death, supposedly closing off the withdrawal option.

This argument is plausible but misleading. For example, there is no doubt that U.S. field commands furnished deceptively optimistic reports from Vietnam, but there is little reason to expect anything else from an action-oriented field organization. The problem of poor reporting did not end with Kennedy's death or the supposed attainment of the object of this alleged conspiracy—the avoidance of early U.S. withdrawal. Poor reporting continued right up to the end of the Vietnam War in 1975, with the U.S. embassy at that time still insisting, with North Vietnamese armies virtually on the outskirts of Saigon, that with a little more aid and a few more guns part of South Vietnam could hold out very well. Thus poor reporting was not aimed at John Kennedy specifically. Moreover, the schedule of withdrawals attached to the Pentagon plan referred to by McNamara and in NSAM-263 has now been declassified. It makes clear that the process would be a gradual one, extending right into 1968.

In the event, U.S. troop strength would instead peak in 1968, at 548,000. Beginning in 1969 the Nixon administration finally began withdrawals, reducing the U.S. presence in Vietnam to 60,000 by 1972. Though Mr. Nixon got 490,000 Americans out of South Vietnam within a three-year period, no one accuses him of carrying out a rapid withdrawal. For Kennedy to have pulled out 16,000 advisers and combat support forces over *five* years ought not to be seen as the dramatic event analysts imply when they write of the Kennedy "withdrawal."

It is true that Kennedy spoke to several associates about withdrawing American troops from South Vietnam. For example, he met with Michael Forrestal, his National Security Council aide for Southeast Asia, who was leaving on a special mission to Vietnam and Cambodia, on the very day JFK departed for Texas on his last, fateful political trip. Kennedy asked Forrestal to warn Cambodian leaders and others that a drawdown in American strength was in the works. But it is not clear from the record whether JFK was talking about getting out of the war, or reducing the U.S. role in the war. Other evidence suggests the latter.

Over the same time frame of the summer of 1963, in which the Pentagon prepared the withdrawal plan that President Kennedy sanctioned in NSAM-263, the administration was in the throes of decisions on Laos that amounted to a mandate for escalation. A July 1962 Declaration on the Neutrality of Laos, agreed upon at Geneva, had reaffirmed the status assigned Laos under the 1954 agreements and pledged the Geneva powers to refrain from "all direct or indirect interference" in Laotian affairs or any use or threat of force. The United States then withdrew most of its military personnel from Laos (secretly leaving some CIA officers with the upland tribes) while the North Vietnamese appear to have made only cosmetic withdrawals. Frustrated by the apparent sterility of the 1962 Geneva Agreement on Laos, Kennedy determined to scuttle that agreement in favor of a CIA paramilitary program and a de facto military alliance with the presumptively neutral Royal Laotian Government. Like the withdrawal plan, the Laos decisions were enshrined in official decision documents, most especially NSAM-249 (June 25, 1963), NSAM-256 (July 31, 1963), and NSAM-259 (August 20, 1963). Planes of the CIA proprietary Air America, which had already made ten clandestine deliveries of arms to the Hmong, upland tribesmen fighting for the CIA, between the Geneva accords and the spring of 1963, increased their level of activity. It is difficult to reconcile this Laos policy with the assertion that Kennedy intended total withdrawal from Vietnam. The most reasonable interpretation is that Kennedy wanted the South Vietnamese to assume more of the burden of their own defense, in effect a form of what would later be termed "Vietnamization," reversing the trend of Americanizing the war.

A second piece of evidence challenges the claim that the version of NSAM-273 approved by incoming President Johnson a few days after JFK's death represented a change from what Kennedy intended. It turns out that the differences between this document in draft form and the text as approved relate primarily to permitting U.S. unilateral control of certain covert action programs. The fact is, there had been a debate in progress in Washington since the spring in which the CIA explained its operational failures by complaining about Vietnamese control. U.S. control, it argued, was a means of ensuring success. A conference at Honolulu that ended during JFK's Dallas trip, one which involved Kennedy's own security adviser, McGeorge Bundy, as well as Secretary of Defense McNamara, approved this idea of greater U.S. participation in covert operations. The now notorious program of covert pressures against North Vietnam, called Operation 34-A, flowed directly from these decisions. There is no reason to suppose that President Kennedy would have refused to approve the amendments in the draft NSAM-273 that reflected the best judgment of his brightest colleagues.

Finally there is the matter of the coup d'état of November 1, 1963, which this time succeeded in overthrowing Diem. American authorities steadily became more dissatisfied with the South Vietnamese leader, to the degree that Diem's wooden response to the Buddhist troubles in August (see Chapter 9) seemed the last straw. But a split developed within the Kennedy administration over how to deal with Diem's obduracy. The State Department was ready to go along with a coup to oust Diem, and for a few days in late August, before a State cable was countermanded, that was the approved policy. Ambassador Nolting was replaced at just this time by Henry Cabot Lodge, who was willing to go along with a coup, though that was opposed by his CIA station chief, John Richardson, as well as by MACV commander General Harkins. In Washington the Pentagon and CIA similarly rejected any notion of support for the coup. The policy changed for the moment, but CIA's case officer to the most prominent South Vietnamese oppositionist generals, Lucien Conein, remained in contact throughout the period.

Some observers argue that by not breaking with the South Vietnamese generals and actively discouraging them from dreams of ousting Diem, the United States became complicit in the coup. At the same time such complicity bound the U.S. closely to whatever regime succeeded Diem's government, in effect trapping the U.S. in the Vietnam War. If so, this maneuver scarcely jibes with a supposed intention to withdraw. Washington's policy on the coup was not a matter of some cabal in Saigon, much as Lodge may have disliked CIA boss Richardson and secured his recall.

Washington was completely aware of the machinations of the Vietnamese generals: between the last week of August 1963 and the coup itself on November 1 there were at least fourteen meetings among senior American policymakers, exhaustively discussing every aspect of the alignment of forces in Saigon, the prospects of a coup, and related matters. Ten of the fourteen meetings involved President Kennedy. Although JFK sometimes only asked questions, the tenor of his comments among the declassified records of these Washington power sessions clearly shows that he was as frustrated with Diem as anyone, and that his concern was to establish political conditions in Saigon that were conducive to prosecuting the war more effectively—*not* getting the United States out of Vietnam. During this period Kennedy gave a television interview publicly expressing displeasure with Diem, and at a White House meeting on October 7 he approved the termination of certain types of aid to South Vietnam, including a halt in military aid to Vietnamese Special Forces, the loyalist troops Diem had used to suppress the Buddhists a few months before. These measures the Vietnamese generals took as signals the U.S. would support their coup, with predictable results. Kennedy also ordered that the thousand-man withdrawal of MACV troops be carried out as a routine action without discussion with Diem, suggesting that the move of which so much is made may have been intended merely as another device to bring extra pressure on the South Vietnamese regime.

In a CIA paper on September 19, as well as in a Joseph Alsop newspaper column the previous day, Washington became aware of political contacts between Ngo Dinh Nhu and the North Vietnamese. Nhu's maneuver must have been aimed at putting the U.S. on notice that Diem had options other than an American alliance, and it succeeded too well. Washington was outraged. Officials at John Kennedy's secret meetings increasingly spoke of South Vietnam breaking commitments made to Washington, tilting the scales even more in favor of American support for a coup. The net result was that when Washington could discourage the Vietnamese generals from acting, it refrained from doing so. These were not men who were busy finding their way out of Vietnam.

On October 29, 1963 (Washington date), that is, a full day before the South Vietnamese generals finally moved, Kennedy held one of his top-secret Vietnam meetings. William Colby of the CIA led off with a detailed briefing on the status of coup versus pro-Diem forces. The CIA even had a nice map on an easel illustrating the dispositions on both sides, which it reckoned to be about equal. The key would be in the actions of the eighteen thousand South Vietnamese soldiers whose political loyalties had not been established. Among them was General Nguyen Van Thieu, the Fifth Division commander who had used his troops to save Diem in the 1960 coup attempt. On November 1 Thieu did not lift a finger for Diem, who was overthrown, temporarily escaped in company with Nhu, but was captured with false promises of a safe conduct out of the country. Diem and Nhu were assassinated the next day.

After the Diem coup the big question was getting the South Vietnamese out into the field to continue the war against the Viet Cong. Any plan for an American withdrawal, however real it may have been, was forgotten. With John Kennedy's death in Dallas three weeks after Diem's demise, the die was cast for the events that followed. Now success in South Vietnam, more than ever, would depend upon the quality of the men and women, American and Vietnamese, who worked on the issue.

4 Profile: George Carver (I)

Many were the men and women who would help make the Vietnam War what it became. Over the years the leaders and the bit players have garnered the most attention—leaders because analysts automatically paid attention to them, and bit players due to the explosion of personal stories put forward in oral histories, interviews, memoirs, and autobiographical novels. But the experiences of an entire layer of middle managers—if that is the right word for them—are less frequently addressed. A number of these officials played roles quite crucial to the evolution of the Vietnam conflict. One is George Carver.

There was little to mark George Carver as a quintessential "spook," argot of the time for an intelligence officer, but still he moved in some circles that James Bond would never have dreamed of. Back-alley spy but colleague of presidents and CIA chieftains, Carver's star rose quickly in the intelligence business and remained ascendant for perhaps too long. Carver was a figure at the Central Intelligence Agency through the late 1970s, when he retired to become a fellow at the conservative Center for Strategic and International Studies, a Washington think tank then associated with Georgetown University.

Carver's outlook was nothing if not international. Born in Louisville, Kentucky, George A. Carver, Jr., was spirited off to China by his parents. George Sr. and his wife Saxon were missionaries determined to preach the gospel in a very dangerous place during the turbulent 1930s. China was crossed and criss-crossed by a nationalist revolution, a Communist revolution, and war, with nationalist, Communist, and Japanese armies all contending for power. Even the relative safety of the International Settlement at Shanghai vanished momentarily in 1937 when Chinese nationalists and Japanese fought a pitched battle for that city and the International Settlement was bombed in error by Chinese planes sent to hit enemy warships. All this must have been an eye-opener for young George, as for other Americans in China during the period, many of whom were harassed, even killed, by Japanese determined to close America's "Open Door." American children were definitely affected. James R. Lilley, George Carver's contemporary and best friend in fourth grade in Shanghai, would also grow up to join the CIA, and would be deputy chief of station in Laos during the Vietnam War years, later becoming U.S. representative or ambassador, successively, to Taiwan, South Korea, and China.

Ultimately it became impossible for Americans to stay in China. George left the Shanghai American School for the States. World War II became a huge international drama punctuating his school years. After the war he went to Yale, which had a famous Divinity School, where young George was a debating champion and was elected to Phi Beta Kappa. Very short and slight, Carver also proved ideal for the crew team and became coxswain. Unknown to him, the crew coach of that era, Allen ("Skip") Walz, who remained at Yale through 1955, was an active recruiter for the Central Intelligence Agency. The Yale classes of 1950, of whom Carver was one, and 1952, were especially heavily recruited. Walz sounded out Carver but decided that George was not cut out to work for the Agency.

Carver meanwhile decided to pursue his doctorate at England's prestigious Oxford University. There too he went out for crew, again being selected coxswain, and went on to cox the Oxford shell on the Thames River for the ninety-seventh running of the Oxford-Cambridge race—the first American to achieve this distinction. His doctoral thesis was a study of the philosophy of Thomas Hobbes, whose proposition that man's innate, unschooled, nature is to exist in a state of war, provided a neat point of departure for Carver to meld his religious and theological background with the conflicts in the world around him. George Carver arrived at the Central Intelligence Agency under his own steam in 1953, beginning a CIA career that would span twenty-six years.

Then as now, the CIA was interested in officers with languages and international experience, and George's childhood in China made him a natural for the Agency. He was employed by the clandestine service as a case officer and reports officer, a manager and chronicler of spies. He did two tours in the Far East in the late 1950s, when America's covert conflict with China was at a peak. On Taiwan during one of those tours, George encountered his old friend Jim Lilley, now also a CIA case officer.

Carver's association with Vietnam began in the late 1950s when Nick Natsios was Saigon station chief and William Colby his deputy. He had diplomatic cover as an economic attaché with the U.S. Operations Mission, but in fact Carver was the case officer to South Vietnamese politico Dr. Phan Quang Dan, the man who was left holding the bag in the abortive 1960 military coup. The South Vietnamese government, possibly through interrogation of Dan or searches of his papers, became aware of the politician's relationship with the CIA and narrowed the list of Dan's possible CIA contact to two names, Carver or Ambassador Durbrow's deputy chief of mission, Howard C. Elting. An infuriated Ngo Dinh Nhu raged at Colby, recently promoted station chief in his own right, that this CIA interference was intolerable and that Carver had to go. Colby insisted that Carver was not an Agency case officer but had simply told the embassy what he learned from Dan without at all encouraging the coup plotters.

The situation was resolved when a sinister letter appeared in Carver's mailbox—Colby thinks arranged by Nhu—which made veiled threats against Carver, his wife of five years, and his family. The letter purported to be from the defeated coup makers in retaliation for the way alleged promises of CIA help had gone unfulfilled as their plot disintegrated. With this scare it became legitimate to withdraw the Carver family from Saigon as endangered, and the helpful Nhu even provided them a motorcycle escort to Tan Son Nhut airport. When Dr. Dan was eventually tried before a South Vietnamese court, prosecutors publicly asserted they had documents to prove that a foreign power had been behind the 1960 coup attempt, but they were not at liberty to discuss the matter further.

By that time George Carver was assigned to CIA headquarters at Langley, Virginia, just outside Washington, where he had been moved into intelligence reporting as a member of the Office of National Estimates (ONE) under Sherman Kent. The work of ONE was to get the best intelligence data from all U.S. government agencies, turn this into draft "estimates" (which were reports representing the considered opinion of the intelligence community), and then persuade the other agency members of the community to concur in the estimates. An estimate approved in this fashion was said to be "coordinated" and would be published as the official opinion of the Director of Central Intelligence (DCI), the chief not only of the CIA but of the rest of the community as well. George Carver was an estimates officer in ONE, one of those analysts who could be called upon to write the first drafts of the National Intelligence Estimates (NIEs), as they were called.

All this is important because George Carver is at the center of the story of one of the key intelligence estimates of the Vietnam War. It was he who was selected initially to draft NIE 58-63, drawn to measure progress in South Vietnam. Colleagues recall Carver's "passionate" desire to rid Vietnam of Ngo Dinh Diem, possibly not unrelated to his treatment following the 1960 coup attempt, but the tone of his draft NIE was balanced. The ONE manager for the NIE thought Carver's draft had some good analysis, some new data, and some organizational problems, but he also observed that the report only implied—it did not come out and say—that Diem had to go. At best, Carver was saying in the NIE, the Vietnam struggle would be protracted and difficult due to the many weaknesses of the Saigon regime, including poor morale and leadership, lack of trust, inadequate South Vietnamese intelligence, obvious penetration of the government by Viet Cong spies, and poor tactical use of available troops.

At the time Carver completed this draft NIE, in February 1963, the CIA's deputy director for intelligence (DDI) was Ray Cline. The DDI headed an entire division of the CIA with responsibility for intelligence reporting other than estimates, but nonetheless had a watching brief over the NIEs. Like Carver, Cline was a clandestine services officer turned analyst, and he was very much an optimist on Vietnam. When the Vietnam NIE had been sent to CIA chief John McCone for his first reading, Cline told the DCI that the paper failed to incorporate the views of the "real" Vietnam experts—the army, Pentagon counterinsurgency experts, the Pacific command, and State Department officials. McCone had ONE throw the estimate open to comment by these people, and they advanced their standard arguments for how the Vietnam War was going so well. Already by 1963 assertions like these were being regarded as boiler plate by the CIA, so despite these comments the national intelligence estimate was sent forward for interagency coordination as it stood.

As would occur in certain instances later in the war, angry conflict developed over the 1963 NIE. Not only was DDI Cline unhappy, but the State Department objected to any analysis that Vietnam had become a *political* problem, since it could then be argued that State had failed in its political role. Of course, the military objected that MACV and other military officials knew better too. Carver's draft NIE, already rewritten once to accommodate Cline and McCone, was revised again in the coordination process. The result was a mishmash, released on April 17, 1963, that warned of political problems with Diem but went on to conclude that "we believe that communist progress has been blunted and that the situation is improving." Considering the South Vietnamese army's recent defeat in the battle of Ap Bac, in which an overwhelming force backed by helicopters, planes, guns, and armored personnel carriers had been unable to drive off a Viet Cong battalion, the conclusions in the CIA estimate George Carver had originally written were laughable. The revisions had in effect falsified the NIE.

Despite the experience of the 1963 NIE, or perhaps because of it, George Carver's stock rose with the CIA front office. When Richard Helms became DCI in 1965 he created a new private staff just for Vietnam and appointed Carver to it. In September 1966, when the first special assistant for Vietnam affairs moved on to another assignment, Helms offered the job to George Carver. Helms said, "I can worry about Indochina or I can worry about the rest of the world. I want you to worry about Indochina."

5   The Covert War

Sergeant Barry Sadler died at a hospital in Murfreesboro, Tennessee, on November 5, 1989. Some people had trouble with what Sadler had been doing during his last years—glorifying mercenaries in a series of novels and training *contra* guerrillas in Guatemala—but there was a time when the sergeant epitomized America's endeavor in Vietnam. That was in the early years, when the war was fresh and heroic and men could still dream of winning it. Barry Sadler then was a twenty-six-year-old guitar-playing medical specialist with the Green Berets, U.S. Army Special Forces. Recovering from a leg wound, Sadler cowrote and recorded a song, *The Ballad of the Green Berets*. Plenty of people who did not know Barry then, and still have never heard of him, remember that song, which reached number one on the hit parade for five weeks in 1966 and sold nine million copies in single and album form.

Sadler wrote of men who were America's best in a war then regarded as a laboratory for counterinsurgency techniques. Until the commitment of major ground forces in 1965, the war was a secret conflict, a shadow struggle waged under cover of a simple military aid program. It was a high point of sorts, participants remember fondly. One officer, later a battalion commander in the First Cavalry Division (Airmobile) and then aide to a senior general in Washington, recalls the careful planning of those days. Like some others, he still believes the U.S. could have won, *if* we had kept the war at that covert, secret warfare level. What about it? This early phase of the Vietnam War should be examined both to answer this question and as an important background to the evolution of the conflict.

In this time at the beginning of the war, Vietnam programs were closely held in Washington, controlled by President Kennedy's National Security Council (NSC) and a subcommittee of that entity known as the Special Group (CI), whose parenthesized acronym stood for counterinsurgency. At his very first NSC meeting, about a week after his January 1961 inauguration, Kennedy spoke of his desire to see plans for covert operations into North Vietnam. The director of the Central Intelligence Agency, Allen Dulles, promptly replied that four teams of eight men each had been trained, but his contingency accounts lacked funds to carry out extensive operations.

Actually Dulles referred to a South Vietnamese special unit, the First Observation Group, formed in February 1956. This unit, the forerunner of South Vietnamese Special Forces (*Luc Luong Dac Biet*), was equipped under the U.S. military aid program but funded by the CIA, and its operations were controlled jointly by the Agency and the Vietnamese. Ngo Dinh Diem complicated this arrangement by holding the First Observation Group outside the regular chain of command, making it directly subordinate to himself; then he complicated things further by creating a separate intelligence organization, the Presidential Liaison Office, also under his direct control, in which every officer was an officer in the First Observation Group as well, and whose director was the group commander. The CIA had nine paramilitary specialists assigned to Observation Group headquarters, but they sometimes did not know where to turn since, in effect, the South Vietnamese unit changed identities depending upon whether the Vietnamese wished to cooperate in a given project.

One American who played a formative role in the creation of this Vietnamese unit was Colonel Edward Lansdale. A political-action specialist in the Philippines, then South Vietnam, Lansdale encouraged Diem to establish the Observation Group. Lansdale had anticipated that the force would perform unconventional warfare missions and organize spy networks in North Vietnam. Instead Colonel Lansdale found a very different situation when he visited Vietnam as part of the Taylor-Rostow mission in October 1961. Although Vietnamese covert operations were "generally well conceived and adequately implemented," Lansdale believed the effort was "much too small" in terms of personnel, equipment, and training. Pacification questions had not been seriously addressed. The government of Vietnam (GVN) had also made "virtually no effective penetration" of the highland areas inhabited by the various tribes of montagnards. Covert strikes against trails and stopover stations used by the Viet Cong had been "too small to accomplish other than minor harassment." Much of the manpower of the Observation Group was tied down providing elite security guards at the homes or offices of friends, cronies, and relatives designated by President Diem.

John Kennedy's earliest Vietnam decisions, recommended by a group under Deputy Secretary of Defense Roswell Gilpatric and formalized in National Security Action Memorandum (NSAM)-52, provided for a 20,000-man increase in South Vietnamese armed forces. Part of this was devoted to increasing the size of the First Observation Group by some 500 men from its early 1961 authorized strength of 305. By July its strength had reached 340. That fall Lansdale found it had sixteen 14-man agent teams. The plan was to build up to twenty 15-man teams backed by two 160-man airborne Ranger companies. While 400 recruits were in training, Lansdale discovered that the company-size assault units had not progressed beyond the planning stage.

In May 1961 Diem had formed a Central Intelligence Organization (CIO) that would eventually grow to more than three thousand personnel. But the CIO was chiefly oriented toward intelligence collection. Ed Lansdale saw the need for a covert-action unit as big as the CIO, but in this he would be disappointed. Lansdale also wanted to emplace a cadre of dynamic Americans at all levels of the Vietnamese bureaucracy who could function as expediters to move the wheels of the GVN machinery when it came to implementing ambitious plans.

Ed Lansdale's notions of what was right for Diem and the GVN were at once sophisticated and naive, the ideas of an advertising man turned political-action specialist. How the United States could pretend to be safeguarding the independence of South Vietnam with Americans working at all levels of the GVN bureaucracy was something Lansdale evidently did not explain to General Maxwell Taylor when he broached this subject with the mission leader. It was typical of Lansdale, who served as the prototype for the protagonists in both the Graham Greene novel *The Quiet American* and the equally well-known *The Ugly American* by William J. Lederer and Eugene Burdick. Military men usually claim that Lansdale was a CIA officer (under air force cover) while CIA veterans insist he was only a military man.

Whatever else is said, Edward Lansdale was exceptional in the attention he paid to the political side of counterinsurgency. Most Americans, even the CIA types, saw the need for political and social programs but remained willing to sacrifice them for security concerns. Paramilitary and unconventional warfare predominated at this stage of America's Vietnam War. At the end of 1961 the 1,209 Americans working on classified projects in South Vietnam outnumbered the Military Assistance Advisory Group's 1,062 regular personnel. Among them were 400 Special Forces, the Green Berets first approved for commitment by President Kennedy in NSAM-52. Most worked on a special border surveillance effort with the montagnards, an effort begun by the CIA. Some, however, worked on the covert war against North Vietnam.

The covert war was one of the toughest assignments imaginable. Then-U.S. ambassador to the GVN Frederick Nolting recalls that "security in North Vietnam was very effective, particularly [around] its military-support installations." Some efforts were attempted anyway. At the end of January 1962 an important cotton-goods depot at Bac Ninh, southwest of Hanoi, was burned to the ground. That spring, according to a State Department airgram, South Vietnamese were "certainly the perpetrators" of sabotage which occurred at a sugar refinery and a factory at Van Diem. That March, North Vietnamese authorities apparently cracked down with arrests of individuals feared to be southern sympathizers or agents.

Although South Vietnamese commandos carried out these activities, the CIA exercised joint control and even had the primary role in furnishing logistics and support. Its organ for doing so was the so-called Combined Studies Group, officially a staff section of the U.S. military advisory group. By the end of 1961 the Agency had provided a fleet of several aircraft, painted black, unmarked, and kept under special guard at Tan Son Nhut airfield, to provide flight services for its covert-action programs. Ambassador Nolting suggests in his memoir that CIA–South Vietnamese operations had proved unsuccessful or too costly and were being discontinued, but this assertion is misleading. Though increasingly overshadowed by larger and more successful programs, such as the montagnard effort, covert action was expanding.

It could hardly be otherwise in a climate in which the war efforts of both the United States and the GVN were rapidly increasing. In January 1962 the military advisory group expanded to become Military Assistance Command Vietnam (MACV), the headquarters that would carry out America's Vietnam War. It was but two months since the Vietnamese Observation Group had been reorganized as the Seventy-seventh Group, LLDB, the beginning of Vietnamese Special Forces. The unit continued to work with the Americans, such as in the CIA's border interdiction effort known as Project Pacific Ocean. As the

LLDB, the Vietnamese also exercised a prominent role in the montagnard effort.

One special problem of the covert plans to strike at the north was transport. Inserting agent teams was more than a mere matter of the CIA providing aircraft. Air crews were critical. Saigon CIA station chief William Colby set up a dummy corporation for cover—VIAT, a private Vietnamese airline—which went to Taiwan to hire nationalist Chinese for pilots and crews. Some American air officers augmented the CIA station as well. Still, Colonel Nguyen Cao Ky, commander of the South Vietnamese air force, insisted upon flying the first mission over North Vietnam himself. Since the Americans intended to use Vietnamese crews as well, Colby felt he had no alternative but to allow it.

Colonel Ky began low-altitude training of his own unit within two days of the initial request. When he asked for volunteers, every one of his seventy to eighty pilots stepped forward. They began to practice flying by moonlight only ten to fifteen feet above the ground. To show his prowess, Ky took Colby along on one flight over the South China Sea. The Vietnamese pilot thought the CIA man looked like a philosophy student. Colby stood in the rear door of the C-47 and finished by promising that next time he would bring along a fishing pole.

There was bright moonlight the night of the first insertion, perfect flying weather. Ky was airborne at about 9 p.m., went in on the deck to avoid the North Vietnamese radar net, and dropped the men at 1:30 a.m. By 6 a.m. the plane had returned to Tan Son Nhut. Colby awaited the crew in the hangar with a case of champagne.

About twenty of the best Vietnamese pilots were selected for the final mission group. They devised a system of double navigation whereby two navigators accompanied each flight, one to sight landmarks, the other to plot the route. Ky outfitted the elite group with black coveralls, but once rumors began to spread about the pilots in black suits, Colby became concerned about mission security. Thereafter the mission group were sequestered in a villa under heavy guard.

Overall responsibility for the agent teams inserted, and for security of the program, rested with the Combined Studies Group, initially under Gilbert Layton, an army colonel on detached service with the CIA. Layton employed a force of Nung tribal fighters to guard Agency assets and for a special mission force, and ran a maritime training center and base in addition to the air operation. The maritime center was located at Da Nang, where Tucker Gougelman was chief of base. Gougelman, a former marine and longtime CIA operative, became so involved in Vietnam he virtually went native, acquiring a family and local interests. He returned to South Vietnam just before its final fall years later, only to be captured by the enemy and never heard from again. Presumably the North Vietnamese interrogated Gougelman and killed him.

Assorted specialists on detached service from the military augmented the CIA for its exotic clandestine missions. These included not only Green Berets but navy underwater demolition experts and Sea-Air-Land (SEAL) soldiers. The marines had an equivalent unconventional warfare unit too, the Force Reconnaissance battalions, and it was not long before the Force Recon specialists were called on to help the covert war.

Operations against North Vietnam continued, but they continued also to present a problem in terms of effectiveness. In January 1963 the CIA presented President Kennedy with revised plans for the activities, designated Projects Haylift and Hardnose. National security adviser McGeorge Bundy told the president that the CIA plan was worth approving even though there was good reason to believe it would encounter "all the difficulties of an operation in a denied area." That May the Joint Chiefs of Staff began planning extended and graduated unconventional warfare operations. Before long the CIA was infiltrating the north with an average of three agent teams a month. By the end of the year the covert air fleet had grown to a dozen aircraft of various types, including modern C-123 twin-engine transports.

Maritime activities were also receiving increased attention from the U.S. navy. The NSC Special Group (CI), at its meeting on September 27, 1962, determined to recommend that fast gunboats be used in the CIA's Vietnam operations. In October the navy directed its Philadelphia Navy Yard to reactivate two aluminum-hulled patrol torpedo (PT) boats in storage there. These craft, PT-810 and 811, were rearmed as gunboats, each with two 40 mm and two 20 mm guns. In May 1963 the navy began using two more boats it purchased in Norway, called Nastys. They were sent to the Far East in the fall of 1963, eventually to join CIA-procured fast craft, also from Norway, called Swifts. Local improvements included removal of the forward 40 mm guns, addition of 57 mm recoilless rifles, .50-caliber machine guns, and 81 mm mortars installed on two of the Nastys. Eight Nastys were in place and operating from Da Nang by June 1964. Except during combat missions, they were commanded by the U.S. Naval Operations Support Group, with training and leadership supplied by SEAL Team One and maintenance from Boat Support Unit One under Lieutenant Burton K.

Knight. During combat the Nastys operated under their Vietnamese crews, though it was not unknown for Americans to accompany them on missions.

During 1963 the CIA relinquished control of most of its activities in South Vietnam. It continued to run the covert war against the north, but that too was coming to an end. Presidential orders to the Joint Chiefs to prepare for nonattributable raids using U.S. advisory assistance, training, and equipment, orders given that May, clearly anticipated transition to military command.

The turning point occurred at a conference among senior U.S. officials in Honolulu on November 20, 1963, just days before the assassination of President Kennedy. There the president was represented by McGeorge Bundy while Secretary of Defense McNamara headed the Washington delegates. William Colby, by now chief of the CIA's Far East Division, just returning from an inspection visit to South Vietnam, briefed the group on the latest developments.

McNamara asked Colby about the covert war against the north and how it might benefit from direct military participation. The secretary of defense thought the transfer of CIA control in the south, called Operation Switchback, could lead to a whole new dimension of pressures against the north.

"They just won't work, Mr. Secretary," Colby told McNamara, referring to the agent teams put into the north. He pointed to the lack of success of similar infiltration efforts against Eastern Europe and the Soviet Union in the early 1950s. Colby's deputy, Robert J. Myers, also spoke of the uniform failure of such missions earlier in both North Korea and mainland China. McNamara listened, a cold look on his face, then rejected the CIA's objections. Lack of effectiveness, the secretary believed, must have been due to the relatively small scale of the operations.

Colby believed in psychological warfare. He advised that U.S. efforts should concentrate on this, including leaflet flights and radio broadcasts that might shake morale in North Vietnam. Instead McNamara ordered the CIA officer, in conjunction with General William C. Westmoreland, commander of MACV, to prepare a twelve-month, three-phase plan for graduated covert pressures against North Vietnam. Colby and Westmoreland huddled and over the following month produced the new plan. It relied on the existing Pacific Command Operations Plan (OPLAN) 37-63 for many of its basic assumptions. The new effort was designated OPLAN 34-A. On December 20, in the course of a visit to Saigon, McNamara approved OPLAN 34-A and directed it to be forwarded to the president.

The president was now Lyndon Johnson, who had taken office in the wake of Kennedy's assassination. Johnson knew little of this background, but he was committed to giving the military every resource it needed to accomplish what it promised in Vietnam. Nevertheless he was warned: "Despite considerable effort, [deleted] very little has come of these operations," NSC staffer Mike Forrestal reported on December 11, "partly because of the tight police control in the North and partly because of their very small size."

Still, Forrestal too went along with the basic thrust of the 34-A concept. Warning that the capacity to carry out large-scale operations did not exist, he thought there was no reason it could not be developed "while we try to work out a diplomatic scenario in which military pressure against the North would play a part." Thus the bottom line, for the president's own NSC staff, was that "it would be worthwhile exploring the possibility of larger-scale operations against selected targets in the North, *provided* we carried them out in connection with a political program designed to get a practical reaction out of Hanoi." Forrestal, it is worth noting, was generally considered a dove in the bureaucratic wars of Washington.

President Johnson approved OPLAN 34-A for execution beginning January 16, 1964.

Under OPLAN 34-A the CIA would continue to help with psychological warfare, as Colby favored, but the major role fell to a new entity created under MACV on January 16. This was the Studies and Observation Group (SOG), commanded by Colonel Clyde Russell, a joint unconventional warfare task force with an initial strength of 150 men, half of them officers. The deputy commander was supposed to come from CIA, but the Agency never named anyone to the post.

To conduct its various operations, MACSOG was subdivided into a number of sections. An Air Studies Group (Op-32) was based at Nha Trang with six specially equipped C-123 aircraft. The crews, who received special training at Hurlbut Air Force Base in Florida, were initially seven nationalist Chinese and three Vietnamese. The Maritime Studies Group (Op-31) and MACSOG's first Forward Operating Base (FOB) were at Da Nang. A Ground Studies Group worked through launch sites that eventually became FOBs. Ground operations were subdivided into Northern Infiltrations (Op-34) and Cross-border Operations (Op-35). Finally, Op-33 was the psychological warfare component. Intelligence support was provided by U-2 flights over

Cambodia, Laos, and North Vietnam averaging one or two a day in February 1964.

The 34-A operations began with an air mission on February 1. An initial maritime operation (a category soon to gain the acronym MAROP) occurred on the 16th. South Vietnamese frogmen tried to sabotage Swatow patrol craft at Quang Khe as well as a ferry at Cap Ron. Later sabotage attempts failed at Quang Khe and against bridges along the coast. Meanwhile, the operations involved many more Americans, starting with Captain Phillip S. Bucklew, USN, commander of the Naval Operations Support Group at Da Nang. The base and associated facilities at Hoa Cam and Dong Ha by now housed both Navy SEALs and Marine Force Recon men. The Force Recon detachments were replaced at six-month intervals for Project Tiger.

April witnessed a flurry of concern over lack of impact of the MAROPs. Echoing Mike Forrestal, Ambassador Henry Cabot Lodge now observed that the missions could not be justified "except as part of a well thought out diplomatic maneuver." Pacific commander Admiral U. S. Grant Sharp reported that "I have been watching this program closely and see . . . some of our early reservations . . . becoming reality." He questioned the competence of the Vietnamese frogmen/ SEALs, a unit that was "not fully developed."

Air operations also suffered difficulties. One aircraft went down over North Vietnam early in the year, to add to the two lost during the CIA phase of the covert war. When MACSOG took over, five agent teams had been active in the north. The military soon added another. Then, between April and July, there were eight air drops with high losses and radio contact with only half the teams landed. Reporting to President Johnson, Mac Bundy wrote "very" in his precise handwriting in front of a memo's assessment that results of the effort had been "moderately successful." The Joint Chiefs reported that one team had been specially targeted against the rail link from Hanoi up the Red River Valley, but were unable to point to any examples of success. It was typical of the air operations, code-named Project Duck Hook, that by the end of November 1964 only one of five air missions approved for the *October* schedule had been completed. Later analysis convinced U.S. intelligence that the teams still in radio contact were all being controlled by the North Vietnamese.

A first success for the MAROPs came only in May, when a North Vietnamese junk was intercepted at sea. Thus began Project Fascination, a CIA contribution intended to cripple the North Vietnamese fishing industry. Fishermen were given gift kits and asked to stop. Over time, like many ideas in Vietnam, this one led to reverse results: eager to be intercepted and receive American largesse, northern fishermen fished even more. Intelligence established that unprecedented numbers of North Vietnamese had become fishermen. At least interrogation of the northerners at Lao Cham island off Da Nang occasionally furnished scraps of useful information.

In June and July 1964 coastal missions also achieved a measure of success. On June 12 a storage facility was destroyed and two weeks later a bridge. On the night of June 30/July 1, Nastys PTF-5 and 6 launched a coastal raid near the mouth of the Kien River. The raiders were seen by a sampan which raised the alarm, however, and the beach security party protecting the raiders' rubber rafts was surrounded and taken under fire. The raiders shelled a water pumping station and got away but had to abandon three 57 mm recoilless rifles and lost two men believed killed. All these incidents the Joint Chiefs reported as successes to President Johnson on July 27.

The month continued with psychological warfare missions against North Vietnamese naval bases at Quang Khe and Ben Thuy, while at Cap Ron on July 15 the Nastys suffered a setback when two more men were lost during an abortive attack on a security post. A mission against Vinh Son was canceled when intelligence detected increased patrol activity by the North Vietnamese navy.

Further raids were scheduled against the islands of Hon Me and Hon Nieu on the night of July 30/August 1, 1964. These involved four Nasty boats, two to shell each island. It was intended to conduct the MAROP against Vinh Son radar station on August 3. According to one account, the July 30 raids were coordinated by Lieutenant "Reb" Bearce of Force Recon. Another account has it that two American SEALs went ashore with landing parties that night, parties that landed at the wrong end of Hon Me and were unable to reach their objective, a radar station. The navy's official history reports that the approach of the raiders was detected, however, and that the raiders knew it, so there was no question of putting ashore landing parties that night.

In any case, the islands were shelled. North Vietnamese naval forces reacted, sending Swatow boats after the Nastys that pursued them but were unable to catch up. The covert warfare craft passed the U.S. destroyer *Maddox* as they headed home to Da Nang, and *Maddox* was then attacked by the North Vietnamese as she cruised in the Tonkin Gulf. This notorious incident of August 2, and the more doubtful one two days later, led to the first American bombing of North

Vietnam. The navy claims there was no relationship between the *Maddox* patrol and the coastal raids, indeed that the United States had nothing to do with these South Vietnamese raids.

Targets for raids were selected and approved by Americans, the boats were readied and supplied by Americans, and Americans may have accompanied them. Without more detailed explication it must be considered farfetched that there was *no* connection. The navy history reports that coordination between the destroyer patrols, which were intended to gather electronic intelligence, and the 34-A boat raids was considered but rejected at the high-command level. On the other hand, at least one former navy communications officer recalls seeing a message to the destroyer commander from the Chief of Naval Operations alerting him to prepare to support the boat raids. The reader must judge for himself.

The CIA, at least, had no doubts. At National Security Council meetings called to consider the incidents in the Tonkin Gulf, John Mc-Cone, CIA director, told the assembled group that "the North Vietnamese are reacting defensively to our attacks on their offshore islands." William Colby, in his most recent account of the war, is equally forthright. "The North Vietnamese attacked an American Navy destroyer," Colby recounts, "in what was clearly a retaliation for a covert raid the previous night by maritime forces the CIA had initiated and turned over to the Department of Defense." Colby seems relieved that the Agency, which had given up its control over the covert war against North Vietnam, cannot be saddled with responsibility for the Tonkin Gulf.

In the aftermath of the incidents, MAROPs were temporarily discontinued, until President Johnson ordered their resumption in NSAM-314 on September 14. Destroyer patrols also resumed at that time. Vinh Son was one of the first targets in the new campaign, Project Timberwork. Additional Nastys with design improvements were ordered in Norway for delivery in the spring of 1965. The biggest MAROP yet occurred with a six-boat raid on November 25, while the last one of 1964 came on December 8. On December 19 McGeorge Bundy concurred with a Westmoreland recommendation that future MAROPs be approved in monthly schedules, as were air operations or sensitive reconnaissance missions. Junk seizures henceforth could be made under local authority without reference to Washington.

In early 1965 Army Chief of Staff General Harold K. Johnson ordered a top-secret study of all aspects of the U.S. military effort in

South Vietnam. Completed in March, the review's analysis of 34-A operations concluded that "the material effectiveness of operations has been marginal." Among 34-A efforts the MAROPs were judged to be most successful, but the study could point to only three successful sabotage missions and admitted a loss rate of 50 percent. The best that could be said for 34-A was that it had a psychological effect in showing Hanoi that the north would not be immune to retaliatory measures.

The covert war could be routinized, but it could not be made effective. This much is demonstrated by the record for the period between January 19 and February 2, 1965. In those days there were two leaflet drops, nine MAROPs, and one insertion of an agent team. Tiger Island was hit three times by MAROPs, the Mach Nuoc radar twice, and there were raids on the naval bases at Quang Khe and Dong Hoi. One raid aborted due to engine trouble, three met heavy return fire, one proved unsuccessful when Nastys collided and incurred heavy damage. As for the resupply of agent team Remus, four agents and four bundles were dropped on the night of January 20. One was killed on landing, one broke his leg, and he and the other two no doubt encountered a North Vietnamese welcoming party. Of roughly eighty agent teams infiltrated into the north during this early covert war, none ever returned.

Radio Hanoi charged the U.S. with another boat raid on February 13 and claimed both Nastys involved had been set afire by defenders. Other broadcasts protested provocative incidents on February 7, 8, and 11. Hanoi used this evident threat as its pretext for demanding withdrawal of the fixed teams from the International Control Commission that were supposed to monitor implementation of the 1962 Geneva agreement on Laos. Although the U.S. remained convinced all along that Hanoi had never observed the 1962 agreement, it was galling that U.S. covert operations could furnish justification for scuttling it. Hanoi also countered with its own operations, most particularly the February 7 shelling of the U.S. air base at Pleiku. The Americans then retaliated with Flaming Dart, the first sustained air attacks against the north, soon to become Rolling Thunder. The cycle of violence continued and sharpened.

The appropriate stopping point for this account of the early phase of the covert war is the Vung Ro incident. On February 16, 1965, an Army helicopter pilot flying over coastal Phu Yen province sighted a steel-hulled vessel under camouflage in a bay. Aircraft were summoned to sink the ship, and divers later salvaged parts of its cargo while exploration of the shores of the bay uncovered additional caches of weapons and supplies. The ship at Vung Ro Bay was held out as an example of how North Vietnam was feeding the war, exhibited to reporters, and featured in the first white paper, called "Aggression from the North," that the State Department issued to justify U.S. armed intervention.

This boat at Vung Ro and the caches found nearby yielded some 3,600 rifles and submachine guns, including some of 7.62 mm. There were 2,000 rounds of mortar ammunition, 1,500 rounds for recoilless rifles, 500 pounds of explosives in prepared charges, and 500 antitank plus 1,000 stick grenades. Five hundred pounds of medical supplies had labels indicating manufacture in North Vietnam, the Soviet Union, the People's Republic of China, East Germany, Czechoslovakia, Bulgaria, and Japan. Documents aboard showed the 130-foot, 100-ton ship as unit K.35 of Naval Transportation Group 125, and included a Haiphong newspaper dated January 23, 1965, military health records, and personal identification for a member of the North Vietnamese 338th Division.

It was an incredible find. Meeting with Westmoreland the next day, Vietnamese leader General Nguyen Khanh showed a photo of the boat and said reprisal bombing of the North Vietnamese navy seemed warranted. Newly arrived U.S. Ambassador Maxwell Taylor cabled a week later that "this discovery is particularly timely in terms of justifying the US/GVN air strikes against North Vietnamese military targets." Air attacks indeed took place.

Years later a former CIA Southeast Asia specialist, laid off during the Carter administration, recalled having seen a very suggestive document himself. It was a carbon copy of a final operating plan, a three- or four-page proposal for a project to fabricate evidence of outside aid to the Viet Cong. The officer, Philip Liechty, in the second of a fifteen-year Agency career, recalls that the plan called for taking large amounts of Communist bloc weapons from CIA warehouses to load them onto a Vietnamese-style coastal boat. In an unusual (and unusually timed) departure from its practice of not commenting on reports of its activities, more than a year later the CIA denied Liechty's claim. Former CIA officer Liechty stood by his original story.

Vung Ro Bay punctuated the move to a new stage of warfare. The covert war continued, but alongside the spooks and secret warriors, large contingents of regular troops moved into South Vietnam to wage a parallel conventional war. It was no longer possible, or even desirable, to keep Vietnam quiet, to conduct that war secretly. Judging from the record, the Vietnam War could not have been won secretly, at least not on the basis of the covert pressures against the north. The Green Berets and other unconventional warfare specialists who labored on this facet of the war worked in vain. The real war had arrived. It began with another mystery, in fact many mysteries wrapped up in one, in the incident in Tonkin Gulf.

Six Mysteries of the Tonkin Gulf

For many Americans, first notice of the Vietnam War came with the Tonkin Gulf incident of 1964. Before that, large though it might loom in White House councils, Vietnam barely registered in the American consciousness. Afterward, Vietnam mattered. What made the difference was the "incident," combat in the Tonkin Gulf between North Vietnamese and the U.S. navy. To hear the Johnson administration tell the story, American vessels innocently plying international waters were attacked without provocation, and when the North Vietnamese repeated the action against a renewed naval patrol, the United States had to respond. Incensed at Hanoi's apparent perfidy, Congress voted a joint resolution authorizing the president to take action, including the use of force. It was the legal authority Lyndon Johnson used to send American boys to fight an Asian war.

Something happened in the Tonkin Gulf in August 1964, but not precisely what the administration claimed. In later years, parts of the administration's story came apart like the layers of an onion. In time the Tonkin Gulf Resolution was repealed while the story of the incident itself became enmeshed in a whole series of controversies. Many mysteries of the Tonkin Gulf have endured; here we examine a few of the most interesting.

■ Practically everyone agrees on one thing, that on August 2, 1964, the destroyer *USS Maddox* (DD-731) came under attack by North Vietnamese naval craft in the Gulf of Tonkin. That is only the bare bones, however. Hanoi acknowledged the attack but claimed the *Maddox* was in North Vietnamese territorial waters. From there the story gets worse: the U.S. destroyer retreated down the gulf, rendezvoused with a second ship, and deliberately returned to the scene of the initial incident to assert a U.S. presence. The two ships together then experienced events they interpreted as a renewed attack. In retaliation, the United States bombed North Vietnam. It was the first overt air action of the Vietnam War.

"It is my duty to the American people to report that renewed hostile actions against United States ships on the high seas in the Gulf of Tonkin have today required me to order the military forces of the United States to take action in reply," President Johnson thundered. He made the declaration from a lectern in the Fish Room of the White House, where television cameras had been set up. It was almost midnight. The timing was intended to permit the navy to get its carrier aircraft into the air for the retaliatory air strike, which hit four North Vietnamese naval bases and a fuel storage site. Two planes were shot down and two more damaged in the strikes, out of sixty-four sorties. Hanoi's oil storage facility at Vinh was judged 90 percent destroyed, and twenty-five naval craft, half its overall force, were destroyed at the four bases.

The first mystery is the question of whether the *Maddox* was in international waters. "On the high seas off North Vietnam," Admiral Thomas H. Moorer, commander of the Pacific Fleet, put it in secret cables at the time. North Vietnam claimed a band of territorial waters twelve miles from the coastline, *but* that claim was never made public until September 1964, about a month after the incidents. Investigations of the *Maddox*'s navigation show the ship closed to within ten miles or less of offshore islands or the Vietnamese coast five times between July 31 and the first Tonkin Gulf incident on August 2. The destroyer captain, Commander Herbert L Ogier, was entirely within his rights to do so: his orders were to remain outside a line eight miles from the coast or four from the offshore islands. Ogier maintained that distance, approaching no closer than 5.1 nautical miles from Hon Vat on the morning of August 2.

At the time the navy recognized only a three-mile territorial limit for North Vietnam's coastal waters.

Regardless of these facts, the August 2 incident took place in midafternoon, hours after the island approach, when the *Maddox* was in fact on the high seas. Thus the PT boat attack was not a *defense* of territorial waters, only a *response* to a *perceived* violation of national sovereignty.

Hanoi was on shaky ground to argue about territorial waters, but Washington overplayed its hand by pretending the destroyer was innocently transiting the Gulf of Tonkin. Therein lies a second puzzle, the *mystery of the passage that was not innocent.* Captain John J. Herrick could tell about that, for Captain Herrick, not the ship's skipper, was in overall command of the *Maddox* that day. Also aboard the destroyer was a van crammed with extra communications gear for a National Security Agency (NSA) spy mission, called a Desoto Patrol, to intercept North Vietnamese radio communications and other electronic emissions. Such NSA intercepts, shared with Herrick, in fact gave the mission commander many hours of warning before the incident of August 2.

A second reason the *Maddox* was not making an innocent passage was Operation 34-A. According to the navy's official history, coordinating these 34-A maritime operations (MAROPs) with the Desoto patrols was considered, but rejected.

Despite this averral, there have long been contentions that the *Maddox* cooperated with MAROPs. These are only strengthened by the official history, which identifies specific MAROPs on July 31, in conjunction with passage of the *Maddox,* and of both the *Maddox* and the *Turner Joy* on August 3. On the former occasion MAROPs Nasty boats, small but heavily armed, hit the North Vietnamese offshore islands, on the latter, Vinh Son and the Cap Ron area. It was thus a matter of arcane and highly classified knowledge for an *American* official to be aware there was no connection between MAROPs and Desoto; that North Vietnamese observers concluded differently is understandable. In actuality there *was* a link between MAROPs and Desoto, if only in the sense that the latter furnished usable intelligence to exploit in 34-A operations, while the MAROPs in turn "tickled" North Vietnamese defenses, tempting them to swing into action, revealing dispositions to waiting technicians aboard the destroyer. In fact, "tickling" and "ticklers" were standard jargon in communications intelligence precisely because these kinds of pinpricks and feint attacks are classic tactics intended to fake the adversary into revealing himself.

Another mystery of the Tonkin Gulf concerns the sequence of events in the mid-afternoon battle. Admiral Moorer, who in 1970 was up for confirmation to be chairman of the Joint Chiefs of Staff, testified that the *Maddox* opened fire only after she came under torpedo attack, insisting that the records back up his recitation of the events. Now the records show that the *Maddox* commenced fire at 9,000 yards at precisely 4:08 p.m. local time, three minutes after firing initial warning shots. During the next sixteen minutes Commander Ogier's destroyer pumped out 283 shells aimed at the Vietnamese boats. As for

Vietnamese fire, the navy's official history shows that the *Maddox* made a positive identification of the PT boats at 9,800 yards, but that the lead Vietnamese warship launched its first torpedo—"unobserved by the *Maddox*"—somewhere between 9,000 and 5,000 yards from the speeding U.S. destroyer. In other words, the *Maddox* could not have *known* she was already under attack when she commenced fire (the torpedo launch was not observed) and very probably (since the torpedo is thought to have been loosed at less than the distance at which the destroyer opened fire) she was not. Thus the best the navy official history can muster for the version Moorer has staked out is very lukewarm approbation.

Captain Herrick's messages to higher command make clear, moreover, that he considered the *Maddox* threatened and expected to defend her. Mission commander and commander of Destroyer Division 192, Herrick had been warned by his NSA detachment of a probable attack, estimated the risk as unacceptable, and asked higher authority to cancel the patrol. Orders to continue the mission left Herrick determined to defend the ship. All evidence indicates the *Maddox* opened fire based on the approach of the North Vietnamese vessels; initiation of engagement was thus on the basis of perceived intent, without reference to an actual attack.

The biggest mystery about the Gulf of Tonkin revolves around *whether there was a second incident at all*. The question subsumes an array of smaller but significant pieces in the puzzle. After the August 2 incident, Captain Herrick had Commander Ogier run the *Maddox* straight down the gulf, meeting the *Turner Joy* (under Lieutenant Commander Robert C. Barnhart, Jr.) next morning. It was then that both ships were sent back up the gulf. Admiral Moorer had a substantial role in shaping the aggressive orders Herrick received for the renewed patrol. Not only was he to return to the scene of the previous incident, but he was to operate in that vicinity for *two days,* spend a further day off Vinh, and one more coming south past Mui Ron and Vinh Son. A two-destroyer force to sail in close proximity to the North Vietnamese coast for ninety-six hours? Rationalize as you may, it was taunting Hanoi to do so.

In any case, Herrick made the patrol, and the destroyers experienced a series of events they interpreted as a second North Vietnamese attack. It cannot be shown from the record, however, that the events were attacks and not other phenomena altogether.

What was the physical evidence for the second incident? That is one subsidiary mystery. The August 2 incident occurred in daylight;

the evidence for it includes photographs of the attacking PT boats, sightings by numerous sailors topside aboard the *Maddox* who witnessed the action, at least three torpedoes (in addition to the "unobserved" one), a bullet that hit the destroyer and was recovered (mounted since, and in possession of Admiral Moorer), and the sightings and gun-camera photos of pilots from the aircraft carrier *Ticonderoga,* who flew up to support the *Maddox* and hit the PT boats themselves. In contrast, the August 4 incident occurred at night, and the physical evidence for it is very thin indeed.

For August 4 there are no photos of attacking boats, shells hitting the American destroyers, or prolonged observation of the enemy by sailors. Four men aboard the *Turner Joy* reported a torpedo wake, perhaps two. On the other hand, Commander James B. Stockdale, a naval aviator who witnessed an hour and a half of the battle from an unparalleled vantage point overhead, saw nothing. An experienced pilot, Stockdale was a squadron commander aboard the *Ticonderoga* and had led the navy's aircraft assisting the *Maddox* in the August 2 attack. He responded to air controllers and looked at all the locations where the destroyers thought there were targets. Nothing. Yet the captain of the *Turner Joy* and some crewmen insisted they had seen a searchlight, boat cockpit lights, and smoke at the place they claimed to have sunk a torpedo boat—one of two said to have been sunk in the alleged three-hour battle.

Underlining this contradiction is the account of Lieutenant John Nicholson, leader of a flight of aircraft that took over air cover from Stockdale's planes. Nicholson's flight had scrambled from the carrier *Constellation,* outbound from liberty at Hong Kong, and mired in the weather front that had just passed over the Gulf of Tonkin. Nicholson found bright moonlit conditions in the incident area and picked up the destroyers easily but could see nothing else. One wingman thought he saw something, but when the planes dropped flares the surface of the sea was empty. Finally the destroyers told them where to attack and then, just as the A-4C jets rolled in to strike, begged the planes to abort the mission. As the jets pulled up they recognized the American destroyers right beneath them—the surface ships had provided erroneous instructions. After that the *Constellation* aircraft were doubly dubious about any radio chatter from the destroyers.

Herrick and Ogier, the mission commander and his flag captain, both refused to certify the authenticity of the engagement to interlocutors in Hawaii. Except for the initial radar contact, Herrick believed, the radar claims were no good, and he thought that many of the reports of torpedoes in the water—of which there were more than twenty—could have resulted from misinterpretation of self-noise. Ogier concurred in doubting the initial impressions. *Maddox* electronic specialists had had a terrible day, with the sonar out in the morning, a radio transponder after that, and the radar performance on the night of the 4th. The most solid contact the *Maddox* picked up all night, the bridge passed to the gun director who, when he had laid the six five-inch guns of the *Maddox* on the target, almost as an afterthought, asked to have the *Turner Joy* identify herself. The accompanying destroyer briefly flashed her running lights. They were squarely in the cross hairs of *Maddox* range finders. On the *Turner Joy*, though Barnhart professed to think the phantom battle a real one, he reported no sonar returns, not even the alleged torpedo seen by ships' company. *Turner Joy* had had plentiful radar contacts, with the two destroyers expending a total of 249 five-inch and 123 three-inch shells, and four or five depth charges.

"For all I know," President Johnson is recorded as having said a few months later, "our Navy was shooting at whales out there."

As a matter of fact, a school of whales is one of the better hypotheses, which would account for torpedo sightings, wake reports, and sonar submarine contact reports during that wild night.

Worth noting is the further fact that the Gulf of Tonkin was a source of spurious electronic signals, beyond the usual level of false returns. In 1945 carrier raids against the Japanese in the South China Sea, the light carrier *Langley* and other vessels experienced false contacts on their radars in this operating area. The exact same occurred in 1954 when a navy carrier group operated in the Tonkin Gulf in conjunction with the battle of Dien Bien Phu. On that occasion at least one U.S. aircraft was lost at sea after being vectored to intercept a false contact. In September 1964 again, when Desoto patrols resumed after the incidents, the destroyers in the mission detected false contacts. Significantly, in the September 1964 incident Washington concluded almost immediately that the radar returns *were* spurious.

The navy's official history is misleading in its claim that the night of August 4 was "particularly good for radar operations." In the era before computer-linked radars (which more easily screen out false images), a period that includes 1964, radar observability was directly related to weather. The weather improved through that night as a storm front moved east past Hainan (so that the *Constellation*'s planes found clear conditions *later*), but observers, from *Maddox* radar and gun-director watches to pilot Stockdale, agree that at the outset of the purported incident the night was one of numerous clouds, a ceiling of two thousand feet or less, complete with rain squalls and thunderstorms. Any form of atmospheric electrical activity plays havoc with radar, and some meteorological phenomena deliver radar returns as well. The problems with this evidence suggest that radar and sonar signals should be discounted for the August 4 incident.

In explanations at the time, and in immediately succeeding years, Robert S. McNamara maintained that the clincher lay in the radio intercepts gathered during the Desoto patrol. Examined in some detail at a February 20, 1968, Senate hearing, the intercepts were numerous, but there were four upon which McNamara especially relied. The first identified the U.S. destroyers as they approached the North Vietnamese coast, the second ordered motor gunboats to make ready for night operations (with one PT also, if it could be repaired in time—it was not), and two messages described action with American vessels.

The first two intercepts were suggestive but by no means conclusive. It was necessary for Hanoi to alert its naval forces to carry out a sortie, but a naval alert did not prove that a sortie had occurred. It is overreaching to infer that this intercept constituted an attack order, in particular in a context in which the North Vietnamese were unable to repair their PT boat, the only one that really had any capability against the U.S. destroyers. It is equally plausible that, finding they would have no PT boat, the Vietnamese canceled the sortie, or, as inferred by CIA analyst George Allen, that it was an order to investigate the American ships rather than attack them.

Another minor mystery of the Tonkin Gulf flows from these same intercepts—what business was the *Maddox* about in the Tonkin Gulf? The communications van was manned by ten navy and five marine specialists who stood watch around the clock. Navy Lieutenant Gerrell D. Moore had orders to share threat information with Captain Herrick and did so. Herrick's message estimating unacceptable risk followed his learning of the sighting report, and his later warning that he expected to be attacked were dispatched after learning of Hanoi's order to its *Swatow*-class gunboats to make ready for sea. In retrospect it seems clear that foreknowledge of a supposed Vietnamese intention to attack predisposed the U.S. vessels to believe they were engaged, a self-fulfilling prophecy.

To avoid creating such problems, usual communications intelligence practice is *not* to share this sort of threat information with the interception platform, a breach of security. Indeed, in the incident that followed, Herrick sent several messages, some of them unencoded with "flash" precedence, that alluded to his information, potentially tipping off the North Vietnamese that they needed to overhaul their codes and communication procedures. Why Lieutenant Moore was permitted to breach security and share threat information is a mystery, but the National Security Agency has never explained its procedures in this instance.

The two other intercepts critical to McNamara's case for the authenticity of the August 4 incident are situation-report type messages. Jim Stockdale comments that these intercepts "were unique in two ways: (1) both described events that in no way resembled the fact situation in the vicinity of the *Maddox* or *Joy* in the Tonkin Gulf on August 4, 1964, but (2) both . . . resembled what a Vietnamese observer standing on the deck of one of the PT boats which attacked the *Maddox . . . might* have decided was the fact situation of *that* day. As the only person in the world who had a good first-hand look at both the episode of the 2nd and the episode of the 4th, I cannot avoid the conclusion that McNamara wound up using August 2nd material when analyzing events of the 4th." Stockdale is not the only one to have come to such a conclusion. Another source, Dr. Louis Tordella, deputy director of the National Security Agency at the time, told Senate committee staff in 1972 that he believed references to aircraft in these intercepts clearly dated them to the previous incident.

There is also the curious case of the North Vietnamese navy prisoner captured with other seamen in 1966, when their PT boat was sunk by another American aircraft. This officer furnished rich intelligence and had rank and position such that no PT mission could have occurred without him knowing of it. Of the August 2 battle, the officer related under interrogation, he had vivid memories and had been a senior subordinate to the North Vietnamese mission commander. According to the historian Edwin E. Moise, who has made detailed investigations of the formerly classified records, the Vietnamese officer specifically insisted he had *no* recollection of any attacks made on August 4. The navy's official history maintains that this very same prisoner interrogation, by confirming allegations of PT boat losses, provides final verification of the August 4 incident.

By the time the sequence of events in the Tonkin Gulf was becoming controversial, along with the reality of the August 4 incident, accounts by the Vietnamese seamen could no longer be checked. The Senate began investigating the incidents in 1968 and held a hearing that February 20. Government censors took months to approve for release a version of the private ("executive session") hearings at which witnesses discussed such items as the intercepted radio messages and prisoner interrogations. That portion of the Senate hearing was released only in December. Meanwhile, that same month, as a goodwill gesture in connection with recently begun peace talks in Paris, Washington sent home the Vietnamese veteran of Tonkin Gulf among a group of fourteen seamen returned at Vinh. The sailors were picked up from a jail in Da Nang and flown aboard the landing ship *Dubuque,* where they had to be protected from angry marines of the Third Battalion, Twenty-sixth Regiment, which had recently suffered at North Vietnamese hands in the battles of Khe Sanh and Dai Do. At Vinh there was a tense local truce in which Vietnamese MiG fighters orbited to one side and U.S. aircraft to the other. The motor junk the seamen were given did not work, and they ended up going home in the *Dubuque's* admiral's barge. The net effect, however, was to put Tonkin Gulf testimony beyond the reach of Senate investigators.

As for the retaliatory bombing of North Vietnam that followed the Tonkin Gulf incident, called operation Pierce Arrow, President Johnson made his decision just five hours after the alleged August 4 incident, when there had been precious little time for confirmatory inquiries of any kind. Perhaps, in the rush to judgment, *it did not matter what the facts were.* And here we come to the deepest mystery of the Tonkin Gulf affair.

Attempting a preemptive defense, the navy's official history blandly comments, "American leaders did not seek to provoke a North Vietnamese reaction in order to secure a *casus belli.*" The evidence presented is simply that the navy expected Hanoi to acquiesce in the face of American naval power. That claim obscures the reality that "American leaders" were managing the coercive 34-A covert action as well as a counterinsurgency program throughout South Vietnam and Laos, not just in the Tonkin Gulf. American leaders had a big problem in South Vietnam where a military strongman, General Nguyen Khanh, demonstrated a pronounced predilection for coup politics, the consequence being shaky political stability in Saigon plus a free hand to the Viet Cong in the countryside. There were rumors that Khanh had put out political feelers toward Hanoi, while the South Vietnamese army suffered a clear defeat at Binh Gia, where the VC for the first time virtually destroyed South Vietnamese elite units in the field. Falling morale in Saigon put Washington under pressure to energize the flagging effort.

Behind closed doors Johnson had put the bureaucracy to work on a Vietnam policy review as early as May. The recommendation that national security adviser McGeorge Bundy gave the president was to approve a decision to "use selected and carefully graduated military forces" against North Vietnam "after appropriate diplomatic and political warning and preparation," and *unless* there was sufficient improvement in South Vietnam and Laos. A draft presidential memorandum prepared for McNamara by his whiz kids summarized the choice: improve the situation in the south with or without "strikes on the North."

These kinds of options were percolating in Washington three months *before* the Tonkin Gulf incidents. A special working group under the National Security Council was planning in detail for various scenarios. It included high-level participants from the Pentagon and State Department, such as William P. Bundy, brother of the national security adviser, who was the leading Far East man at State. The Special Southeast Asia Working Group concluded that some congressional authorization was politic in escalating to overt force in Vietnam.

The argument put to LBJ in June 1964 was to try for a joint congressional resolution, and to do it immediately, before presidential politics (1964 was an election year) took over everything. With advisers and at NSC meetings, President Johnson seemed visibly perplexed about what to do to shore up Saigon, but he could not bring himself to surface the Vietnam War as a political issue by going to Capitol Hill for authority to go to war.

In this framework occurred the August 2, 1964, incident in the Gulf of Tonkin. It undoubtedly appeared to LBJ as a heaven-sent opportunity to try for the authority his advisers wanted without committing himself to responsibility for the initiative. Note that Johnson took no initial action following the August 2 incident *except* to declare that U.S. forces would resume their patrol, defend themselves, and disarm attackers. This sequence of events conforms closely to the NSC planning of May and June, meeting the perceived need for diplomatic warning to Hanoi. Then the August 4 "incident" followed. No wonder Captain Herrick and his subordinates were under such pressure to certify that an attack had occurred. If nothing happened on August 4, Admiral Moorer's orders to assert U.S. presence in the Gulf of Tonkin ensured that the Desoto patrol would remain close to the North Vietnamese coast for another three days.

Washington had motive. The Tonkin Gulf furnished occasion. Task Force 77 in the South China Sea generated the capability. Jim Stockdale, when he woke up aboard the *Ticonderoga* on the morning of August 5, felt sick when told they were summoned to retaliate for the "second" North Vietnamese attack. Days later senior Pentagon aides came to the *Ticonderoga* to hear him affirm there had been nothing out there in the second incident. Washington knew within days, probably by August 10, when Congress completed passage of the Gulf of Tonkin Resolution (Public Law 88-408). It would take years, with the executive fighting every step of the way, for the contrary indications on Tonkin Gulf to come out.

For conspiracy fans there is a final mystery of the Tonkin Gulf. This involves a purported back-channel cable from the chief of naval operations, Admiral David L. McDonald, direct to Captain Herrick, before the start of the Desoto mission. The cable is said to have ordered Herrick to *make sure* he got in harm's way by going in prepared to support MAROPs, and is connected with parallel orders through special warfare channels to the MAROPs craft that they could rely on destroyer support. The source, who had access to relevant navy communications files, later heard an intriguing account of the origins of the message. Late one July night, according to this account, the CNO was summoned to the White House to be met by Lyndon Johnson accompanied by two of his NSC staff. LBJ virtually ordered Admiral McDonald to send the *Maddox* into action, reportedly saying he had reason to know of the Desoto patrol and the MAROPs, their closeness, and the potential for an incident.

The story amounts to hearsay, a secondhand report. Expert sources lend it little credence. For example, McGeorge Bundy recalls no meetings between the CNO and the president, much less late-night sessions on Tonkin Gulf, and does not think other NSC staffers could have met with LBJ without him knowing of it. Navy sources scoff that McDonald would never have gone so far outside the chain of command. But diary notes kept for President Johnson *do* indicate a meeting with Admiral McDonald on July 31, 1964, though it was in the daytime (1:00 to 1:45 p.m.) and Admiral McDonald sat in the cabinet room in company with the other members of the Joint Chiefs of Staff. No record of this meeting has yet been found. The session with the Joint Chiefs may have been innocuous, and this story apocryphal, but it remains true that more than one former communications operator recalls strange traffic during those days up to and through the Tonkin Gulf incident.

Whether or not there was a conspiracy at Tonkin Gulf, deception occurred there, if not in the events surrounding the purported battles off the North Vietnamese coast, at least in the halls of Congress in Washington, D.C. There the Johnson administration, without mentioning its extensive private discussions on the steps to be taken in

Vietnam, asked for a straightforward grant of powers as if the Tonkin Gulf incidents had happened in a vacuum. No one admitted that for months, at least since June, leading American officials had been working specifically on an action scenario that could be used if there were a congressional resolution on Southeast Asia. Stampeded by supposed North Vietnamese aggression, Congress obliged with a resolution, passed in splendid ignorance of the administration's secret contingency plans. The nation moved closer to war without thought to America's allies, the South Vietnamese for whom this war was to be fought. American soldiers, sailors, and airmen were ultimately deceived as well—ignorant of the Vietnamese, they were not prepared for what followed.

Profile: Generals and Politics in South Vietnam

If you move one tank one foot more, I will have you bombed." That is what Air Vice-Marshal Nguyen Cao Ky says he told another South Vietnamese general who had begun moving troops, Ky supposed, for a coup d'état. This is only one of the stories, and not the most important, that Marshal Ky tells of participating in or busting up coups during the period before 1965, when Ky himself emerged as military strongman of South Vietnam. In the wake of the fall of Ngo Dinh Diem, there was no stabilization of South Vietnamese politics and no sense for Americans that they could work alongside steady allies. The roiling controversies of Vietnamese politics pitted faction against faction, generals leading them, creating a strange military alliance for Americans. Torn between a desire to stay out of Vietnamese politics, and the feeling that supporting one faction or another was the best way to halt the political infighting and get on with the war, Americans were anything but happy with their lot in South Vietnam. American advisers, especially those who served at a high level with the Vietnamese, could not help but become aware of the fragility of the coalitions under the surface of the South Vietnamese war effort. Despite the importance of the Vietnamese allies to the conduct of a war in their own land, however, very few American writers on Vietnam have paid much attention to the texture and qualities of the South Vietnamese military leadership. Considering that in the wake of the overthrow of Ngo Dinh Diem that leadership became South Vietnam's political leaders as well, the oversight is an important one.

■ The Army of the Republic of Vietnam (ARVN), as the Saigon leadership named the South Vietnamese army, was more than the defender of the government. The reasons lay in the origins of the military in the French colonial period. It was France that had first formed a Vietnamese National Army for the express purpose of fighting the Viet Minh in the war that had ended at Dien Bien Phu. Before that, and in fact until World War II, Vietnamese had merely served in the French Colonial Army, and as mere privates. In colonial Vietnam one could get ahead as an official of the administration or as a landowner. Anticlerical at home, for the most part the French favored Catholics in Vietnam; Catholic missionary priests had played an important role in creating the pro-French constituency that had given France a foothold in Vietnam. Eventually the pro-French Catholic elite of Vietnam themselves demanded that Vietnamese be permitted to rise to noncommissioned officer (NCO) and officer ranks in the Colonial Army. Nevertheless, by the time of World War II, when the Japanese occupied French Indochina and watched over the French administration, there were but a handful of Vietnamese officers among the forty thousand indigenous troops serving with the Colonial Army.

The availability of the military as a pathway to the Vietnamese elite was immeasurably broadened by the Franco-Vietnamese war. The French absolutely *needed* the Vietnamese National Army, both as a token of Vietnamese sovereignty (hence a demonstration that the war France fought was not a colonial one) and as an addition to their own troop strength. From its formal founding in 1949 through Dien Bien Phu, the Vietnamese National Army increased from a strength of 25,000 to about 240,000, and from just a single battalion to 172 such units. This rapid growth generated an acute need for officers that had to be met by commissioning Vietnamese. France lent plenty of officers and NCOs to the National Army throughout the war, but charges of continuing colonialism were hard to refute when critics could say, as they could in 1952, that Vietnamese officers commanded no more than a third of the battalions in Vietnam's own army. As a matter of fact, with 126,000 persons in the Vietnam National Army at that time, there were just four Vietnamese with the rank of colonel and seventy-six others who were majors or captains. Even by the time of Dien Bien Phu, only 40 of the 172 battalions were commanded by Vietnamese. Since about 40 officers were needed to lead each 800-man battalion, the Vietnamese had a requirement for almost 7,000 officers in their army. There were about 4,500, including only three generals. Clearly many opportunities were open to a Vietnamese officer.

A quick look at civilian life reveals a contrast that helps to show why the military might represent an attractive alternative for upward social mobility. From 1941 to 1951, the last decade during which France continued to administer the educational system in Vietnam, the number of students who were passed after taking examinations for a secondary-school degree averaged about a thousand a year, even though the number of Vietnamese in schools grew from 1,389 (1937) to about 25,000 (1951). The number of Vietnamese studying in France in 1951—college students who presumably had their degrees and were from families well enough off to afford this—stood at about 5,000. Those who lacked the money to live in France found themselves in great demand in the army, which required that its officers have secondary-school degrees. Vietnamese who joined the military during the French war would become the military elite by the time the Americans arrived. Vietnamese society during the time of the American war would be characterized by a military elite, on the one hand, and an economic and commercial elite on the other. By and large, the political elite comprised individuals drawn from these others.

A survey of the lives of South Vietnamese generals provides an interesting snapshot of this military elite which, aside from Ngo Dinh Diem, dominated Vietnamese politics throughout the American war in Southeast Asia. The following remarks are based on biographies of ninety-three individuals who attained the rank of senior colonel or brigadier general or above in the Army of the Republic of Vietnam, most of them by 1969. They have been compiled by the author over a long period during and since the war. Biographical data is less plentiful on ARVN officers promoted to this rank in 1972 and after, and these latter would probably shift the picture more toward one showing the impact of U.S. training beginning in the 1950s; but it would not appreciably change the picture regarding geographic and class origins of the generals, or that reflecting the differences between the military elite and South Vietnamese private soldiers.

We must also make the caveat that our snapshot is based upon less than comprehensive data. We cannot supply every ARVN general's complete biography. In many cases we have some but not all relevant information, although our data is largely sufficient for a broad survey of this type. As a matter of history, however, it is perplexing that for Vietnam, that most quantified of all wars, Americans should be ignorant of the class origins of a third of the South Vietnamese generals, or of the religious persuasions of fully two-thirds of them. This lack of key data about America's own allies underscores one reason for the U.S. defeat—that the United States believed it could fight this war without necessarily understanding Vietnam. That notion proved to be a delusion.

Now to our snapshot of the ARVN elite. First, in common with armies the world over, elite breeds elite. That is, people who had received the proper "sacraments"—the right training schools and assignments—stood a much greater chance of rising to the top. During the French time in Vietnam, an officer training school had briefly been located at Tong in 1940, and was recreated at Hue in 1948 and then moved to Dalat. This school was the Vietnamese West Point, its initial nine-month course of study raised to a year early on, to two years in 1956, and to a full four-year college program in 1966. This officers' academy graduated about two-thirds of the South Vietnamese generals. When graduates of the specialized Vietnamese naval school are added, the proportion is almost exactly two-thirds.

By way of contrast, reserve officer academies were a much poorer route to power, as was getting a commission out of NCO schools. As many officers were commissioned directly from the ranks in ARVN as graduated from both these sources, and all of them together accounted for the training of only about 12 percent of the men who rose to become generals in the South Vietnamese army. Nevertheless, these sources accounted for some key ARVN officers. For example, the reserve officer schools of the Vietnam National Army were located at Nam Dinh, in northern Vietnam, and at Thu Duc, a little to the north of Saigon. South Vietnamese military strongman and air force commander Nguyen Cao Ky was a 1952 graduate of Nam Dinh. Ky also became president of an association of officers from the reserve schools that helped form the base for his later political power. Four generals were graduates of Thu Duc, and every one of them became a key figure: Ngo Quang Truong, often pictured as the ARVN's best fighting general; Tran Van Minh, commander-in-chief of South Vietnamese armed forces; Nguyen Ngoc Loan, national police chief (infamous as the result of a photograph taken of him executing a Viet Cong prisoner during the Tet offensive); and Nguyen Duc Thang, who became a corps commander and also minister for pacification.

As with Ky and his reserve officers association, the Vietnamese generals became adept at creating and utilizing power bases from cohorts of their associates. Nguyen Van Thieu, Ky's nemesis and South Vietnam's last president, was a graduate of the officer academy when it was still at Hue, and a good half dozen of his classmates were later ARVN generals given important assignments, many of which they probably owed to Thieu.

One place *not* to be if you hoped to become a general was in the militia. The French started a militia with 1,500 men when they returned to Indochina in 1945, a force that grew to some 55,000 during the French period, and, under various names like self-defense corps or regional forces/popular forces, to 535,000 by 1972. Just one man was promoted out of the militia to become a South Vietnamese general. Indeed, one had a much greater chance of becoming a general in the ARVN if he had fought *for the Viet Minh revolutionaries.* A good 10 percent of the senior officers in our ARVN sample had been with the Viet Minh, some for extended periods. The case that has been written about to some degree is that of Colonel Albert Pham Ngoc Thao, now buried in a cemetery for heroes of the revolution, who by 1949 led the entire Viet Minh espionage network for the Saigon region. But Thao represents only the tip of the iceberg. According to journalist Richard Critchfield, Nguyen Van Thieu himself had been a Viet Minh district chief in 1945–1946. Though that is not reflected in other records, another Vietnamese military strongman, Nguyen Khanh, who controlled South Vietnam in 1964–1965, had been an aide to the Viet Minh logistics chief for the south. Other senior ARVN officers with Viet Minh service included corps commander Nguyen Huu Co, division commander Lam Van Phat, intelligence chief Do Mau, pacification czar Nguyen Be, and Nguyen Van Khiem, chief of staff to President Thieu from 1968 to 1971. Fighting for the Viet Minh clearly did not preclude high rank in the South Vietnamese army.

Another way to analyze the ARVN generals is with respect to birthplace. Much is made in Vietnam of the regional differences among those who live in the south, versus the central part of the country, versus the north. Politically it is well known that Ngo Dinh Diem, during his years in power, attempted to create a power base among northerners who came south following the 1954 Geneva agreements. Looking at ARVN generals as a group, however, it is evident that almost half (44 percent in our sample) were born in the south, with another 23 percent coming from central Vietnam.

This data creates a surface paradox—the supposed favoritism shown northerners compared with the preponderance of others who rose to high rank. A different criterion helps to explain that paradox—religious persuasion. Vietnam is a country that is mostly Buddhist; if one combines Buddhism with the rough animism that often is seen in practice, estimates range as high as 80 or more percent of Vietnamese who, if asked, would say they are Buddhists. Yet only four ARVN generals openly acknowledged being Buddhists, and one of them was a scion of the Vietnamese imperial family. Two of the others, Nguyen Chanh Thi and Pham Van Dong, were thought to be among the best fighters in the South Vietnamese army. Put differently, only those who were the best fighters could openly admit to Buddhism. Such an impression is strengthened by the large number of ARVN officers (about 15 percent of those whose religion is known) who converted to Catholicism during Diem's time in power. These officers could not change their place of birth, but they *could* try and fit themselves into a group Diem was known to favor by changing their religion. Conversely, the very paucity of data on religious practice among the ARVN generals can be taken as an indication that, knowing Diem's partiality to Catholics, the Vietnamese officers who were Buddhists kept that fact as quiet as they could.

Five of the men who rose to the rank of general in the ARVN were born outside Vietnam altogether. These included Cao Van Vien, a corps commander and longtime chief of the Vietnamese Joint General Staff, who was born in Laos. Two generals, Tran Van Don and Le Van Kim, were born in France. Coincidentally, or perhaps not, Don and Kim grew up to be brothers-in-law, and both were principal planners of the military moves taken in the November 1963 coup d'état that overthrew Ngo Dinh Diem.

One ARVN general, Nguyen Van Hieu, was born in China, where his father was an official of the French *Sûreté* in Shanghai, and later in Hanoi. Hieu studied to become a priest but ended up in the ARVN instead, commanding two different divisions. He headed the investigation of corruption within the army savings fund, contributions to which were mandatory for ARVN soldiers, which forced the 1972 resignation of Thieu ally and defense minister General Nguyen Van Vy. In 1975 Hieu was deputy commander of the ARVN military region which included Saigon; he committed suicide when the collapse of South Vietnam became apparent.

As much as any other, one fact that helps explain why the ARVN often fought poorly against the Viet Cong and the North Vietnamese Army is that there were real differences in regional outlook between the body of generals we have just surveyed and the group of soldiers under their command. As of 1964, even in the ARVN Fifth and Seventh divisions, which spent the entire war fighting in the Mekong Delta and Saigon areas, northerners comprised 48 percent of the manpower, a fact consistent with Diem's coddling of the northern refugees and his desire to surround Saigon with troops more loyal to him. Southerners accounted for only a quarter of the soldiers, and among them Vietnamese born in Saigon made up just 6 percent. Even the ARVN Airborne drew 37.2 percent of its men from the north and just 15 percent from either Saigon or the Mekong Delta, primarily the latter. Only the Vietnamese Marine Corps provided a relatively close fit with the generals, drawing 32.5 percent of its personnel from the Mekong, 13.6 percent from Saigon, 29.6 from Central Vietnam (Annam), and 22.6 percent from the north.

Naturally, regional origins changed over time, with casualties thinning the ranks of northerners and war with its inevitable destruction generating refugees who filled Saigon and other cities. Already in 1964 some of the change was evident in the backgrounds of recruits then in training: almost two-fifths were from the Mekong area, 5 percent from around Saigon, about half from central Vietnam, and only 5 percent from the north. Two significant conclusions can be drawn from this data. First, rural Vietnamese from Annam and the Mekong furnished the bulk of South Vietnamese soldiery. Second, the low representation of Saigonese can only be interpreted to mean that the urban kids were staying in school or getting into commerce, not entering the army. (It was not happening only in America!) An unusually high presence of Saigonese in the Marine Corps lends weight to this observation by suggesting that the self-proclaimed Saigonese elite *were* more willing to serve in a high-prestige organization like the Marines.

Years later a Vietnamese antiwar activist and scion of the Saigon elite, a man from the best Saigon circles who had studied at the best French-run schools, provided unwitting confirmation of this thesis when he told a friend how he had become a marine officer, only to be turned against the war after witnessing the slaughter of almost his entire unit at the battle of Binh Gia. This battle occurred over the New Year of 1964–1965 and featured the first instance of a coordinated attack by many Viet Cong battalions and regiments. The VC 514th Battalion—whose archives, captured later, would become the heart of a bitter intelligence dispute over the size of the Viet Cong military—delivered the coup de grace at Binh Gia.

Such trends could not be countered until after the summer of 1968, when South Vietnamese leader Nguyen Van Thieu decreed universal conscription.

The class origins of the South Vietnamese generals also speak to the issue of who was leading the fight. In contrast to the predominantly peasant troops, only three of the ARVN generals were the sons of farmers. Only one, Pham Van Dong, came from an ethnic minority (the Nung of North Vietnam), and he had already become an officer under the French and had, in fact, been the first Vietnamese commander of a *groupe mobile,* a medium-size multibattalion combat formation. Fully a third of ARVN's generals, in contrast, were the sons of *landowners* (and 17 percent of our entire sample the sons of *large* landowners). Another fifth of the generals were sons of officials, either mandarins (as was Ngo Dinh Diem himself) or administrators for the French colonial authorities. Another tenth were from families of military men, sons who could become officers where their fathers could do no better than NCO. In combination, two-thirds (63.3 percent) of South Vietnamese generals came from these three sources.

By way of contrast, only five generals (less than 8 percent) among those officers whose backgrounds are known were sons of professionals, including teachers. Only eleven in all were the scions of what could be termed the urban middle and upper classes.

In sum, there was a marked divergence between the interests of the South Vietnamese military leadership and the perspectives of the soldiers who did the fighting. If the military was to be a pathway for upward social mobility, one that furnished an alternative to professional or commercial entrepreneurship, the mechanisms for gain had to be found within the system of command. This realization goes a long way toward explaining the many instances of corruption that occurred during the war, everything from territorial commanders (district and province chiefs) charging fees for services, to battalion commanders padding their payrolls with nonexistent soldiers ("ghost armies"), to corps commanders charging money for recommendations for promotion to divisional command. The truth is that the practice was systemic, and *that* is why corruption could never be eliminated. For American strategists this meant that one of the objectives of counterinsurgency plans was by definition impossible of accomplishment.

■ This survey of backgrounds brings us to the question of political involvement. The various cliques continually jockeyed for positions of influence within the ARVN and, once it had virtually become a military preserve, the South Vietnamese government. The element of opportunism was quite strong—in contrast to an ideologically driven system of control, the South Vietnamese military cliques *never* attempted to wipe one another out. Ngo Dinh Diem and his brother Nhu were the only ones ever executed in a Vietnamese coup, with the probable exception of Pham Ngoc Thao, who was recognized as having become such a troublemaker that someone wanted him liquidated. Even Thao's death was staged to appear as something other than an execution. Reluctance to kill officers persisted in spite of the fact that *six* coups took place in Saigon between the overthrow of Diem and the final emergence of Nguyen Cao Ky and Nguyen Van Thieu as paired military strongmen. Thieu and Ky retained the leadership for a decade, from the spring of 1965 until the final collapse of South Vietnam in April 1975.

Political maneuvering between Ky and Thieu sheds further light on this point about the opportunistic nature of clique competition. In 1965 Ky was the dominant figure on the Armed Forces Council, the committee of generals behind the juntas that ran the country. By 1967, when the generals had promulgated a constitution and held an election for president, Thieu had the primary leadership role. Much of what Thieu did to eclipse Ky consisted of manipulating military personnel assignments as well as the range of candidates permitted to run in the elections. Although Thieu's activities had the same effect as a coup d'état, no one lost his life in these machinations. An incident that underlines the point occurred in mid-1968, during the second battle of Saigon which punctuated a Viet Cong follow-up to their Tet offensive. During that engagement an armed helicopter firing rockets at a VC-occupied building mistakenly hit the place where a number of senior ARVN officers and police officials were conferring. Most of these men were important figures in the Ky clique, and Ky lost a great deal of his influence within the South Vietnamese police apparatus as a result. Though dark rumors were heard afterward about the helicopter incident, no one was ever able to pin the action with surety upon the Thieu clique.

The bottom line is that South Vietnamese generals were able to act with relative impunity to support those clique leaders they thought would help them. They could switch allegiance with equal facility. For the most part, the worst danger was that they might be sent into a comfortable exile or, as a lesser sanction, dispatched as military attachés to some foreign post. A few generals who fled were sentenced to death in absentia, but there is no instance, except for Thao, of such a sentence being carried out.

A typical example of a general in politics is that of Dang Van Quang, born in Ba Xuyen province at the edge of the Mekong Delta. Quang first served the French as an NCO from 1947 to 1949, then received his officer training at Hue, where he was a classmate of Nguyen Van Thieu. Like other Thieu classmates, he later benefited from this connection. Under Diem the rising officer converted to Catholicism and was appointed director of the civil guard, the militia of that era.

Quang moderated his support for Diem in the early 1960s, then shifted to support the coup plotters who overthrew Diem in November 1963. As an old friend of Nguyen Khanh, Quang supported Khanh's coup in January 1964 and was then appointed to command the ARVN Twenty-first Division in the southernmost part of the country. Khanh swiftly found himself opposed by Vietnamese Buddhists, then Catholics, then army cliques. Reaching for loyal supporters, Khanh promoted Dang Van Quang to command the IV Corps, covering the entire Mekong Delta.

General Quang recognized the growing weakness of Khanh's leadership and shifted his own loyalty to Nguyen Cao Ky. Thus he supported Ky's intervention to counter an anti-Khanh coup in February 1965, but just two days later he sided with Ky in the Armed Forces Council that ousted Nguyen Khanh. Meanwhile, General Quang ran his corps area like a satrapy, ignoring directives from Saigon and gradually developing differences with Ky, now prime minister. Dang Van Quang then shifted his loyalties to General Thieu. Even though Ky succeeded in relieving Quang of command in November 1966, Thieu was able to shift Quang into the South Vietnamese government as minister for planning and development.

Dang Van Quang remained within the Thieu camp from 1967 on, but his actions—three changes of allegiance in three years—were characteristic of the political gymnastics of the ARVN generals. Quang became secretary to the new generals' organization, the National Leadership Council. He then was named national security adviser to President Thieu, a position in which he played power broker and exercised authority over South Vietnamese intelligence and security services. That position Quang kept right through the fall of Saigon, when he was evacuated by helicopter from the U.S. embassy roof, later settling in Canada.

So it was, and so it continued; the generals played their games at the top while Americans wondered why the South Vietnamese army was not effective. In 1965, according to Pentagon data, the average ARVN combat battalion had a paper strength of 640 men present for duty, but could put just 370 troops in the field. The "ghost armies" reigned. Not only did this phenomenon persist, but the expansion of the South Vietnamese army that occurred as the war continued, just as had happened during the French war, created a requirement for more officers, in effect a "seller's market" for upwardly mobile Vietnamese. A major study of the war sent to the Nixon White House in 1969 concluded that it would take at least two and a half years for the ARVN to train even the number of officers it had needed in mid-1968. The same study remarked that "the promotion system responds to the politics of the senior generals rather than to the needs of the professional military service." According to Pentagon figures, fewer than 2 percent of Vietnamese officers who received promotions during 1966 and 1967 got them for combat victories. The South Vietnamese military as a whole "has been unable to relate to the population and is neither a politically unifying nor a modernizing force. "

Beyond these structural problems was the question of the degree to which the Viet Cong had penetrated the South Vietnamese military. American sources in 1970 speculated that there could be as many as thirty thousand Viet Cong agents in the South Vietnamese government and armed forces. It was virtually impossible to create major plans or conduct significant actions without knowledge of them leaking to the adversary. Penetration reached the highest levels of the ARVN and in some cases remained unknown until the collapse of South Vietnam. This is what happened, for example, with General Phan Dinh Thu, who had begun his career in the French army in 1948 and had been with Nguyen Van Vy, future army commander-in-chief and defense minister, on a key parachute drop to save a northern Vietnamese Catholic bishop. Thu himself rose to command ARVN's Special Forces after the demise of Diem, and later was deputy commander of a corps in the 1970 invasion of Cambodia. As South Vietnam disintegrated in the spring of 1975, Thu appeared at the Saigon Radio and Television Center and told its startled former director that he was a member of the VC's Saigon Revolutionary Committee.

Americans whose visions of victory in Vietnam centered on massive, or massively effective, utilization of the South Vietnamese military were promoting strategies that started out with two strikes against them. Some Vietnamese officers were just not that interested in the war; others were perhaps more interested in the other side. The combination proved devastating. The Vietnam War would continue, but more and more fueled by Americans, keeping the ARVN in the field, keeping the South Vietnamese in clover, supplying some of the more imaginative ideas for mobilizing South Vietnam for the war. Some of the more innovative American solutions were put into practice by the CIA and the Green Berets among the montagnards of South Vietnam's Central Highlands.

8   # Special Warfare in the Central Highlands

While Barry Sadler was popularizing U.S. Army Special Forces with his song *The Ballad of the Green Berets*, these American unconventional warfare specialists were engaged in Vietnam in what was perhaps their most ambitious and successful program. It grew out of a collaboration between Special Forces and the Central Intelligence Agency in some of the earliest American programs in South Vietnam. Special Forces' raison d'être in the Vietnam War had much to do with these early endeavors, which it pursued long after the CIA had moved on to other projects. In the process the Green Berets went some distance toward fulfilling their motto of liberating peoples from oppression—albeit the liberation of native minorities from their own South Vietnamese government. Military and political obstacles prevented that ideal from reaching fruition and defined the limits of the Green Berets' success. The story of that effort is a major aspect of Special Forces activity in the Vietnam War.

Green Berets first went to South Vietnam because the Vietnamese armed forces had requested special trainers for the Ranger units they wished to form. Mobile training teams of ten men each began trips to Vietnam in May 1960. Three of these teams, together with ARVN instructors who had graduated from U.S. Ranger training programs at Fort Benning, Georgia, ran three new ARVN ranger schools.

Such training missions were bread and butter for the Green Berets, the kind of job they had done many times in many countries. More exotic action awaited them as the Vietnam War began to heat up. There was increasing evidence that South Vietnamese rebels fighting the government of President Ngo Dinh Diem were receiving support from North Vietnam. It is now known that Hanoi issued orders for the establishment of a supply route to the southerners as early as May 1959. In the theory of counterinsurgency established by the dynamic new Kennedy administration in 1961, isolating guerrillas from outside support assumed central importance. In Saigon the CIA was the American organization most concerned with this problem. Agency officers devised the concept of a "mountain scout" program under which native tribesmen inhabiting Vietnam's Central Highlands would be recruited in small numbers and given Ranger-type training to conduct quiet surveillance missions against the North Vietnamese moving their supplies across southern borders.

The mountain scouts were a small-scale operation, and though the ARVN had combat units stationed in the Central Highlands, these did relatively little to ensure the security of the settlements of mountain tribesmen—"montagnards," after the French word for mountaineer. Thirty major tribes, almost a million people, were at stake in the Central Highlands. Perhaps that was not how Saigon viewed these people, at least during Diem's time in power. "Montagnard" previously had carried no connotations; it was extracted from the geographic label that French colonial administrations had applied to the area before 1954—*Plateaux Montagnards du Sud,* or Southern Mountain Plateaus. Thus the term montagnard was not at all like the Vietnamese term used for the tribal peoples—*moi*—which translates as "savage." Far from being savage, though, there were many similarities between montagnards and lowland Vietnamese. Beneath the patina of modernity Vietnamese had acquired from the French, they were, like the montagnards, animists who honored extended families and ancestral homelands. Likenesses also abounded between the village cultures of Vietnamese and montagnards, and there were similarities between the traditional Vietnamese mandarinate and the highly developed legal and court system that existed among the mountain tribesmen. The montagnards might still acquire most of their food from hunting and slash-and-burn agriculture, but their small societies, primitive though they might be, were not savage.

In colonial days the French preserved a measure of tradition among the tribes by administering them separately from lowland Vietnamese, under province officers who maintained direct but loose supervision. Vietnamese revolutionaries in the anti-French war saw this as a policy of divide and rule but proved unable to make substantial inroads in montagnard areas, where numbers of tribesmen actually served in the French auxiliary forces. But after the 1954 Geneva agreement, when Ngo Dinh Diem, an anti-Communist Vietnamese nationalist, took over the political leadership of the south, the situation for montagnards changed radically.

President Diem worked on the premise that he could "assimilate" the peoples of the Central Highlands, but that notion really served as cover for the insertion of a dominant elite of lowland Vietnamese. For example, montagnards had governed their own districts and villages under French province chiefs, but Diem now installed not only Vietnamese province chiefs but district leaders as well. Montagnards had occasionally taken actions opposing the French, whose plantations encroached on tribal lands and extracted forced labor from the tribespeople, but reaction to the Vietnamese reached new levels of intensity. Vietnamese traders and money lenders enraged the montagnards; Vietnamese settlers began to appear in great numbers. In particular, Vietnamese immigrants from the north, entering South Vietnam in the wake of Geneva, were funneled into Dalat and Ban Me Thuot, and many others settled in Kontum and Pleiku.

Vietnamese images of the montagnards followed from the *moi* appellation. Official reference materials seem to have underestimated the numbers of tribespeople, carrying the figure 700,000 when a million would have been closer to the mark. Private attitudes were typified by that of one young Vietnamese woman who later told an American, in all seriousness, that montagnards had tails. Even progressive Vietnamese had limitations. Miss Tu, a provincial school inspector in Dalat in the early 1960s, was widely considered to be among the best lowlanders. Unlike her successors from 1967 on, Tu actually visited the hamlet schools, took supplies to the villages, and sat with tribal leaders, yet after years of this degree of involvement continued to believe that montagnards carried around inferiority complexes.

Miss Tu nevertheless was perfectly aware of Vietnamese discrimination against the tribal peoples. She compared it to attitudes toward African Americans in the United States before desegregation. William Colby, CIA station chief in Saigon from 1960 to 1962, made a similar comparison, likening Vietnamese regard for the montagnards to the way frontiersmen had treated Native Americans in the nineteenth century. Diem's resettlement of Vietnamese to the highlands proved insufficient to alter the balance of population in the upland provinces, but it confirmed montagnard fears of Vietnamese encroachment.

In 1958 the montagnards exhibited an unprecedented degree of unity when members of four different tribes joined to form a single autonomy movement. The peoples involved—Bahnar, Jarai, Rhadé, and Koho—later became familiar to a generation of Green Berets alongside whom they fought in America's Vietnam War. At that time, though, the montagnards remained virtually unknown and their movement, called the BaJaRhaKo, seemed quite exotic. Its leaders included Nay Luett, a montagnard educated in France who spoke six languages; Y'Bham Enuol, a former French functionary; and Paul Nur, offspring of a Frenchman's union with a Bahnar tribal woman and another former official. In late 1958 the BaJaRhaKo surprisingly seized and held the provincial capital of Pleiku. The Diem government sent troops to quell the uprising. According to some sources, the ARVN went so far as to issue operations orders for the extermination of montagnards. In any case, leaders like Nay Luett, Y'Bham, and Paul Nur were imprisoned and held for more than five years. One montagnard leader, Y'Bih Aleo, a Rhadé tribesman, escaped to join the nascent National Liberation Front, which made him a vice-president and chairman of its ethnic autonomy effort designed to attract montagnard support. Far from moderating its policies toward the upland minorities, the Diem government continued to exploit the tribes, exacting tax payments in exchange for few services, permitting no self-government above the hamlet level. The accent remained on "handling" the montagnard "problem," not on helping the uplanders help themselves.

■ This situation continued as Americans filtered into the Highlands. The first Americans were civilians: missionaries, relief workers, or professional observers. Best known among the latter were the assorted crew of anthropologists, political scientists, and other specialists sent by Michigan State University under contract to the U.S. government. Anthropologist Gerald C. Hickey, originally of the Michigan State group, assembled some of the earliest detailed looks at montagnard medical practice and village life, and went on to do the same for small communities throughout South Vietnam. Among relief workers, David A. Nuttle of International Voluntary Services (IVS) was notable for his efforts not only to assist the Rhadé in the hills above Ban Me Thuot, but to inform others through monographs put out by IVS. It was one of the IVS workers, whose name is recorded as David A. Norwood (possibly the same person), who became concerned with evidence of apparent inroads among the Rhadé by the National Liberation Front. The IVS volunteer went to Saigon and contacted the CIA station, where he encountered Gilbert Layton, an army colonel detached to the Agency as chief of paramilitary operations for South Vietnam.

Layton and Norwood came up with a plan to arm Rhadé villagers to defend themselves, and they took the idea to station chief Colby.

The CIA liked the concept and thought it might be more generally applicable, but decided to try it first as a pilot program. In October 1961 the IVS volunteer, a U.S. embassy (doubtless CIA) representative, and a Green Beret medical sergeant went to the Rhadé elders to convince the tribe to throw in with the Americans and the South Vietnamese. This was not an easy decision for the montagnards, who had been shown little consideration by the Saigon government. Saigon, in fact, had used the deteriorating security situation as an excuse for halting its medical and educational activities among the tribes. Nevertheless, the Rhadé elders decided to go along and selected Buon Enao village to be the first outpost for what the CIA now termed its Village Defense Program. Colby then went to Ngo Dinh Nhu, whom Diem used to supervise his intelligence and security services, and received South Vietnamese approval to proceed.

The CIA stipulated that the village to be armed must enclose itself with a fence and dig shelters inside, both as preparations for defense and as a visible token of the new alliance. Buon Enao had readied itself by December 1961. The CIA meanwhile went to the U.S. army to borrow Green Berets for the actual training and advisory mission; Special Forces initially provided half of its Detachment A-113 from Okinawa under Captain Ron Shackleton. After further consultation between the Rhadé elders and the CIA's Layton in January, the A-113 team members were brought to Vietnam, stayed briefly at a safe house, and flew up to Ban Me Thuot in an unmarked C-46 transport with a Nationalist Chinese crew on February 14, 1962. From there they climbed the foothills of the Highlands to reach Buon Enao, where fifty Rhadé tribesmen awaited them.

Montagnard village defense proved a hugely successful endeavor and would soon expand. With Buon Enao as a center, a security zone radiated outward, increasing in diameter almost weekly. There were other zones as well, spreading out from other nuclei. By April 1962 village defense encompassed forty villages within fifteen kilometers of Buon Enao, with 14,000 Rhadé defended by 975 montagnards. Within a year 60,000 Rhadé were under the protection of 10,500 defense force montagnards, colloquially called "yards" by Americans, with another 1,500 Rhadé in units of "mobile strike forces," whose troopers were called "strikers." By December 1963 there were 43,376 village militia and 18,000 strikers. Other montagnard irregulars, many trained at a Special Forces facility at Hoa Cam, near Da Nang, included 300 border surveillance trailwatchers, 2,700 mountain scouts, and about 5,300 Popular Forces troops.

These force levels were not reached merely by arming the Rhadé who, though they were among the largest tribes, were estimated to number only 100,000 to 120,000. Many of the "yard" tribes were also incorporated, and so were river pirates, religious sects, and the Cambodian minority as the village defense program spread to all four of Vietnam's corps areas. Typical was the experience of the Sedang, another tribe (like the Rhadé) of the Mon-Khmer group who numbered 40,000 to 80,000 and lived in northern and western Kontum. The Sedang were among early recruits to the program, when it was still under CIA auspices. By mid-1962 there were two battalions of armed Sedang, with platoons of about 10 men each distributed among 57 armed villages. Concerned by these developments, the Viet Cong tried to teach the Sedang a lesson. That June a VC force attacked a village armed with only traditional weapons—spears, swords, and crossbows. Incredibly, the VC were driven off. Two days later they returned in greater force, overwhelmed the village, and carried off all its young men, but the gesture simply backfired—outraging the entire tribe, which enlisted in the montagnard program in ever greater numbers. The Sedang were soon rated as superb montagnard fighters.

There were many more tribes than these. Among others rated superb were the Rengao and the Nung, tribesmen from the north, along the Vietnamese-Chinese border, who had emigrated after the Franco-Vietnamese war. Among the effective fighters were the Bahnar, Bru, Jarai, M'nong, and Stieng. Those rated merely capable included the Halang, Hré, Hroi, Jeh, Koho, Ma, Muong, and Raglai. The ratings come from an army ethnographic study compiled a few years later by area specialists at the Johns Hopkins University.

As the montagnard militias and strike forces expanded, their Special Forces support kept pace. At first there had been half of a single Green Beret field unit with the tribes and another half at Hoa Cam; then one was committed specially to Buon Enao; then five units supported the forty-village cleared area reached in the spring of 1962. By the time the Buon Enao experiment was declared successful and Darlac province reverted to South Vietnamese civilian administration, Green Beret presence was substantial, sometimes outstripping the South Vietnamese in their commitment of LLDB Special Forces.

The growing Green Beret presence also eclipsed CIA participation in the program. Soon there were so many American military that the effort could not be claimed as a covert operation, a clandestine activity, even a pilot program. Moreover, the Kennedy administration wanted to turn the CIA back toward more traditional intelligence work. After the Bay of Pigs failure in Cuba in early 1961, President Kennedy had issued orders that future large-scale paramilitary operations be controlled by the military. At a certain point the montagnard program in South Vietnam fell into this category. Toward the end of 1962 the U.S. implemented Operation Switchback, under which the CIA turned over the montagnard program to the military. In September the Green Berets, in turn, activated a provisional Special Forces Group Vietnam to direct this and all other Special Forces activities. The turnover was completed on July 1, 1963, though for a couple of years, under a project called Switchback-Parasol, the CIA continued to procure weapons and equipment for Special Forces using army funds, enabling the Green Berets to avoid the cumbersome army logistics system. By the end of 1963 Special Forces Vietnam (Provisional) had thirty-six Green Beret field units, four B Detachment command elements, and a C Detachment at Nha Trang for command and service support. Altogether 674 Special Forces men were assigned, many of them to the montagnard program.

South Vietnamese participation also mushroomed with the growth of the montagnard effort. Before the anti-Diem coup, one of the first trips into the countryside made by Ngo Dinh Nhu had been to Buon Enao, and Nhu made expansion of the training activity contingent on an enlarged South Vietnamese role. Knowing that South Vietnamese participation was critical in the long run, the CIA's Colby envisioned an ARVN component from the very beginning. Under the final scheme the ARVN's own Special Forces (LLDB) would provide one of its teams to each montagnard camp in parallel to a field unit of American Green Berets. The LLDB commander would be in overall control of the camp. This arrangement would often be honored in the breach by Americans, who retained effective command, but the situation symbolized the struggle between South Vietnamese power and montagnard aspirations that lurked just beneath the surface of the verdant highlands and apparently placid villages.

Surface texture was what Americans saw first—the seeming success of the alliance with the uplanders. Every month the numbers for montagnards under arms grew, with strike forces eventually so large that Colby decided they needed a distinctive name: Civilian Irregular Defense Groups (CIDGs). A regular pattern of organization emerged at Special Forces camps, with each typically garrisoned by four CIDG companies and one or more platoons of reconnaissance troops. The CIDG companies usually comprised members of the same tribe, and those at any particular camp corresponded to the ethnic composition of the settlements around them. The growth of the military role and transition away from CIA participation was symbolized in the experience of Peer de Silva, Colby's successor as station chief, who once visited one of the montagnard villages. Sitting with the village headman, de Silva was horrified to see the montagnard pick up a frog, snap its neck, and take a bite. The headman then handed the frog, ostentatiously, to the CIA officer. De Silva escaped from the situation as best he could, but, as any Special Forces adviser could have told him, one gained the confidence of the montagnards by participating in their rituals and rites. Anyone incapable of absorbing the rice wine the uplanders imbibed on every imaginable occasion might as well request a transfer.

Meanwhile, the Viet Cong tried again to derail the CIDG program. The first CIDG base to undergo a pitched attack by the VC was Plei Mrong, in Jarai country, during the early morning hours of January 3, 1963. The VC waited until half the camp strike force was out on patrol, while VC agents were apparently successful at sabotaging the camp mortar and its primary radio. Plei Mrong's LLDB unit showed little initiative in the battle while the ARVN Twenty-second Division refused to take its assigned Ranger battalion out of reserve to rescue the CIDG camp. Plei Mrong nevertheless held out despite considerable losses. During the six months following the battle, CIDG patrols encountered Viet Cong units 374 times, while the VC probed or mortared Special Forces camps 94 times and attempted infiltrations on 11 occasions.

It was a Green Beret officer who won the first Congressional Medal of Honor awarded during the Vietnam War. He was Captain Roger Donlon, for his defense of Nam Dong camp on the night of July 6, 1964. Donlon commanded detachment A-726 with three hundred Nung strikers. The Nung strikers were semiprofessional mercenaries frequently employed by both Special Forces and the CIA. Typically Nung troops provided defense forces while a tribal militia and strike force was being trained and formed. At Nam Dong, in southwestern Thua Thien province, the Green Berets had concluded that there were few prospects for local recruiting and were preparing to close the camp when a reinforced battalion of VC hit in the middle of the night. Eighty percent of the casualties occurred during the first fifteen minutes, in which the communications bunker, Nung barracks, and medical hut were blown up. Wounded in the stomach and shoulder, Captain Donlon nevertheless dragged others to safety, wiped out VC infiltrators, saved and moved a camp mortar, retrieved a recoilless rifle, and continued to direct the defense through a five-hour battle. Additional hits in the leg and face did not stop him. A most unlikely participant in the Nam Dong battle was Gerald Hickey, now a RAND Corporation social scientist who was to write some of the most perceptive anthropological studies of the Vietnamese village.

Battles like those at Plei Mrong, Nam Dong, and Dong Xoai, where Lieutenant Charles Q. Williams of Special Forces earned another Medal of Honor in June 1965, made it clear that a big problem for the montagnard camps was the availability of reaction forces. As likely as not, the available ARVN units would not be sent to help a camp under attack or, if they were, would not arrive in time. Later, when U.S. troops were also fighting in the war, very few of them had tactical areas of responsibility corresponding to the montagnard zones. Strike force units had already been consolidated into the CIDGs, which usually were deployed with several company-sized units per Special Forces camp. Now, as reaction forces, the CIDGs were supplemented with battalion-size Mobile Strike Forces, usually called "Mike" Forces. Each corps area in South Vietnam began with one Mike Force while Nha Trang headquarters (after October 1964 redesignated the Fifth Special Forces Group) had two Mike Force battalions. The latter units were manned by Nungs.

Thus was created the basic system of warfare in the Central Highlands. The ARVN had its units (principally the Twenty-second and Twenty-third divisions) and large bases in the upland valleys, at towns like Pleiku and Kontum. These regular units carried out large sweeps that rarely made contact with the elusive Viet Cong. The Special Forces used border surveillance posts and teams, plus mountain scouts during the early years (later these were folded into the CIDGs), to detect VC movements and activities, then sent out CIDGs to patrol the hinterland. The VC in turn struck back with repeated assaults on the Special Forces camps. If attacked, the Green Berets brought up Mike Forces, which could also be committed in operations to bolster the CIDG companies. It was a war of posts, alarums, and excursions. In search of even faster reaction times, Fifth Special Forces eventually designated elements of their Mike Forces as airborne and air assault units, which could parachute or be helicoptered into operating areas. While the Vietnamese Special Forces, the LLDBs, held titular command in the montagnard camps, the Mike Force units were a purely American concern.

This much of the montagnard story, though perhaps not widely known, is at least familiar. Virtually unknown, or known only to a small circle of Special Forces and CIA sympathizers and American pacification enthusiasts, is the story of the evolving political framework within which CIDGs functioned.

■ Symptomatic of the undercurrent of tension between the Saigon government and the montagnards was, again, Buon Enao. Once the area was declared secure and reverted to standard government administration, the Darlac province chief took away the special status of the Rhadé villages, funneled support and funds elsewhere, and in general treated the montagnards with the degree of contempt lowland Vietnamese reserved for their supposedly primitive mountain brethren. Over time the security situation deteriorated. In the end, security was a little better because more villages had defenses and because of the CIDGs and Special Forces camps, but the province was no longer to be considered pacified. What remained was a program mobilizing additional auxiliary forces.

Unfortunately, though Americans could take heart from montagnard distaste for the Viet Cong, they could also readily see the disdain of the lowland Vietnamese. It was not easy to be in the middle. It was almost as if the South Vietnamese wished to spark a conflict with the tribes. Sympathetic Vietnamese officers who went out of their way to learn something of the "yards" would be transferred away, as happened to Captain Nguyen Van Nghiem, psychological warfare officer for the Twenty-second Division in the 1962 period, or to Lieutenant Colonel Nguyen De, a province chief somewhat later. After the fall of the Diem regime, when a succession of military juntas ruled Saigon, South Vietnamese policy became even more inept.

Montagnard desire for something better again manifested itself in a unity movement, a kind of thrust for indigenous nationalism. This was the creation of FULRO, the Unified Front for the Liberation of Oppressed Peoples, in mid-1964 by tribal leaders headed by Y'Bham Enuol, now out of prison. A manifesto on August 1 promised a struggle to end Vietnamese domination of the uplanders, including the Rhadé, Bahnar, Jarai, Bru, Raglai, Sedang, Hre, Kebuan, Chauma, Hadrung, Mnong, Siteng, Cham, and other peoples. The formation of FULRO is often neglected, but an understanding of its appeal is vital in explaining the mutiny that took place on the night of September 19/20, 1964, in five CIDG camps around Ban Me Thuot. Beginning at the camp of Buon Sarpa, montagnard strikers raised the FULRO flag, imprisoned their American advisers, and captured or killed their Vietnamese overlords. In an eight-day revolt in which more than eighty

Vietnamese died, the montagnards from Buon Sarpa and several other camps marched on Ban Me Thuot, which they almost captured from regular South Vietnamese troops. They did gain the radio station, from which Y'Bham proclaimed the FULRO message, denouncing Vietnamese genocide and demanding autonomy. American advisers with the Buon Sarpa band finally convinced the strikers to return to their CIDG camp.

A few days later a South Vietnamese army unit, the Forty-seventh Regiment, a larger force than was usually seen in the field against the VC, invested Buon Sarpa. Then General Nguyen Khanh appeared. Montagnards hauled down the FULRO flag, replacing it with Vietnamese colors. General Khanh and rebel leaders exchanged pistols and promises. Khanh rejected autonomy but made other concessions: montagnard customs courts would be restored; villages received increased farm lands; local languages would be taught in school with Vietnamese to be introduced only in higher grades. The Vietnamese also promised preferred admission for montagnard candidates to high schools, the Thu Duc Infantry School, and the Dalat Military Academy. The last CIDG camp to surrender was given a commander of Rhadé descent, and Rhadé officers were appointed to two other CIDG camps as well.

Montagnard nationalists assessed the postmutiny changes as cosmetic. Y'Bham, his staff, and several hundred armed strikers made for the Cambodian border. Their analysis was quite right: in fact the Saigon government made a formal diplomatic protest to the United States that the U.S. had armed the montagnards without Saigon's knowledge or consent; that it had interposed itself between the rebels and the Saigon forces; and that as a result the Saigon regime had lost face throughout Southeast Asia. All five of the CIDG camps involved in the disturbances were closed within the year.

In October 1964 General Khanh convened a congress of the tribes at Pleiku at which he signed a decree granting a number of FULRO demands in principle. His government fell shortly thereafter, however, and no attempt was made by any of its successors to implement the Pleiku accords. By July 1965 frustration was such that almost two companies of Rhadé strikers from the Buon Brieng CIDG camp defected to FULRO with all their weapons and equipment. Only then were montagnard courts restored as had been promised. In September timely intervention by South Vietnamese troops prevented another uprising at the Buon Ho CIDG camp, where four hundred strikers were disarmed before any bloodshed.

Meanwhile, Y'Bham continued his attempts to negotiate and attract attention to his peoples' plight. In March 1965 he was at Pnom Penh for the Indochinese People's Conference sponsored by Prince Norodom Sihanouk. The FULRO leader praised Cambodian assistance but denounced the Saigon government. Leaflets by FULRO exhorting CIDG soldiers to revolt were found in many places, and by the end of 1965 Y'Bham had achieved a sufficient degree of coordination to execute a sophisticated operation. On December 17 the provincial capitals of Quang Duc and Darlac were captured and held for a time while district towns and CIDG camps in five widely separated provinces were simultaneously seized. Two CIDG camps in Darlac fell, and thirty Vietnamese, including a district chief, were killed.

It is against the backdrop of the FULRO challenge that one should see the changes that came about in the CIDG program in the mid-1960s. The Vietnamese insisted upon phasing out village defense per se, resulting in the disbanding of militia whose weapons were collected. Only the better-organized and -trained CIDG companies with their Special Forces/LLDB leadership remained. This move clearly aimed at closing off a large potential source of arms for FULRO adherents. Still the movement continued to grow, while Vietnamese charged that FULRO was allied to, and launching military operations in conjunction with, the National Liberation Front. No evidence supports this charge.

More quiet contacts in 1966 brought additional promises from Saigon. At one point authorities thought they had licked the montagnard autonomy drive, convincing FULRO to surrender its arms in a three-phase ceremony at Ban Me Thuot. Ambassador Henry Cabot Lodge optimistically reported to Washington that 2,757 FULRO troops had gathered to lay down their arms on the anniversary of the Pleiku congress of 1965. Y'Bham smelled a rat at the last moment, however, and only 250 soldiers actually came to the rendezvous. An estimated 7,000 FULRO troops remained at large in Cambodia and along the remote border.

Montagnard desires to have an army, a semi-autonomous force free to ally itself with the U.S., received but a pale reflection in Vietnamese practice. In 1965 there were twenty-two tribesmen enrolled as officer candidates and another forty-six aspirants to noncommissioned rank. It would take a long time to man an army at that rate of training. By 1967 one Jarai, Nay Lo, had achieved the rank of lieutenant colonel and was installed as chief of Pleiku province. He was regarded by montagnards themselves as incompetent, unimaginative, and incapable of handling a complex job. Within two years he had been replaced by another montagnard, Colonel Ya Ba.

In the wake of the 1965 uprising, the Vietnamese government sponsored a further meeting to address montagnard concerns. This time tribal representatives presented the lowlanders with a draft bill of rights, an idea believed to have come from friends among U.S. Special Forces. A major outcome was the formation of an office for montagnard affairs at Ban Me Thuot, headed by the tribal leader Paul Nur. At Saigon followed a General Directorate for Montagnard Affairs, a job to which Nur was soon promoted. Nur told U.S. officials in mid-1967 that it was precisely General Vinh Loc, commander of Vietnamese II Corps and the officer with civil and military responsibility for the Central Highlands, who was the most difficult to work with. Nur had become quite disappointed and contemplated resigning. He felt himself under continual pressure from Vinh Loc to pay less heed to the advice and counsel of Americans.

When Vietnamese held a secret meeting with Y'Bham on April 14, 1967, Paul Nur was invited only as an afterthought and was given no real role to play. Thus Vinh Loc lacked Nur's advice when he later assembled a set of recommendations on a new minorities policy that was turned into a speech and a formal government decree by President Nguyen Van Thieu. Nur could have told Loc and Thieu that their proposals did not go far enough to attract the renewed loyalty of FULRO. As Nur expected, the FULRO executive committee met in Cambodia toward the end of July and rejected the government decree as not even matching the promises Thieu had put in his speech. By November 1967, when the General Directorate was in the process of being converted into a full Ministry for Ethnic Minority Development, it had some 725 employees. In the fashion that had come to be typical, however, only a third of the office's employees were montagnards, and of the group's Saigon staff only three were uplanders: Paul Nur himself, his director of administration and finance, and one other.

When the ministry was activated the top post went to Nay Luett, another of the old-guard montagnard activists who had been imprisoned with Y'Bham in Hue during the late fifties and sixties. Emerging after the fall of Diem, Nay Luett reportedly found himself marked for assassination, not by the Viet Cong but by the Saigon government, and was forced to drop out of sight. He sought security among the Americans, proceeding to Buon Beng CIDG camp where he volunteered for a job as a truck driver. Encouraged by Lieutenant Jim Morris, one of many Special Forces men to turn a benign eye toward montagnard nationalism, Nay Luett thrived, suddenly emerging as a member of the Vietnamese cabinet.

Tet in 1968 found FULRO quiescent but the National Liberation Front and North Vietnamese on the move throughout the country. In Pleiku, II Corps authorities had several weeks' advance notice of an intention to attack because of a document disclosing the attack plan that had been captured by the U.S. Fourth Division. There, as well as at Ban Me Thuot and at Kontum, a coordination error led the North Vietnamese and Viet Cong to attack a day ahead of the time they jumped off in the remainder of the country. There was hard fighting, but the issue was never in doubt. At Cheo Reo in Phu Bon province, where former Green Beret Ed Sprague had just returned to Vietnam, working for the State Department as province senior adviser, his montagnards detected the Viet Cong as soon as they tried to cross the airfield, pinned them down, and drove them off. For them the Tet offensive lasted less than an hour.

In the aftermath, General Vinh Loc was reassigned from II Corps to head the national defense college, replaced by Lu Muong Lan, from a well-to-do family in Quang Tri whose schooling had been at Hue. Lan had previously held several jobs in the highlands, including commander of the Twenty-third Division and II Corps chief of staff. He did not present the same obstacles as had Vinh Loc, a prince of the old royal family. With the impetus of the new Ministry for Ethnic Minority Development, quiet contacts were initiated with FULRO in August 1968. Y'Bham and other tribal representatives met secretly with the Vietnamese at Ban Me Thuot, and talks moved to Saigon. By February 1969 sufficient progress had been made that President Nguyen Van Thieu planned a change of allegiance ceremony in Ban Me Thuot where he would preside over FULRO's laying down of its arms. But as in 1967, the montagnards did not trust the Saigon government, and Y'Bham never surrendered. Just a handful of FULRO soldiers showed up to swear allegiance to the Republic of Vietnam. A sort of secret war continued between FULRO and the Vietnamese. In 1970 the South Vietnamese took over the last CIDG and Mike Force units from the Americans and made them ARVN Ranger units. It is not coincidental that the ARVN Rangers consistently posted desertion rates among the highest in the South Vietnamese army. The American Fifth Special Forces Group disbanded and its Green Berets headed for home.

Among their greatest battles during the last years were the CIDGs' fight at Lang Vei, during the Khe Sanh campaign, and at Kham Duc in the summer of 1968 (see Chapter 18). Later there were desperate defenses of the montagnard camps near the Cambodian border, particularly Ben Het and Bu Prang. Americans who advised the CIDG and ARVN Rangers during these later years cannot recall any instance of a significant Viet Cong penetration of a montagnard unit in the Central Highlands, though there was plenty of FULRO presence in the striker units. During the Easter offensive of 1972, when the North Vietnamese army mounted large-scale attacks in the montagnard zone and the ARVN virtually collapsed there, strikers were the backbone of the defense that saved Kontum.

Although the Paris cease-fire agreement of 1973 brought an end to America's direct role in South Vietnam, in the Central Highlands it merely began the so-called War of the Flags, in which the sides sought to demonstrate control over the land. Montagnards fought hard in Pleiku and Kontum during 1973 and 1974. By 1975 they had little to show for years of war. According to Ed Sprague, by then a senior pacification adviser and possibly the American closest to the montagnard leadership, during those last months the Saigon government again began to make overtures toward the tribes. President Nguyen Van Thieu met with montagnard leader Nay Luett and offered autonomy to the tribes in their Highlands provinces. Luett had no idea at the time that Thieu was considering a complete South Vietnamese withdrawal from the Highlands, which would have left the montagnards to fight on alone against the North Vietnamese. Luett was ecstatic at the offer, but soon afterward the NVA began their final offensive, Thieu's withdrawal in the Highlands turned into a rout, and South Vietnam literally disintegrated. Some 200,000 montagnards perished in this terrible conflict.

There are reports that the United States offered to extend covert assistance to the montagnards if they would continue fighting the NVA in the Highlands. In truth the tribes needed little encouragement. But the 1975 collapse was nothing less than a montagnard tragedy. Americans like Ed Sprague did what they could—he got two thousand "yards" to Nha Trang where they stood on a beach awaiting an American ship that never came. Nay Luett, still minister at Saigon, was able to move some montagnards to Phu Quoc island (ironic, that this formerly notorious prison island should be seen as a refuge), but there they languished. Nay Luett himself was arrested by the Liberation Front and is reported to have died in a reeducation camp. Ksor Rot, token montagnard member of the Saigon Senate, was publicly executed. North Vietnamese forces began a regular military campaign in the Highlands against the tribesmen, who had once been promised autonomy by the National Liberation Front.

With FULRO the montagnards were ready with an experienced underground network. Initially at least, they were also well equipped—one source estimates they must have had 1.5 to 2.0 rifles available for every fighter; others believe FULRO's weapons situation was even better. Ed Sprague, who was at Cheo Reo when the South Vietnamese disintegration began, thinks fleeing ARVN troops must have abandoned two thousand rifles in just one pile near his compound. Under Y'Kpa Koi, a former montagnard civil servant, FULRO began its resistance in fairly good shape. But rifles break, or jam, or are lost, and ammunition runs out. Aside from captures, the only new supplies were five thousand weapons supplied by the Chinese in the early 1980s. The montagnards could scarcely replace weapons, could barely replace soldiers, and were left to conduct a sort of broken-backed war.

The end of the montagnards' war came late, not in 1954 or 1973 or even 1975, but in the wilds of Cambodia's Mondolkiri Province in 1992. The man on the other side when they laid down their weapons was not Vietnamese or Cambodian or Khmer Rouge but Uruguayan Army Colonel Lenel Milone, assigned to a United Nations peacekeeping force. The FULRO band was led by Colonel Y Peng Ayun, and it gave up 194 weapons with just 2,567 rounds of ammunition, enough for only a few minutes of sustained battle. By then Y'Bham was long dead—he had taken refuge in the French embassy at Pnom Penh during the final days of Cambodia's fall to the Khmer Rouge, who then coerced the French into handing over Y'Bham and others, all quickly executed. Victims across the border in Vietnam included the montagnards who had reached relatively high rank in the ARVN: Lieutenant Colonel R'Com Pioi; Major Rmah Crai; Major Rmah Jok; Major Nay Phun; Major Nay Kueo; and others. Thousands more died then or later. Montagnard refugees taken into the United States included a band of 209 accepted from Thailand in 1986, and Y Peng's group in 1993—in all, fewer than a thousand. The United States never carried out promises, witnessed by certain Americans, of covertly arming the montagnards, and the U.S. has done precious little for montagnard refugees. If anything, the betrayal is greater than that suffered by America's Hmong allies in Laos (see Chapter 22).

In the early, heady days of the war, when anything seemed possible, mobilizing the mountain peoples was seen as a way to play guerrilla warfare back at the Viet Cong and North Vietnamese. Strategists hypothesized that a strong effort along the border would raise the price to North Vietnam of supporting the insurgency in the south, and at a minimum help keep track of North Vietnamese activity in the hinterland. But tribal mobilization ran head-on into the interests of the Saigon government, which stood to lose any authority gained by the montagnards. Thus the CIA and Green Beret programs fundamentally ran counter to the dominant United States interest in supporting Saigon. Because America's alliance was with Saigon, the outcome for the montagnards could hardly have been other than it was. Those whose Vietnam "winning" strategies hinge upon the recruitment of such small groups of superb fighters as the montagnards have never explained how this was to be accomplished without Saigon's short-circuiting the entire exercise, as indeed it did. This might not have mattered so much if the South Vietnamese people had been unified in the face of the war, but politically, with their own people, South Vietnam's military leaders had grave difficulties, as we shall now see.

Bullets, Bombs, and Buddhists

In a war fought for the hearts and minds of the Vietnamese people, it is odd that Americans tended to pay close attention to South Vietnamese political and social dynamics only in crisis situations. The best illustration of this propensity is probably the case of the Buddhist religious movement, which had marked political effects in South Vietnam between 1963 and 1966. Many aspects of this experience proved tragic. There was tragedy for American policy in the way the Buddhist upheavals in Vietnam contributed to locking the United States into the Vietnam War. Tragedy also lay in store for certain South Vietnamese leaders, even some who used the Buddhist factor to manipulate U.S. policy. Finally, it proved tragic for the Vietnamese people that the Buddhist revival occurred at a moment in history which swept it into a maelstrom of conflict and ultimately led to religious oppression greater than what had existed before.

Worship of ancestors and animal spirits, later to become loosely integrated into Buddhism, were the first religious movements in Vietnam. The Chinese introduced Confucianism and Taoism after their conquest of Vietnam in the second century B.C. In the second century A.D. the Chinese monk Mou Po is credited with being the first major apostle of Buddhism in Vietnam. Mou Po's Buddhism was of the type known as Mahayana. The other major strain of Buddhism, Theravada, came to Vietnam through Cambodia, where Indian missionaries had introduced it. Japanese-style Zen Buddhism came to Vietnam in the sixth century. Between the tenth and twelfth centuries Buddhism was actually recognized as the state religion of Vietnam, while Christianity followed the arrival of Portuguese and French priests beginning in the sixteenth century. By modern times there were no fewer than sixteen different varieties of Buddhist teaching in Vietnam, in addition to the contributions of Buddhism to the syncretistic Cao Dai and Hoa Hao religious sects. It is commonly accepted that 70 to 80 percent of Vietnamese subscribed to the faith represented by the amalgam of Buddhism and animism (though brochures put out by the South Vietnamese embassy in Washington in the early 1960s put the figure as high as 90 percent), with perhaps a quarter to a third of nominal Buddhists active in church ceremonies and affairs.

The political troubles in South Vietnam in the 1960s that revolved around Buddhism were the product of two factors that emerged from this earlier history. One of these was the appeal of Christianity, the other the renaissance of Buddhism. European missionaries had made quite significant inroads in traditional Vietnamese society, to the degree that anti-Christian religious persecution had appeared at times in the eighteenth and nineteenth centuries. French colonial rule began during the latter half of the nineteenth century, and the French openly favored Catholic Vietnamese, who were enlisted as allies in colonial administration. Over time this had the effect of ensuring a disproportionate concentration of educational attainment and wealth in the hands of Vietnamese Catholics. When colonial rule gave way to Vietnamese government in the 1950s, it was the Catholics who were best placed to take advantage of the change.

President Ngo Dinh Diem's South Vietnamese government should be seen in this context. Diem was appointed prime minister under the last Vietnamese emperor, Bao Dai, in the wake of the 1954 Geneva agreement, and concentrated sufficient power to supplant the monarchy within two years. Diem was a devout Catholic, as were all the Ngo family. Diem also presided over a massive influx of Vietnamese from the north after Geneva, of whom perhaps 700,000 of more than 900,000 were Catholics, eventually making up almost half the entire Catholic population of South Vietnam. It was natural for Diem to take advantage of this population movement to create an especially loyal constituency. In view of the argument advanced by Italian cleric Piero Gheddo, the primary chronicler of Catholicism in South Vietnam, that cultural conditions created a "ghetto mentality" among Vietnamese Catholics, a Diem policy of alignment with the Catholics became even more understandable.

At the same time, it is important to note that Diem's government was not a theocratic one. The mishmash ideology he developed and called "personalism" was avowedly secular, not in any sense religious. The Can Lao party formed by his brother Ngo Dinh Nhu had a large degree of Catholic participation but was not a religious movement. Diem personally had contributed money to Buddhist fund-raisers for renovation of their Xa Loi pagoda, and his government similarly assisted the Buddhists' program. Still, the provincial and local officials Diem appointed were overwhelmingly Catholic, as were the military officers he promoted. Diem is most accurately seen as a patron of Catholics, not a mobilizer of Catholicism.

The second factor in the political troubles that began in 1963 was the renaissance of Vietnamese Buddhism. This rebirth had been proceeding for more than four decades, and Buddhist associations had been formed in south, central, and northern Vietnam in 1931, 1932, and 1934 respectively. Between 1956 and 1962 the number of higher schools for monks more than doubled; of the 4,766 pagodas in the country, 1,295 were renovated and 1,275 built during this period. Membership in Buddhist associations increased by a third. Among key developments were the founding of the An Quang pagoda in Saigon in 1950, and creation of the General Association of Buddhists in 1951. Headquartered at the Xa Loi pagoda after 1958, by 1962 the General Association, which represented only six of South Vietnam's sixteen Mahayana sects, claimed to have some 3,000 monks, 600 nuns, and 3 million lay members, including 70,000 to 90,000 in youth groups.

Behind the raw numbers, significant things were happening within the Buddhist faith. The older, entrenched hierarchy of the General Association were conservative and maintained the contemplative stance of traditional Buddhism, but younger, dynamic, and assertive bonzes (monks) were increasingly moved by the notion that Buddhism could play a constructive role in Vietnamese society. This kind of engaged social activism was not fundamentally different from the ecumenical movement that swept Roman Catholicism worldwide during this same period, but it was the misfortune of Vietnamese Buddhism that the struggle between engaged social reformers and the traditional hierarchy would be played out against a backdrop of revolutionary war.

Because the Diem government tried to preserve a monopoly on political action, it made early efforts to coopt emerging Buddhist reformers. For example, one young Buddhist laywoman, Cao Ngoc Phuong, worked actively in the Saigon slums helping poor Vietnamese start businesses and obtain education for their children. Madame Nhu, the wife of Ngo Dinh Nhu, first attempted to recruit Phuong into her Vietnamese women's auxiliary to the Can Lao party. When that failed, attempts to arrest the Buddhist activist followed. The same thing was happening elsewhere in South Vietnam, particularly in the Hue area, where reformist Buddhists were the dominant strain.

Until 1963 the traditional Buddhist hierarchy continued to oppose the activists, but the hierarchy was forced into uneasy alliance by actions of the Diem government. This was the real meaning of the "Buddhist crisis" which began in the late spring of that year. The catalyst was an incident at Hue that directly involved the Ngo family. Early in May the bishop of Hue, Ngo Dinh Thuc, Diem's brother, was celebrating his twenty-fifth anniversary jubilee, and Catholics paraded through the city carrying religious flags. Since 1957 President Diem had had laws against bearing other than national flags, ordinances reiterated in 1958 and 1962, but they were not enforced against Thuc's Catholic parade. May 8 was the date Buddhists celebrated as the 2,507th birthday of Buddha, and when it arrived Buddhists attempted to carry their religious flag (coincidentally, a flag designed by the American Henry Steele Olcott in 1885) despite the law.

Ngo Dinh Can, another of Diem's brothers, the Thua Thien province chief, ordered police and army units to break up a demonstration of some ten thousand Buddhists who marched on the radio station after the bonze Thich Tri Quang was denied the opportunity to broadcast an anniversary message to Buddhists. Accounts differ as to whether Major Dan Sy's troops made any preliminary effort to disperse the crowd, but they then fired upon the Buddhists, and an armored car crushed some of the demonstrators. Eight persons died. The Diem government showed its colors by putting out the story that the Buddhists had been killed by a grenade rolled into the crowd, ostensibly from a Viet Cong operative. West German doctors, however, had witnessed the entire event and confirmed the Buddhist account of the incident.

This Hue disaster led to Diem government intransigence, outraging Buddhists who then mounted more demonstrations, leading to a cycle of protest, repression, and mobilization familiar to any veteran of the American antiwar movement. The demonstrations soon spread to Saigon. Buddhist elders met Diem with a list of demands for redress—that the government accept responsibility, pay compensation, prosecute the responsible officials, and permit use of the Buddhist flag. Diem remained obdurate. On May 28 Buddhist activists showed how well organized they were when several hundred bonzes materialized out of nowhere in front of the National Assembly building to protest and announce the start of a two-day hunger strike. A week later *New York*

Times correspondent David Halberstam reported that the religious crisis had developed political overtones.

Tuesday, June 11, brought an event that caught the attention of the entire world. Halberstam was sleeping late when he received a phone call from a Vietnamese friend urging him to come to the site of the demonstration. Fellow *New York Times* reporter Malcolm Browne, advised by one of the Buddhist spokesmen, arrived earlier, to be told by Thich Duc Nghiep, "I advise you to stay until the very end of this, because I think something very important will happen." A little over an hour later, Thich Quang Duc, a sixty-six-year-old bonze from one of the pagodas at Hue, who had traveled for days in an old car to reach Saigon, emerged at the busy intersection of Phan Dinh Phung and Le Van Duyet streets to immolate himself in protest against Diem. Other monks and Buddhist nuns chanted, burned incense, and sang as Quang Duc was first doused with gasoline, then set himself aflame. Browne snapped a series of photographs that became graven images of the Vietnam era.

It mattered not that the self-immolation of Quang Duc had been a premeditated affair—Browne remembered later that he had been told before the end of May that two monks were considering sacrificing themselves, one by immolation. (On the day of Quang Duc's death, other bonzes physically blocked fire trucks when they arrived at the scene.) The image of the serene Quang Duc burning in the Saigon street ignited a storm of anti-Diem protest in Vietnam and much criticism of the Diem regime throughout the world. On the day of Quang Duc's funeral, the South Vietnamese government suddenly agreed to a provisional settlement with the Buddhists, a measure it then undercut by the most lethargic efforts at implementation.

Meeting with reporter Browne, President Diem later asked if it was true that Browne had bribed the Buddhists to set up the event so he could take pictures of it. Madame Nhu cemented the now-mutual hostility with her ill-considered remark that all the Buddhists had done was to "barbecue a monk." Later Madame Nhu compounded that offense, telling another reporter, "Let them burn more, and we shall clap our hands." Over the following days security units used force to break up Buddhist demonstrations; Ngo Dinh Nhu circulated a statement to the Can Lao party impugning Buddhist motives and accusing them of affiliation with the Viet Cong; and the spiral of hostility ascended still higher.

President Diem belied his periodic claims of having no quarrels with the Buddhists by the action he took in the third week of August, when he sent Colonel Le Quang Tung's Special Forces to raid Buddhist pagodas. In Saigon both Xa Loi and An Quang were struck, with significant destruction and hundreds arrested. At Hue's Tu Dam pagoda, Thich Tri Quang's seat of authority, an eight-hour pitched battle ensued between troops and demonstrators armed with sticks. Thirty were killed and seventy injured. According to a CIA cable, ten South Vietnamese generals participated in planning the pagoda attacks, which if true indicates Diem's intent to spread responsibility for the anti-Buddhist strike. Many of the generals who were named later participated in the military coup that overthrew Diem in November 1963, in the wake of which Diem and Nhu were murdered and Colonel Tung executed. By forcing the generals into complicity with the anti-Buddhist campaign, Ngo Dinh Diem helped seal his own fate. At the same time, United States horror at the Diem actions resulted in the withdrawal of support for his government and acquiescence in the generals' coup. That action, in turn, virtually locked the U.S. into the Vietnam War.

American accounts of this period that emphasize the role of the CIA in the anti-Diem coup tell only one side of this story. The degree to which President Diem engineered his own fate is often overlooked.

Yet another result of the pagoda attacks and the Diem coup was its impact within the Buddhist movement. The conservative church hierarchy that had resisted calls to activism was silenced by the August raids while Buddhists throughout the country were radicalized by the government's show of force. The success of the November coup seemed to affirm the arguments of the radicals. Leadership by bonzes like Tri Quang and his associates, Thien Minh and Tam Chau, were cemented by the victory. And because Diem had permitted no *political* opposition, the net effect was to make activist Buddhists the primary political movement in South Vietnam.

In the months following the overthrow of Diem, the Buddhists made a number of moves to consolidate their power. A national congress held at the Xa Loi pagoda in December 1963 and January 1964 created a new umbrella organization, the Unified Buddhist Church. The same congress adopted a proposal by Thich Nhat Hanh to create a School of Youth for Social Service, giving formal expression to aspirations for social change. After April 1964 a cadre of Buddhist militants were trained in martial arts at Saigon in the Quang Trung Judo School, which reportedly had a capacity for three thousand students. Desires for higher education were fulfilled by the Institute for Higher Buddhist Studies, a Saigon affiliate of the UBC's Institute for the Execution of the Dharma headed by Thich Tri Quang. Lay education was the function of the Van Hanh University established in February 1965.

Buddhist political power became manifest in the two years after November 1963. The succession of military juntas and civilian puppet cabinets organized by strongman General Nguyen Khanh in 1964–1965 made successive concessions to the religious movement even as demonstrations continued over one issue or another. American officials observing this scene were aware of underlying Buddhist strength. CIA reporting of the period demonstrates that the U.S. government held a far more sophisticated view of the Buddhist situation than those American pundits who tried to minimize the problem by attempting to show that Buddhism was a minority religion in Vietnam or that the Buddhists were Viet Cong allies.

In June 1963 a special report by the Office of Current Intelligence (OCI) of the CIA predicted that the Buddhist confrontation with the Vietnamese government "seems certain to have lasting political repercussions" (indeed, that "it could even lead to Diem's overthrow"). Although the Viet Cong had at least two bonzes among their higher leadership, the CIA noted, "there has been no evidence that the Communists instigated or influenced the Buddhist demonstrations or demands." But Hanoi and the Viet Cong had made propaganda use of the Buddhist crisis as an example of repressive tactics by the South Vietnamese. At the height of the Khanh government's Buddhist troubles, in September 1964, U.S. authorities compiled a formal Special National Intelligence Estimate (SNIE) on the prospects for government in South Vietnam. The SNIE concluded that "at present the odds are against the emergence of a stable government capable of effectively prosecuting the war." The estimate also found that Khanh seemed to be seeking Buddhist support and had some at that moment, while having little backing from Vietnamese Catholics (of whom Khanh himself was one). There were signs of continuing internal divisions among the Buddhists, a comment which indicated the CIA was aware of the differences both between factions of the Buddhist activists and those between the activists and the traditional hierarchy, which had begun to reemerge by this time. As for the militant leadership, "there continues to be no firm evidence that Tri Quang is pro-Communists [sic], or proneutralist."

When President Johnson sent his national security adviser McGeorge Bundy on a mission to Saigon in early February 1965, Bundy took with him a further SNIE from the CIA on South Vietnam's short-term prospects. That report stated that "dominant power obviously rests with the military, but the Buddhists are strong enough to make unworkable any set of political arrangements their leaders care to oppose. . . . The military and the Buddhists will almost certainly retain an effective veto power." In examining the Buddhists the CIA concluded that "they do not appear to desire the responsibilities of office or direct participation in government." As for Thich Tri Quang, "on balance we incline to the view that he is probably not now deliberately working for a Communist victory," although, the CIA believed, Quang's "disruptive actions thus far are serving these ends." On his Vietnam trip Bundy carried biographical data on Tri Quang, Tam Chau, and other Buddhist activists, plus a set of talking points for a meeting with Tri Quang. The bonze missed his meeting with McGeorge Bundy, but another was arranged. An aide who accompanied Bundy felt their session had aspects of a seance, as Tri Quang played the mystic and his pronouncements oozed past Bundy's Western logic. The meeting left Bundy "reeling."

Meanwhile, the Buddhists had turned decisively against General Khanh, who was replaced in February 1965 by a new junta whose strongman, Air Vice-Marshal Nguyen Cao Ky, became the first Buddhist to lead the government. By that summer the OCI unit at CIA was reporting that although "the basic political and religious conflicts have not been resolved . . . influential public figures appear reluctant to provoke new turmoil, and inclined to give the new government programs a chance." This period of relative tranquility gave way in the spring of 1966 to renewed political crisis, as a Buddhist Struggle Movement formed at Hue to demand fresh recognition. The crisis crystallized in March when Marshal Ky attempted to oust the popular Buddhist General Nguyen Chanh Thi, who commanded South Vietnam's I Corps and the region surrounding Hue. Thi was placed under house arrest while political conflict swirled around him. Military activity in I Corps ground to a halt as South Vietnamese army commanders and units began taking sides. On March 19 Buddhists staged a mass rally at Da Nang and paralyzed the city for three days with a general strike. At Hue students seized the radio station which had been the focus of the 1963 troubles, ironic since shortly before emergence of the Struggle Movement the military commander in the earlier incident, Major Dang Sy, had been taken to trial and sentenced to life at hard labor. A key difference in 1966, however, was the presence of the U.S. III Marine Amphibious Force (III MAF) commanded by General Lewis W. Walt, who thought he saw in the Struggle Movement "a danger signal of likely Viet Cong infiltration of the opposition."

Washington took the most serious view imaginable of this new episode in the Buddhist crisis. It led the U.S. government to one of its few recorded instances of considering withdrawal from Vietnam. William P. Bundy, brother to McGeorge and at this time assistant secretary of state, remembers the crisis well: "I always viewed it as a terrific setback, a very, very negative development in every possible way." At a White House meeting on April 2, President Johnson gave instructions that U.S. ambassador Henry Cabot Lodge get in touch with Thich Tri Quang and "get tough with him," that the U.S. support Ky, but that a "fall back position" be prepared. "If necessary," LBJ remarked, the United States ought to be prepared to "get out of I Corps . . . and even Vietnam," and he spoke of the need to "perhaps take a stand in Thailand." Two days later, after a demonstration in Hue by three thousand South Vietnamese soldiers, LBJ warned that it was important to keep U.S. troops and equipment out of the riot area, but he opposed "appeasement" and declared the "time has come when the alternative is to get out—or do what we need to do to get the government shored up." On April 6, at another crisis meeting, Secretary of Defense McNamara warned that the "Struggle Movement may be too strong to throw off. . . . They obviously have strength we didn't know about." McNamara ruminated that the U.S. did not know enough about Buddhist objectives but concluded, "I don't want to go to war against them."

The United States did help Marshal Ky shore up his government, providing airlift to move two Vietnamese marine battalions to Da Nang (statements that these troops traveled by sea do not appear to be accurate). Vietnamese armored units loyal to General Nguyen Chanh Thi then marched against Da Nang, but III MAF intervened at the crucial moment, with General Walt defusing several key situations and blocking a vital road bridge with F Company of the Ninth Marines. Hue remained tense throughout the period, culminating on June 1 when the United States Information Service library there was burned down, a day after demonstrators had sacked the U.S. consulate. General Thi eventually left the country for exile in the United States.

As a political sop, Marshal Ky appointed a quasi-legislative body and then held elections for a constituent assembly in the fall of 1966. Catholics, who made up a little over 10 percent of the South Vietnamese population, provided 19 percent of the 542 candidates in the 1966 election and 29 percent of those elected. Ky exulted at a press conference: "As a political force in Vietnam, Buddhism can be considered to be liquidated for all time."

Ky's elation proved premature. After all, almost half the delegates elected in 1966 were Buddhists, even though their representation did not reflect the proportion of Buddhists in South Vietnam. Similarly, Buddhists posted a strong showing in the 1967 elections for a National Assembly (52 of 137 delegates), and in the presidential elections that gave Nguyen Van Thieu and Nguyen Cao Ky 34.8 percent of the vote, Buddhist candidates Truong Dinh Dzu and Phan Khac Suu (a Cao Dai who nevertheless had the support of Thich Tri Quang's faction) together posted 28 percent of the vote. Dzu even outpolled the Thieu-Ky ticket in Quang Ngai province just south of Da Nang, and in several provinces of III and IV Corps areas. Truong Dinh Dzu had run on a peace platform and advocated negotiations with the National Liberation Front. For his trouble Dzu spent much of the remainder of the war in prison. Buddhism, however, continued to be a political factor in South Vietnam.

That Buddhists remained a political factor did not mean that their clergy were politically active. The Theravada Buddhists of the Mekong Delta, with their Cambodian roots, had never become especially militant. The traditionalist hierarchy of the Mahayana strain, never comfortable with the maneuvers of Tri Quang, Tam Chau, and their cohorts, had been silenced by the apparent successes of 1963–1965, but growing factionalization among the activists gave them the opportunity to reassert themselves. The defeat of the Struggle Movement in 1966 was a clear setback for the militants. Tri Quang and Tam Chau were forced to yield up their senior institute posts. They and others like Thich Thien Minh were put under house arrest or spent much of their time trying to stay one step ahead of South Vietnamese security forces. Buddhist social reformers, to whom politics had been a distraction anyway, focused anew on their primary interests. Walt W. Rostow, by 1966 President Johnson's national security adviser, had thought there might be more fallout from the Struggle Movement. Aware of the historical differences between southern, central, and northern Vietnam, at the height of the disturbances he had told Washington colleagues, "We may be seeing the emergence of a nation from this tripartite mess." William Bundy had shot back, "Walt, are you mad?" There can be little doubt that Washington heaved a collective sigh of relief as Vietnam's Buddhist crisis receded and the war intensified.

Those who argue that America ought to have won the war in Vietnam almost universally postulate military strategies that presume a stable South Vietnamese society united in opposition to the National Liberation Front and North Vietnam. In fact, Buddhist political troubles were symptomatic of the *dis*unity of the Vietnamese polity. Deep political differences lurked just beneath the surface even at those moments—like 1968 after the Tet offensive, or 1970 during the invasion of Cambodia, or 1972 when the ARVN was regaining Quang Tri—when militarily the war appeared to be going well. The political condition of South Vietnam can best be described as metastable, in the same way that Rumania appeared stable just before the overthrow of its Communist rulers in 1990, or as the Soviet Union appeared in 1991. The finest of the South Vietnamese were those who refused to permit political potentates to stop them from doing what they knew to be right. A good example is the Buddhist monk Thich Nhat Hanh.

10 **Profile: Buddhist in a Sea of Fire**

One Buddhist thinker whose life well illustrates the sad effects of the Vietnam War is Thich Nhat Hanh. Among those bonzes who responded to the calls for an "engaged Buddhism" that assisted social reform, Hanh became a key theoretician and is known today as the exponent of the philosophy of "Mindfulness" and founder of the Interbeing movement. Nhat Hanh's repeated tours of the United States and Europe, and the Buddhist communities he has established in France, have had an impact on religious practice in the West as well as some effect in supporting continued efforts of Vietnamese Buddhists to achieve free practice of their religion in socialist Vietnam. Along the way, Thich Nhat Hanh's stormy life stands as an example of just how difficult has been the path of Buddhism in Vietnam.

Born in the central area of Vietnam in 1926, he began early to study Buddhist texts and was ordained a monk at age sixteen at the height of World War II. Becoming Thich Nhat Hanh, he wrote poetry and sermons (Buddhists call them "dharma talks") that were among the most popular presented by bonzes of his generation. Hanh was among the founders of the An Quang pagoda in 1950 and subscribed to "engaged Buddhism" even before the time of Ngo Dinh Diem. When An Quang became the Buddhist Institute, Hanh was one of its first professors, having lectured at the pagoda since 1954. It is a measure of antagonisms between traditional and engaged Buddhism that lay authorities at both the An Quang and Xa Loi pagodas struck Hanh's name from the *livrets de famille* of those temples, in effect preventing Hanh from presenting courses or residing at them.

Thich Nhat Hanh first traveled to the United States in 1961; he studied comparative religion at Princeton and taught at Columbia

University. In New York at the time of Diem's demise, Hanh was torn by the urge to return to his native country, but he felt put off by the lack of support for his earlier reform efforts, especially a lack of support from Thich Tri Quang. Columbia asked Hanh to stay and offered to create a department of Vietnamese studies around him. But Hanh received a letter from Tri Quang, who said he had grown too old and old-fashioned to be the intellectual leader of the new Buddhist movement (though he was just three years older than Hanh). Hanh returned to Vietnam, where he became a principal drafter of the program of the Unified Buddhist Church adopted by a national religious conference in January 1964, as well as a prime mover in forming the Vanh Hanh University and the School of Youth for Social Service, whose first head was one of Hanh's former students. Thich Nhat Hanh himself became the first director of social studies at Vanh Hanh University.

Resuming his social activism, in early 1964 Hanh began leading teams of disciples, activists, and experts to remote villages damaged by the war. During one such mission, after devastating floods at the New Year of 1965, Hanh's team had to thread its way carefully between South Vietnamese troops and Viet Cong fighting in the area. The bonze's protégés continued this work, helping villagers build schools and health clinics, and even setting up pilot villages. Some School of Youth for Social Service adherents died in various incidents, including at least one grenade attack on the school itself. The work continued despite later action by the Vanh Hanh University severing its affiliation with the school. By 1975 some ten thousand persons were involved in the social work, and the school had been written up in the American press as a "little" Peace Corps.

Thich Nhat Hanh also continued his writing and became chief editor of the La Boi Press, a Buddhist publishing house, as well as editor of the official publication of the Unified Buddhist Church. In February 1966 he founded a religious order, Tiep Hien, formally consecrating his philosophy of Interbeing. Later that year he was invited to undertake a lecture tour of the United States by the Fellowship for Reconciliation and Cornell University. Advocating negotiations and "peace"— which by this time South Vietnamese government circles regarded as Communist provocation—brought an edict against Hanh's return to Vietnam, a ban continued by the subsequent Communist government of unified Vietnam. Thich Nhat Hanh has lived in exile ever since.

From Hanh's point of view, peace was necessary to stop the suffering of the Vietnamese people, and he continued to press these views throughout the remainder of the war. His best-known political work, *Vietnam: Lotus in a Sea of Fire,* was published in the United States in 1967. He also pressed his views in meetings with Secretary of Defense McNamara, in audiences with Pope Paul VI, and on lecture trips in Europe and the United States. Assisted by Chan Khong, a dedicated nun of his Tiep Hien order, Hanh formed a Buddhist peace delegation in Paris to press for an end to the war during the period of the Paris negotiations from 1969 to 1973. Throughout this period they collected donations and furnished support for Buddhist social activists still engaged in Vietnam. Hanh also met with American political figures, including Robert F. Kennedy and Senator J. William Fulbright, and in 1967 he was nominated for the Nobel Peace Prize by Martin Luther King, Jr.

Since the war Hanh has founded a Buddhist collective, called Plum village, near Bordeaux, France, and has continued his efforts in behalf of Buddhists in Vietnam while focusing on more general religious teaching. In 1976 and 1977 Hanh and Chan Khong sailed in the Gulf of Siam, helping in the rescue of Vietnamese boat people. The two have made appeals to the current Vietnamese government in favor of Buddhists and freedom of religion, and Chan Khong continues to raise money for social and religious projects in Vietnam.

At last count Thich Nhat Hanh had published more than ninety books and pamphlets, mostly on religious themes and in Vietnamese. The bonze continues to tour and to present dharma talks to interested audiences, including more than seven tours of the United States since the early 1980s. Where a dharma talk at Berkeley, California, in 1985 drew an audience of four hundred, in 1990 avid listeners in the same city packed a four-thousand-seat auditorium. That year Hanh held a special retreat only for Vietnam veterans, and he came away appreciating their particular problems in working through their Vietnam experiences. "The veterans have something to tell their nation about how to deal with problems that are likely to happen," Hanh later wrote, "problems that will not look different from Vietnam."

Thich Nhat Hanh was probably not one of those people who believed that American soldiers who came to South Vietnam in huge numbers beginning in 1965 were fighting for him. The forces were deployed without regard for those Vietnamese who opposed the war, and the conflict would not end before the soldiers had their chance. How quickly those soldiers arrived in Vietnam ultimately figured in arguments about why the war turned out the way that it did.

Parameters of Victory

In a widely read and highly influential book he titled *On Strategy,* Colonel Harry G. Summers analyzed how the principles of war had served America in the Vietnam conflict. Summers began with the question of national commitment, showing how this had been incomplete, then proceeded to demonstrate how conventionally understood principles of war had been applied (or misapplied) in military strategy. Among Summers's most significant observations are several that, as the years have passed, have entered our public consciousness in a rather different and somewhat distorted form. Behind this supposed conventional wisdom, the facts suggest a different reality.

Summers maintains that during the most active phase of the American war in Vietnam, Lyndon Johnson made a conscious decision *not* to invoke our national will for the war—LBJ would not mobilize and would never seek a declaration of war, preferring instead the more nebulous and ultimately unsatisfactory cloak of the Tonkin Gulf Resolution passed by Congress. Summers argues that this more restricted invocation of national will limited the means that could be committed to the Vietnam War. In his explicit consideration of specific military strategies, Summers goes on to posit that American military officers were mistaken in perceiving that time was on their side because of their advanced technological means. Instead, says Summers, time played in favor of the North Vietnamese. Then, in his discussion of the principle of surprise, Summers notes the difficulty of achieving this given the military buildup that necessarily precedes action or intervention.

History has distilled Harry Summers's arguments into one of the more prominent recipes for "what ifs" in the Vietnam War, the notion of "decisive" intervention. The thought is that Hanoi would have been defeated if only the United States had intervened instantaneously with overwhelming force. The notion has been repeated so often that it sometimes figures among lists of the supposed lessons of the Vietnam War. It finds echoes in the Persian Gulf, where in the space of a few months in 1990 the United States dispatched hundreds of thousands of troops to Saudi Arabia to confront Iraq while theoretically avoiding the pitfalls of Vietnam.

The problem with the decisive-intervention school of thought is that it pushes a panacea, divorced from reality, similar to all those other panaceas that were offered while Vietnam was still in progress and that were supposed to bring victory to the United States. This interpretation is placed on Harry Summers's work even though one can search *On Strategy* in vain for an actual claim that instantaneous, decisive intervention would have brought success. History has embroidered the original source. The faults in the logic of decisive intervention, however, reside not in the locus of the claim that it would work, but in the concrete realities of Vietnam. The inadequacies of decisive-intervention logic become apparent once one examines the logistic factors, those inconvenient but real barriers to a great many armchair strategies.

■ Contrary to the claims of latter-day critics, the Vietnam buildup was not all that slow. President Johnson deliberated at length, but once he made his decision McNamara's Pentagon executed it with considerable efficiency. After Johnson announced his decision for a buildup on July 28, 1965, the Pentagon deployed its first division-equivalent of combat troops that same month.

Coincidentally, the late-summer decision for Vietnam intervention permits a close comparison with the 1990 Persian Gulf intervention by the Bush administration, now touted as the strategic ideal. In 1990 the Iraqi invasion of Kuwait resulted in an early August determination by President George Bush to commit American forces on a large scale to Saudi Arabia. In November Bush followed with a decision to further expand U.S. deployment. Nevertheless, in both 1965 and 1990 the initial phases of military buildup began in late summer and extended through the end of the year.

The part of the deployment most Americans remember from the Vietnam War is the commitment of the First Cavalry Division (Airmobile) to the Central Highlands. This is likely due to the division's then-novel helicopter-based tactics and its early engagement at the battle of the Ia Drang Valley. Yet the Cav commitment represents but a small part of the 1965 deployment. Between July and December 1965 the United States deployed roughly thirty-three combat battalions to South Vietnam to join five already in place—in numerical terms about 150,000 troops. The 23,000 Americans in Vietnam at the end of 1964 became 184,000 a year later, with almost all the increase coming between August and December.

In the Persian Gulf in 1990 the United States built a force of 240,000 men between August and December. The numbers do not tell the whole story, however, because in 1990 the figures included large numbers of sailors afloat in naval vessels in the Gulf and the Indian Ocean, and relatively larger numbers of men in support units. In addition, in 1990 the United States was furnishing few military advisers to large local military establishments and thus not contributing (at least in this fashion) to allied military capability.

Counting only the available combat units, the 1990 Gulf deployment put four reinforced divisions in place within the equivalent time period, a force amounting to some fifty-one battalions. Even at first blush this pace of deployment runs at only 50 percent faster than that of 1965, and several factors combine to make comparative performance closer than first apparent. Most important, during the Vietnam buildup of 1965 American military transportation was also responsible for moving allied military units, so-called "Free World Forces," to the theater of operations. During the period of comparison, allied forces sent to Vietnam included an Australian battalion and a South Korean division plus a marine brigade, a total of thirteen battalions. The 1965 Vietnam buildup thus amounted to fifty-one battalions—the same number deployed in the Persian Gulf in 1990.

Not to put too fine a point on this comparison (involving a military establishment separated by many years), one can accept that the Persian Gulf buildup was faster without conceding much difference, certainly not enough to make for "decisive" intervention.

■ The Vietnam buildup, like that for the Persian Gulf, should be seen as a masterpiece of rapid action and the ad hoc resolution of seemingly insoluble problems. To say less denigrates the creative talents and resourceful activities of those Americans who made the buildup happen, for the fact is that South Vietnam was not prepared for a military buildup of this magnitude and could not have accommodated American forces without herculean efforts by U.S. support troops. Although it was fashionable during the war for grunts on the front lines to deride support personnel as "rear-echelon mother-fuckers" (REMFs), without the much-maligned REMFs the war as it evolved would not have been possible. The unglamorous statistics of supply and the requirements of military forces make this quite clear.

At the time of President Johnson's intervention decision, South Vietnam had exactly two ports capable of handling deep-draft (that is, large oceangoing) cargo ships. By far the larger one was Saigon, whose design and construction dated from French colonial days. Saigon had four deep-draft berths and had been handling an average of 150,000 short tons of goods per month. This figure included war supplies for the South Vietnamese military, supplies for U.S. components of the Military Assistance Command Vietnam (MACV), American foreign aid administered by the Agency for International Development, and (the largest single share) general goods destined for the South Vietnamese economy. Although Saigon had a good reputation as a port, it nonetheless was counted among the ports of underdeveloped countries. The second deep-water port at Cam Ranh was not even in the same league, having but a single deep-water berth. Shallow draft and coastal traffic could use the ports of Nha Trang and Qui Nhon, and a number of beaches could be used to offload materiel. South Vietnam had just three airfields capable of handling large jet aircraft that could bring in American troops for the buildup. *And that was it.* It was typical of this period that when the First Cavalry Division arrived in Vietnam, except for an advance party it landed on the beach at Qui Nhon.

A standard benchmark for logistics planners is that it requires roughly fifty pounds of supplies each day to keep a single soldier in the field. Thus the roughly 184,000 American troops in South Vietnam by the end of 1965 would have required some 138,000 tons of supplies per month. And more must be added to the supply requirement to account for ARVN regular troops (276,900 in January 1966). If the ARVN were supplied at a scale of, say, twenty-five pounds per day, that would add 100,462 to monthly supply traffic. In addition there were South Vietnamese militia forces numbering 260,000 in 1965–1966; if these were supplied at twelve pounds per person per day, an extra 46,800 tons a month would be needed. In sum, these supply requirements would total 285,262 tons per month, exclusive of the needs of (supply-intensive) naval and air forces. Such a requirement exceeded South Vietnan's entire port capacity.

By way of comparison, in World War II, during the high-intensity combat for Leyte Island in the Philippines in November 1944, supply people landed 340,000 tons of supplies for the U.S. Sixth Army, whose average strength that month amounted to about 138,000 troops. During the Korean War in 1953, the Military Sea Transportation Service moved an average of 626,000 tons a month. Thus the Vietnam supply requirement was by no means out of line with historical experience.

To complicate matters further, the entire order of battle of the United States Army in 1965 contained exactly *one* port construction engineer company.

It should be obvious that difficulties such as these were overcome only by considerable ingenuity and a great deal of impromptu, ad hoc action. Engineering units of all kinds were drafted to work on the logistics infrastructure while civilian contractors were brought in to supplement military resources. Numerous expedients were adopted to increase the handling capacity of the available ports. Barges and lighters, in particular, were of great use in unloading large cargo vessels without access to a deep-water berth. Here too civilian contractors were of considerable assistance, such as the Alaska Barge and Transport Company, which assumed full responsibility for cargo discharge at Nha Trang in April 1966.

Hardly surprising under the circumstances is the fact that an engineer higher command, the Eighteenth Engineer Brigade, became one of the first formations to deploy to Vietnam, in September 1965, simultaneous with the First Cavalry Division. A survey of countrywide requirements for engineer work, not only on the logistics infrastructure but on camps, storage facilities, and other works, resulted in a detailed briefing presented to MACV commander General William C. Westmoreland on November 4, 1965. According to that briefing there were existing requirements for 170 "battalion-months" of construction work. More than 62 percent of the full requirement could be attributed to work necessary on four ports—Cam Ranh, Dong Ba Thinh, Qui Nhon, and Tuy Hoa. Since the 7,900 engineers then in Vietnam amounted to the equivalent of 8.4 engineer battalions, component commander Major General Robert R. Ploger estimated that it would take two years to accomplish the required construction, even if the engineers were completely freed from field and combat engineering tasks during the interval.

Ingenuity became a significant factor helping to solve the construction nightmare. For ports a major innovation was the DeLong pier, originated by the company of that name, which involved a specially equipped barge that converted itself into a pier when caissons were drilled into the harbor floor by pneumatic jacks built into the barges. Each DeLong pier barge provided a berth for two deep-draft cargo vessels and could be installed by sixteen men in forty-five days. A conventional wooden pile pier of the same dimensions, according to General Ploger, would have consumed the efforts of forty men for six months, requiring special equipment to boot.

The first DeLong pier was installed at Cam Ranh. By 1967 that port had at least six deep-draft berths plus more capacity provided by lighterage. Thus in September 1965 Cam Ranh landed 34,909 tons of military cargo (and 46,751 in December), rising to 137,158 tons by July 1966. The DeLong pier essentially made this possible.

Beyond all the other engineering projects was the port of Saigon, which had to be greatly expanded to accommodate MACV's military traffic. This would be left out of the military engineering survey and instead handled by private contractors, among them the large concerns Brown and Root, Raymond International, Morrison-Knudsen, and J. A. Jones, which formed a consortium to operate in South Vietnam. The Vinnell Corporation handled electrical and water plants. An entire new facility called Newport was constructed upstream from the old Saigon port facility. Newport became a primary port of entry for U.S. military supply traffic, with the Saigon Port Authority adopting streamlined procedures to facilitate clearance of cargo from the facility. By such means Saigon's capacity rose to more than 600,000 tons a month at the height of the war.

Large-scale increases were also the rule elsewhere. Da Nang went from only lighterage to six deep-draft berths by 1968 for a capacity of 316,000 tons a month. Qui Nhon, formerly a coastal port, got four berths and could land 180,000 tons. Cam Ranh ultimately reached ten berths with a capacity to discharge 210,000 tons a month plus 900,000 barrels of fuel. By early 1968 the throughput capacity of the logistics system had risen to almost 1.2 million tons a month. Of course, by that time supply requirements were commensurately greater than in 1965. Rough calculations indicate a MACV logistics requirement of about 650,000 tons a month, one of perhaps 470,000 tons for the South Vietnamese armed forces and militias, and a civilian requirement of 200,000 to 300,000 tons. In other words, supply requirements continued to consume all the capacity that had been generated.

In 1965 all that lay in the future. The *existing* level of supply capacity limited the pace of the buildup. It is a tribute to the energy and ingenuity of REMFs throughout South Vietnam that the buildup went as fast as it did. Nha Trang began operations in September, landing 5,000 tons; over the last three months of 1965 it averaged 11,000. Phan Rang went into service that November with an over-the-beach supply operation that handled 10,059 tons that first month but thereafter fluctuated from 2,000 to 8,000 before settling at an average of about 5,000 tons a month.

Despite all efforts, however, the equipment and supplies for 184,000 troops, not to mention the 22,000 "Free World Forces" present by January 1966, simply could not be handled within the limits of the existing logistics infrastructure. Soon there developed a backlog of ships awaiting unloading, a backlog that rose to 122 cargo ships on November 26, 1965. These vessels idled at a cost to the United States of $3,000 to $7,000 a day, so-called demurrage costs.

Barge operations became crucial as an intermediate stage in reducing demurrage costs. Supplies could be offloaded from the oceangoing vessels, sending them on their way, and then held on the barges until such time as the cargos could be landed. In addition to Alaska Barge, civilian contractors that became important to the lighterage operation included Sea-Land Corporation and the indigenous Chinese concern Han Jin.

In one sense, barge operations postponed the problem but did not solve it. Instead they moved the bottleneck from the deep-draft ships onto the barges. Thus by November 1966, when the MACV force levels stood at 470,000 Americans and 59,000 "Free World Forces" in eighty-three battalions, 1,600 loaded barges were waiting to discharge cargos. Of those, more than a thousand had already been waiting a month or longer. Monthly logistics requirements were then approaching 650,000 tons for the MACV components alone.

Logistics problems would not go away, partly because General Westmoreland asked for and received additional increments of strength about as quickly as his REMFs—engineers and the rest—could increase the system's capacity. Thus in January 1967 at Saigon there were 35 deep-draft ships in waiting and hold status, ships containing 202,754 tons of cargo. At the same port in the third week of February there were 979 barges waiting to unload, 642 of which had been waiting for over a month. When, in March, planners studied the age of barge cargo, they discovered that fewer than a third of the barges—32 percent—had been awaiting unloading for less than a month. Slightly more than a third of barge cargo was one to two months old; 16 percent had been sitting for 61 to 90 days; 13 percent for 91 to 120 days, and a final 4 percent of cargos had been awaiting unloading for over 120 days.

A contrasting survey of materiel in transit sheds at Saigon port showed that fully 73 percent of the tonnage moved within the first month. Almost two-thirds of the remainder moved within the second month. Only a minuscule proportion of supply tonnage in the warehouses had been there for longer than three months. A similar survey a month later showed different, slightly less favorable percentages, but the basic distribution pattern remained the same. Much maligned as they were, the REMFs did well at moving the supplies once they got ashore. The bottleneck clearly lay in getting the materiel into South Vietnam.

Special efforts began in the spring of 1967 to reduce the logistics backlogs. These bore such fruit that Ambassador Ellsworth Bunker was mightily impressed—at Saigon only 581 barges were then under load, with just 359 of them waiting longer than a month. "I think what has been accomplished in the case of the port is a near miracle," Bunker reported to Washington.

By the fall of 1967, finally, the logistics system reached a point where handling became instantaneous—no loaded ships awaited berths. Even then there remained regional or local weaknesses in the system. For example, northern I Corps lacked any serious port capacity, leading to the ad hoc establishment of an over-the-beach facility at the mouth of the Cua Viet River. The supply-handling capacity in that area emerged as a specific factor in timing the arrival of reinforcements that Westmoreland requested to meet the Tet offensive.

The story of airfield capacity is similar to that of the ports. The margin was slim to begin with, although the infrastructure was improved rapidly. The three jet-capable airfields of 1965 increased to eight a year later, and those were ultimately improved to have a total of fifteen runways. Fields capable of handling C-130-type aircraft grew from nineteen in 1965 to forty-five near the end of 1966 and sixty a year later. Still, the nature of this beast was such as to be more useful for personnel movements than for supplies, excepting emergency or critical items. More than 90 percent of supplies for South Vietnam entered the country by sea. Where air had been handling roughly 16,000 tons a month during 1965, this reached 83,000 tons by 1968, a figure nevertheless dwarfed by seaborne supply tonnages.

■ Ellsworth Bunker quite rightly felt impressed by the achievements of the REMFs at Saigon port. What he called a near miracle was a reflection of South Vietnam's full logistics infrastructure. In the relatively short space of two years the REMFs' prodigious efforts had multiplied South Vietnam's import capacity by a factor of ten, a full order of magnitude. That they did this in the midst of a war, and in spite of the commercial schemes and corruption prevalent in Saigon society, only adds to the achievement. The engineers and logisticians and transport specialists may never have gotten their utilities wet in the mud with the rest of the grunts, but they made life in the field possible for American soldiers in Vietnam. Moreover, they constructed an array of facilities unmatched in previous American wars which made life on base between operations relatively comfortable for GIs. These base facilities helped maintain the morale of MACV's forces. The REMFs' contributions to the war effort may not have been obvious, but they were important nonetheless.

Yet even the near miracle in South Vietnam could not make the impossible happen: the buildup of American military power in South Vietnam occurred only as fast as was possible. Increased logistics capacity was matched by increases in force levels; conversely, the levels of MACV's military power could not be raised faster than they were.

There are two ways one can interpret the facts regarding the American military buildup in South Vietnam. Looking at numbers of battalions deployed, the rate at which they moved into the country, their straining at the margins of the existing logistics infrastructure and the U.S. army order of battle, it is possible to argue that the intervention and buildup in South Vietnam was as decisive as it could have been. Emphasizing only the limitations of South Vietnamese infrastructure, one could argue that truly decisive intervention lay beyond the realm of possibility. Either way, latter-day critics who argue that the United States could have won the Vietnam War with a faster, more decisive intervention are engaged in wishful thinking.

These kinds of basic factors are almost entirely ignored in arguments that the war should have been won. Analysts who make such "winning" arguments prefer to focus on the military tactics used in Vietnam. That some of these tactics were ill conceived, few analysts would deny, as the experience of Binh Dinh Province will illustrate.

12

White Wing to Pershing: The Failure of Large-unit War

As 1965 drew to a close, the American command in Vietnam reached a crucial decision. Military Assistance Command Vietnam (MACV) was riding the crest of a wave, high on its successful defeat of the North Vietnamese Army (NVA) in the Central Highlands in the Ia Drang battles. The victory prevented the NVA from cutting South Vietnam in two and turned back Hanoi's response to American intervention and the commitment of ground troops. The Ia Drang achievement was won by the "Cav," the First Cavalry Division (Airmobile), self-styled as the army's "First Team." Indeed, perhaps Ia Drang earned them their nickname. The big decision made by General Westmoreland, MACV commander, in the waning hours of 1965 was what to do next with his First Team.

Westmoreland naturally operated under certain constraints. As soon as it landed the First Cavalry Division had been sent to a base at An Khe, along Route 19, which connected Pleiku in the Highlands with Qui Nhon, a port city on the central Vietnamese coast. Space for the base had been cleared by a brigade of the 101st Airborne Division, while Cav support people soon planned a large facility they named Camp Radcliff. The airmobile division's great mass of helicopters provided incredible mobility but also established a certain range of choices for Westmoreland, given the unit's location at Radcliff.

The decision Westmoreland reached, perfectly reasonable under the circumstances, was to order an offensive in the coastal region at the foot of the Highlands below An Khe. This province, Binh Dinh, long considered a problem area, had become a special concern since the responsible ARVN formation, the Twenty-second Infantry Division, was thinly dispersed from this lowland area up to Pleiku in the hills.

111

Concerned about security for the central Vietnamese coast, as soon as he had any disposable force, Westmoreland sent it to Qui Nhon. The new formations arrived between September and November 1965 and were the first combat units to come from the Republic of Korea (ROK), specifically the ROK Capital ("Tiger") Division less one regiment, and the Second Marine ("Blue Dragon") Brigade.

South Korean troop presence improved security around Qui Nhon but could not solve all Westmoreland's problems. The tactical terrain of Binh Dinh, dominated by single-planting paddy and sudden hill masses, provided numerous areas suitable for guerrilla bases close to the peasant villages of the coastal plain. The lowlands were important both as rice-producing areas and because of Highway 1, the north-south road (and nearby railroad) that provided the transportation backbone of South Vietnam. The roughly half-million people of the province also represented a significant stake in pacification—the contest for hearts and minds.

Westmoreland conceived a lightning offensive that would utilize the best capabilities of his elite forces, drawing not only on the Cav but on ARVN, the ROKs, and the U.S. marines. Under this operational concept the South Koreans would expand their perimeter northward out of Qui Nhon toward the Suoi Ca. An ARVN airborne brigade would be committed at the critical point of the offensive. The Cav would leap in from the Highlands, suddenly flooding the Binh Dinh plains around Bong Son. If the guerrillas had any thought of escape across the provincial line to Quang Ngai, they would be met by an almost simultaneous marine amphibious landing at Duc Pho. The amphibious elements could link up with the airmobile ones while the ROKs provided security for a forward operating base, making the Cav's airmobile operations even more effective.

It was a dream plan. Even better, the American lineup was first-rate. Major General Harry W. O. Kinnard of the Cav had virtually improvised a division of 15,800 officers and men plus 434 aircraft and 1,600 vehicles. Kinnard had deployed his scratch unit successfully to a distant theater of operations, to a remote battlefield there, and straight into a pitched battle with some of the best troops the NVA had to offer. Division commander Kinnard chose his Third Brigade to make the Bong Son air assault. Colonel Harold G. Moore, commanding that brigade, was the newly promoted battalion chief who had led Cav troops in one of the most notable Ia Drang engagements. The only sour note was that his brigade included the Second Battalion, Twelfth

Cavalry (2/12), which had been severely mauled on a forsaken landing zone west of Pleiku.

The marines were under Lieutenant General Lewis Walt, leader of III Marine Amphibious Force (MAF), who planned to put two battalions on the beach just at the demarcation line between his III MAF (and ARVN I Corps) command and that of II Corps, the ARVN headquarters responsible for Binh Dinh. Another battalion would air assault inland. Later the seaborne component was increased to three battalion landing teams, with a further one in reserve afloat. The heliborne assault was cut back to two rifle companies with their battalion command element. The invasion took place on January 28 despite heavy seas, low overcast, and light rain.

The marine operation went forward under the code-name Double Eagle. Colonel Moore's endeavor carried the slug Masher when it jumped off on January 24, but it didn't last long. On the first day Moore encountered an accidental setback when a C-123 transport crashed at the Deo Mang pass near An Khe. At the White House in Washington, where President Johnson habitually watched the press tickers, he read the wire service flashes that forty-two American soldiers had died in a crash in Masher. Johnson did not like the code-name, fearing it might raise the wrong connotations among Americans. The word came down the chain of command to change the name. General Kinnard thought up a new one—the air assault from the hills became White Wing. The changeover went into effect on February 4.

The Cav were first off the mark at the end of the Vietnamese Tet holiday. Colonel Moore's orders were to find and destroy a major NVA/VC supply and recruiting center near Bong Son. As often happened in Vietnam, the rumor went ahead of The Word, so Cav infantry and helicopter crews began gossiping about Bong Son as soon as they learned the 1/9th Cavalry, the division air cavalry unit, had sent reconnaissance ships there. Rumor had it that every recon ship had been damaged; one senior pilot, a warrant officer and old-time airman, was said to have turned in his wings.

On its first day Moore's brigade assaulted into its first objective, Landing Zone Dog, which turned out to be a defended VC village, and as hot as the recon boys had been saying. The lift was huge, more than a hundred ships; fully twenty were damaged and five shot down (losing only two pilots and two gunners) during the approach and initial assault. The assault itself, into an ancient graveyard, was successful enough that helicopters were stationed forward at the landing zone (LZ) from the first night. For a time, though, it had been a near-run thing, as the 2/7 Cavalry took the hits and one of its rifle companies landed scattered. This was the battalion that had been chewed up in the Ia Drang, and coincidentally the same unit that had suffered the loss from the C-123 crash outside An Khe. At Cu Nghi, just west of Tam Quan, one Cav company won through by bore-sighting a 105 mm howitzer at a charging enemy.

Viet Cong machine guns on the ground took a steady toll of the helicopters. The Cav's 228th Aviation Battalion lost four of its CH-47 Chinooks in an hour; within a few days ten Chinook pilots were killed or wounded. In the 227th and 229th Assault Helicopter Battalions, consisting of UH-1D "Hueys" to carry infantry troopers, forty-five ships took damage in the initial days of Masher.

Colonel Moore used classic airmobile tactics in Masher. When 2/7 encountered resistance at Cu Nghi, the Cav opened a new LZ north of the village and fed in a battalion to take a blocking position. Reinforced by 2/12 Cavalry the next day, Moore's command smashed into the village, thought to have been held by the Seventh and Ninth battalions of the NVA Twenty-second Infantry Regiment. The Cav took the village with heavy losses—121 killed and 220 wounded—but believed it had annihilated the North Vietnamese, counting 660 bodies. Meanwhile, Colonel Moore began to use LZ Dog as a point from which to radiate. On January 31 he opened up a new LZ Quebec, all the time working his forces north toward the An Lao Valley.

Everyone agreed they were up against substantial opposition. Cav estimates put the defenders at about seven thousand, the equivalent of a division of mixed NVA/VC troops. Units included the Eighteenth and Twenty-second NVA regiments and the main force VC Second Regiment. In their own estimates of the situation, marines carried two of these units, plus the NVA Ninety-fifth Regiment, the VC Thirty-eighth Independent Battalion, a transport unit, and eleven VC local force companies ranging in strength from 90 to 150 men each. At the interallied joint services conference before Double Eagle, held by ARVN I Corps commander General Nguyễn Chanh Thi, most agreed that these NVA/VC forces stationed themselves in the hills in southeast Quang Ngai Province, with their base structure behind them in the An Lao Valley of Binh Dinh.

Force Recon Marines and scouts from the ARVN Second Division staged reconnaissance forays into the Duc Pho area for two weeks before Double Eagle. General Hoang Xuan Lam, the division commander, detailed two battalions of his Fourth Regiment as Task Force Bravo to man-blocking positions north of Duc Pho. This auxiliary operation, code-named Lien Ket-22, went off without a hitch. Aside from the dismal weather on January 28, the Double Eagle assault proceeded well. There were air strikes, naval gunfire support by the cruiser *Oklahoma City* (CLG-5) and the destroyer *Barry* (DD-933), and arrangements for B-52 Arc Light strikes inland, beyond the Special Forces camp of Ba To, where the Double Eagle heliborne component would assault. The worst obstacle proved to be surf that built to swells of six to eight feet after midmorning. Courtesy of the Cav, the marines benefited from the aerial scouting of the First Squadron, Ninth Cavalry. Weather continued to plague the landing buildup for two more days, then broke on the last day of January.

Double Eagle's tactical commander was Brigadier General Jonas M. Platt, an assistant commander of the Third Marine Division, otherwise responsible for the U.S. base at Chu Lai. Platt put two battalion landing teams (BLTs) across the beach, the 3/1 and 2/4 Marines, with BLT 2/3 afloat as a special landing force. An abbreviated "battalion," really only two rifle companies with a command element, 2/9 marines (down from Da Nang for the occasion), made the heliborne landing at Ba To. Only one landing force unit encountered serious opposition, and that only late in the afternoon of the first day. Again weather proved an obstacle to Platt, who was prevented from launching ground probes to follow up the preplotted Arc Light strikes in the interior. Circumstances obliged Platt to adopt the 2/9 disposition, originally forced upon him by marine helicopter limitations, with the whole force. After the landing Platt found the two-company expedient quite flexible. He added 81 mm mortars for heavy weapons support and formed six or seven maneuver elements with the available marines. The original invasion site, Red Beach, had now become "Johnson City," a busy forward operating base. Contact with the enemy continued to be sporadic. On February 3 General Platt ordered an advance southward to link up with the Cav in Binh Dinh. Recon Marines, from B Company, Third Recon, or from First Force Recon, conducted more than forty patrols and sighted over 1,000 enemy during Double Eagle. The operation officially claimed 312 VC killed plus 19 captives (with 18 weapons and 868 rounds of ammunition among them). Marine losses were 24 killed and 156 wounded.

On Colonel Moore's White Wing front, after the carnage of the first day, a pattern of operations asserted itself similar to what the marines experienced: few contacts, mostly frustrations. The public relations people had made something out of the Binh Dinh-Quang Ngai offensive, especially in claiming victory at Cu Nghi, but thereafter the enemy faded away. By the end of January Colonel Moore was telling reporters of his regret that the North Vietnamese refused to be drawn into a sizable battle. In early February he expressed disappointment with the results of Arc Light strikes. Meanwhile, the marine PR people began to talk of Double Eagle, involving ten thousand men and eighteen major vessels, as the largest amphibious operation since Inchon. Cav "Headhunters" from the 1/9th Cavalry recall the marines as giving scant credit to Cav scouting.

Credit or not, the marines could not afford to have so many maneuver battalions engaged in unproductive operations. They called a halt to Double Eagle in mid-February. The Vietnamese marines also recalled Task Force Bravo.

Reports following White Wing saw it progressively draw in quantities of new troops. A greater Cav commitment induced General Kinnard to assume direct command from Moore on February 4. The ARVN sent a second regiment of their Twenty-second Division into Binh Dinh, committed the reserve airborne brigade, and threw another airborne brigade in after that. The offensive sweeps continued until March 6, in all, forty-two days. Operations created a mass of refugees from the villages in the path of battle; 3,421 were evacuated from the An Lao valley alone. Final claims have been variously reported as 2,839 "known casualties," or at 1,342 Vietnamese dead, 633 captured, and 1,087 VC suspects detained. Moore had claimed 660 KIAs, 357 captured, plus the recovery of 49 individual and 6 crew-served weapons in the initial phase of the campaign. Colonel Moore's Third Brigade of the Cav sustained 75 killed and 240 wounded. General Kinnard later reinforced Binh Dinh with his Second Brigade to free Moore for the An Lao Valley thrust, which brought a link-up with the Double Eagle marines. Artillerymen from Battery B, First Battalion, Thirtieth Artillery made the first contact on February 4 with Marines of Company G, Second Battalion, Fourth Marines near Tam Quan.

What is clear from all this is that the North Vietnamese and Viet Cong engaged only so long as they thought it advantageous to do so. They then broke contact regardless of the flexibility of airmobile or amphibious forces. One may also question how much they knew of the impending plans for Masher. Despite the offensive posture of American forces, the enemy retained the tactical initiative.

In a nutshell that was Binh Dinh—a dream operation, a fine lineup of commanders, plenty of support, determined execution, and the enemy got away.

■   White Wing did not end the war in Binh Dinh. Far from it. When the extra U.S. and ARVN troops were pulled away by the exigencies of war, the adversary regenerated. In May the VC struck back with a two-battalion attack on the ARVN bridge guard at Phu Ly bridge, a critical Highway 1 crossing on the Suoi Ca River. That post also happened to cover LZ Hammond, turned into a forward base for the Cav.

In mid-May the division developed a minor contact outside Vinh Thanh Special Forces camp into another flash operation, Crazy Horse. It began with a painful encounter near An Khe by A Company of the 1/12 Cavalry. A large enemy force inflicted heavy casualties in a hot firefight; the company's weapons platoon was overrun before it was all over, with all but one man killed or wounded. When 2/12 assaulted in to help, they were unable to deploy properly in the difficult terrain. The enemy escaped again.

During June 1966 the enemy returned with a regiment-size attack at Tam Quan against ARVN Task Force 140, in a permanent base camp deployment. The ARVNs were wired in, had trenches, some mines, a platoon that was APC-mounted, and two platoons of 105 mm howitzers. The compound contained two ARVN regular infantry battalions and the equivalent of another in Regional and Popular Force units. The NVA struck hard out of the night but were beaten back with the aid of an AC-47 gunship, a type often nicknamed "Spooky" or "Puff the Magic Dragon."

In the fall of 1966 the Cav, now under the command of Major General Jack Norris, went back on the offensive in Binh Dinh, throwing its units into operation Thayer. The Headhunters, Cav air scouts of the First Squadron, Ninth Cavalry, one day made a chance sighting near Hoa Hoi village. Quick-reacting scout infantry touched off a firefight, whereupon the Cav command fed forces into the engagement. There had been no reason to suspect Hoa Hoi; 1/12 Cav had already passed nearby and found little opposition. Behind Hoa Hoi the Phu Cat Mountains loomed and sheltered the enemy, whom the Headhunters immediately identified as NVA by the density of their fire.

Again the American reaction was prompt, dynamic, and something of a model. Norris interrupted Thayer to improvise an entirely new major operation, Irving, which lasted twenty-two days beginning October 2, 1966. The main striking force was Lieutenant Colonel James Root's First Battalion, Twelfth Cavalry, reinforced by two companies of the First Battalion, Fifth Cavalry. Hoa Hoi had not previously been exploited as a reconnaissance objective because it had not been considered a logical choice as a base area. The hills lay smack up against the sea and an inshore lake. The Cav first blocked off the promontory, then systematically swept the entire area. Combat intelligence in due course identified the adversary as the Seventh and Eighth battalions of the NVA Eighteenth Regiment. The operation created 10,779 new refugees in the Hoa Hoi district, but Irving was widely regarded as successful, and Westmoreland recalls it as a "classic" meeting engagement and encirclement. The tally sheet included a body count of 681, another 128 possibles, 220 prisoners, and 1,172 detained VC suspects. The Cav's operational system of airborne fire support, immediate reaction, and follow-on reinforcement proved devastating to the North Vietnamese.

In other combat action further south in Binh Dinh, close to LZ Hammond, the Second Regiment, Third VC Division reconnoitered and planned an attack with both direct and indirect fire weapons. General Truc, commander of the Third Division (also called "Yellow Star"), disapproved on the grounds that neither of his other two regiments were available to support an attack. Lieutenant Colonel Xoan's Eighteenth Regiment was the force around Hoa Hoi, while Major Diep's Twenty-second Regiment was in the An Lao Valley. Major Khanh of the Second VC conducted an intense ten-minute mortar barrage of LZ Hammond on the night of September 23 but subsequently withdrew to the Kim Son Valley.

The Cav riposte began October 25 and lasted into February 1967, a total of 111 days. This offensive into the Kim Son and Luoi Ci valleys was called Thayer II. It tallied some 1,757 enemy killed, of whom 657 were claimed as confirmed NVA. The Americans captured ammunition and food, 479 weapons, and other equipment. The attacks were backed by naval gunfire support, B-52 strikes, and 1,126 fighter-bomber sorties (a sortie is one flight by one plane). Combat operations created 1,000 refugees, after which authorities decided on resettlement and evacuated the remaining population of the Kim Son Valley. After-action reports by Cav units referred to the enemy's ability to accept or reject combat at will. Viet Cong and North Vietnamese leaders still retained the initiative.

The high point of the operation was the battle for LZ Bird, once more at the enemy's initiative, in the last days of 1966. According to an NVA officer taken prisoner in the battle, the Twenty-second Regiment commander, Major Tin Phuong, had intended to attack just before Christmas and then have the agreed truce time to effect his withdrawal. Instead, preparations were delayed, and the cease-fire time was used to assemble. The NVA attack on Bird, a fire base in the crow's foot of Kim Son Valley, began soon after midnight December 26. The regiment struck with about 1,300 North Vietnamese troops against a well-bunkered position that was capably sited in a bend of the Kim Son River. Bird contained the twelve guns of two understrength artillery companies plus an understrength rifle company in defense, altogether barely 150 men with fourteen machine guns. The NVA swarmed over the perimeter, capturing more than half the Cav position before they were stopped, then slowly driven back. The Americans called in artillery fire on their own positions and fought on, finally inflicting so many losses the North Vietnamese recoiled.

Thus ended a year in Binh Dinh province, about as it had started. A major difference was that by December 1966 the province was dotted with 85 refugee centers housing some 129,202 Vietnamese. The Vietnamese Revolutionary Development (RD) ministry was then in its infancy, with trained RD teams for villages hardly beginning to emerge from Vung Tau. There were few pacification resources to pour in after the soldiers left, while Saigon had precious little infrastructure to implant and few programs that were really effective. As always seemed true with pacification, success was mostly a matter of local initiative and method, and therefore not readily transferable.

For 1967, coastal portions of Binh Dinh and selected districts around Qui Nhon were put on the "priority" pacification list for the newly inaugurated national campaign plan. The Cav resumed its large-scale operations in February 1967 with Pershing, the first phase of which lasted into 1968, until January, just before Tet. Claims for almost a year's operations were 5,343 KIAs. Finally, concern for the threat to I Corps and the situation at Khe Sanh induced Westmoreland to shift the Cav northward, where they fought around Hue and Quang Tri and in the thrust to reestablish the overland link to Khe Sanh. The Cav, now commanded by Major General John J. Tolson, were probably glad to be leaving Binh Dinh. Stay-behind elements of the airmobile division launched Pershing II, high-intensity operations to cover the departure of the major part of the division. The second-phase operation claimed another 614 KIAs and coincided with the Tet offensive.

In secret assessments made of Tet's effect on pacification in South Vietnam's provinces, Binh Dinh figured among those where pacification suffered a "moderate" setback. With the "Accelerated Pacification Program" initiated later in 1968 to regain the ground lost at Tet, Binh Dinh moved into the category of provinces counted under government control. Even so, a GI stationed at Bong Son in November 1969 recalls that he and his buddies took no chances because "the province had a history of being very sympathetic to the VC." By August 1971 public reports placed Binh Dinh back on the list of provinces in which government control was threatened. In the heavy Vietnamese battles of 1972, Binh Dinh was unsettled. During the debacle of 1975, one of the reasons for the loss of so many trying to escape from the Central Highlands and An Khe was that Binh Dinh fell before the evacuation convoys could make it down Route 19 from the hills to Qui Nhon.

By that day Binh Dinh had been the locale for countless operations like White Wing. The large-unit operations, even those as flawless as Irving, seemed to settle little. Certainly Binh Dinh, where commanders complained that the adversary could readily evade contact, illustrates large-unit war in Vietnam. It was like sweeping water that flows back as soon as the brush passes. American firepower and tactics were devastating, and could hardly lose in battle, but they could hardly win "the Nam." It was one more paradox of Vietnam.

Perhaps the reason the tactics would not work was that the enemy was not who the U.S. supposed he was. A debate on this very matter, carried out secretly within the American intelligence community, would not be understood until years later, when it became the focus of controversial court cases. This dispute over the enemy, and the way it was resolved at the time, warrants examination because it reassured commanders that the strategy they *were* using was the right one.

War of Numbers: Westmoreland Case Reprise

A mong the more intense controversies of the Vietnam experience is the question of the size of the adversary the United States fought in the war. While Americans were still in combat in South Vietnam, that controversy formed the stuff of a secret dispute between military authorities in South Vietnam and civilian intelligence experts in Washington. After the war the dispute over the size of the North Vietnamese and Viet Cong forces, the so-called order of battle, became the subject of a television documentary screened by the Columbia Broadcasting System in January 1982. In turn the documentary, titled "The Uncounted Enemy: A Vietnam Deception," became the focus of a libel suit by former Vietnam commander General William Westmoreland, who charged he had been defamed by the broadcast's allegation that he had been at the center of a deliberate deception to prevent Washington from understanding the reality of the Vietnam War. The case of *Westmoreland v CBS* was settled out of court in early 1985, but not until after a long and bitter trial in which both sides fought hard, CBS to prove its charges justified, General Westmoreland to show he had been libeled and damaged by the television broadcast.

Westmoreland v CBS became one of the most celebrated court cases of the Vietnam War, as important as the Pentagon Papers (where the issue was prior restraint to obstruct press publication of a secret war study) or the court-martial of Lieutenant William Calley for his role in the My Lai massacre (where war crimes were the subject). Unfortunately, the very intensity of the controversy over *Westmoreland v CBS* has been an obstacle to understanding the real events involved. Many veterans and some others reacted as if questioning General Westmoreland's intelligence appraisals was the same as attacking

American and Vietnamese veterans for their sacrifices in the war. Accounts of the trial typically criticize the structure of the CBS documentary, deplore the motives of one side or the other, or detail the testimony and cross-examination of the various trial witnesses like a baseball box score. But the box score approach is purely speculative since the case never went to the jury, and anyway press interviews with jurors immediately following the settlement indicated that the jury favored the CBS version of events.

Lost amid the welter of charges and countercharges in the heat of the public relations competition was the record of actual events during the Vietnam War. Some treatments of the subject are entirely silent on the order of battle controversy in its proper historical context of 1967, as if the issue exists only due to a television program and not to events during the war itself. The inside of the intelligence dispute over the order of battle is brought out in *War of Numbers: An Intelligence Memoir* by Sam Adams. For the first time, the Adams memoir provide an account of where the order of battle dispute came from, when it began, and how it percolated to the top levels of the Central Intelligence Agency and Westmoreland's Military Assistance Command Vietnam (MACV). Shorn of the rhetoric of public relations and the hyperbole of the CBS trial—which may relieve those who worried about what Adams might say in the wake of the legal case (he was the key consultant to CBS in framing its documentary)—*War of Numbers* is a disturbing story that shows where several skeletons are buried. Sam Adams not only shows why he became upset enough about this issue to start a virtual one-man campaign over it, but he also permits us to reconstruct an intelligence shift that amounted to an enormous reevaluation of the threat facing every American in South Vietnam.

The sense of urgency that impelled Sam Adams was acquired during his first trip to South Vietnam, in January 1966, when Viet Cong saboteurs set off a bomb outside his Saigon hotel. Author of a recent CIA study arguing that increasing numbers of VC defectors portended a drop in Viet Cong morale, Adams was startled that the Vietnamese Communists could be dangerous in the heart of the south. It was the first of a series of events that jarred Adams out of complacence. Another was a highly successful South Vietnamese sweep against the Viet Cong 506th Battalion in Long An Province—shortly after a battle that was supposed to have knocked the guts out of this VC unit, it had returned to full strength and was making spirited attacks. Adams then discovered a huge discrepancy between the numbers of Viet Cong guerrillas Long An Province officials believed they were fighting and the figure for guerrillas in that province carried on the official order of battle. At the same time, reviewing captured documents, Adams continued to turn up evidence that the Viet Cong suffered from significant rates of desertion.

The genesis of the order of battle dispute lay in the dawning realization that two trends could not both be correct at the same time if the order of battle was accurate—the VC could not be losing men to desertion and combat at a high rate and yet maintaining and increasing its strength. Long An became a microcosm of the mystery of Vietnam. Late in the summer of 1966 the CIA received a bulletin from the MACV Combined Documents Exploitation Center reporting a VC document taken in Binh Dinh province listing local guerrilla strength, giving a figure *eleven times* higher than what appeared in the order of battle. The first discoveries surprised CIA analyst Adams, the next ones disturbed him. Adams began searching specifically for guerrilla strength in the captured documents. He encountered data for Phu Yen and Phuoc Long provinces that duplicated what had been learned in Binh Dinh. Adams and other analysts of the Indochina Division of CIA's Office of Current Intelligence (OCI) began to press for reevaluation of the MACV order of battle, revising numbers to reflect their evolving knowledge of the size of Viet Cong guerrilla forces. Eventually the CIA used its revised guerrilla figures in several different reports in 1966–1967.

Questions about the order of battle rose to the level of a formal inquiry in February 1967, when a CIA delegation led by Dean Moor, Indochina Division chief, traveled to Honolulu for a conference with MACV intelligence boss Major General Joseph A. McChristian. The latter wore two "hats" as Westmoreland's intelligence chief, or J-2, and as head of the Combined Intelligence Center Vietnam (CICV). As they would have said at the CIA, the order of battle was his "paper." That was in fact the line McChristian took at the Honolulu conference, insisting that any necessary revisions would be his to make, at the same time assuring CIA representatives that his own studies confirmed that changes in the guerrilla figures included in the order of battle were indeed necessary. In fact, according to Colonel Gains Hawkins, then CICV's chief for this type of analysis, Saigon's estimates were similar to those of the CIA.

So far so good, but the obstacle proved to be General Westmoreland himself. Acutely aware of the erosion of public support for the Vietnam War, rather than putting his superiors on notice that they had to do something or MACV's difficulties would multiply, the general chose to take an active part in the debate, with press conferences, interviews, and the like. Westmoreland's concern was magnified by a development we can now reveal for the first time: on March 9, 1967, the chairman of the Joint Chiefs of Staff, General Earle Wheeler, put Westmoreland on notice that statistical revision of recorded numbers of battalion-size or larger attacks by the VC and NVA was a politically sensitive matter. In an "Eyes Only" cable, Wheeler told Westmoreland that upward revision (doubling, tripling the old figures, or more), "If these figures should reach the public domain . . . would, literally, blow the lid off Washington." Westmoreland insisted on going ahead with revisions in the secret figures on numbers of attacks; but when the order of battle dispute surfaced, it was obvious that this involved an even more sensitive matter, because the order of battle numbers were often cited and quoted in public to justify various measures in the war.

General Westmoreland had additional difficulties as a result of his own efforts at public advocacy. In April 1967, and again that November, he traveled to the United States on barnstorming tours designed to restore a favorable public view of the war. Lending his prestige to arguments that encouraged Americans to support Vietnam policy, Westmoreland insisted that the war was being won, that there was, in fact, "light at the end of the tunnel" (Westmoreland's phrase)—victory was beginning to come into sight. To buttress his claim, the general asserted that the North Vietnamese and Viet Cong had passed a "crossover point" at which their losses were greater than the numbers of recruits available in South Vietnam plus infiltrators sent down from the north on the Ho Chi Minh Trail. Thus intelligence became involved in the hortatory argument, the claim that the size of enemy forces in the south was dwindling. This claim flew in the face of evidence the CIA was turning up, and therein resides the problem with Sam Adams's discoveries.

In the spring of 1967 there occurred a series of MACV J-2 studies which produced the larger Viet Cong numbers that General McChristian had promised would be inserted into the MACV order of battle. A review of the figures was boiled down into a reporting cable. Several of the military witnesses in the *Westmoreland v CBS* case, including Westmoreland himself, have confirmed the fact of a meeting in which McChristian sought Westmoreland's approval for a cable to Washington outlining his new estimates for the numbers of Viet Cong self-defense and secret self-defense forces. McChristian remembers Westmoreland complaining that the report would be a political bombshell. In West-moreland's testimony he says he argued that the war was not against civilians (like the members of these VC formations), and that he asked McChristian to leave the cable with him. Shortly thereafter, General McChristian came to the end of his Vietnam tour and left. The new chief of MACV intelligence was Brigadier General Phillip B. Davidson, and his chief of estimates Colonel Daniel O. Graham.

Questions of Viet Cong strength came to a head during the summer of 1967 when the U.S. intelligence community began to work on a high-level report on Vietnam. This kind of report, termed a special national intelligence estimate (SNIE), is *the* premier product of the CIA and all other agencies, including the military, spearheaded by its Defense Intelligence Agency (DIA). The Vietnam report was numbered SNIE 14.3-67 and was drafted by Robert Layton, author of an important CIA analytical study a year earlier. In it Layton had mentioned the evidence that the Viet Cong self-defense forces were larger than previously thought. Order of battle figures were needed to go into the SNIE. When interagency meetings to coordinate the special national estimate began in June, DIA representative George Fowler steadfastly rejected all attempts to insert higher order of battle figures. The impasse led to an August visit to CIA headquarters by a MACV delegation, then a further conference in Saigon a month later. At the latter meetings the CIA group was led by George Carver, special assistant for Vietnam affairs to CIA director Richard Helms. Carver went to this conference prepared for a fight and he got one.

Phillip Davidson has left an account of these events in his book *Secrets of the Vietnam War*. Davidson writes that this September 1967 discussion of Viet Cong order of battle in Vietnam was the most acrimonious of hundreds of similar meetings during his career, and that the CIA ultimately backed down due to MACV's "rock hard" determination. The MACV intelligence chief remembers his experts objecting to the way Sam Adams had extrapolated numbers for Viet Cong militia from only twenty-eight documents. Adams's results applied to the whole of South Vietnam whereas his evidence drew on materials written in many different times and places by officials at different levels of the Viet Cong hierarchy. Davidson contrasts this to MACV intelligence which based itself on all sources of data. In Adams's *War of Numbers* he notes this incident, then goes on to describe how a MACV officer proceeded to extrapolate a much lower countrywide figure for service troops. When CIA analysts questioned MACV's source for this estimate, it turned out that the military had based their figure on *one* single document, and had then excluded on various pretexts some of the Viet Cong personnel listed there. What's more, according to Adams, MACV adjusted its numbers in such a way that its overall estimate for service troops, despite the purported addition, was even lower than before. Under the MACV projections the total North Vietnamese and Viet Cong order of battle in all categories was only cosmetically different than it had been.

Despite CIA misgivings, George Carver eventually caved in to MACV's united front and went along with order of battle numbers that Saigon accepted while also excluding self-defense and secret self-defense forces from the numerical estimates. Carver sent Helms a cable, which Adams quotes, that "the circle has been squared." The level of concern at MACV is suggested by the fact that attendees at the final session of the conference included Westmoreland himself, his deputy commander General Creighton W. Abrams, pacification chief Robert Komer, and MACV *public relations* director Brigadier General Winant Sidle.

When MACV prepared a press briefing describing the "refined" order of battle that had been prepared, this was put through several drafts before the VC militia figures were judged to be presented with just the right inflection to escape notice. In fact, the order of battle briefing drafts were a subject of discussion in Lyndon Johnson's White House, where national security adviser Walt Rostow led a group attempting to manipulate the media on Vietnam. Rostow and his military assistant canvassed alternatives and made changes in the briefing.

The eventual MACV briefing on the order of battle described the self-defense and secret self-defense forces as "home guards, primarily for . . . control and light defense." The VC militia were seen as fixed, part-time, partly or even unarmed, with "personnel of all ages" and "a high percentage of females," in sum "essentially low-level fifth columnists" who "do not represent a continual or dependable force and do not form a valid part of the enemy's military forces."

Soon after this draft briefing the CIA director finally approved SNIE 14.3-67. According to Adams the CIA's most senior estimators were outraged by the results of the order of battle dispute; he quotes Sherman Kent, chief of the Board of National Estimates, as asking, "Sam, have we gone beyond the bounds of reasonable dishonesty?" Ludwell Montague, one of the CIA's oldest hands, is quoted as having said, "It makes my blood boil to see the military cooking the books."

Nor were the CIA the only people concerned. When he saw the proposed MACV briefing in its final draft, William Bundy, a leading

State Department official, told Walt Rostow that the language about how the VC self-defense forces were not a military threat ought to be deleted "in light of the intelligence judgment that these forces do inflict casualties and are also included in military loss totals on a regular basis."

Those who knew best were naturally the American boys on the ground in Vietnam. The troops had no doubt whatever that the booby traps, grenade ambushes, and similar activities of part-time VC militia were among their worst perils. At least one commander of the Twenty-fifth Infantry Division north of Saigon in the 1970 period ran his forces on very complex schedules in part precisely to keep them alert to these dangers. A battalion commander further north during 1966 performed clever time studies and got his men out of the field every day at midafternoon because he reasoned the troops became careless at that time of day. General H. Norman Schwarzkopf, when he commanded a battalion near Chu Lai, found booby traps his worst enemies. It was the VC militia, not the North Vietnamese or main forces, who were responsible for most of this type of activity, and according to 1966 statistics booby traps, mines, and grenades accounted for 37 percent of America's Vietnam casualties. Nor was this some historical anomaly. In the Franco-Vietnamese War mines accounted for 75 percent of deaths and 56 percent of wounds in the Tonkin Delta during 1953–1954. Perhaps it was not coincidental that General Westmoreland chose to abandon his lawsuit just after two Vietnam veterans, PFC Daniel A. Friedman and Captain Howard Embree, testified at the trial as to just how dangerous it was in the field in South Vietnam.

The legal controversy over the intelligence order of battle did not begin until long after the war, but it was during the Vietnam conflict that intelligence games contributed to mistaken assessments that cost lives. For example, in February 1968, at the height of the Tet offensive, the CIA reported that as far as it could determine, the North Vietnamese 304th and 320th divisions, then fighting U.S. marines at Khe Sanh, had yet to be added to MACV's confirmed order of battle holdings. Although those units would, in fact, be included in the MACV totals before the end of that month, total Viet Cong and North Vietnamese strength estimated in February stood at 204,126, compared with 224,581 in December 1967. The order of battle estimate sunk even lower before recovering toward the late spring and summer. By then the CIA had given up on presenting any consensus order of battle and began publishing its own figures, much higher than MACV's. By·

then, too, Sam Adams had become thoroughly disgusted with the whole exercise and had begun the crusade that eventually led to *Westmoreland v CBS*. Meanwhile, an open and quite obvious intelligence issue developed over whether the United States had been "surprised" by the Viet Cong/North Vietnamese Tet offensive, the event that colored everyone's thinking through the remainder of the Vietnam War.

14

What Surprise? Whose Prediction? Intelligence at Tet

We were not surprised by the fact of the Tet offensive," the general shot out in his stentorian voice, his gaze roaming over the assembled legislators as he testified on Capitol Hill. "We were not surprised by the massiveness of the numbers of troops committed. What surprised us was the rashness of the Tet attacks." Thus remembered Lieutenant General Daniel O. Graham on December 3, 1975, a few months after the downfall of Saigon. Graham, a career intelligence officer since 1959, ought to have known—when Tet occurred on January 31, 1968, he had been chief of the Current Intelligence and Estimate Division on the MACV staff.

Predicting an offensive such as Tet had been, in 1968, Colonel Graham's primary job. His boss, MACV intelligence chief Brigadier General Phillip Davidson, had the ultimate responsibility. Both had made certain predictions. What were they doing on the night the Tet offensive flared? Graham, with other majors and colonels billeted at his BOQ, hastily organized themselves into scratch infantry squads for emergency defense. Davidson, with two other senior officers and three enlisted men at his own billet, made plans for a last-ditch defense of the house and settled into a fitful sleep. Vietnamese guards responsible for their security did not show up for work that night.

Ever since Tet the question of whether it represented an intelligence failure has been controversial, lurking in the wings, provoking heated arguments. Who knew what when, and what they did about it has been the stuff of many a long talk, and even a court trial as the Tet intelligence question became enmeshed in the larger dispute over the North Vietnamese Army and Viet Cong order of battle. Graham's position represents one extreme in the Tet intelligence debate. On the other side is a general officer colleague, David R. Palmer, who maintains that Tet represented an intelligence failure on a par with Pearl Harbor. Sorting through the particulars of intelligence performance at Tet is useful to understanding the Vietnam War.

■ The record, along with the pattern of operations across the south, indicates that Hanoi and the Viet Cong began planning for the Tet offensive sometime in the summer or early fall of 1967. General Westmoreland dates the moment from the time in July 1967 when a B-52 Arc Light strike near the Cambodian border caught a top NVA headquarters and gravely wounded General Nguyen Chi Thanh, NVA senior field commander in the south. The loss was a grievous one for Hanoi but coincidental in terms of its timing of the offensive, as the determining factors had necessarily to be the intervals necessary to get supplies and reinforcements in place for operations. Since troops had to come down the Ho Chi Minh Trail and supplies either down the trail or by sea through Cambodia, the necessary preparation time was considerable. From an intelligence standpoint, at some moment during this process of preparation it became possible to learn Hanoi's intentions. Certainly a great many GIs doing their jobs in South Vietnam would have appreciated knowing.

There was a complication, however, in Vietnam and Washington in the fall of 1967. President Johnson and General Westmoreland wanted to show they were winning the war. Johnson personally sanctioned what reporter Don Oberdorfer has called the "Success Offensive," in which the administration pulled out all the stops to convince America that the war was being won. Westmoreland himself returned to Washington in mid-November. Arriving at Andrews Air Force Base, the general said that in four years he had never been more encouraged. Addressing a rare joint session of Congress, Westmoreland declared, "We have reached an important point when the end begins to come into view."

Only the media product came before the public; the press was unaware of the administration's efforts to orchestrate the news it was reporting. Oberdorfer later learned of a "Psychological Strategy Committee," sometimes called the Monday Group for the day of the week on which it met, chaired by national security adviser Walt Rostow. The group included representatives of the White House press office, the departments of State and Defense, the CIA, and the United States Information Agency. In fact the committee was called the Vietnam Information Group (VIG), and it did indeed plan a psychological strategy. Here, decades ago and with another name, were LBJ's "spin doc-tors."

Because of the importance of public opinion to the war effort, the VIG had an impact on intelligence in Vietnam. One area in which this was especially true was with the order of battle estimators. Another was with the intelligence estimators, whose responsibility it was to pre-dict an NVA/VC offensive if they saw one coming. In view of public re-lations considerations, a threat too large or a predicted offensive would be decidedly inconvenient. This was no MACV conspiracy, as alleged by the CBS documentary, but the practical effect of a position taken at the highest level of the United States government. MACV's in-telligence system either succeeded or failed in rising above this political obstacle in some decidedly interesting ways.

■ The adversary generally controlled the pace of operations in Viet-nam. What led to Tet began in Binh Long and Phuoc Long provinces in late October 1967. Shortly after midnight on October 27, the NVA Eighty-eighth Regiment hit the command post of the Third Battalion, Ninth Regiment of the Army of the Republic of Vietnam Fifth Divi-sion just south of Song Be. With about 800 to 1,000 soldiers, the NVA outnumbered ARVN by about four to one but were still driven off after three assaults, with an estimated 134 killed to an ARVN loss of only 13.

Two days later, at 1:15 a.m. on October 29, the 273rd Regiment of the VC Ninth Division attacked the town of Loc Ninh, about twenty-seven miles to the west. Two Regional Force companies and a Popular Force platoon, together with two American advisers, defended the town. Just to the south, across Highway 13 from the airstrip, was a Civilian Irregular Defense Group (CIDG) camp with three companies of CIDG strikers and another half-dozen American advisers. Alto-gether there were about six hundred defenders at Loc Ninh. The attack began with a heavy mortar and rocket barrage and within an hour had penetrated the northern part of the ARVN Captain Tran Minh Cong's command post. Captain Cong, the district chief, called in air strikes and artillery fire on his own position. He kept the enemy at bay until daylight.

Meanwhile, Major General Pham Quoc Thuan, ARVN Fifth Divi-sion commander, requested helicopters that moved up two companies of ARVN reinforcements, and then brought up two of the CIDG com-panies, along with General Thuan. By the afternoon they had cleared the immediate environs of the town. Also quick to respond was the

First Brigade of Major General John H. Hay's U.S. First Infantry Division, one of whose battalions took up a blocking position to the west between the town and the Cambodian border (about nine miles away). Two more American companies plus two artillery batteries set up a fire-support base at the Loc Ninh airstrip.

So far this had been a typical engagement, but Loc Ninh soon became rather unusual. Rather than fading away as the enemy was wont to do, the VC division commander came back with more troops, feeding in his 272nd Regiment for repeated attacks on the airstrip and CIDG camp, despite the U.S.-ARVN buildup, the scale of which is suggested by the expenditure of artillery ammunition: 611 rounds on October 29 against 2,326 the following day. The battle continued until the adversary broke off on November 8. By that time General Hay had air assaulted two more battalions into the sector, General Thuan had brought up more men as well, and tactical intelligence had identified elements of the 141st and 165th NVA regiments in addition to the VC forces engaged. The battle ended with a claim of 850 enemy killed against 50 friendly dead and 234 wounded. Artillery had fired 30,125 rounds, and there had been 452 sorties by tactical air plus eight Arc Light strikes.

Before the Loc Ninh battle sputtered out, another significant engagement began. This was further north in the same corps sector, II Field Force, under Lieutenant General Frederick C. Weyand. It began on November 4 when a patrol from the Third Battalion, Twelfth Infantry of Major General William R. Peers's Fourth Infantry Division ran into North Vietnamese troops dug in on a ridge southwest of Dak To, in Kontum Province. Attempting to hold the initiative, Americans and Vietnamese quickly committed truly major forces, making Dak To one of the largest battles of the year. General Peers continued to control the battle for the Americans, with his own First Brigade plus Brigadier General Leo H. Schweiter's 173rd Airborne Brigade. The ARVN II Corps put in its own Forty-second Regiment and two battalions from the general reserve, the Second and Third paratroops. There were also CIA Mobile Strike (Mike) Force companies in the area.

This division-equivalent nevertheless experienced considerable trouble in a battle that lasted more than two weeks. American airborne and ARVN troops were repeatedly attacked, and a mortar barrage at Dak To on November 15 blew up a large Fourth Division ammunition dump and virtually leveled the CIDG camp there. Helicopters of the Fifty-second Aviation Battalion of the First Cavalry Division supported the battle operations, flying over 10,000 hours in 22,000 sorties, and carrying 40,000 passengers and 6,000 tons of cargo. Artillery fired 151,000 rounds, and there were 2,096 tactical air sorties and 257 B-52 strikes. The troops identified elements of four North Vietnamese infantry regiments.

Mystery again reared its head in the Dak To battle. Once more the enemy stood and fought rather than disappearing into the jungle. Significant grist for the intelligence mill was also added during the Dak To battle, when the Fourth Battalion, 503rd Infantry (Airborne) captured enemy documents in a heavy firefight on Hill 823. One of the documents turned out to be a directive from the NVA B-3 Front, their headquarters for the Central Highlands, laying down instructions for a winter-spring campaign. Hurriedly translated in Saigon by the Combined Document Exploitation Center (CDEC), MACV deputy commander General Creighton W. Abrams cabled its contents to Westmoreland, who was in Washington as part of the public relations push.

Westmoreland held a press briefing at the Pentagon on November 22 in which he quoted the objectives section of the B-3 Front directive. These included "annihilating a major U.S. element"; encouraging improvements, in combat, of techniques of massed attack; liberating an important area; and effecting "close coordination with various battle areas throughout South Viet Nam." Among the characteristics of the expected campaign would be "many large-scale, well-coordinated combat operations," most of which would be conducted far from VC/NVA base areas.

Following Westmoreland's presentation, *New York Times* reporter Neil Sheehan asked, "You don't think the battle of Dak To is the beginning or the end of anything particular for the enemy?"

"I think," Westmoreland countered, "it's the beginning of a great defeat."

The MACV commander did think that Hanoi might have made major decisions already. He had said as much to the press on previous occasions. What he had not said publicly was that he thought they could be preparing for an attack around Christmas in northern South Vietnam, perhaps at Khe Sanh. Westmoreland had ordered his logistics people to prepare for additional reinforcements to this northern area and was already preparing to establish a forward MACV headquarters element there, for command of the constantly increasing numbers of U.S. army troops in what had been a marine sector. When marines at Khe Sanh found North Vietnamese troops reconnoitering their positions just after the New Year, Westmoreland, who had in the interval abandoned the hypothesis of a Christmas attack, put even more stock in his prediction of trouble in the northern provinces.

The nearest thing to a dead giveaway was the notebook of a political cadre, one Vu Sinh Vien, captured in Quang Tin on November 19 by an element of the 101st Airborne Division. Vien's notebook contained the significant entry that "Central Headquarters concludes that the time has come for a direct revolution and that the opportunity for a general offensive and general uprising is within reach." The document further noted that military attacks would be used in conjunction with risings of local populations in actions against cities and towns. Still, this was not, as maintained in the generally accurate account of Colonel Herbert Y. Schandler, the capture of the actual attack order, but rather a commentary by a subordinate cadre on what he had heard—which might have been an order, might have been someone talking about an order, or perhaps someone speculating upon what the order would be. General Westmoreland, who also quotes this document in his memoirs, fails to characterize it at all, which may have contributed to the misunderstanding. In any case, the Vien notebook was treated as an ambiguous indicator, ambiguous enough to be released to the press, rather than closely held for exploitation, as early as January 5, 1968.

■ Gathering indicators is only the first step toward warning of surprise. Equally critical is predicting enemy intentions. This was of primary concern both in the field and in Washington. In both places there was evidence that the VC and NVA intended to carry out an offensive "winter-spring" campaign, but the indicators could not be seen as conclusive until a very late date. For example, with respect to the "attack order" question, the text of such an order was actually captured in Tay Ninh Province on February 3. Hanoi and the Liberation Front, depending on sector, had distributed their final orders only twenty-four to seventy-two hours before the attacks.

Moreover, as frequently happens in intelligence work, indicators can be misleading or even represent deliberate deception. In this respect the question of timing (the lunar new year) is a significant one. On December 16, 1967, a Vietnamese marine battalion on operations in the IV Corps tactical zone had captured another document, a province directive with standing equal to the one taken near Dak To. When translated at CDEC, the directive ordered a cease-fire to be observed from midnight, January 27, 1968, to midnight, February 3, a period that clearly includes the moment when the VC and NVA unleashed their offensive. The directive could have been superseded, or it might have been deliberately intended as a deception. Sorting out this kind of chaff is a major difficulty of intelligence analysis.

Who did what with the available information?

Echoes of several of the captured documents may be found in the report completed on November 24 by the CIA's Saigon station analytical team of Joseph Hovey, Bobby Layton, and Jim Ogle. This CIA analysis predicted a three-phase campaign (October–December 1967, January–March 1968, and April–June 1968) with "military and political ambitions which surpass anything previously attempted in such a relatively short period of time," specifically by "an all-out attack." Efforts on all battlefronts would be intended to create conditions for the general uprising. Even the CIA felt drawn to Khe Sanh, however, for the report emphasized that the VC/NVA would "conduct large-scale continuous, coordinated attacks by main force units, primarily in mountainous areas close to border sanctuaries," with the aim of forcing MACV and ARVN to redeploy major units to the borders. But the Agency did predict "widespread guerrilla attacks" on large units in "rural/heavily populated areas" as well as attacks on key "agencies and rear service bases."

Of great import was the CIA's summary conclusion: "The war is probably nearing a turning point and . . . the outcome of the 1967–68 winter–spring campaign will in all likelihood determine the future direction of the war." This was not exactly a prediction of Tet, but it came pretty close.

In Washington, meanwhile, at LBJ's right hand, Walt Rostow was growing restive with the length of time required for the evaluation of captured documents. In late November or early December he made arrangements for copies of captured documents to be pouched from CDEC through to the White House. In fact, the CIA analysis detailed above may have begun as a demonstration of the Agency's capacity for quick interpretation. In any case, Rostow heard of the CIA report, asked for a summary to be cabled ahead, then asked the top Vietnam analytical office at CIA, the Special Assistant for Vietnamese Affairs (SAVA), to comment on the Saigon station product. Analysis at SAVA found nothing objectionable about the report, save for low numbers projected for the VC/NVA order of battle. Their evaluation went to the White House on December 15. Rostow passed both reports to the president, with his own covering memo.

Rostow himself, with his military assistant Brigadier General Robert N. Ginsburgh, went over a number of the captured documents as they arrived. The gist of these, and sometimes the full texts, he sent on to the president. Doing his own evaluation, Rostow told LBJ that Hanoi was talking as if it was shooting for a general uprising or a restaging of the battle of Dien Bien Phu at Khe Sanh.

Soon after seeing the Saigon CIA report, Lyndon Johnson flew to Australia for the funeral of Prime Minister Harold Holt, who had drowned while swimming. Accorded the privilege of addressing the Australian cabinet, LBJ warned of dark days ahead, of the possible use of "kamikaze" tactics in Hanoi's effort to achieve a breakthrough. Again, however, the major threat was put in the Khe Sanh context, as became clear when a senior Australian cabinet minister asked Rostow for more information on the move of two NVA divisions toward Khe Sanh.

During Johnson's trip, on December 20, Westmoreland weighed in with his own prediction of an intensified effort, a countrywide one, "perhaps a maximum effort" over a relatively short period. Meanwhile the indicators continued to pile up. Aerial reconnaissance detected a 200 percent increase in truck traffic down the Ho Chi Minh Trail. This appeared logical to SAVA at Langley, where the CIA had data suggesting that infiltration rates were up to twenty thousand to thirty thousand a month at the end of 1967. At MACV the J-2 analysts accepted the truck traffic but insisted on much lower projections for infiltration, a monthly average of less than ten thousand. At the same time, desertion (Chieu Hoi) from the enemy was down, pacification statistics stagnated, and the ratio of enemy to friendly weapons lost dropped during November and December, despite battles like Loc Ninh and Dak To.

What about MACV intelligence? General Davidson's November J-2 summary, which arrived on Walt Rostow's desk only on January 9, 1968, predicted that Hanoi would commit units from its strategic reserve while continuing a "peripheral" strategy of maintaining most troops near border sanctuaries. MACV felt the enemy "retains the objective of winning at least one significant, exploitable victory for propaganda purposes," and that he would initiate major offensive action "when he sees a high probability of success, or when he deems it militarily, psychologically, or politically necessary to do so." This estimate was so broad it could cover almost anything. In effect it was just so much boiler plate.

Things refined themselves somewhat in December. Two months earlier a new J-2 director of intelligence production, Colonel Charles A. Morris, had established attack warning as the top intelligence priority, but now J-2 was slow to go beyond generalities. At the Combined Intelligence Center Vietnam (CICV) a sharp analyst put together the scattered indications and warned specifically of countrywide attacks on the cities at Tet. Incredulous, the junior officer supervising the analyst turned and asked what his Vietnamese counterpart thought. The ARVN officer agreed there would be attacks on the cities, especially Saigon. When the CICV section chief took this evidence to his boss, he was told J-2 knew of it, as did MACV, which didn't wish to make overt preparations for fear of being seen to take Viet Cong propaganda seriously.

Actually CICV's responsibility lay in the order of battle area. Under Colonel Morris it was the current indications and estimates shop, headed by Daniel Graham, that was supposed to predict an attack. Lieutenant Colonel Graham, some years after the congressional testimony quoted at the beginning of this chapter, actually softened his own claims about intelligence at Tet: his account in 1982 was that MACV believed in an attack either the day before or the day after Tet, not on Tet itself, and that the adversary's attack on cities and towns was a surprise. Graham and Phillip Davidson believed that attacks on the cities would be foolhardy and discounted any such strategy. General Davidson's own account concedes that the VC and NVA achieved tactical if not strategic surprise. The surprise in timing was relatively minor, and offset by the fact that forces of the enemy Military Region 5 attacked a day early, enabling MACV and Seventh Air Force to declare final alerts at many crucial locations. More surprising—and here Davidson uses Graham's own word, "rash"—was the scale of the attacks on the cities and towns. The degree of their surprise is suggested by what they had to do the night of Tet.

Something similar occurred at Fred Weyand's II Field Force. There, once again, the order of battle section made an important discovery. In this case it happened that documents captured during the Loc Ninh battles contained new post box numbers for VC units plus evidence of a realignment in command boundaries. When plotted on a map, the new boundaries revealed that the VC were radically redesigning their system so that no single unit had responsibility for the Capital Military District, Saigon. Rather, all of a sudden *all* the unit sectors *included* Saigon, like daggers pointing at the heart, or slices of a pie. The corps intelligence chief, however, would not allow his subordinates to write an estimate predicting urban attacks. When subordinates drafted such an estimate anyway, he demanded it be rewritten.

A major reason why II Field Force would not allow the prediction of an offensive was that its order of battle holdings had been reduced. Seemingly the enemy order of battle could not sustain major offensive operations. General Weyand is considered a hero by some subordinates for nevertheless taking precautions, not only against an offensive but specifically against urban attacks.

According to Graham, Weyand was not entirely sure of his ground. At a Weekly Intelligence Estimate Update meeting the subject came up. "You know," Weyand said, "some of these people are acting like they really might try to attack the cities . . . maybe we ought to pay more attention to that."

Graham believes that Weyand was acting on the basis of human intelligence reports supplied by an agent net run by Lieutenant Colonel William Pietsch, later to achieve momentary infamy in Cambodia as an irritant to the press.

But Davidson's own chief of production, Charles Morris, supported Weyand's fears, though most senior officers resisted such an interpretation. Weyand and Morris did not press their case to the level of a dispute; they simply raised the possibility as one to consider.

Westmoreland went along, after speaking again with Fred Weyand on January 11. Westmoreland permitted the II Field Force commander to cancel planned offensive sweeps into Phuoc Binh province and to redeploy maneuver battalions closer to Saigon. Before the Tet offensive began, Weyand had doubled his forces close to Saigon.

For their own part the Vietnamese, according to an official monograph, received a senior *Chieu Hoi* (Viet Cong defector) who, under interrogation, revealed plans to attack Saigon. Still, ARVN intelligence issued a specific warning only sixteen hours before the start of the offensive, and by that time half the army had gone home on leave for the Tet celebrations. President Nguyen Van Thieu had gone to celebrate Tet at his wife's family home in My Tho. As for intelligence cooperation between allies, Phillip Davidson claims he first heard of the deserter with his Saigon information when he read about it in the army monograph, completed in 1976.

Westmoreland's official position remains the best indication of the J-2 estimates he was given, which themselves have yet to be declassified. On January 15 Westmoreland reported a 60-40 chance the campaign would commence *before* Tet. The military moves he planned clearly revealed his perceptions: transfer of two ARVN airborne battalions and two brigades of the First Cavalry Division to the northern provinces while accepting a "calculated risk" around Saigon. These forces would be added to a stream of reinforcements already sent north.

On January 22 Westmoreland reported enemy actions in the preceding forty-eight hours as "the initial attacks of the expected enemy offensive in northern I Corps." MACV saw these actions as "probably" preliminary to a full-scale attack on Khe Sanh. On the other hand, he noted, "I believe that the enemy will attempt a country-wide show of strength just prior to Tet, with Khe Sanh being the main event." Also endangered, the general felt, were Pleiku and Kontum, three CIDG camps in those provinces, and province towns in III and IV Corps which would be "likely targets for renewed attacks by fire." This cable, MAC 01049, also contains the first specific mention of Saigon: "Terrorism will probably increase in and around Saigon."

A second cable, MAC 00967, sent "Eyes Only" the same day, reported the enemy displaying "a very unusual sense of urgency" and suggested that Hanoi planned "a coordinated offensive designed to seize and hold key objectives in the northern two provinces." Westy added Hue and Quang Tri to the list of localities anticipated to be in danger. Two days later Westmoreland and Ambassador Ellsworth Bunker jointly recommended that the Tet truce not be observed in the northern provinces. Westmoreland had already asked that it be limited to thirty-six hours. Both requests were granted. Later MACV reported that January 25 was "shaping up" as the big day.

But January 25 passed without the widespread attacks that had been expected. So did four more days. Some lucky intelligence finds at Pleiku and a few other places enabled individual commanders to issue alert orders, and an MACV alert went out on January 30. That night some of the enemy jumped the gun and attacked too soon. This event was critical in demonstrating that the warnings should be taken quite seriously. The next night came the offensive.

■ Was Tet a surprise? Yes and no. The CIA report, the Westmoreland cables, show that there was no strategic surprise. A number of specific urban attacks were also anticipated. But the precise timing and scale of the attacks certainly were a surprise. General Davidson himself concedes the enemy a tactical surprise. At Saigon, where Westmoreland anticipated terrorism, there was a multibattalion attack that would have been even larger had not Fred Weyand insisted on getting many of his II Field Force battalions into what turned out to be blocking positions. In the end it was a close-run affair.

In many intelligence failures, later investigation shows that information necessary for predictions was in the system but could not be discerned for the noise. Tet was different. This time, as a study by the President's Foreign Intelligence Advisory Board confirmed, both Washington and Saigon were fully aware that the enemy planned a major offensive. What happened at Tet was people succumbing to preconception. Saigon expected an attack but anticipated it would center on Khe Sanh, so Davidson and Graham found themselves holding rifles in the middle of the night. Washington failed to appreciate the urgency of the reporting from MACV, and hardly did so until the American embassy in Saigon came under attack. The American people, prepared so assiduously by the administration spin doctors to expect a great victory, light at the end of the tunnel, instead experienced the darkest days of the war. Their confidence was shaken. Hanoi's ability to carry out a countrywide offensive, unsuccessful as it proved militarily, suggested that the much-touted MACV war effort might in reality be bankrupt. Things would never be the same.

No theory of victory in Vietnam can be considered successful, as a theory, unless it credibly accounts for how a psychological shock like Tet could be prevented. The prospect of such a shock was in fact inherent in the situation—the daily lengthening war, the Viet Cong and North Vietnamese presence throughout the country, and the mind-sets of American officers and officials. These were factors that could not be changed by strategy, no matter how ingenious. As a consequence soldiers would have to fight some of the toughest battles of the Vietnam War.

15   Tet!

Vietnam was a war of novel places, names, and things, often so exotic that GIs share experiences more by comparing unit assignments than by asking each other where they had been. But the war had a few moments that so seared themselves into the collective consciousness that everyone, even those who had already left "the Nam," remembers exactly where they were and what they were doing when it happened. The greatest of those moments was Tet in 1968, when the Viet Cong and North Vietnamese unleashed a countrywide offensive and abortive general uprising. What follows is a reconstruction, excluding the battle for Hue, of some of the main actions of the offensive.

Tet was a time for the Vietnamese to relax and celebrate the lunar new year, a sort of high holiday season, indeed Christmas, New Year's, and Easter all rolled into one. Fighting traditionally took a back seat during Tet. In 1967, in fact, both sides declared and largely observed cease-fires at Tet. But 1968 was different, even though cease-fires were again set for the occasion.

The North Vietnamese knew what was coming and made slightly different arrangements for their own celebration of Tet. North Vietnam moved the date ahead a day so that their Tet would commence at midnight of January 29/30. Only in South Vietnam would the most important initial hours of the festival be disrupted.

Viet Cong and North Vietnamese troops made many more careful preparations for the offensive. Units and equipment quietly moved into position near their objectives; detailed intelligence information was gathered and battle plans drawn up. The NVA and VC fought several pitched battles in late 1967, drawing South Vietnamese and allied troops away from the cities they intended to attack. For the Americans of General Westmoreland's Military Assistance Command Vietnam, the NVA created a diversion by massing forces to threaten the combat base at Khe Sanh. As the time for action approached, the VC carefully smuggled weapons into heavily guarded cities like Saigon and Hue. The preparations were thorough and intense, down to instructions to manage the mass uprising of South Vietnamese citizens that the VC hoped to elicit.

The Tet offensive came on a truly massive scale throughout South Vietnam. North Vietnamese and Viet Cong units committed between 67,000 and 84,000 troops in attacks on 39 of 44 provincial capitals, 71 district seats, Saigon, every ARVN corps headquarters, and several major air bases—altogether some 166 cities and towns.

Although the degree of coordination achieved by the VC and NVA was impressive, perfection eluded the enemy given the scope of his undertaking. In the ARVN I and II Corps tactical zones, which corresponded respectively to the U.S. III Marine Amphibious Force and I Field Force zones, VC or NVA units attacked eight cities or towns a day early. This provided MACV and ARVN with a final warning and an opportunity to cancel the Tet cease-fire and alert their formations.

Action began at Nha Trang on the Central Vietnamese coast. There, at 12:35 a.m. on January 30, the VC opened an attack with mortars firing six shells at the Vietnamese navy training center. The mortars missed the target; moreover, a planned ground attack was unaccountably delayed and began only at 2 a.m. The Nha Trang attack has to be viewed more as harassment than a serious effort, for the NVA B-5 Front committed to it only elements of five sapper companies plus one hundred locals from the VC infrastructure. This was very little for a city with a population of 119,000.

The Nha Trang attack was parried successfully. Alert ARVN guards caught some of the enemy parties before they reached assembly positions. Warned by radio intercepts, an ARVN Ranger battalion, returned from an operation earlier in the day, quickly intervened at the points of main effort. Three Special Forces detachments (Nha Trang was headquarters for both U.S. and Vietnamese Special Forces) also engaged the enemy in the city. By midafternoon Nha Trang was cleared after twelve hours of fighting. ARVN claimed to have killed 377 of the enemy, captured 77, and taken one *Chieu Hoi*; it admitted to losses of 88 killed and 220 wounded. Thirty-two civilians were killed and 187 wounded while 600 homes were destroyed, leaving 3,192 homeless.

Meanwhile, at 1:35 a.m. on the 30th, the fighting spread to Ban Me Thuot at the southern edge of II Corps. Here too the harbinger was a barrage of mortars and rockets, but it was followed by a ground attack of two battalions' strength. At the same time, northwest of Pleiku, a battalion attacked Tan Canh, a district town near Dak To. Three more battalions moved against Kontum City at 2 a.m. On the coast at Hoi An, another ground attack went in at 2:55.

The ARVN II Corps and U.S. I Field Force quickly found themselves fully engaged. Headquarters at Pleiku came under attack by the VC H-15 Battalion at 4:40 a.m. Here troops of the American Fourth Infantry Division had been on alert since January 26 when their commander, Major General Charles P. Stone, ordered full precautions. Two days before the attack, ARVN security forces had apprehended eleven VC agents at a local safe house and captured a tape recording exhorting the population to rise. II Corps chief of staff Colonel Le Trong Tuong then put some forces on alert too, and on the night of January 29/30 ordered a section of tanks into the city, "Tet or no Tet," as he told the reluctant unit leader. The VC were readily defeated at Pleiku and Hoi An, but fighting sputtered on for several days at Kontum and Ban Me Thuot.

In I Corps, Tet opened with a bombardment of the large U.S. air base at Da Nang plus an attack on corps headquarters at the outskirts of the city. The bombardment killed one American but destroyed five aircraft and damaged twenty-five more. The ground attack involved a company of VC infiltrators, of whom perhaps a dozen penetrated the compound. Overriding objections from his American advisers, the ARVN corps commander ordered air strikes with heavy ordnance close to his own position. The VC were driven back and then pursued by helicopter gunships.

At 4:10 a.m. two more VC battalions struck at Qui Nhon along the coast further south. There the Viet Cong briefly captured the radio station but were unable to put anything on the air before they were driven out.

These attacks on January 30 provided unmistakable indications to MACV and ARVN that battle was impending. At 11:25 a.m. on the 30th a MACV "flash" message canceled the cease-fire, mandated resumption of normal operations, and ordered a maximum state of alert "with particular attention to the defense of headquarters complexes, logistical installations, airfields, population centers, and billets." That day Westmoreland either saw or talked on the telephone with every senior American commander in Vietnam to discuss the likelihood of upcoming widespread attacks. He arrived home late and tired, only to be awakened at 3 a.m. on the 31st by the shrill ring of a field telephone—

Tet was in progress. That night five of the six autonomous cities in Vietnam came under attack, along with Saigon, 35 provincial capitals, 64 of 242 district seats, and 50 other hamlets.

Saigon and the surrounding provinces, in the MACV structure, were under II Field Force, commanded by General Weyand. This corresponded to the tactical zone of ARVN III Corps, although a separate special security zone with a radius of twenty-nine miles had been established around Saigon in October 1967. The ARVN had had full responsibility for the special zone since December 15, 1967. This zone contained fully 75 percent of the population in III Corps and 90 percent of South Vietnam's industrial facilities. Only one U.S. battalion, the 716th Military Police, was stationed within the city itself.

General Weyand responded to the border battles of late 1967, especially that at Loc Ninh, by drawing down the forces within the Saigon security zone. By early January there were fourteen II Field Force battalions within the zone but thirty-nine outside it. As we have seen, Weyand, a former chief of army intelligence, developed suspicions of an impending VC offensive and began to redistribute his maneuver battalions. Before the day of Tet he had virtually doubled, to twenty-seven battalions, II Field Force strength inside the special security zone. This had an important bearing on the outcome of the Tet battles.

The Tet action that received the most attention, both from the press and at the White House, was the attack on the United States embassy, four blocks down Thong Nhat Boulevard from the Presidential Palace. The embassy attack was carried out by 19 sappers of the 250-man C-10 Saigon City Sapper Battalion, a Viet Cong special unit consisting of men living in Saigon under various cover occupations. The C-10 battalion, whose men were promised promotions immediately after the offensive, executed a wide range of actions in Saigon, ranging from terrorist incidents to intelligence gathering, but for Tet they came into the open. C-10 sappers not only attacked the embassy but also the Presidential Palace, Vietnam navy headquarters, and a range of other targets.

Action opened at the U.S. embassy, according to chronologies, at 3:15 a.m. The Sate Department duty officer that night, however, recalls being awakened in his quarters in Room 433 by a loud explosion shortly before three. The duty officer, E. Allan Wendt, then heard automatic weapons fire and determined the embassy was under attack, after which he phoned embassy political officers. Though nineteen VC sappers might seem an absurdly small number to send against an objective as large as the embassy, in fact the VC must have had precise intelligence to which they calibrated the size of their force. The night contingent at the embassy consisted of Wendt, a State communications specialist, one from the army, one Vietnamese, a CIA duty officer, and two communications people, plus three marine guards. Outside the building were two American MPs on duty at the main gate plus a South Vietnamese police detachment of four men. The VC outnumbered the Americans and had a two-to-one margin over the armed security men around the embassy.

The sapper strike began with an assault on the gate, where the MPs were shot down, but not before taking a toll of the enemy and managing to close the gate itself. The VC blasted through the compound wall with plastic explosives, then used a B-40 rocket against the main door. This wounded the one marine at the security post in the lobby and knocked down the guard leader, Sergeant Ronald W. Harper, who was down the hall gathering additional weapons from the armory. Except for one man who popped into the embassy building at the first sign of trouble, the Vietnamese police disappeared and took no part in the battle. More rockets and grenades burst in the lobby, then it became an exchange of fire between sappers sheltered behind potted trees on the grounds and Sergeant Harper inside. Harper's radios had been smashed by the fire, but he was in touch with Wendt on the centrex telephone at his station.

The sounds of battle in Saigon were unmistakable and the press quickly learned of the embassy battle, erroneously reporting that the VC were inside the U.S. embassy. This caused a flurry of concern at the White House, where early reports of the attack through State had already reached the National Security Council. President Johnson, always concerned over Vietnam, had been briefed about the premature Tet attacks of the 30th and was pressing for more information. Late in the afternoon of the 31st, Westmoreland had had a telephone conversation with White House Situation Room chief Art McCafferty, to update the NSC and LBJ's information. Only hours later, when it was the afternoon of the 31st in Washington, first reports of the embassy attack began to arrive.

While confusion abounded at the White House, the embassy battle developed into a stalemate, with the VC on the grounds but unable to enter the building past Sergeant Harper. The delay allowed MP reinforcements from the 716th battalion to arrive and surround the VC from the outside. By 4 a.m. Wendt was in touch with MACV by phone and was told that a medevac helicopter would be sent for the wounded marine and another copter would bring ammunition. It was the ammunition chopper that came in first, but not until about 6:45 a.m., and it took off the wounded man. The helicopter brought three cases of M-16 ammunition, which was useless to Sergeant Harper who was armed with a pistol, a shotgun, and an Italian Beretta submachine gun. There were no M-16s in the embassy.

At dawn the MPs outside managed to shoot off the locks on the main gate while another man found the hole the VC had blasted through the compound wall. Reinforced by the remainder of the marine guard detachment, the MPs crashed into the compound behind a jeep that finally opened the gate. At 8:15 a.m. almost three hours after MACV's promise of reinforcement, the first of a platoon of 101st Airborne troopers under Major Hillel Schwartz began to land from helicopters onto the embassy roof. By that time the VC sappers were mostly dead or dying. One darted into the house next door to the embassy in the compound, which was being used by Colonel George Jacobsen, an adviser to the CIA on pacification. The unarmed Jacobsen was thrown a pistol by marines outside and got the VC as he came up the stairs. The embassy was declared secured at 9:10 a.m.

Meanwhile, Washington's concern continued unabated. At 5:45 a.m. General Westmoreland received a call from Joint Chiefs of Staff chairman General Earle Wheeler on a secure line, directing him to call the White House and report to NSC adviser Walt W. Rostow. At the embassy Wendt or communications specialist James A. Griffin took several calls from Assistant Secretary of State Philip C. Habib in the White House Situation Room. There were also calls from the CIA. All were grateful to learn that initial press reports had been inaccurate.

For all the attention it garnered, the embassy attack was but one of many actions around Saigon. Another was an attempt by a dozen sappers against Vietnamese navy headquarters. The sappers rode in two civilian cars and were stopped at a checkpoint in Lam Son Square. The alert detachment at the headquarters was in combat position in bunkers and immediately defeated the VC when the attack began at 3 a.m. At the Philippine embassy an attempt to kidnap the ambassador failed when he managed to escape with a light injury. A second attempted kidnaping failed at the residence of Prime Minister Nguyen Van Loc. A thirty-four-man platoon of C-10 sappers also opened an attack on the Presidential Palace at 1:30. They fired B-40 rockets at the staff entrance gate on Nguyen Du Street and tried to crash through. The presidential guard, MPs, police, and two tanks drove off the VC, who holed up in an unfinished high rise across the street. Over the next two days the unit was wiped out to a man.

Although initially successful, a C-10 attack on the National Broadcasting station also miscarried. This VC element came disguised as police field force troops and quickly overwhelmed the police field squad defending the station. But this radio station contained studios only, the transmitter was remotely located several miles away, and the chief of the transmitter station immediately cut the audio feed from the downtown studios, substituting prerecorded programming. Saigon radio transmitted without interruption and with no indication of anything amiss. At 5 a.m. a company of the ARVN Eighth Airborne Battalion arrived and began a counterattack that recaptured the studios, which resumed normal operations within two hours.

A number of Viet Cong actions, ranging from shelling to small arms fire, were directed at U.S. billets in Saigon between 3:00 a.m. and 6:13 a.m. At least fifteen Bachelor Officers' Quarters (BOQs) or enlisted quarters reported these actions to the 716th MP Battalion or requested assistance. Several claymore mines were detonated at the Saigon Motor Pool. At the Rex BOQ, which reported fire at 3:21, the majors and colonels billeted there organized themselves into scratch infantry squads. One of them was Colonel Daniel Graham, chief of the Combined Intelligence Center Vietnam. It was the closest he had come to being shot at in the Vietnam War. The ad hoc infantry was soon relieved by 716th Battalion military police.

In Go Vap two VC local force battalions attacked the Co Loa artillery base which they overran, capturing twelve 105 mm artillery pieces. They also seized nearby Camp Phu Dong, headquarters of the ARVN Armor Command. The enemy had plans to use captured artillery and tanks in other Saigon actions, and brought trained tank crews along as part of the assault force. These plans too miscarried—ARVN's tanks had been sent elsewhere in November 1967 while, at Co Loa, ARVN gunners had removed the breech blocks of their pieces before pulling back. Both objectives were later recaptured.

Northeast of Saigon, one regiment of the VC Fifth Division had the mission of attacking the II Field Force headquarters at Long Binh. Another was to assault ARVN III Corps headquarters and Bien Hoa city plus the nearby major air base. Here the VC became confused because one designated assembly point, a rubber plantation, had been cleared by Rome plows the preceding month. In the confusion the VC missed a chance to liberate a prisoner camp and diluted their main attacks. At the III Corps compound the enemy was unable to penetrate, while at

Long Binh they did no better than blowing up several ammunition storage bunkers. The VC 274th Regiment was able to penetrate the eastern perimeter of Bien Hoa air base, reaching the runway, but was stalled by fire from a defending Regional Force battalion. Two aircraft on the base were destroyed and seventeen damaged, but the 274th lost 139 killed and 25 captured. A vital 199th Brigade force reacting to these attacks was Lieutenant Colonel John B. Tower's Second Battalion, Forty-seventh Infantry (Mechanized). Elements of the 101st Airborne Division also defended Bien Hoa air base, while the coup de grace came from the Eleventh Armored Cavalry Regiment (Colonel Jack MacFarlane), which moved more than a hundred kilometers to Bien Hoa in eight hours. By the evening of February 1 the VC and NVA were completely neutralized.

Potentially most damaging among the VC/NVA efforts on Tet were the several attacks at Tan Son Nhut on the northern edge of Saigon. This was not only a major air base but functioned as Saigon's international airport and housed MACV headquarters, ARVN Joint General Staff (JGS) headquarters, and the residence of Vice-President Nguyen Cao Ky. Defense forces here included U.S. Air Force security police, Vietnamese air force base defense forces, an ARVN headquarters battalion, and Ky's personal guard.

Although its perimeter was divided into defense sectors equipped with multiple wire barriers, mine fields, and more than 150 bunkers, Tan Son Nhut had inevitable security problems. The flow of personnel was too heavy to prevent VC intelligence gathering—designed for 3,000, the base typically had a daytime work force of more than 25,000 persons. Moreover, there could not be a cleared field of fire outside the perimeter due to the dense, encroaching settlements of Saigon's population. For Tet the VC/NVA committed elements of their C-10 sappers plus five other battalions to strike Tan Son Nhut from three directions.

The first Tan Son Nhut attack began at 2 a.m. on Gate 5, which gave access to the JGS compound. A VC support element had already infiltrated the Long Hoa pagoda just across the street. A commando for the main assault suddenly drove up in a bus—but just as it began to unload, a jeep of U.S. MPs arrived at the gate and the VC opened fire. This distraction gave the ARVN gate guards just enough time to shut the gate and reply to the fire from a side bunker. The gate guards were rapidly reinforced by U.S. MPs from BOQ No. 3 and other installations. The C-10 platoon commander, promised promotion to battalion commander after Tet, had been tasked to occupy the ARVN general officers' quarters and capture them or their family members as hostages. Instead the man himself was taken prisoner.

The Viet Cong intended to mount a simultaneous attack at Gate 4, but their Go Mon battalion was delayed in reaching its assembly position until 7 a.m. Nevertheless, the VC knocked down the gate with B-40 rockets and swarmed through, taking the buildings housing the Armed Forces Language School and JGS Headquarters Company. With only the ARVN Honor Guard battalion plus an armor troop for the entire JGS complex, South Vietnamese reaction was weak and uncoordinated. Had the Go Mon battalion pursued, it could have overrun the JGS building and the Joint Operations Center; instead the VC dug in to defend a perimeter, mistakenly believing the JGS building itself was already in their hands. At 9 a.m. the ARVN countered with two paratroop companies, and that afternoon committed a marine battalion, hurriedly flown up from the Mekong Delta as reinforcement. The JGS compound was secured at 10:30 a.m. on February 1, and VC remnants were driven back into Saigon city.

Perhaps the most dangerous of the Tan Son Nhut attacks was that against the western perimeter of the base, closest to the airfield. Here the enemy committed two local force battalions plus one from the 271st Regiment of the VC Ninth Division. A U.S. air force security man, noticing that his buddy in the adjacent bunker had failed to answer calls on the internal radio net, assumed he had fallen asleep and went to wake him up. At that instant B-40 rockets smashed the bunker the man had just left, killing its other Vietnamese occupants, and the attack came across the perimeter at Gates 51, 10, and 2 at 3 a.m., advancing about two hundred meters. Two platoons of air force security police reacted to the attack along with some of Ky's guards and managed to contain the VC long enough for the ARVN to bring up its last reserve—two more companies of the Eighth Airborne Battalion. Despite heavy losses, these troops held off the Viet Cong until dawn.

About 9 p.m. on the 30th, meanwhile, Lieutenant Colonel Glenn K. Otis, commanding the Third Squadron, Fourth Cavalry at Cu Chi (about twenty-five kilometers northwest of Saigon), had been ordered to send one troop to Tan Son Nhut in anticipation of VC action. This was modified at 4:15 a.m. the next morning with orders to block the regiment equivalent then attacking the base. Captain Leo B. Virant's Troop C was under way in fifteen minutes and in action by 6 a.m. The unit hit the VC assault force from the rear but met a hornet's nest of fire, though it cut off some of the VC inside the perimeter. Four tanks and five APCs were quickly hit and burning, with Captain Virant suffering a head wound. Otis ordered up a detached platoon of Troop C, then Troop B (Captain Malcolm Otis), which made a forty-seven-kilometer approach from Trang Bang in forty-five minutes. The reaction forces were supplemented by gunships and air strikes, and the VC driven back from Tan Son Nhut.

A number of the VC took refuge in the nearby Vinatexco Textile Factory, South Vietnam's newest industrial plant, where a command post and antiaircraft positions had been set up to support the original attack. This was plastered with air strikes from 9 a.m., followed by ground attacks. Some 157 VC were killed and 9 captured inside Tan Son Nhut, about 300 bodies left near Gate 51, and another 162 bodies later counted in the Vinatexco plant, which was destroyed. American forces lost 23 dead and 86 wounded with 13 planes damaged, while ARVN losses amounted to 32 killed and 89 wounded.

Other attacks in the Saigon area had less impact. In general, efforts of the VC Seventh Division to impede reaction force movements throughout the II Field Force area failed. Although the Viet Cong did not attain their objectives, enough of their forces infiltrated into Saigon to require clearing operations for about two weeks after Tet. The battle at Hue also, of course, continued. And a battle ensued at Quang Tri in I Corps, successfully held by the ARVN with intervention from Colonel Donald V. Rattan's First Brigade of the First Cavalry Division (Airmobile).

Expectations of a second round of Viet Cong attacks did not materialize. Nevertheless, Tet did inaugurate an extended series of standoff attacks on U.S. and Vietnamese air bases throughout Vietnam. Fifty of these barrage attacks occurred through February and March, involving some 1,030 recorded rounds on nine air bases; Tan Son Nhut was hit eighteen times, Bien Hoa four, and Da Nang once. Another eighteen barrages were directed at Binh Thuy. Some 24 U.S. and Vietnamese aircraft were destroyed and 165 U.S. and 71 Vietnamese planes damaged.

Official statistics for the Tet period of January–February 1968 show U.S. losses of 3,326 killed and 16,947 wounded plus ARVN losses of 7,930 killed, 18,270 wounded, and 1,474 missing. Claimed enemy battle deaths were 55,084. Of these, Westmoreland estimates in his memoirs, the VC/NVA incurred 37,000 killed between January 29 and February 29. At the same time he minimizes friendly losses by restricting himself to the period from January 29 to February 11, for which he reports 1,001 Americans and 2,082 Vietnamese killed.

Based on casualty and prisoner figures, and on the VC/NVA's inability to take and hold the cities and towns, many accounts of the Vietnam War hold that Tet was a great military victory for MACV and ARVN. Many of these accounts also concede that Tet was a political victory for the North Vietnamese and Viet Cong. It is worth concluding with the words Ambassador Ellsworth Bunker reported to Lyndon Johnson on February 8, 1968: "The primary [VC/NVA] objective of winning the war in one great series of attacks on the cities does not preclude a lesser objective. Hanoi may well have reasoned that in the event that the Tet attacks did not bring the outright victory they hoped for, they could still hope for political and psychological gains of such dimensions that they could come to the negotiating table with a greatly strengthened hand." If that was the thinking in Hanoi, it proved to be quite correct.

For all the trauma of the night of Tet and the couple of days that followed, one intense battle was still in full swing, even when Ambassador Bunker wrote the cable quoted above. That battle was for Vietnam's great old imperial capital, on the Perfume River of central Vietnam, the city of Hue. The fighting for Hue was the longest and most intense engagement of the Tet offensive.

16　Red Tide at Night

If there was anything about the Tet offensive of 1968 that should have come as no surprise to the American and South Vietnamese commands, it was the fighting in the north, in I Corps, specifically the battle for Hue. For years General Westmoreland had been anticipating efforts by the North Vietnamese army to overrun the provinces adjacent to North Vietnam. These were the provinces assigned to the South Vietnamese I Corps command. Thua Thien province, the second of them, contained Hue, imperial capital of Vietnam, a city of 140,000 people and headquarters of the ARVN First Division.

For over a year the NVA had had a military region headquarters, "Tri-Thien-Hue" (MRTTH), explicitly aimed at Thua Thien, its city Hue, and the northernmost province, Quang Tri. During the run-up to the truces that marked Christmas 1967 and Tet, Westmoreland had been specifically concerned that the NVA might resort to all-out attacks to achieve psychological success. At first he had been preoccupied with the Demilitarized Zone (DMZ) area of Quang Tri and the Christmas truce, but once that passed the general focused his concern on Tet. He asked General Robert E. Cushman, Jr., commanding the III Marine Amphibious Force (III MAF) in this area, corresponding to ARVN's I Corps, to prepare a plan to minimize potential American casualties in such an eventuality.

Westmoreland anticipated an NVA offensive in I Corps, albeit around Khe Sanh. In mid-January 1968, as we have seen, the MACV commander predicted that the North Vietnamese would likely begin their offensive before Tet, and on January 22 he reported NVA actions of the preceding two days as the start of the anticipated offensive. Also on the 22nd, Westmoreland sent an "Eyes Only" cable to General Earle Wheeler, chairman of the Joint Chiefs of Staff, adding Hue (and Quang Tri city) to the list of localities thought to be endangered by the projected NVA operation. After meeting with Ambassador Bunker on January 24, Westmoreland placed limits on the observance of a planned Tet cease-fire by troops in I Corps.

So much for what the intelligence specialists call "strategic warning." There was also specific warning ("tactical" warning) of a threat to Hue. In mid-November 1967 intelligence authorities in Saigon received a document captured by the ARVN I Corps Reconnaissance Company, a notebook maintained by a Viet Cong functionary. The notebook contained remarks on a resolution adopted by the MRTTH regional committee, which had ordered special efforts to control several villages immediately east and southeast of Hue, "in order to provide favorable conditions [for the revolution]." Exactly a month later an agent working for the American 525th Military Intelligence Group reported on a meeting of high-level VC cadre held to plan the "spring offensive." There word had been given that local VC "would be reinforced with a battalion which would be armed with modern weapons, supported by experts." Furthermore, attacks were to be "large scale" and intended to make "echoes" (such as propaganda results from attacks on large U.S. or ARVN units), "in spite of possible heavy casualties." Most suggestively, the agent mentioned a VC intention "to disturb the safety of Hue City by sabotage operations."

On January 28 South Vietnamese soldiers of the First Division Reconnaissance Company observed an NVA force leave its mountain bases for the coastal plain on which stood Hue. North Vietnamese strength was estimated at three battalions, perhaps a thousand to fifteen hundred troops, a large enough force to pose a real threat somewhere. In addition, on January 30 American radio listening posts at Phu Bai, southeast of Hue, picked up NVA transmissions. That night Viet Cong and North Vietnamese troops elsewhere in South Vietnam jumped the gun and launched their Tet attacks prematurely. Westmoreland canceled the remainder of the Tet cease-fire and put MACV forces on full alert.

Given this high-level interest, plus strategic and tactical warning, it is a measure of the intelligence failure at Tet that Hue city was taken by surprise. One may attribute this to an American fixation with Khe Sanh, or to failure to disseminate intelligence properly. Either way, the consequences were tragic.

■ Details of who surprised who, and how, mattered little to Philip W. Manhard, senior civilian adviser in Hue for the Civil Operations and Revolutionary Development Support (CORDS) unit, the U.S. pacification agency. Formed with CIA assistance, and employing personnel from the Agency, the State Department, and the military, CORDS was supposed to have its finger on the pulse of the war. Instead Manhard, a foreign service officer detailed to the organization, was now radioing Saigon that his home was surrounded and that he and two aides were retreating to a hiding place within.

For several days there was open concern as CORDS chief Robert Komer and Westmoreland pulled every string they could think of to save the man. Westmoreland specifically discussed the Manhard case in phone calls with Ambassador Bunker, III MAF staff, and ARVN officers. When Manhard's house was recaptured days later, there was no trace of the local CORDS chief. Only in 1973, when the sides exchanged prisoners, was Manhard heard from again. As for his organization, North Vietnamese troops also captured its Hue offices and overran districts containing the houses in which CORDS personnel lived. Another American captured and held by the North Vietnamese, even interrogated by the Soviets before his release in 1973, was Hue-based CIA officer Eugene A. Weaver. During the first days of the battle as many as thirty CORDS people were missing and not accounted for. Many turned up later, fortunately safe, but most with stories to tell.

Such became common experience at Hue at Tet 1968. Equally typical of these trials was what happened to the Vietnamese province chief for Thua Thien, Lieutenant Colonel Pham Van Khoa, who also happened to be mayor of Hue. According to Marine General Cushman, Khoa's entire family was murdered by NVA soldiers. Khoa and a bodyguard fled to a hospital, where they hid in an attic. The North Vietnamese took over that building and actually set up a command post in the room immediately below Khoa's hiding place. While ensconced in the attic, Colonel Khoa heard NVA officers saying they had captured CORDS chief Manhard and were going to kill him. The ARVN officer and his bodyguard spent a week breathlessly awaiting rescue.

Unlike the Coleridge poem, which promises delight if the sky is red at night, on the night of Tet a red tide brought weeks of misery to Hue. The stories of Manhard and Khoa are only the best known. A captured document, which amounted to an eight-page plan for the NVA city administration, set as one goal the disruption of the Saigon government machinery at every level. North Vietnamese troops apparently worked from lists of Hue residents, complete with addresses, which told them whom to arrest. The NVA had ready access to such detailed information, in part because their chief of administration had been, until the Hue Buddhist troubles of 1966, the city's chief of police.

In the months after the battle, mass graves were found in various places. The first, found just east of the Citadel, a Vauban-style fortification just north of the Perfume River and the site of the former imperial palace, contained 150 bodies. Another, by a creek in Nam Hoa district, was found to contain 250. No one knows exactly how many were executed during the Hue fighting. Some 3,500 citizens were missing at the end of the battle, while the number of bodies exhumed, according to different accounts, ranged from 2,300 to 3,000. After the battle it had always been the official line from Hanoi that civilian casualties were people caught in the crossfire or killed by bombing. As late as 1988, for example, Colonel Nguyen Quoc Khanh, who commanded the 806th Battalion of the NVA Sixth Regiment at Tet, insisted that "there was no case of killing civilians purposefully; those civilians who were killed were killed accidentally." In addition, some proportion of the civilians who disappeared must have gone willingly—members of the secret Viet Cong infrastructure who joined openly when their forces came to town.

South Vietnamese and American historians now generally agree that a massacre of civilians occurred at Hue, the city on the Perfume River. This tragedy gives dimensions to the intelligence failure that permitted the North Vietnamese to gain control of the city. These macabre events should be kept in mind as the backdrop for the military heroics of the battle for Hue.

■ Carefully planning their attack, the North Vietnamese began with a 122 mm rocket bombardment into the Hue Citadel and other key locations. North of the Perfume River the 800th and 802nd battalions of Colonel Nguyen Trong Tan's NVA Sixth Regiment attacked the western face of the Citadel, hoping to overrun Tay Loc airfield and the headquarters of the ARVN First Division. These NVA troops were assisted by the Twelfth Sapper Battalion which had been infiltrated within the city. South of the Perfume the attacking force consisted of two battalions—the 804th and K4B of the NVA Fourth Regiment. South of that, beyond the Phu Cam canal and the An Cuu bridge crossing it, the K4C Battalion of the Fourth Regiment had set up a blocking position, while north of the city the block was Nguyen Quoc Khanh's 806th. Rockets began the action at 3:40 a.m. on January 31, 1968.

The North Vietnamese intended to capture more than two hundred specific objectives in Hue, ranging from individual homes like that of CORDS chief Manhard to ARVN headquarters and the counterpart compound of the MACV advisory team assigned to the First Division, under Colonel George O. Adkisson. At the prison the NVA liberated more than two thousand inmates, many of whom presumably joined in the battle.

Not all the North Vietnamese efforts were successful. The best-known defense was that mounted by Captain Tran Ngoc Hue and his *Hoc Bao* or "Black Panther" Company of the First Division. Captain Hue and his men defended Tay Loc airfield, driving off the attackers of the NVA Sixth. Major General Ngo Quang Truong and his two-hundred-man divisional staff of the First Division also defended their compound against the same North Vietnamese troops, while the men of the Eighty-first Ordnance Company, just eighty soldiers guarding a stock of fourteen hundred brand-new M-16 rifles, not only defended the armory for over two weeks but moved the weapons out of harm's way before the NVA could reach them. At the MACV compound Colonel Adkisson also held off the enemy. Although the NVA failed to capture the local radio station, they did get its power and broadcast facility, temporarily putting the Saigon government off the air. One major headache for MACV officials during the early days was moving a fifty-watt mobile transmitter to the area to make up for the lost broadcast capability.

Meanwhile, the American command was in a certain disarray, due to the evident threat at Khe Sanh, to the north in Quang Tri province. In coping with that threat III MAF was moving its entire Third Marine Division to Quang Tri while extending the First Marine Division tactical area of responsibility to include Hue. This activity, called operation Checkers, was in full swing at the moment of Tet. As a result the major marine base at Phu Bai, eight miles southeast of the imperial city, was much weaker than usual. Phu Bai had Task Force X-Ray under Brigadier General Foster C. LaHue, a deputy commander of the First Division. LaHue had with him two full regimental headquarters (those of the First and Fifth marine regiments) but only two and a half rifle battalions, less than the complement of a single regiment. The marine units comprised elements of both regiments, not a single integral formation. Indeed, marine practice in Vietnam now conformed to the army custom of tailoring brigades by assigning different kinds of battalions—the Corps was using its regiments much like army brigade headquarters, shifting battalions around as required. Thus, when Tet came, Task Force X-Ray had two companies of the First Battalion,

First Marines, plus the First and Second battalions of the Fifth Marines.

First to be tapped for Hue was Alpha Company of 1/1, under Captain Gordon D. Batcheller. At the time General LaHue was responding to early reports of attacks on the MACV advisory compound. Sleeping in a tent at Phu Bai when he was first alerted, Batcheller's initial orders were simply to join ARVN units outside the base. His company was not familiar with the terrain or objectives, having been helilifted from Quang Tri just hours before as part of a battalion redeployment. Garden-variety snafus had left two platoon lieutenants plus part of First Platoon behind. Supported by a couple of truck-mounted quad-.50-caliber "Dusters," the force moved south of Phu Bai for a rendezvous with an ARVN unit that never appeared. Task Force X-Ray then changed Batcheller's mission to send him north through Hue to link up with Vietnamese units north of the city. Before he came anywhere near accomplishing that task, new orders sent him to relieve the MACV advisory compound.

As A/1/1 moved up Highway 1 and neared Hue, it encountered a fortuitous reinforcement—the Third Marine Division embarkation officer in a jeep leading a large crane escorted by four tanks of the Third Tank Battalion. The tanks furnished vital armored support for what followed. Then the marines had a second bit of incredibly good luck. As Hue is laid out, the portion of the city south of the Perfume River is separated from the land south of that by another water barrier, the Phu Cam. Highway 1 crosses this by the An Cuu bridge, the main avenue of approach for U.S. forces entering the battle. At the outset the enemy had set its Co Be Sapper Battalion to blow up the An Cuu bridge, but that effort had failed. Marines found holes in the concrete, but the structure stood and was solid. Batcheller was able to enter Hue South Side without further ado. Had the NVA successfully blown the An Cuu bridge it would have retarded, perhaps decisively, the entire American response to their operation against Hue.

As it was, things were far from simple. The single reduced marine company faced one NVA battalion in blocking positions while two more battalions of the NVA Fourth Regiment busily besieged the MACV compound. Before long Batcheller had to request help. Task Force X-Ray sent its battalion commander, Lieutenant Colonel Marcus J. Gravel, with the other available rifle company of the unit, Bravo, under Lieutenant C. B. Matthews. Soon afterward Phu Bai attached Golf Company of 2/5 under Captain Charles Meadows. The latter company made the link-up with A/1/1, to find Captain Batcheller wounded by shrapnel. He was replaced by Second Platoon commander Lieutenant Ray L. Smith. The combined force pushed ahead and reached the MACV compound, where a couple of hundred beleaguered advisers were glad to see them—but Colonel Adkisson, at least initially, was not glad enough to open the post exchange. The First Marines also secured a boat dock and helicopter landing zone on the bank of the Perfume plus the approach to the Nguyen Hoang bridge. Hue's Citadel was directly across the river.

This was the beginning of the longest sustained infantry battle of the Vietnam War to that date. Yet despite the agonies to which American and South Vietnamese soldiers were subjected, their commands seemed to play the battle as a public relations exercise rather than as serious combat. The second day of the action, the ARVN corps commander spoke of an NVA force holding out in the Citadel but claimed it was a mere "platoon" (say thirty men); MACV spokesmen told reporters that U.S. and ARVN troops were "mopping up" in the city. In reality the NVA had committed most of a division and occupied much of the city. Initially such claims may have been based upon ignorance, but this cannot account for the repetition that went on day after day. On February 2 the MACV spokesmen reported "pockets of resistance"; by the 4th the pockets were "small." On February 7 it was "a" small pocket at the extreme southwest corner of the Citadel. The public relations claims disappeared only after the battle had gone on so long that reporters began to reach the scene and file directly.

Nor was the line of myopic optimism strictly for public consumption. In "Eyes Only" cables to Pearl Harbor and Washington in which he reported MACV's daily progress, General Westmoreland was not entirely forthcoming about Hue. His February 1 report adverted that "the Citadel portion of Hue continues to remain partially occupied." This corresponds to the press briefing Westmoreland gave that day, in which he admitted that the NVA held just "a portion" of Hue. But in his "Eyes Only" report for February 2 it was merely the northeast and southwest portions *of the Citadel* that Westmoreland conceded remained "partially occupied." The National Military Command Center was independently informed that the NVA had slightly *expanded* its area of control in Hue due to darkness. In a secret summary of the Tet offensive he prepared for Joint Chiefs of Staff chairman Earle Wheeler on February 4, Westmoreland positively asserted that the U.S. response had "prevented him [the NVA and VC adversary] from taking a single city." Not only did Westmoreland's secret reporting parallel the disingenuous public relations effort, but both cloaked the reality that

ARVN and American soldiers were having to claw their way into a city the NVA did indeed occupy. This cannot have been a service to Washington-level policymakers.

While the generals played with the big picture, at Hue individual soldiers made the difference in fighting from house to house, even room to room. Vietnamese division commander Truong had an advantage in the buildup for a counterattack, as he had intuited an impending attack on the eve of Tet and had summoned reinforcements. One battalion came to the aid of his command compound, Mang Ca, then helped secure the airfield and other north side positions. The Second and Seventh Airborne Battalions brushed aside NVA blocks to reach Hue the day after Tet. By February 4 Truong had five maneuver battalions on line, most from his division's Third Regiment. By then, Task Force X-Ray had one battalion up front and another in the city, while MACV had also deployed a three-battalion brigade of the First Cavalry Division (Airmobile) to the west to obstruct NVA access to Hue in operation Jeb Stuart.

Clearing the south side became the mission of marines of 2/5 under Lieutenant Colonel Ernest C. Cheatham, Jr. By the time the main effort got under way on February 4, the marines faced a well-concealed and protected adversary who had had days to prepare. By then the marines had claimed a body count of 33, but had taken some serious losses themselves, with Lieutenant Colonel Gravel's 1/1 so weakened it was reduced to holding open Highway 1 and capturing the Joan of Arc School, a mere hundred yards from the MACV compound.

Poor weather posed a serious obstacle to allied combat operations. The Americans wanted to mount air strikes, with irritating gas not so much as bombs, but were continually forced to scrub missions. Weather hampered the insertion of the First Cavalry too, forcing some units to deploy on foot. When ARVN corps commander General Hoang Xuan Lam complained that the marines were not giving him the support he wanted, the culprit was again found to be weather. On February 4 Lam had asked for a helicopter lift of some 105 mm howitzers; the marines ran into cloud cover down to four hundred feet, forcing them to fly so low that ground fire broke up the sorties. The chopper carrying the first gun took eleven hits; its crew was wounded and forced to give up. Similarly, Lam wanted the U.S. to bomb Hue, but the *Vietnamese* air force had not flown a single sortie. Day after day the weather continued to be a problem.

On February 5, to put the cap on the poor weather, the ceiling was down to just fifty feet. By then, however, the Americans had two

destroyers offshore to provide naval gunfire support, making up somewhat for the lack of aircraft. General Lam was also more satisfied with
his supply situation, having begun to receive material by boat and
truck and giving up some of his more extreme requests, including one
for M-16 ammunition that would have required the marines to hand
over fully half of all the rifle ammunition they held in inventory in
Vietnam.

Still the battle continued on the ground. In the fighting for Joan of
Arc School on February 4, the able Sergeant Alfredo Gonzalez of
Alpha Company, 1/1, won the Medal of Honor while commanding
Third Platoon. Suppressing enemy fire on his men with Light Antitank
Assault Weapons, Gonzalez fired at the NVA, pinning them down. He
was an Alpha Company sparkplug, at least until the North Vietnamese
killed him. Meanwhile, 2/5 attacked along a southwest axis, culminating with a nasty fight on February 6 for the two-story province headquarters building. Spearheaded by Captain Roy Christmas's Hotel
Company, the marines triumphed, but not before the NVA Twelfth
Sapper Battalion finally succeeded in blowing the An Cuu bridge. By
then the marines claimed a 736 body count. They declared the south
side secure on February 10, but North Vietnamese snipers and isolated
resistance remained, and none of this action touched the NVA forces
inside the walled city.

General Truong's First ARVN Division had the greatest chance at
the enemy inside the walled city. Truong had begun the battle by holding out while the NVA swept past him to occupy the Citadel and other
points. Afterward he had been steadily reinforced. The Second and
Third battalions of the Third Regiment advanced along the northern
bank of the Perfume River, but the NVA prevented them from getting
inside the wall, confining them to Gia Hoi district. Two more battalions joined up over the next days, the First relieving the division command post. The Fourth Battalion, Second ARVN Regiment reinforced
Tay Loc airfield, and was in turn relieved by an ARVN airborne task
force. On February 6 the Americans even managed to air-drop 105
mm howitzers to the South Vietnamese in spite of the poor flying
weather.

By this time the North Vietnamese were concentrated in the southern portion of the Citadel, including the old Imperial Palace. Neither
side fought for that, but the city walls, the buildings, and the former
moats provided excellent cover and protection. The North Vietnamese
troops were tough. A French photographer who was permitted among
them and then allowed to leave furnished III MAF with pictures that

showed well-uniformed NVA troops with the latest equipment. This included AK-47 assault rifles, rocket-propelled grenades, and good web gear (from which equipment could be hung) that appeared "stuffed to the hilt with ammo and grenades." The NVA even had good haircuts. Four battalions were estimated to be in the walled city—the Sixth Regiment plus sappers.

Tough fighting wore out the ARVN troops perhaps faster than their adversaries. By February 7 the First Division still seemed to be making little progress. That day General Westmoreland telephoned General Cao Van Vien, chief of the ARVN Joint General Staff. Vien cited the ARVN Seventh Airborne Battalion as an example of the heavy losses his men were taking—the unit was now little more than a company in strength. Westmoreland proposed pulling out the ARVN units inside the walled city and substituting a fresh task force of two airborne and two Vietnamese marine battalions. Vien thought it a good idea and took it the next day to President Nguyen Van Thieu. By February 12 the ARVN had brought up their Ninth Airborne, along with the First, Fourth, and Fifth Vietnamese marine battalions.

Meanwhile, the NVA actually counterattacked. On the night of February 6/7 they used grappling hooks to scale the inner walls and hit the Fourth Battalion, Second ARVN, driving it back to Tay Loc. General Truong was widely regarded as an effective ARVN leader, and his division as the best in the Vietnamese army. If the ARVN First Division plus general reserve units like the airborne could not shake the NVA out of the Citadel, it seemed there would be no alternative but to have Americans do the job. The battle of Hue could not be allowed to drag on indefinitely. On February 7 Truong requested U.S. assistance in the Citadel. This was the origin of the instructions to III MAF to get Americans north of the Perfume River.

As the orders went down the chain of command through Task Force X-Ray, they translated into a mission for Major Robert H. Thompson's First Battalion, Fifth Marines. One company was helilifted to take over part of the former ARVN airborne sector along the southeast wall. Thompson, with a reinforced company, crossed the river by landing craft to link up with the other force. The ARVN paratroops were withdrawn despite the fact that the Vietnamese marines had been delayed and had still not arrived to take up their positions. This culmination of operation Hue City began on February 13, when the NVA continued to occupy 60 percent of the Citadel.

Captain J. J. Bowe's Alpha Company operated on the northeast wall. They came under fire within moments of jumping off and in less than ten minutes took thirty-five casualties, including the company commander. Charlie and Bravo companies advanced around noon with little effect, except that two supporting marine tanks took rocket hits on their turrets. By midafternoon 1/5 had been ordered to hold in place and reorganize. The battalion also spent February 14 hunkered down while artillery and naval bombardment worked over known NVA positions. General Creighton Abrams, deputy MACV commander, supplemented the available artillery support when he insisted the marines move some of their heavier guns, eight-inch artillery, to bring them into range of Hue.

Accounts sometimes note that only at this relatively late phase of the battle was authorization given to use all types of weapons. But General Truong spoke of using all kinds of firepower from the first moments of the battle, and General Lam, according to Westmoreland's telephone records, was asking for air sorties as early as February 5. The marines feared air strikes might result in unwanted collateral damage and refused Lam's request. Westmoreland confirmed that, but with orders that applied only to the walled part of the city and may have exempted "strong points." In any case, artillery and naval gunfire were in use from the earliest days while the air restrictions were rescinded on February 12. Weather should be seen as the major reason air power was not brought to bear sooner. This improved during the U.S. phase of the Citadel fight, and F-4 Phantoms were in evidence when Colonel Thompson's 1/5 returned to the attack on February 15.

For four days Thompson's battalion battered at the northeast wall of Hue. On the night of the 16th communications intelligence intercepted a message from the local NVA commander to headquarters, and instant direction-finding permitted immediate artillery and naval fire that is thought to have killed the officer and his communications men. Later that night NVA headquarters received a recommendation from the successor that North Vietnamese troops withdraw. Headquarters refused permission. Both Americans and South Vietnamese claim to have intercepted this traffic.

Whatever the reality of the artillery shoot episode, it is clear that by late February the North Vietnamese days in Hue were numbered. The MRTTH command had committed four battalions of later reinforcements for more than a division in all, perhaps six thousand to nine thousand troops, a total of sixteen battalions according to ARVN sources. Losses were substantial. An NVA document captured later listed among those killed a regimental commander, eight battalion and twenty-four company commanders, and seventy-two platoon leaders.

Still the North Vietnamese fought doggedly. On February 19 two NVA battalions struck back at the Vietnamese First Marine Battalion, which held its ground but apparently failed to prevent the escape of certain NVA elements.

In fact the Vietnamese marines proved generally disappointing at Hue, and Westmoreland was soon talking with Vien about replacing them in the north with newly reconstituted Airborne units. In a message to Westmoreland on February 23, General Abrams reported he had sent a letter to Cao Van Vien noting the poor Vietnamese marine performance and insisting that if they could not rise to the occasion they should not form part of the South Vietnamese armed forces.

Meanwhile the U.S. marines and other ARVN troops ground ahead foot by foot. Between February 13 and 20 Thompson's 1/5 sustained 47 killed, 240 seriously wounded, and another 60 wounded but still in action. No company had more than half its strength left, the battalion had only three platoons still commanded by lieutenants, and all four platoon commanders in Bravo Company were corporals; even the battalion chaplain had been killed. Against this the unit had a confirmed body count of 219 North Vietnamese soldiers and gained complete control of the northeast wall on February 21. Lima Company of the Third Battalion, Fifth Marines, under Captain John D. Niotis, went in to reinforce 1/5 for the last stage of the battle. Suddenly the marines found themselves advancing against light opposition.

Another NVA attack took place that day against the Vietnamese marines, who repulsed it. The Vietnamese marines then launched a surprise night attack of their own on February 23/24. At about 5 a.m. on February 24, soldiers of the ARVN Third Regiment put their flag in place of the North Vietnamese flag on the Citadel wall. Later ARVN and 1/5 troops captured the Imperial Palace, which had scarcely been damaged in the long battle. Fittingly, it was the *Hoc Bao* (Black Panther) Company of the ARVN First Division that finally raised the South Vietnamese flag over the palace.

Destruction was substantial and losses were heavy all round. Figures used for determining relief payments for Hue residents list 4,456 housing units as destroyed, another 3,360 as more than 50 percent damaged, and 2,757 additional homes as damaged to some degree. Some 116,000 refugees were left from the former population, while ARVN estimated that 944 civilians had been killed and 784 wounded as a result of military action in the battle. American marine losses were 147 killed and 857 wounded; army casualties included 74 dead and 507 wounded. South Vietnamese losses totaled 384 killed and 1,830 wounded. Claimed North Vietnamese casualties were 5,113 dead, and there were 89 prisoners. The ultimate costs, the pain and agony of these things, can never be known. It was paid then, and still today, by Vietnamese north and south, and by Americans who fought alongside them.

Even as this fierce battle continued on the Perfume River, and as the Tet fighting elsewhere in South Vietnam died away, one more fight continued. This engagement, which endured so long that it became known as the great siege of the Vietnam War, was the fight Westmoreland had originally expected in place of the countrywide Tet offensive. Westmoreland's fight was the battle of Khe Sanh.

No Damned Dinbinphoo! Khe Sanh and the U.S. High Command

Route 9 begins at Dong Ha near the Vietnamese coast. Hugging the Mieu Giang past Cam Lo, the road heads west toward the mountains. As it ascends the Annamite chain to cross into Laos, Route 9 becomes little more than a one-lane dirt road. The encroaching tropical vegetation beyond its shoulders has to be cut away periodically just to keep the passage open. Perched astride the road a few miles before Route 9 enters Laos is the village of Khe Sanh. The accidents of war made it the scene of one of the climactic battles of Vietnam.

Khe Sanh was a battle of images warring for the mind. Images clashed not only on the plateau and in the hills surrounding the combat base, but in Saigon and in Washington, D.C. One image was brave marines holding an isolated position, another the unseen enemy. Each man at Khe Sanh carried away images uniquely his own. The story of the battle at that place has been told from these points of view—by journalists at the time, by marine, air force, and other historians, and by participants in the campaign. Much less known is the story of Khe Sanh at command levels, from the perspectives of the men at MACV and in Washington who made the decisions that sent men into action at Khe Sanh and sent others to support them.

■ Khe Sanh became important precisely because of its location on Route 9 near the Laotian border. In the early years of the war, as we have seen, Military Assistance Command Vietnam followed a strategy of border surveillance and denial, using detachments of U.S. Army Special Forces to organize and train Vietnamese montagnard tribesmen. The Khe Sanh border camp, opened in July 1962 at a time when the CIA ran this program, actually predated the assumption of command responsibility by MACV. It was still in place in 1965 when U.S. marines came to the northern provinces of South Vietnam, the I Corps Tactical Zone (I CTZ), making that area a marine preserve. There was little fighting at Khe Sanh in those years. Only in January 1966 was the camp subjected to a heavy mortar barrage by the enemy for the first time.

Marines came to Khe Sanh in April 1966 when the First Battalion, First Marines moved in to conduct Operation Virginia. The Marine command for I CTZ, III Marine Amphibious Force (III MAF) subsequently decided to garrison Khe Sanh on its own, after Operation Prairie that September, and the Special Forces camp was moved a few miles west to the vicinity of Lang Vei, where navy seabees constructed reinforced concrete bunkers for the montagnards. Special Forces Detachment A-101 moved to the camp with its Bru tribesmen toward the end of the year. Lang Vei was declared operational on December 21, 1966. It was the only hardened Special Forces camp in I CTZ.

During these years of intensifying warfare, the North Vietnamese across the border in Laos worked assiduously, improving and expanding the road network known as the Ho Chi Minh Trail. With the trail work and the growing utilization of this route for infiltration came North Vietnamese Army units to defend it. The presence of these NVA forces provided a built-in capability to surge NVA troops onto the Khe Sanh plateau and the surrounding mountains if the enemy wished to challenge American control of the area.

An early indication that Khe Sanh was becoming a sensitive sector was a series of engagements in the spring of 1967 known as the Hill Battles. That February the marine battalion at the base was replaced by a company whose mission was to defend the airstrip and patrol the surrounding area to a depth of fifteen thousand meters. There were patrol contacts in late February, a squad-size NVA probe of the combat base from the northwest on March 5, and a series of ambushes on the slopes of Hill 861 on the 16th. III MAF shuttled companies through the base, deployed armor, antitank sections, and two army heavy weapons sections, and kept up vigorous patrols, leading to another ambush battle on April 23. In the early morning of May 4 a reinforced company of the NVA 325C Division attacked Lang Vei and escaped with light losses. By then more than a battalion of marines were in position and another was added to conduct assaults that cleared Hill 861, Hill 881 South, and Hill 881 North. Intelligence indicated that the NVA then withdrew, and the Khe Sanh sector again turned quiet.

In the summer and fall of 1967, III MAF's attention was drawn to the area south of the Demilitarized Zone (DMZ) that separated North from South Vietnam. Following directives from Washington, General Westmoreland had ordered the emplacement of a fortified line to prevent the NVA from moving upon Dong Ha or Quang Tri. There was fierce fighting around Con Thien and north of Dong Ha. Near the end of 1967 intelligence began to discover signs that the enemy might attempt a major offensive action in the new year. The NVA had not forgotten Khe Sanh—marine patrols that December found evidence of two full enemy divisions moving into position nearby—325C to the north of the combat base and the NVA 304th Division to the southwest. Also within a twenty-five-kilometer radius were the entire NVA 320th Division and another regiment of the 324th.

Nor had General William Westmoreland forgotten Khe Sanh. The MACV commander had been concerned about the base from a very early date, and not just because the NVA might pose a threat to it. Westmoreland did worry about that—as early as September 1966, visiting III MAF to review the results of a war game that Marine General Lewis Walt had conducted at the request of MACV, Westmoreland became convinced that III MAF "were particularly underestimating an enemy threat to the CIDG-Special Forces camp at Khe Sanh." This recollection, in Westmoreland's memoirs, dovetails neatly with the rationale for the defense of Khe Sanh given in the June 1968 CINCPAC-MACV *Report on the War in Vietnam,* which states that "were we to relinquish the Khe Sanh area, the North Vietnamese would have had an unobstructed invasion route into the two northernmost provinces from which they might outflank our positions south of the Demilitarized Zone."

But Khe Sanh was also important in basic MACV ground strategy for a second reason, an offensive one. The plateau was seen as a base for special operations into Laos and a takeoff point for reconnaissance planes. Further, as Westmoreland writes in his memoirs, "I still hoped some day to get approval for a major drive into Laos." These intentions go unmentioned in the official CINCPAC-MACV report, but they were arguably at the heart of Westmoreland's strategy. In the early years of U.S. combat involvement, deployments first focused on stabilizing the overall situation and then began to shift north toward I CTZ. MACV had plans for an offensive into Laos by early 1966.

One effect of Westmoreland's strategy was to insert the U.S. army into what had been a marine preserve. III MAF commanded in I CTZ, but if the force levels were to continue rising while the number of available marines remained limited, there was no alternative to "grunts."

The closest MACV could come to getting marines was a South Korean marine brigade, which went to Chu Lai in 1966. The first army battalion (from 173rd Airborne Brigade) went north that same year, followed in 1967 by the division-size Task Force Oregon (later to become the American Division). In mid-1967 MACV began planning for the commitment of the First Cavalry Division (Airmobile) in I CTZ as well.

In cables to Washington on September 27 and 28, 1967, Westmoreland explicitly used the justification of "improving the military situation in the DMZ" for a series of further troop requests. As Defense Secretary Robert McNamara reported to President Johnson on October 4, these included accelerating deployment of the Eleventh Infantry Brigade (which became part of American) from February 1968 to December 1967, accelerating deployment of the 101st Airborne Division to bring in all major elements before December 20, 1967 (an objective not entirely met), retaining in Vietnam parts of the Ninth Marine Amphibious Brigade, and increasing the level of B-52 Arc Light sorties from eight hundred to twelve hundred per month.

This program of activity antedated the major NVA threat to Khe Sanh and the Tet offensive. The I CTZ buildup was *not* a response to those enemy actions. Planning for displacement north of the airmobile "Cav" was already in hand; MACV had ordered acceleration of logistics improvements in I CTZ, and other new troops were flowing in as well. Further, Westmoreland projected for 1968 a series of four operations, codenamed York, that would sweep the Vietnamese side of the Laotian border and set up a possible offensive from Khe Sanh into Laos. The contingency plans for a Laotian offensive were updated in early 1968 by MACV General Bruce Palmer with the code names El Paso I and II. Both York and the El Paso actions were recommended by Westmoreland in cables to the Joint Chiefs of Staff on January 6 and 8, 1968.

Thus Westmoreland's own strategic intentions made him especially sensitive to any threat to Khe Sanh. Although intelligence discovered indications of enemy offensive intentions against South Vietnam's cities, which were reported to Washington, it was the threat to Khe Sanh that seemed salient. Walt Rostow, President Johnson's national security adviser, reported "increasingly solid evidence of [a] major North Vietnamese buildup against I Corps area." This January 5, 1968, cable added that "Westmoreland's best estimate is that [the] North Vietnamese army [is] massing for another major offensive in this area, perhaps targeted this time on Khe Sanh." Westmoreland's stated reasoning for a defense of Khe Sanh, given to JCS chairman Earle Wheeler a week later, remained that the combat base was the western anchor of the DMZ defenses, that its loss would allow the enemy into areas contiguous with the heavily populated coastal zone, and that its abandonment would be a major propaganda victory for the enemy.

Defending Khe Sanh meant reinforcing it. Under Colonel David E. Lownds's Twenty-sixth Marine Regiment, the forces in place in December included artillery and weapons units, his First Battalion, a 100-man Vietnamese Regional Force company, and the four company Bru CIDG force at Lang Vei. The Third Battalion, Twenty-sixth Marines was added in December. In January came the regiment's Second Battalion (the first time the regiment's three battalions had operated together in Vietnam), the First Battalion, Ninth Marines, more artillery, and the Thirty-seventh Vietnamese Ranger Battalion. A covert action group was also sent, about 450 men of Forward Operations Base 3. Total strength in the area on January 23, 1968, amounted to almost 5,800 marines, 228 naval personnel, about 75 army, and perhaps 700 Vietnamese and CIDG tribesmen. These forces held the Khe Sanh Combat Base, Lang Vei, and outlying positions on Hill 881 South, Hill 861, Hill 556, Hill 861A, Hill 950, and the Rock Quarry.

Colonel Lownds soon saw indications that the North Vietnamese too had an abiding interest in Khe Sanh. The day after New Year's 1968 five enemy officers, including an NVA regimental commander, were killed while making a personal reconnaissance of the combat base perimeter. They had been wearing marine uniforms. On January 17 a patrol moving north in heavy fog ran into an NVA ambush. On the 20th another patrol from M Company of 3/26, probing out of 881 South, encountered a strongly defended bunker line. An NVA antiaircraft company commander who surrendered that day gave the marines information that attacks would be made that night on Hill 881 South and Hill 861. The latter strongpoint was indeed attacked, followed on January 21 by probes against Khe Sanh village and rocketing of the combat base that destroyed a helicopter fuel dump and the base's largest ammunition dump. The historical "battle" of Khe Sanh is considered to have begun that day.

Lownds's Twenty-sixth Marine Regiment immediately hunkered down in anticipation of what was to come. The Vietnamese Regional Force company pulled back to join FOB 3 in the combat base. First Battalion, Ninth Marines arrived the next day and the last reinforcement, the Vietnamese 37th Rangers, on January 27. Patrols into the hinterland were discontinued. There was a big push to improve defenses with better bunkers and trenches, an effort hampered by scarce engineering materials, especially lumber. Khe Sanh base had originally been laid out for a single battalion; its rapid reinforcement drove the necessity for additional fortification. Constant enemy shelling confirmed the wisdom of the effort.

The marines refused to consider the Khe Sanh battle a "siege." Lownds even professed ignorance of the earlier Franco-Vietnamese War siege of Dien Bien Phu, noted reporter Michael Herr, at a time when many among the press corps in Vietnam, struck by the analogy, were busily studying books on that 1954 French defeat. The Dien Bien Phu analogy was not lost on Saigon and Washington, however. At MACV Westmoreland even formed a panel of staff officers specifically to study the similarities. Lyndon Johnson had played a central role in determining U.S. policy in the earlier crisis, and in Washington he turned to his military advisers exclaiming, "I don't want no damned Dinbinphoo!"

LBJ closely followed events at Khe Sanh, ordering detailed reports, including daily situation reports from Westmoreland personally. The White House Situation Room wall was hung with an aerial mosaic map of Khe Sanh while the Pentagon provided the president with an elaborate terrain model of the base and surrounding area.

Johnson's concern led to the best-known instance of high-level attention given to Khe Sanh—his insistence on a memorandum from the JCS, "signed in blood," promising defense of the combat base. That memorandum, dated January 29, 1968, in fact amounted to little more than a two-page summary of a Westmoreland telephone conversation with Earle Wheeler that morning. Westmoreland asserted that all possible preparations had been made, that everyone was confident, and that Khe Sanh could and should be held. The entire JCS contribution to this memo was a two-sentence addition: "The Joint Chiefs of Staff have reviewed the situation at Khe Sanh and concur with General Westmoreland's assessment of the situation. They recommend that we maintain our position at Khe Sanh."

Westmoreland was quite correct about his extensive preparations. Not only had Khe Sanh been reinforced but U.S. maneuver battalions in I CTZ had been increased by almost two division equivalents, to thirty-eight battalions, about 40 percent of MACV's *total* strength, so many that a MACV Forward headquarters under General Creighton W. Abrams was established to supplant III MAF. The equivalent of an ARVN airborne division was also slated for movement within the next few days. Air support had been reorganized under MACV's deputy for air operations and increased since January 17 to an average forty B-52 and five hundred tactical air sorties into the Niagara area, the air designator for Khe Sanh and its environs. Around Khe Sanh itself a sophisticated electronic sensor system code-named Muscle Shoals had been emplaced between January 19 and 25, helping offset the loss of tactical intelligence from patrolling.

With so many eyes on Khe Sanh, on January 31 the North Vietnamese and Viet Cong suddenly unleashed a series of powerful assaults throughout South Vietnam, including celebrated battles in Saigon and Hue, which collectively became known as the Tet offensive.

At Khe Sanh nothing happened.

While fierce fighting continued throughout South Vietnam, Khe Sanh stayed quiet. LBJ remained concerned and pressed General Wheeler about the Dien Bien Phu analogy on the evening of February 2. Wheeler replied, based on another talk with Westmoreland, in a memorandum the next day. Wheeler quoted Westmoreland to the president: "Although not ideal, the tactical situation at Khe Sanh as well as our improved combat techniques and capabilities are considerably different from those at Dien Bien Phu." Westmoreland nevertheless asked for additional C-130 transport aircraft and expedited delivery of replacement helicopters and U.S.-issue small arms (M-16 rifles, M-60 machine guns, M-29 mortars) to the South Vietnamese. During this conversation Westmoreland also raised the question of the use of tactical nuclear weapons or chemical agents which "should not be required" but would be "active candidates" if "the situation in the DMZ area change[d] dramatically."

Though Khe Sanh had not been attacked, that was still the expectation. On February 4 Ambassador Ellsworth Bunker reported the enemy "apparently preparing momentarily to launch extremely heavy [attacks] in Northern First Corps." That day at the White House an NSC military staffer whom LBJ trusted implicitly, General Robert Ginsburgh, reported that "we might expect the battle for Khe Sanh to start within the next three days." He speculated that B-52 and tactical air attacks might have upset NVA timing or that the NVA might be intending to coordinate Khe Sanh attacks with a second round of city attacks. NSC adviser Walt Rostow asked Wheeler to begin filing daily reports and arranged for General Ginsburgh to be on duty that night. Meanwhile, thirty-nine B-52 Arc Light sorties in four strikes code-named Uniform were scheduled for that day.

Fighting near Khe Sanh did begin on February 5 with elements of the NVA 325C Division attacking Hill 861 in conjunction with a four-hour rocket, mortar, and artillery barrage on the combat base. The marines replied with 7,788 mortar and artillery rounds, and there were 33 B-52 sorties, bringing the total of Arc Light sorties in that area to 654 since January 15. Rostow spoke with Westmoreland by phone early on February 6 (Washington time) and advised that MACV "had nothing spectacular to report." Soon afterward (February 7 in Vietnam) the Sixty-sixth Regiment of the NVA 304th began a massive assault on the Lang Vei Special Forces camp. For the first time in the history of the war the enemy used armor in his attack. Lang Vei resisted heroically but was overrun—of twenty-four Green Berets, thirteen were wounded and ten missing and presumed dead. Three-quarters of the Bru CIDGs were unaccounted for when CIA sent a spot report to the White House. Survivors moved into the FOB 3 compound at Khe Sanh where inquisitive marines were turned away at gunpoint. The next day came a daylight attack on a platoon of the 1/9 Marines near the Rock Quarry, countered by a relief force of two reinforced companies with two marine tanks.

Everyone now believed the climactic phase of the war had come. Commenting that day on Hanoi's position in possible peace negotiations, Ambassador Bunker cabled, "What their final position will be remains to be seen, and indeed may not be determined pending further developments—Khe Sanh for instance." South Vietnamese President Nguyen Van Thieu's opinion, according to a Bunker cable on the 8th, was that "the enemy will endeavor to keep up pressure throughout the summer in the First Corps and the Central Highlands." Westmoreland's cable on February 9 predicted that "the third phase [of the Tet offensive], which is yet to begin, would involve consolidation of his position and strong attacks across the DMZ and against Khe Sanh with the objective of establishing military control over the two northern provinces." This "third phase" offensive, Westmoreland asserted in an "Eyes Only" cable to CINCPAC and CJCS on February 12, "has just begun." It would be "a maximum effort by the enemy." MACV appealed: "I desperately need" reinforcements to avoid a "major risk" throughout the south as he sent troops to I CTZ.

These views only added to the considerable unease in Washington. General Maxwell D. Taylor, former JCS chairman and ambassador to Vietnam, whom LBJ had called upon for advice, remembers a luncheon meeting on February 3 at which "an air of gloom" surrounded the discussion. Taylor "tried rather feebly to make the point that Khe Sanh was only an outpost, and no one should expect an outpost to be a Verdun." Others accepted that the U.S. itself had done much to build up the psychological importance of Khe Sanh, and meetings on February 11 and 12 agreed to emergency augmentation of MACV forces. LBJ meanwhile asked Taylor to review Westmoreland's cables. In a memorandum of February 12 Taylor agreed that MACV augmentation was necessary but warned "there is a real danger that the defense of Khe Sanh will require resources better used elsewhere."

In a second memorandum two days later, Taylor went even further: "My review of Westy's cables does not convince me of the military importance of maintaining Khe Sanh at the present time if it is still feasible to withdraw. Whatever the past value of this position, it is a positive liability now. . . . My present opinion is that Khe Sanh probably can be held but that it will be at a heavy price in casualties and in terms of other ground troops necessary to support and reinforce it. I have real doubt that we can afford such a defense." Taylor stated he would feel "greatly relieved" if the JCS saw fit to give MACV guidance along these lines: "Khe Sanh appears to the Joint Chiefs of Staff to be an exposed position difficult to supply by air and expensive to supply overland . . . it is less clear that [Khe Sanh's] present value now justifies the cost of an all-out defense. . . . The effect of a costly defense absorbing forces badly needed elsewhere could in the end be far more disadvantageous to our cause than a withdrawal now." Taylor recommended leaving the final decision up to Westmoreland, framing his suggested JCS message as an opinion rather than an order, but he wrote "in full realization of how wrong one can be at a distance about a military situation such as this." He further noted that it could be too late to do anything about Khe Sanh, and that if this were so, "we should put all doubts behind us and prepare for the fight."

General Taylor provided this striking commentary at the very moment President Johnson was considering emergency augmentation of MACV, in which Taylor also concurred. What is most curious, however, is that these deliberations in Washington and fears for Khe Sanh occurred at a time when the fighting there had again diminished. For two weeks after the Lang Vei and quarry engagements, enemy shelling and aerial resupply were the dominant concerns at Khe Sanh. Not until February 21 was there another ground attack, and then it consisted of a company-size NVA probe against the perimeter held by the ARVN 37th Rangers. On the 22nd the combat base was subjected to the heaviest shelling of the battle—1,307 rounds (the marines themselves fired an average of 2,063 rounds per day throughout the battle; during March the NVA managed an average of only 150 daily).

A major NVA attack finally occurred on February 29, with three reinforced battalions striking again at the ARVN Rangers. Once again Colonel Lownds's tactical intelligence furnished timely warning, while Arc Light strikes devastated the NVA assembly areas. The enemy proved unable even to breach the wire and left seventy-eight bodies behind when they retreated. Bru patrols reported hundreds more bodies left in the assembly areas.

The NVA assault on the Rangers proved to be the climactic episode of the Khe Sanh battle and the only major attack on the combat base itself. It too was anticipated at the White House—LBJ asked General Wheeler about Khe Sanh after breakfast on the 28th (February 29, Vietnam time). The JCS chairman maintained that the NVA would pay "a terrible price" to take the base and declared Westmoreland was confident he could hold it. A few days later the president received intelligence reports that some NVA forces were pulling back from Khe Sanh, and on March 9 the enemy force was estimated at six thousand to eight thousand, about half the previous level.

Throughout March artillery bombardments and aerial resupply continued as Lownds's chief concerns at the base. The marines replied in kind, greatly overmatching enemy firepower. The supply situation was so good the marines considered they had excess ammunition; they celebrated Saint Patrick's Day by firing off three hundred rounds of green smoke. The air force developed low-altitude parachute methods to improve supply while the marines utilized new "super gaggle" helicopter tactics to supply the hilltop positions. Westmoreland continued his I CTZ buildup, to fifty-four battalions on March 13, a little over 50 percent of all U.S. maneuver battalions. Two weeks later the famed "Cav" under General John Tolson, with the First Marines and an ARVN airborne task force, began Operation Pegasus, which reopened Route 9 and relieved Khe Sanh on April 9. The battle was over. Later, in the summer of 1968, Khe Sanh was quietly abandoned.

■ The defense of Khe Sanh is a credit to the tough marines, Special Forces, Vietnamese, and CIDG Bru troops who fought there. American losses amounted to 205 killed, 852 medevaced, and 816 other wounded. Air power also deserves a large share of credit for evacuating casualties, bringing in replacements, and delivering more than 14,000 tons of supplies plus almost 85,000 tons of ordnance on the enemy, to account for a good proportion of his losses. Lownds's forces found 1,602 enemy bodies and estimated more than 10,000 NVA wounded, though LBJ was told in late April that calculations using three different methodologies estimated NVA losses between 14,600 and 28,900.

For all their losses, the enemy too achieved something significant at Khe Sanh. They made the combat base a sensitive position that fixed the attention of the American command, mesmerized Washington, and flung the Americans into a previously unmatched state of uncertainty. Westmoreland moved half his U.S. maneuver battalions into I CTZ but still felt obliged to postpone a planned offensive into the Ashau valley in favor of Pegasus. As late as March 13, after the NVA began to pull back, the CIA was predicting that "the large North Vietnamese forces in I Corps *will* seek a clear cut victory against ours in the weeks and months ahead in something like conventional warfare." While Washington waited for massive attacks that never materialized—and could not explain why they did not—the enemy felt free to pursue his Tet offensive throughout South Vietnam. Both sides could claim victories of sorts from Khe Sanh.

Because the decision was made by President Johnson in the early days of the siege, one final result of Khe Sanh was the dispatch to South Vietnam of the last reinforcements MACV would receive. The war reached a clear peak during those early months of 1968. For many Americans serving in Vietnam it was a time of unparalleled danger. There were dangers everywhere, for old hands as well as fresh reinforcements. The experience of one of the marines who arrived among the post-Tet wave of reinforcements furnishes a good example of the personal sacrifices and costs that Vietnam represented.

18   Profile: Tim Brown's Vietnam

At the moment of the Tet offensive, marine Timothy Brown was having an ordinary day at the Marine Barracks at Kaneohe, Hawaii. An artilleryman with the Second Battalion, Thirteenth Marines, Brown could have had no idea the events of Tet would affect him. But just over a week into the battle, General William Westmoreland cabled Washington asking for extra reinforcements to meet the threat. President Johnson promptly consented, and one of the units slated for the mission was the First Marine Amphibious Brigade, which included Tim Brown's artillery battalion. President Johnson actually visited some of the marines who would be leaving from Camp Pendleton, California, but the men from Hawaii went by sea, aboard the transport *USS Bexar*, arriving at Da Nang in late February or early March 1968. The firing batteries of Brown's unit were posted to several hills surrounding the bustling Da Nang base, which had been attacked by rocket fire during Tet.

At twenty, Tim Brown was a little older than the average marine. He was also exceptional in having attended college before volunteering for the Corps. Born in Atlanta, he moved with his family to Dallas a couple of years later and was bred a Texas boy, patriotic and practical. His brother went to West Point and did a Vietnam tour as a young officer in 1967. Tim kicked around after high school but soon decided to get his military service out of the way. Rather than waiting around to be drafted, he chose the Marine Corps. Now he found himself in South Vietnam.

The climax of Artilleryman Brown's Vietnam experience came barely more than two months "in country." That was due to North Vietnamese activity in Quang Tin Province, southwest of Da Nang, where the Special Forces camp at Kham Duc guarded the Laotian border. The U.S. command anticipated a move against Kham Duc and had begun preparations for a fight there, sending engineers to perfect the airstrip and endow it with all-weather landing capability. Kham Duc was also strengthened by a platoon of two 105 mm howitzers, assigned to work with the Fifth Special Forces Group, which had control of the camp. It was Tim Brown's platoon, of D Battery, 2/13, that was chosen for the task. Platoon leader Lieutenant Robert Adams learned of the mission in mid-April. By late April U.S. intelligence had information the North Vietnamese Second Division intended to hit Kham Duc. The intention was confirmed by interrogation of a prisoner captured on May 3.

Kham Duc had a satellite camp, a smaller outlying position called Ngok Tavak, perhaps seven kilometers away as the crow flies but closer to a dozen by the rugged mountain trail that passed for Route 14 in this part of Vietnam. The Special Forces decided to deploy the marine artillery to Ngok Tavak in an effort to retard North Vietnamese preparations for their attack. Around the beginning of May 1968, Tim Brown suddenly found himself at a forward outpost facing imminent assault. Ngok Tavak was an "Old French Fort," not the abode-walled or concrete Foreign Legion post popularized by Hollywood but a simple dirt-walled compound with sandbag-and-wood bunkers, foxholes, and some barbed wire. It had been garrisoned off and on since French colonial times. Brown and his thirty-three buddies reinforced a Mobile Strike Force ("Mike" Force) company of 122 Nung tribesmen commanded by Australian Captain John White, assisted by a dozen Australian, American, and Vietnamese officers, enlisted men, and interpreters. Over the following days Captain White was further strengthened by a thirty-five-man CIDG mortar unit, whom the Nungs did not trust. Captain Christopher J. Silva, commanding the Kham Duc camp, helicoptered forward to adjudicate the dispute, only to be caught at Ngok Tavak by the North Vietnamese attack.

Marine Brown and the other men of D/2/13 set up their two guns on the old parade ground outside Ngok Tavak fort and fired a number of times, especially during nights, at likely North Vietnamese road-building sites and places they might assemble for an attack. But ammunition supply was a problem—bad weather restricted helicopter access, so only very limited artillery strikes were conducted, and those were not far-ranging because the guns had to be fired at maximum elevation to clear the tops of surrounding hills and mountains. Then Captain

White asked Lieutenant Adams to move inside the fort, and the marines worked a full day to manhandle the guns into position. The next day, May 10, after midnight, the North Vietnamese hit Ngok Tavak with a full battalion plus extra specialist elements like sappers, who led the attack, blasting through the fort's wire barriers.

In nine minutes North Vietnamese soldiers overran half of Ngok Tavak, driving back the Nung strikers and marines who had to regroup along one wall of the position, losing their cannon in the process. Only the appearance overhead of a gunship—the renowned "Puff the Magic Dragon" AC-47—saved the camp by forcing the North Vietnamese to the ground. After dawn Captain White got more help from fixed-wing aircraft and was able to organize a counterattack that temporarily regained the camp, but without reinforcements he could not hold and instead made preparations to execute a fighting withdrawal. Tim Brown recalls that the North Vietnamese stopped shooting to let three medical evacuation helicopters into the landing zone, but then they opened up when CH-46 choppers tried to land with more Nungs. Two helicopters were shot down, blocking the landing zone, making overland evacuation unavoidable, a retreat possible only because of intense air support.

Of forty-four Americans and Australians, fifteen were dead, twenty-three wounded, and two missing. There were similarly heavy casualties among the Nung and CIDG strikers. The same thing happened to the Kham Duc camp itself over the next few days. Before it was all over the Kham Duc–Ngok Tavak affair accounted for fully five to six Americans missing in action and thirty-two killed whose bodies were never found, the highest ratio of missing for any battle in Vietnam.

Tim Brown suffered only light wounds at Ngok Tavak and went on to other duties in Vietnam, but that action stayed with him long after he left the marines in April 1969. Brown completed college at Southern Methodist University, went to work as a financial analyst for Dun and Bradstreet, and later started and ran several different businesses on his own or with partners. He still wondered what had happened to his marine buddies, and felt especially bad for having had to leave the bodies of the dead, and not having been able to search for the missing, at Ngok Tavak. Partly to feel he was doing something about this, Brown became involved with Vietnam veterans' issues in the early 1980s, eventually becoming active at the local, state, and national levels of Vietnam Veterans of America, Inc. In 1987 he and two others founded

Vietnam Veterans Foundation of Texas, which continues to do charitable, educational, and health work in behalf of vets and their families.

Still Ngok Tavak beckoned. When VVA planned a "Veterans' Initiative" and sent a delegation to Vietnam in 1994, Tim Brown went along and was so persistent in his appeals and requests to be allowed to visit Kham Duc that eventually the Vietnamese gave him a land rover and a guide for the six-hour drive. Kham Duc is a thriving montagnard village today; it has electricity and even some buildings of concrete. At Kham Duc, Brown was able to persuade reluctant village elders to let him go on to Ngok Tavak despite the late hour and impending darkness. Overcome by emotion after climbing halfway up the hill, colleagues went the rest of the way for him and collected soil, also finding artifacts like fragments of a marine flak jacket. Brown and his companions held a memorial service for the dead of both sides at Ngok Tavak, and he was surprised to learn from villagers that the Vietnamese too regard the hill as a sort of holy place, for they suffered many dead there. A month or so before his May 1994 visit, Tim Brown was told, the commander of the North Vietnamese regiment that had gone up against Ngok Tavak and Kham Duc had himself come back on pilgrimage. Perhaps we can ultimately be united, not merely divided, by the Vietnam experience.

 **19**

Victory Through Air Power

In 1914 air enthusiasts dreamed that the airplane could be made a true weapon of war. In 1941 air power theorists believed that aim had been accomplished and set out to show that an enemy nation could be brought to its knees solely or primarily by means of the airplane. Despite a massive postwar investigation in Germany and Japan, the so-called United States Strategic Bombing Survey, the jury remained out on the efficacy of air power, at least in the absence of the atomic bomb, as instrument of total victory. In 1961, in Vietnam, the air power theorists were back, this time with the expectation that Southeast Asia could be made a laboratory for the development of techniques for tactical air warfare. As the Vietnam conflict deepened, so too the promises of the air power theorists broadened and became confident, even proud. By 1965, with President Lyndon Johnson under considerable pressure to approve a program of sustained bombing of North Vietnam, his air marshals were quite confident their weapons would work as advertised. Ten years later Saigon fell to the North Vietnamese and the United States stood, defeated, amid the shambles of the most destructive war in its history. One of the most pernicious of the myths that have grown up in the aftermath of the Vietnam War is the argument that all would have ended differently if only air power had been given a free rein. No review of Vietnam can be complete without considering this matter of air power, and a good place to begin is with an outline history of the air war.

During the early, laboratory phase of the Indochina war, the airplane was merely one more technology played in low key. In the late 1950s the number of U.S. air force (USAF) personnel in South Vietnam and Thailand combined stood at just about one hundred. In South

Vietnam most of the USAF people were trainers or maintenance specialists helping the Vietnamese air force (VNAF) keep its 150 aircraft flying. The VNAF then consisted of a combination of light liaison-type aircraft, twin-engine transports, and propeller-driven trainers and fighter-bombers, almost entirely of World War II vintage. In short, the VNAF constituted a typical Third World air force of the period—an obsolescent armed service of marginal capability.

Of course, the older-type aircraft that mostly made up the Vietnamese air force became immensely more useful in the context of guerrilla warfare, where they seemed more suitable in many respects than modern jets. The first USAF combat unit deployed to South Vietnam, the 4400th Combat Crew Training Squadron, nicknamed "Jungle Jim," operated precisely the same sorts of aircraft and for the same reasons. Jet B-57 bombers were later added to make up the rest of a covert air unit code-named Farm Gate, which comprised the major element of United States air strength in South Vietnam until the 1964–1965 period of large-scale intervention. In fact, the first plane lost in the Vietnam War was of the older type—a C-47, its crew a mixture of air force men and army and CIA psychological warfare experts.

The nature of the early air commitment is notable in comparison with the army's side of the military assistance program, for it is widely acknowledged that the army at that time had focused almost entirely upon building up a Vietnamese army that would be a purely conventional force suited for conventional warfare against an invader, not for a guerrilla conflict. Jungle Jim, in contrast, was an *un*conventional air force, an outgrowth of the so-called air commando concept, pioneered in Burma during World War II for the support of tribal partisan units. Thus the air force and army were preparing for *different wars* in South Vietnam, an early clue to the war's ultimate outcome.

In 1964–1965 the first steps toward intervention were covert, as the army and navy moved to emulate unconventional warfare techniques in their own spheres of activity. The first significant military action, however, was an air strike, the Gulf of Tonkin reprisal carried out by 64 naval aircraft against North Vietnamese naval bases after alleged (and some real) attacks on U.S. navy ships. This early use of air power illustrated the great flexibility and operational dexterity of the airplane, one of the characteristics that earned air power a great role in the Indochina war. Through the fall and winter of 1964 and 1965 there followed a succession of provocations and reprisals, almost a vicious cycle of gradually escalating violence, which led Washington decision-makers to order matching increases in air capabilities. By early 1965, when a real air campaign was initiated, USAF had deployed 222 aircraft and 6,604 airmen to South Vietnam with another 83 planes supported by 2,943 airmen in Thailand. At the same time the navy had three aircraft carriers (the *Coral Sea*, the *Hancock*, and the *Ranger*) off the coast with some 240 more planes available.

The air campaign that began in February 1965, at first called Flaming Dart, ostensibly retaliated for Viet Cong actions in South Vietnam, in particular mortar attacks on U.S. Farm Gate bases at Pleiku and Qui Nhon. At the high command level, however, the air attacks were justified as a gambit to shore up support for the South Vietnamese government, helping to create a modicum of political stability for southern leaders who were then promising a "March North." It is significant that a special requirement for the early Flaming Dart raids was that they be accompanied by parallel strikes from VNAF aircraft. On several occasions when for technical or weather reasons the VNAF planes were unable to participate in strikes, American authorities scrubbed the contemplated missions.

Vietnamese participation was dropped as a mission requirement when the air campaign moved to a new phase of steady strikes no longer contingent upon Viet Cong provocations. This air campaign carried the nickname Rolling Thunder for the assault on the north, the Democratic Republic of Vietnam (DRV), or Barrel Roll where it was aimed against the eastern portion of Laos through which the North Vietnamese were funneling supplies down the Ho Chi Minh Trail. Approval for the first Rolling Thunder raid came on February 18, 1965, and the bombing took place on March 2. After that came a break until March 14, but then a regular bombing program commenced five days later. Through March, 529 attack sorties were mounted against North Vietnam, followed by 1,498 sorties during April, 1,511 in May, 2,307 in June, and 3,162 in July. Thereafter the number never dropped below 3,000 a month until December 1965, when President Johnson ordered a bombing halt in support of a peace initiative he continued through the end of January 1966.

The Rolling Thunder bombing campaign continued under the auspices of the commander-in-chief Pacific (CINCPAC), at that time Admiral Ulysses S. Grant Sharp. Under Sharp both air force and navy units conducted the bombing. The USAF component consisted of the Second Air Division (later the Seventh/Thirteenth Air Force) with headquarters in Saigon. The navy component was Task Force 77 stationed in the Gulf of Tonkin. The aircraft carriers of this unit assumed a southerly position, called "Dixie Station," when they intended to strike targets in South Vietnam, and a northern position, "Yankee Station," when the targets were located in the DRV. Rather than exercising strong positive command, Admiral Sharp left control of operations in the hands of his subordinate commanders, which resulted in some overlap and duplication, and in a degree of confusion until December 1965 when the air force and navy made an administrative agreement to divide DRV territory into a number of "route packages," assigning each package to one of the services.

As the Rolling Thunder and Barrel Roll air campaigns proceeded, qualitative as well as quantitative changes were made in the program. The first mission approvals from Washington were quite specific—in the initial strikes, a one-day attack on two fixed targets. By the fall of 1965 programs were being approved for two-week periods including up to 1,200 sorties at a time. The total sorties then flown in Rolling Thunder alone stood at more than 19,000. A year later program approvals came at monthly intervals. Rolling Thunder 51 provided for a level of 10,000 sorties a month, Rolling Thunder 52 for 13,500. Actual numbers of sorties flown, usually lower due to weather and maintenance factors, nonetheless stood at more than 5,000 a month.

The air campaign had important qualitative elements as well. Targets embodied in the strike plans were selected from target lists approved by the Joint Chiefs of Staff and submitted to the president. Such lists had existed even before the inception of Rolling Thunder and represented the compendium of targets thought to be significant. As the campaign continued and more and more targets came under attack, the target list expanded to include more facilities and locations of lesser military importance. The length of the target list became a continuing subject of policy debates at the command level.

Another qualitative aspect of the bombing program, the existence of so-called sanctuaries, also constantly affected command decisions on the air campaign. Very early in Rolling Thunder, President Johnson established circles around the major North Vietnamese cities of Hanoi and Haiphong, within which any air strike required his special sanction. Johnson also created a similar buffer zone along the DRV's border with the People's Republic of China.

Yet a third qualitative limitation on the air campaign concerned means of destruction. Certain *types* of munitions were ruled out (such as nuclear weapons) or were not permitted except with special approval that was normally not given (such as mines). On the other hand, a wide variety of aerial munitions were available, and operational commanders were free to choose the means with which to strike a target.

Finally, there were restrictions as to the type of target that could be attacked, even within the approved target list. For example, North Vietnamese oil installations (in military jargon called Petroleum-Oil-Lubricants, or POL) were kept off the strike list until mid-1966. Through that year the U.S. command engaged in an intense debate over whether to attack Hanoi's POL, with Secretary of Defense McNamara opposing the move while Admiral Sharp, the Joint Chiefs of Staff, and national security adviser Walt Rostow all favored it. Rostow in particular, who had been an analyst of bombing in Europe for the OSS and Eighth Air Force during World War II, pressed strongly for the president to approve this course. At length he did so. The Rolling Thunder 50-Alpha program, approved on June 24, 1966, provided for a range of POL strikes that were rapidly carried out. Within two weeks of the start of this phase of Rolling Thunder, Rostow was telling President Johnson that targets representing 86 percent of the DRV's POL storage capacity had been attacked and an estimated 57 percent of that capacity destroyed. Nevertheless this achievement, plus continued attacks under the Rolling Thunder 52 program, had no discernible impact on Viet Cong or North Vietnamese combat performance in South Vietnam.

The POL campaign of 1966 is a good example of the air theorists' enthusiasm for panaceas. Time and again extravagant claims were made for the efficacy of using certain techniques or attacking certain types of targets. Armed reconnaissance, for example, was supposed to catch North Vietnamese truck traffic, forcing the supply flow down the Ho Chi Minh Trail to grind to a halt. This was not some latter-day notion but a conscious goal from the earliest days of Rolling Thunder—accounting for roughly two-thirds of the sorties during the campaign's first six months. Official claims for 1966 include 4,084 trucks destroyed or damaged, another 5,587 in 1967, plus an additional 4,704 vehicles destroyed or damaged over the first three months of 1968. During this period railroad yards were destroyed 13 times and damaged on 301 occasions, and there were claims of 2,311 railroad cars destroyed and 2,862 damaged. By late 1967 armed reconnaissance missions consumed fully 90 percent of the attack sorties flown outside South Vietnam.

Again this level of destruction occurred without apparent effect on combat in the south. Events proved positively embarrassing at the Pentagon, where the Defense Intelligence Agency kept a computerized count of the DRV's estimated truck inventory. According to one officer who held the DIA's North Vietnam desk during this period, the inventory number dropped to zero at least *seven or eight times* during his tenure there. Each time the Joint Chiefs wanted to know why we were still seeing trucks in the DRV. The Joint Staff J-3 section, which worked directly for the JCS, refused to accept any explanation that questioned the accuracy of pilot reporting.

Armed reconnaissance and POL were just two of the panaceas that were supposed to lead to victory through air power. Other suggestions included striking the DRV's electric plants, mining its ports and waterways, blowing up North Vietnamese bridges, and bombing the dikes and dams that protected its agricultural land from flooding. Except for the last, every one of these measures was included in the Linebacker air campaign of 1972 which was designed to blunt a North Vietnamese conventional offensive in the south. In 1972, however, it was a toss-up whether the true effects were not the product of strikes in South Vietnam rather than in the north. Moreover, the controlling factor in the impact of air power in 1972 seems to have been that the North Vietnamese Army was *more vulnerable* during that year. That is, Hanoi's shift to a pattern of conventional combat operations made the NVA's lines of supply, and especially its petroleum stocks and pipelines, much more crucial to its combat capability. Had identical air assets and techniques been applied against the guerrilla and semiregular adversary during 1965–1968, air power's impact would not likely have been any greater than in fact it was.

Political and *diplomatic* conditions applied during 1965–1968 made a 1972-style air campaign impossible during the earlier phase of the war. President Johnson was actively concerned about the danger of Chinese and Soviet intervention during his stewardship of the war, and there was no reason to risk a superpower conflict in Southeast Asia with an air campaign *he* intended as a tool of coercive diplomacy. Richard Nixon benefited from his own prior overtures to China and Russia, which in 1972 gave him the ability to order a maximum air offensive without worrying about outside intervention. Earlier, in 1969, Nixon had specifically considered but ultimately rejected the same option of a go-for-broke air offensive.

Meanwhile, Rolling Thunder rolled on, limited by its deficiencies in some respects but still a display of enormous combat power. The North Vietnamese Army, though not crippled by the incessant bombing, was not immune to American air power. Cadres and reinforcement cohorts, who spent a month or two on the Ho Chi Minh Trail wending their way south, developed a healthy respect for the American fighter-bombers, especially the B-52 heavy bombers that struck from above the clouds. These too were active in the southern portion of the DRV, the North Vietnamese panhandle, most notably the Demilitarized Zone.

What success the air campaign had has led some, notably the air enthusiasts, to claim that it should have had even more, and to blame Washington for the failure. Lyndon Johnson's micromanagement, the argument runs in one version, or Robert McNamara's steadfast opposition to the views of the Joint Chiefs of Staff in another, were primarily responsible for the shortcomings of the air campaign. Admiral Sharp has been a major proponent of this opinion, noting that he "strongly" shared the feeling that "civilian politico decision makers have no business ignoring or overriding the counsel of experienced military professionals in presuming to direct the day-to-day conduct of military strategy." Sharp concedes having been "harsh in my judgment of those civilian, political decision makers who chose out of flagrant arrogance or naive wishful thinking to ignore the sound, time-vindicated principles of military strategy in their direction of the Vietnam air war." Even in the midst of the war, in a summer 1968 report published just a few months after the end of Rolling Thunder, Sharp advanced the view that "there was no doubt that our past efforts had hurt North Vietnam and that continued support of the war in South Vietnam was causing severe hardships. From a purely military view, additional operational latitude for air and naval forces would have enabled the execution of campaigns against North Vietnam which would have brought about a more rapid deterioration of the enemy's total war-supporting structure."

Admiral Sharp's strident critique of the air war has received a far more sympathetic reception than warranted by its superficial analysis. In the first place, this argument assumes the existence of immutable and well-recognized principles of air strategy. The whole history of strategic bombing in World War II demonstrates otherwise. Far from adhering to immutable principles, generals were seizing upon targeting panaceas, whether city bombardment, attrition of the aircraft force, railroad bombardment, industrial strike, or POL, one panacea that had its start in 1944–1945 when it was credited with bringing the German war machine to a halt. After the war, another war in Korea again failed to demonstrate that air power could by itself (utilizing nonnuclear weapons) paralyze the communications of the adversary on the battlefront. To others, the air theorists' vision of immutable strategic principles seemed no better than one of many aspects of technique.

Implicit in the assumption of principles of air strategy is that the specific plans for air war against North Vietnam reflected the one and correct strategy. In fact this was never the case. Even within the military, for example, the *army* had a different vision of air strategy than did the services executing Rolling Thunder. This disparate view formed the basis for the strategy contained in the Joint Staff ad hoc study group concept of operations for Vietnam, elaborated in mid-1965 when American combat troops were first being committed to the war in significant numbers. The concept was not one of directly defeating the adversary through air attack, as the air theorists supposed could be done at a sufficient level of violence, but using air attacks and interdiction of North Vietnamese supply lines to raise the cost to the DRV of supporting the conflict in the south. Ground combat by itself, as Vietnam veteran Larry Cable argues convincingly in his study *Unholy Grail*, could be used to raise the expenditure of men and equipment by the Viet Cong and North Vietnamese to a level at which the air campaign would really begin to affect them. Robert McNamara happened to agree with this view of Vietnam strategy rather than the one espoused by Admiral Sharp. Holding such a view did not in itself make Secretary McNamara naive or flagrantly arrogant, any more than Admiral Sharp's views endowed him with the same attributes.

The air war critique is pernicious both because it assumes that micromanagement from the White House governed the air campaign, and because it assumes that such micromanagement as may have existed was necessarily bad. The truth in both these matters lies elsewhere. First, micromanagement from the White House was President Johnson's *right* as commander-in-chief of the U.S. armed forces. The Constitution makes it exactly that way. LBJ, however, did not choose to exercise that right in quite the fashion critics often imply. The image they convey is of a crafty and conniving president, huddled over a plotting board, approving one proposed bombing mission, rejecting another, almost like Adolf Hitler in his bunker pushing pins around on a map of the Russian front. In fact, President Johnson rode close herd like this only on the very first installments of Rolling Thunder. In February and March 1965 such attention to detail was entirely appropriate.

A year later LBJ had neither the time nor the inclination for the kind of micromanagement portrayed by the critics. During 1966 American aircraft flew 81,000 attack and 48,000 combat support sorties against the DRV, plus 48,000 attack and 10,000 support sorties in the Laotian panhandle. As a practical matter there was no way for the White House to command such a campaign *except* by the general periodic approvals and series program approvals that LBJ in fact gave. The president gave specific consideration to *qualitative* changes—whether or not to approve a POL plan, whether or not to have a bombing halt, whether or not to increase or eliminate the sanctuaries surrounding Hanoi and Haiphong—but he did not micromanage the program. He behaved intelligently as a strategic commander.

The periodic program approvals ensured President Johnson the means to see that his strategic directives were being observed, and to make sure that certain specifics he marked for inclusion or exclusion were being executed. Moreover, the device of periodic program approvals was *exactly the same* means used by the Pentagon and the CIA in administering the strategic reconnaissance program, or the navy the naval deployment and exercise program, or other features of U.S. military activity. This device had not been initiated by Lyndon Johnson. To accuse him of micromanagement for using it smacks of gross indifference to the president's particular needs.

Nor is it accurate to claim that there was no high-level management of the air campaign in the comparative case, the Persian Gulf War. In that war the air attacks against the Iraqi capital of Baghdad are highly instructive. Due to Iraqi subterfuge, an error in target identification, or both, one of the Baghdad strikes hit a suspected command bunker which turned out to be a crowded civilian bomb shelter, producing heavy loss of life and embarrassment for the United States. In fact, bombers struck twenty-five downtown Baghdad targets in the weeks before the bunker attack, and just five such targets through the remainder of the war. For four days immediately following the bunker strike no air attacks were permitted on Baghdad. These restrictions originated in Washington and outside the air force, according to several serving officers.

In Vietnam, so-called micromanagement was not forthcoming from the one place it ought to have been—the CINCPAC headquarters of Admiral Sharp. Rather than exercising a strong leadership role as the theater commander responsible for the air war, Sharp left the conduct of operations to his subordinates. CINCPAC acted as an interface between local commanders and Washington, and an adjudicator for the internecine squabbles of component commanders. Sharp advocated his preferred strategy to Washington, but that merely preached to the choir of the Joint Chiefs, who also believed in an unrestricted air campaign and in late 1966 warned of an "aerial Dien Bien Phu" if their advice was not taken. It was not, but no Dien Bien Phu happened. Perhaps that indicates the validity of the strategic visions held by JCS and CINCPAC. Sharp does not seem to have been an admiral in the style of Chester W. Nimitz, bravely seizing the moment for command decision, or a theater commander like Eisenhower, delicately balancing the competing interests of sensitive national contingents. Sharp seems more in the style of Civil War theater commander Henry W. Halleck, blustering from the sidelines in the catbird seat.

Whatever the degree of White House micromanagement, could it have been justified? That depends upon U.S. intentions and the goals of the air campaign. If Vietnam had been World War II, with the objective to deal a knockout blow to the adversary's industrial economy, perhaps it would have been less appropriate for civilian leaders to question military opinions. But this was Vietnam; the DRV's was an agricultural economy, a subsistence one at that, and the United States pursued an air campaign in the midst of a guerrilla war against the guerrilla enemy. No one had ever fought a war like that before; neither Admiral Sharp nor the Joint Chiefs nor their various operational commanders knew any more about strategy in this context than Lyndon Johnson himself. To put a point on this, one could argue that with his acute political awareness LBJ had a *better* feeling for strategy in this profoundly political war than did his generals.

Another aspect of the air power question concerns the technical nature of the campaign's objectives. Admiral Sharp's criticism is misleading in implying that the U.S. intention was to wage an air offensive à la World War II. That was never the design of the air campaign. Rolling Thunder always had goals that were explicitly *political* in nature. It was supposed to encourage the DRV to go to the negotiating table while raising the price to Hanoi for continuing the war during the interval. If one accepts the goals advanced in March 1965 by Assistant Secretary of Defense John T. McNaughton, the air campaign really had very little to do with North Vietnam. McNaughton's formulation was that U.S. aims were:

70 percent—To avoid a humiliating U.S. defeat (to our reputation as a guarantor).

20 percent—To keep SVN (and the adjacent) territory from Chinese hands.

10 percent—To permit the people of SVN to enjoy a better, freer way of life.

ALSO—To emerge from crisis without unacceptable taint from methods used.

NOT—to "help a friend," although it would be hard to stay if asked out.

Whatever may be said of the rest of McNaughton's rationale, President Johnson agreed with the notion that the United States ought to come out of Vietnam without taint from the methods it had used. Barry Goldwater adopted the rhetoric of unlimited force in his race for the 1964 presidential election. Lyndon Johnson had won that election using the language of restraint. It was not realistic to have expected the president to wage an unrestricted air war.

A related point concerns the use of an air campaign as a diplomatic tool. The whole theory of limited war and coercive diplomacy, which lay at the heart of Vietnam air strategy, *necessarily required restraints.* That is, it was not possible to send a signal through bombing *except* by means of ordering changes in the level of violence, the kinds or locations of targets, the types of weapons used, and so forth. In order to *have* a diplomatic function, the changes ordered *had* to be discernible to the adversary; they could not be so subtle that the signal was lost. Thus, for example, LBJ could order or withhold air strikes within the Hanoi and Haiphong "no strike" zones, and that action would send a definite message to the North Vietnamese. Eliminating those zones would have comforted Admiral Sharp, and perhaps improved the efficiency of Rolling Thunder, but it would have vitiated the diplomatic function of the air campaign. The fact is that the president ordered air strikes against sanctuary targets on numerous occasions, so we are not simply talking about a mindless restriction imposed by the White House. Rather, Johnson tailored his military strategy to his diplomatic approach. Observers who care to investigate will discover many instances in which specific bombing restrictions were directly linked with peace initiatives in progress. Admiral Sharp's complaints are understandable, but they reflect the narrower vision of a military specialist.

Finally, it is worth asking whether the air campaign restrictions had any positive benefit for the American military. A more detailed review of data would be necessary to answer this question definitively, but a prima facie argument can be made that air restrictions had at least some benefits. Naturally the North Vietnamese built up their air defenses once the bombing began, ultimately achieving the thickest air defense network since the Ruhr in World War II, with more than 8,000 antiaircraft guns, 25 surface-to-air missile battalions, and about 250 interceptor aircraft. The DRV's air bases and a considerable portion of their most sophisticated defenses were concentrated in the Hanoi-Haiphong area. Thus restrictions on strikes in this area helped limit U.S. air losses. Considering that the air force logged by far the highest total of Americans missing in action in Indochina (722 by December 1972, with another 138 navy that can be added), and that the majority of these were lost over North Vietnam, one can well imagine that the American MIA problem today would be even sharper had restrictions been lifted in the air campaign.

In *The Limits of Air Power,* a detailed examination of Rolling Thunder, Mark Clodfelter points to an important factor that helped determine the thinking of air force officers—their training at the (pre–World War II) Air Corps Tactical School. This training was based largely on the strategic warfare theories of such air enthusiasts as Billy Mitchell and Giulio Douhet. No doubt these theories influenced officers who had become senior air force generals by the time of Vietnam, but it does less to explain the acceptance of similar thinking by naval officers like Admiral Sharp, whose World War II experience had been quintessentially in air power as a tactical and operational instrument.

Clodfelter also argues that Rolling Thunder was limited by what he terms Lyndon Johnson's "negative objectives"—preventing a third world war and keeping both domestic and international opinion focused elsewhere than Vietnam. The 1972 bombing called Linebacker is seen as effective because Richard Nixon supposedly did not have such negative objectives behind his air campaign (and because the North Vietnamese had shifted to a pattern of conventional ground operations). This particular argument is something of an intellectual construct. For LBJ, bombing North Vietnam in fact encouraged Soviet and Chinese participation, both to replace assets destroyed by Rolling Thunder and to help man the DRV's air defenses. It was constantly at the back of the president's mind that if he escalated too far, he would bring the Communist powers in openly for a larger war; but this is scarcely the same as pursuing a "negative objective." As for Richard Nixon, the 1972 strategy most assuredly did have equivalent negative objectives—avoiding domestic political backlash in the midst of an election campaign—and part of the reason for his selection of air power as the instrument of intervention was precisely because it was seen as the least costly option in political terms. Again, the reason for the relative success of bombing in 1972 comes back to the differences in North Vietnamese military practice, not to an improvement in the nature of air war strategy.

Despite all the arguments about target lists and strategy, the way the air war ended reveals most dramatically its true nature as a diplomatic tool. For the fact is that Lyndon Johnson simply called off the air war, just as he had ordered bombing pauses a half-dozen times before, to create an opening for diplomacy. His order came on March 31, 1968, when he simultaneously withdrew from that year's presidential election. Disgruntled generals and admirals have never forgiven the president his decision, but they seem to have forgotten the purpose of the air war, not to mention the president's prerogative to make the decision that he did.

By the end of March 1968 tactical aircraft had flown approximately 304,000 sorties in Rolling Thunder and B-52s another 2,380. North Vietnam shuddered under the impact of 643,000 tons of bombs, while the Barrel Roll area of Laos had been struck by about 220,000 tons more, with a further 45,000 tons of ordnance dropped on northern Laos. Roughly 500 aircraft had been lost to North Vietnamese defenses, including 46 to missiles and 11 to aircraft. American planes had downed 124 DRV aircraft (a further 71 North Vietnamese and 22 American planes were lost in the Linebacker campaign).

The weight of ordnance expended during this "restricted" air campaign (not counting the 1972 bombing, which was even more destructive) was about a third greater than the total tonnage of bombs dropped in the *entire* Pacific Theater in World War II, including both the strategic bombing of Japan and the atomic bombs dropped on Hiroshima and Nagasaki. There must have been something wrong with the air war strategy other than the restrictions placed upon it. Left to another war in another time and place was the air enthusiasts' dream of proving their arm the sole decisive weapon of warfare.

The failure of air strategy left the war managers with that perennial Vietnam conundrum, finding an effective way to blunt the enemy's main effort. Some felt the North Vietnamese themselves could provide the solution, that interception of NVA and VC radio transmissions would furnish the knowledge necessary to meet and smash the enemy on the ground. This story is another hidden facet of the Vietnam War.

20 **Spooks in the Ether**

In the same way that many veterans believe the part of the Vietnam War they saw has to be the authentic one, there were indeed many Vietnam wars. In some cases the rivalries that existed, say between front-line infantry and support troops helping to keep them in the field, hinged precisely upon ignorance of the others' real contribution to the war effort. The war of the line-doggies, of the bombers and big battalions, was obvious. A level beneath that was the secret war of covert operations. There was another war too, even more secret than the covert one, a war of radio waves that took place entirely in the air, where victories and defeats were gained by men and women hunched over hot electronic components or tables of figures and charts. For a time, at the dawn of the war, some senior policymakers believed that the combatants in this war of the ether would decide the victors in the battle of the bombers and big battalions. This is the story of the spooks in the ether.

One mainstay of the French war in Vietnam had been their Radio Technical Service, a unit which despite its name had nothing to do with radio technical support other than what was required to use the air waves to intercept Viet Minh communications. The French had broken the Viet Minh logistics code as well as other operational codes at various times during the first Indochina war. One of the reasons for French overconfidence heading into the battle of Dien Bien Phu was precisely that their intelligence would know everything the adversary was up to. Things did not work out that way, of course; it was the French who were ultimately defeated, forced to leave Vietnam. They took their communications intelligence organization with them, including most of its equipment.

The infant Army of the Republic of Vietnam (ARVN) had grown from French colonial roots and was well aware of the capability the radio service had provided the French Expeditionary Corps. But they began with nothing more than three old, cranky, and hard-to-fix radio direction finder (RDF) units. In April 1957 the Vietnamese created their own radio intelligence service, calling it the Technical Study Center. This center was commanded by a lieutenant, had just sixty-five persons assigned to it, and opened radio listening posts at Saigon and Da Nang. President Diem followed in 1958 by asking United States assistance for its radio intelligence efforts.

President Eisenhower refused Diem on radio intelligence help. Washington feared compromise of the top-secret code-breaking techniques of its National Security Agency, notwithstanding the fact that the U.S. was actively helping the Vietnamese military in other respects. Diem renewed his request in early 1960 when he sent an emissary to a political officer of the U.S. embassy, this time asking for little more than equipment. That August the U.S. replied in the affirmative, and the war in the ether escalated.

When John Kennedy assumed the presidency, the communications intelligence (COMINT) program was little further along than the previous summer. President Kennedy was looking for ways to galvanize the South Vietnamese, and one of the recognized problems ARVN had was poor combat intelligence. A sophisticated COMINT capability might well be the answer, or at least part of it. This time the idea was not just U.S. equipment but an actual American COMINT unit. The idea became one of a menu of recommendations considered by a panel of senior policymakers headed by Deputy Secretary of Defense Roswell Gilpatric. The Gilpatric group reported on April 27, 1961, and two days later Kennedy discussed its recommendations with his senior advisers on the National Security Council. He approved the program, including the proposed COMINT unit, and directed that there be no public acknowledgment of any part of the new program, which also included Green Berets, the air force "Jungle Jim" unit, and other exotic measures. Apparently because of its top-secret treatment, the Gilpatric committee program received its formal approval in a memorandum from Secretary of Defense Robert S. McNamara; it was never consecrated by a National Security Council directive.

The Gilpatric committee program led swiftly to consideration of a Vietnam initiative at the United States Intelligence Board (USIB). The board, then headed by Allen W. Dulles, was the chief authority over all American intelligence programs, and USIB had previously been a key obstacle in the provision of COMINT assistance to South Vietnam. This time the USIB approved two new projects, codenamed Whitebirch and Sabertooth, one to provide Vietnam with help on communications intelligence, the other for communications security (COMSEC). Whitebirch was authorized three officers and seventy-four enlisted men, Sabertooth one officer, two warrant officers, and a dozen men. The unit arrived at Saigon, where it was constituted as the 400th Operations Unit (Provisional) of the United States Army Security Agency, with the cover identity of Third Radio Research Unit (RRU). The code-breakers set up shop in a heavily guarded compound at Tan Son Nhut airfield.

Not long afterward a Third RRU man became the first American soldier killed in action in South Vietnam. That happened on December 22, 1961, when Specialist-4 James T. Davis with an ARVN mobile radio direction finding team was ambushed by Viet Cong. Davis's truck was blown off the road by a mine, after which the American and his ARVN companions were killed by the ambushers.

Getting the drop on the Viet Cong turned out to be more difficult than anyone had imagined. Augmentation of the Third RRU naturally followed, and in January 1962 it was authorized to expand to 25 officers and warrants and 358 enlisted personnel. The real problem, as the American code-breakers were not yet aware, was that there was not much Viet Cong radio traffic to intercept. For example, the key North Vietnamese intelligence organization, called the Research Bureau, maintained its agent networks in the south with minimal use of radios. Radios were assigned to the nets, but for the most part these were simple transistor radios, such as Japanese models that could be bought anywhere. The operators' only function was to listen to Hanoi broadcasts at certain times and dates and copy down Morse code messages to be passed along to the agents, who would know their meaning. The agents' own messages were given to couriers, preventing the network from ever being compromised by radio transmissions. Only in a dire emergency or with a highly urgent message would Research Bureau nets actually broadcast messages, and then they would pass these along to operators of a few clandestine transmitters maintained in South Vietnam for this purpose.

These kinds of organizational security measures to a great extent compensated for Hanoi's inability to protect its radio traffic with sophisticated equipment or codes. In both these departments North Vietnamese and Viet Cong capabilities were strictly limited. For example, although the North Vietnamese Army considers it was created as early as 1944, was active in 1945, and had fought against the French beginning in December 1947, it was not until June 1950 that the merger of smaller units created the NVA General Staff Cryptographic Bureau. The codes used were standardized only within relatively small entities, such as regions or single army divisions, and all were substitution codes. Some of the better ones split words in two, three, or four parts for more involved encoding, but there was nothing resembling the machine encryption devices common in the U.S. military, and there would not be such sophistication in Hanoi's methods right through the war with the Americans. The basic code used in the early 1960s was a development of one innovated by the Cryptographic Bureau as early as 1951. Similarly, radio equipment was a hodgepodge of French, Chinese, Russian, Japanese, and American gear, hard to keep spare parts for, and relatively primitive. Channel switching, frequency seekers, and secure voice devices were unknown to North Vietnamese practice until late in the American war, when military aid and the simple theft of American equipment made more advanced radios available.

The North Vietnamese were wise to focus upon the kinds of security measures they could safely implement. One was their careful separation of communications personnel, not only from agents but also from encoding and decoding personnel. The various specialists were not only separated on duty but forbidden to associate when not working. In May 1961 Hanoi sent two infiltration groups into the south composed entirely of code cadres; in a sense their move to increase COMSEC matched the American commitment of a new communications intelligence unit.

Without doubt the United States had the capability to increase its COMINT effort more rapidly than North Vietnam's. The increase was visible in terms of personnel and units. By June 1964—just before the incidents in the Gulf of Tonkin—the Third RRU was fielding 43 officers and 543 enlisted men. There was also an independent Detachment J of the RRU with another 270 officers and men plus 10 Vietnamese personnel; a detachment of the marines' First Composite Radio Company with 48 officers and men; and the Seventh RRU, committed in September 1962, with another 37 personnel. Given that the North Vietnamese committed two communications battalions to operate their entire radio net along the Ho Chi Minh Trail, the number of Americans working against NVA communications must have matched pretty closely the strength of the *entire* opposing organization.

Meanwhile, the South Vietnamese were building their own radio intelligence capacity as well. The offensive radio effort (COMINT) was concentrated in 1963 in an entity called Unit 15, while the so-called First Radio Control Unit formed to handle COMSEC. Continuing problems existed in that the ARVN units were forced to compete for scarce radio operators with all other South Vietnamese communications users, and, unlike American practice, ARVN radio intelligence operators were not awarded extra pay or any other distinction. Competition for limited amounts of equipment existed as well. Nevertheless there was progress, and Unit 15 went into the field beginning in October 1962 with forward bases at Da Nang, Nha Trang, Pleiku, and Ban Me Thuot.

■ Regardless of growing pains and drawbacks, communications intelligence scored real successes. General Nguyen Khanh recounts that in early 1964 his radio intelligence, presumably Unit 15, was able to establish the location of a key Viet Cong command post—it may have been the headquarters of Military Region 5. General Khanh mounted a lightning operation, dropping ARVN paratroops on the site and surprising the Viet Cong, most of whom barely had time to escape. The South Vietnamese captured the command's senior doctor but, more important, a radio set and a complete set of code charts. The Vietnamese photographed this material, then left it exactly as it had been, hoping the Viet Cong would think ARVN had missed this installation. The VC reportedly went on using those codes for months.

Meanwhile, North Vietnam, still dependent upon primitive communications networks, nonetheless created certain problems for the COMINT experts of the Americans and South Vietnamese. Seven thousand miles of French open-wire telephone lines predominated in the north, which also had an old civil radio net. Foreign aid, by this point in the war, had yielded little more than some radio-telegraph equipment used by the Communist party, the military, and police units, and a three-thousand-line automatic telephone switchboard promptly installed at Hanoi. The phone lines did not produce emissions that could be intercepted at long range. This became an advantage in tactical combat in the south when NVA forces used only runners and telephone for their unit-level tactical nets. Radio served only to communicate with higher headquarters, and those contacts were made strictly upon a time and frequency schedule, after which both emitters would again go silent. These techniques severely limited the volume of traffic accessible to American COMINT receivers, though "limited" is a relative term. In 1965, for example, the number of messages handled daily by the headquarters of North Vietnamese Military Region 4, which covered the panhandle area just above the Demilitarized Zone, averaged about 200. As North Vietnamese and Viet Cong troop levels rose, the need for rapid communication, faster than that possible by courier or telephone, inevitably grew enormously. By 1966 Hanoi perceived enough of a problem with its communications security that the General Staff issued a special directive setting COMSEC standards. The army also held a conference of cryptographic experts in an effort to improve the security program. That year the General Staff handled 1,982,225 secret messages; Military Region 4 itself sent or received another 274,708. Clearly there was a potential for compromise of secret information.

What was true for the North Vietnamese was so in spades for the Americans, who were used to radio at every level and for virtually every purpose, and who had radio transmitters much more widely distributed among their forces than the NVA. As a test of friendly COMSEC, the Seventh RRU furnished a monitoring team that augmented the radio research company assigned to the First Cavalry Division (Airmobile) soon after that unit arrived in South Vietnam. The idea was to listen in on friendly transmissions and see how much the Viet Cong or NVA could have learned from them. The radiomen monitored 10,902 transmissions over a three-week period as the "Cav" made its initial deployments, and found little concern for security precautions, compromise of net frequencies and call signs by sending them in the clear, and hardly any use of preplanned authentication systems. The COMSEC specialists recommended improvements, but shortly afterward the First Cavalry became embroiled in the fierce battle of the Ia Drang Valley. During that engagement COMSEC teams went on to listen to 28,023 more radio transmissions. They found that security was almost completely ignored in the heat of battle: the only codes ever used were unauthorized, homemade ones easily broken by the NVA; actual army codes and encryption devices were never used in practice. The Ia Drang battle alarmed National Security Agency officials and impelled the NSA and military contractors to design new equipment to scramble the sound of a voice on the radio, so-called secure voice transmission.

These kinds of lapses made it easy for North Vietnamese and Viet Cong operators to pick up detailed pictures of the opposing forces and data on upcoming attacks, even an ability to come up on American radio nets with false messages, calling off attacks or artillery bombardments. When the signals officer of the First Cavalry tried to change all the division's radio call signs in the midst of the battle to restore security, the attempt caused so much confusion among Cav units that the change was called off in order to restore combat effectiveness.

Both sides could play at the radio deception game, as Major General William E. DePuy's First Infantry Division demonstrated north of Saigon in the summer of 1966. DePuy's intelligence officer had initiated an effort to achieve close coordination with the RRU supporting the division, in this case the 337th Army Security Agency (USASA) Company. Learning that the opposing VC Ninth Division was on the move, DePuy had messages sent over the radio to the effect that a weak troop of armored cavalry would be on the Minh Thanh Road at a certain time. In actuality, four infantry battalions with plenty of artillery were poised to spring a trap. The resulting battle of the Minh Thanh Road in July 1966 ended with more than three hundred dead Viet Cong counted on the battlefield.

The battle of the ether rocked back and forth as troops of both sides fought it out on the ground. North Vietnamese interception efforts were hampered at first by their primitive radio equipment—at one point more than two dozen different types of radios were being used in field units—equipment largely not compatible with the AN/PRC-25 radios employed by American tactical communications nets. Here VC agents came in handy, stealing PRC-25 sets whenever possible anywhere in South Vietnam. First priority went to North Vietnamese COMINT units, but by 1969 the NVA had captured so many PRC-25 sets that this equipment was becoming standard in North Vietnamese combat units. The Americans then took a step lead by introducing the AN/PRC-77, the long-awaited secure voice radio. In any case, deception was common throughout this period. Instances of the NVA entering U.S. or South Vietnamese radio nets with deceptive imitation messages, in the northernmost provinces alone, averaged ten a month during the first four months of 1967.

Meanwhile, American radio spooks inaugurated a new effort to permit instant tactical exploitation of intercepted messages, an effort to repeat successes like that on the Minh Thanh Road. Project Dancer was the program, and it involved putting Vietnamese nationals to work alongside the radio operators to supply instant translations that could be passed to field units as intelligence. Later Project Dancer expanded to the air, and Vietnamese flew planes with American intercept operators. Dancer involved significant security risks because the Vietnamese nationals, if they were VC spies, would be getting very close to some of the most highly secret equipment and techniques imaginable. The extra precautions taken to enhance security, such as investigating recruits and isolating their working spaces, retarded expansion of the program and, daily, slowed the rate at which intelligence could be passed to combat forces. Thomas Ferguson, an intelligence officer with the Twenty-fifth Infantry Division, which worked with the 372nd USASA Company at Cu Chi, complained that Saigon's review ("sanitization") of data collected this way robbed it of timeliness. Ferguson also argued that with the number of troops Cu Chi could send into the field and the small size of typical VC units, the Viet Cong usually had to move only a half-mile or so before a sweep operation would miss them. Moves of that length could be made in the time necessary for a message to be sent from Cu Chi to Saigon and back, not including what 509th USASA Operations Group, the overall COMINT command, would need to decide how to reply.

At the strategic level the spooks of the ether could contribute to intelligence appreciations of the enemy's intentions and capabilities. A most notable instance of this occurred in late 1967 and early 1968, in the months before the Tet offensive. At that time the North Vietnamese brought two new infantry divisions down the Ho Chi Minh Trail to take part in the war, and they also redeployed forces to threaten the American combat base at Khe Sanh. Radio intercepts revealed some of these troop movements and helped alert General Westmoreland to the NVA maneuvers. It is too much to assert, however, as is sometimes claimed, that COMINT predicted the Tet offensive. Rather, the radio spooks added data that helped Westmoreland fix his focus upon Khe Sanh. As intercepts indicated threats to other South Vietnamese targets, particularly the cities and towns, the intelligence prediction shifted only to something that might be called "Khe Sanh–Plus," *not* to any expectation of a countrywide offensive without Khe Sanh. A report circulated by the National Security Agency on January 25, 1968, is said to have warned that points throughout South Vietnam were threatened. But a member of the CIA's Office of the Special Assistant for Vietnam Affairs who saw this report construes it differently. Agreeing that the NSA report observed an "almost unprecedented volume of urgent messages . . . passing among major commands," the CIA officer notes that the document merely termed as "possibly related activity" what it could pick up in the area of Saigon and southernmost South Vietnam. This scarcely constitutes an explicit prediction of Tet.

Then the Tet attacks began, with intensity seldom before seen in the war. The radio spooks did not escape North Vietnamese attention. At

Phi Bai, location of the 1,076-man Eighth RRU, the radio intelligence compound was the target of a rocket bombardment late in the afternoon, just before the main attacks—apparently an attempt to short-circuit COMINT observation of NVA activity during the offensive. Fifteen heavy rockets hit the compound but missed all the key targets. Instead the rockets completely demolished the bachelor officers' quarters, but no one was hurt.

Tet was also the occasion for acts that resulted in the award of a Legion of Merit medal to Private First Class Edward W. Minnock, Jr., who became the only enlisted soldier ever given this honor. Minnock was an analyst of COMINT intercepts with the 404th Radio Research Detachment, working alongside the 173rd Airborne Brigade in central Vietnam. Having earlier supplied valuable intelligence during the November 1967 battle of Dak To, this time Minnock helped in the defense of An Khe and Tuy Hoa, and a couple of months later explicitly warned of a planned NVA attack against Tuy Hoa in time for this to be broken up in defeat.

Managing the many activities of Tet no doubt forced the North Vietnamese to unprecedented levels of radio traffic. One Hanoi publication notes that the number of messages handled by the General Staff Cryptologic Directorate rose from the previous average of five thousand per month to a new peak of thirteen thousand. With all those messages there was more to intercept and more possibilities for radio direction finding (RDF). At the height of this period, just before Tet proper, when Westmoreland thought he was fighting a battle of Khe Sanh, the RDF specialists tentatively identified a senior NVA headquarters in Laos. Some insisted it was the main NVA command and that General Vo Nguyen Giap himself was there (certain intercepts apparently indicated that Giap had left Hanoi for the south). Westmoreland ordered the cave location plastered by a massive B-52 raid—almost nine hundred tons of bombs dropped in two waves. Although several accounts date this raid on January 29, 1968, Westmoreland actually reported its results to Ambassador Ellsworth Bunker at a meeting on January 24. In any case, Giap was not at the command center, and the bombing did not stop Tet. But it is interesting to note that after 1968, North Vietnamese practice ensured significant separation between a communications unit and the command post it served.

So the war of the ether continued. Harve Saal, a field man with MACV's Studies and Observation Group (MACVSOG) reports that his covert unit had great success listening in on North Vietnamese radio nets, so much so that troops would joke that going on actual missions was unnecessary. At the same time the MACVSOG men grumbled that the NVA always seemed to be able to pick up on their patrols virtually as soon as they landed from helicopters. In May 1970 ARVN Rangers in Kontum province recovered from enemy bodies copies of key codes (one-time pads) of a type used by MACVSOG, and with date markings on certain pages suggesting they could recover any traffic they held for those days.

The Americans and South Vietnamese mounted a special effort against North Vietnamese communications intelligence during 1969, for by then adversary COMINT was evaluated as a major impediment to combat operations. A Pacific Command study of operational security that spring estimated that the NVA and VC might have as many as four thousand persons working just to break into friendly communications; some suspected the number to be as high as five thousand. The North Vietnamese enjoyed success too. Documents captured in July 1969 included worksheets showing solutions for a number of recovered groups in a widely used U.S. field code, plus no fewer than fifteen solved ARVN three-digit codes. That December an infantry platoon of the First Brigade, First Infantry Division actually overran a Viet Cong radio intelligence unit called "A3," capturing a dozen VC codebreakers and their equipment and documents. Project Touchdown was then inaugurated as an intense effort to get the most information possible about the adversary COMINT effort. The Viet Cong proved to have extensive experience, had copied more than two thousand American or ARVN field radio conversations, had broken codes—in short, they were thoroughly professional.

The war of the ether briefly became a public issue in 1970, at the time of the American–South Vietnamese invasion of Cambodia. As part of Washington's justification for that operation, President Nixon told the American people that the armies were going after COSVN— the Central Office for South Vietnam—the Viet Cong high command. But COSVN was not to be found. As had been the case with tactical information in Project Dancer, the intelligence was dated before it could be put to use. Former Viet Cong official Nguyen Nhu Thang confirms that COSVN had at one time been in the area the Americans suspected, but it had begun moving away long before the invasion started. Attempts to track COSVN by radio direction finding were also frustrated by more sophisticated Viet Cong operating techniques; the several radio units that worked for COSVN took turns handling messages, and while one unit worked the radios all the others would be moving. Thus Viet Cong radio traffic constantly emanated from new locations and could not be used as valid data for the location of COSVN headquarters.

Vietnamization affected the radio intelligence war quickly. The Army Security Agency thinned out its units at an early stage, though most of the radio research units pulled out of South Vietnam only in 1971 or 1972. By that time ARVN and the South Vietnamese air force were supplying 95 percent of the intelligence from radio interception. While the flow continued to be voluminous, the quality of COMINT gathered was diminishing. In 1969 the North Vietnamese held another army-wide conference on improving communications security, and that year they actually moved to a new system of general codes. It took time for the Americans and South Vietnamese to regain their former degree of understanding of the NVA codes; meanwhile their resources were being reduced by withdrawals from Vietnam. Ultimately Americans could not win the war of the ether—COMINT did not bring victory in Cambodia in 1970, or in Laos in 1971, and it did not predict the massive Easter offensive launched by the North Vietnamese in 1972. Communications intelligence became one more supposed path to victory in Vietnam that merely terminated in a dead end.

21   Phoenix: The War Against the Viet Cong Apparat

The war in Vietnam was a conflict shrouded in ambiguity. Most obviously there were the ambiguities of objective and, at the level of main forces, of what all those firefights really contributed, of what "victory" meant when the enemy *always* disappeared. Most ambiguous, perhaps, was the ambiguity of pacification: a war assertedly being fought for the hearts and minds of the Vietnamese people being waged by large units that crisscrossed the country.

Pacification was an effort by the United States and South Vietnamese governments to gain dominance in the villages of rural Vietnam. It involved such varied components as police and security programs to deny Viet Cong access to the villages, at one extreme, and cooperative economic programs and the rooting out of government corruption at the other. The ultimate objective was to convince villagers to give their loyalty to the South Vietnamese government, thus creating secure, or "pacified," conditions in the countryside. Like most everything else in Vietnam, American leaders were aware of the pacification problem from an early date and repeatedly came up with formulas supposed to provide the solution. There were "new life hamlets" and "strategic villages," revolutionary development and civil operations. But while the military prosecuted the large-unit war with élan, their commitment to pacification remained rhetorical.

Part of the difficulty was due to the nature of the target. With the large-unit war the military command, while it could not "see" the North Vietnamese army or the Viet Cong, could keep relatively good tabs on the adversary. In the pacification war, on the other hand, the opposition was a shadowy network of Viet Cong village authorities, informers, tax collectors, propaganda teams, officials of community groups, and the like, who collectively came to be called the Viet Cong Infrastructure (VCI). Supported by local VC guerrilla units, the VCI was for many years beyond the reach of South Vietnamese or American forces.

The solution to the VCI proved elusive even within the broader mystery of pacification. It was not difficult, after all, to postulate that relocating peasants and creating local civil guard detachments might complicate the VCI's task in gaining the support of the population. Even Ngo Dinh Diem, resistant to so much else, had gone along with the early proposals for a strategic hamlet program. It was much more difficult to figure out how to come to grips with the underground VCI.

The sheer lack of resources devoted to pacification was telling. With the war seen as a contest between major military forces, those forces continued to absorb more than the lion's share of both South Vietnamese and U.S. expenditures. True, the conventional forces were inherently more expensive; nevertheless, if one accepted the rationale for the war as one for the loyalty of the Vietnamese people, programs directly aimed at the people ought to have commanded a greater share of resources. These relatively cheaper programs offered greater returns for less money. As the Central Intelligence Agency found with its montagnard effort, major gains could in fact be made with very little in the way of spending.

Probably the most expensive element of pacification was the creation of the Civil Guard and the village Self-Defense Corps, later to become respectively the Regional Forces and People's Self-Defense Force. These two forces would ultimately comprise about a million troops, beginning with a twenty-thousand-man Civil Guard increase approved as one of the Gilpatric recommendations in 1961. This cost just 3.7 percent of what the U.S. was spending in Vietnam. Between 1961 and 1965 this item in U.S. expenditures exceeded 10 percent only once (12.6 percent in fiscal 1964) and averaged less than 6 percent. In terms of operational use, however, South Vietnamese commanders felt the Civil Guard to be an adjunct force and most often employed it in conventional sweep operations.

Still, in the early years even the presence of local units and the incipient village program did not greatly inhibit the VCI, which continued to work underground according to its own directives from Viet Cong authorities. The deteriorating situation at the main force level, which led to the open commitment of American combat troops, also diverted the attention of many away from the pacification war.

■   It was American civilians, from the CIA, the Agency for International Development (AID), and elsewhere who pressed for rededication to pacification during the period of the ground troop deployment. In Washington the CIA presented a twelve-point program to improve the situation in South Vietnam, much of which revolved around pacification measures. In Saigon, AID pressed for American province and corps pacification advisers with signatory authority over money for local projects. A counterpart fund also evolved to provide more resources for civil programs, now focused on medical, educational, and economic projects. The Vietnamese Regional and Popular forces, totaling 256,700 in July 1965, increased to 284,500 by April 1967.

As the American commitment deepened, with increased ground forces and a more widespread advisory network, the military also showed greater interest in pacification matters. One of the most significant initiatives came from General Lewis Walt, marine commander in I Corps, who started a Combined Action Program. This effort united marine volunteers with Vietnamese militiamen in companies that managed districts, with platoons for villages and hamlets. The units assisted villages with self-help projects and were much more able in the security role of running patrols and ambushes against the local VC. The program began as an attempt to ensure security around the base at Phu Bai. The initiative soon spread throughout I Corps, or, as this area was known to U.S. marines, III Marine Amphibious Force, which included the five northernmost provinces of South Vietnam. By July 1966 there were thirty-eight of these Combined Action platoons in Walt's command area. Although the Vietnamese did not furnish Walt enough of their Popular Forces manpower for the marines to meet their goal of forming seventy-four platoons by the end of that year, that objective was reached in July 1967, and before Tet the number had reached seventy-nine. Unique experiments in civil cooperation for pacification included that run by Lieutenant Colonel William R. Corson of the Third Marine Tank Battalion. Corson joined with local villagers in joint fishing and other commercial projects as a means of building villagers' incentives to side with the South Vietnamese government.

While the marines registered successes in their mission, Walt's programs still aimed at general pacification, not directly at the Viet Cong infrastructure. Nevertheless it was in the I Corps area that the Viet Cong's own actions spawned South Vietnamese interest in fighting the infrastructure. That happened in 1964–1965 around Qui Nhon, where

VCI activities so enraged locals that they approached CIA officials to ask for weapons to kill Viet Cong. Peer de Silva, CIA station chief (who was soon thereafter wounded and invalidated out of the country when the Viet Cong planted a car bomb outside the U.S. embassy), recognized the potential for an anti-VCI program and agreed to arm the Qui Nhon citizens. This experiment proved so successful around Qui Nhon that the CIA wished to expand it to the rest of South Vietnam. The Agency coined the term "People's Action Teams" (PATs) for the local strike groups and created a training center at Vung Tau. Some of the Qui Nhon participants went to Vung Tau as instructors. The PAT program then formed one of the CIA's twelve action proposals handed to President Johnson in 1965. Vung Tau became a kind of mecca for "other war" types, since the South Vietnamese pacification training facility was also located there, as were certain other unconventional warfare activities.

Intelligence was naturally the primary stumbling block in any effort to combat the VCI. The Qui Nhon villagers had *known* who was the enemy. But pacification efforts aimed at general area security did not develop the type of information necessary to identify the VCI. Concentrating on conventional patrolling, Vietnamese army units and regional forces did not develop this information either. Borrowing a concept from the VC, who used "action militia" for both security and propaganda, in 1966 the Saigon government began a new "Revolutionary Development" (also called Rev Dev, or simply RD) or Rural Development program. A cabinet-level Ministry of Revolutionary Development under Major General Nguyen Duc Thang was created in July 1966. Training centered at Vung Tau, which expanded to accommodate 5,000 trainees and graduated a class of 4,500 that May. By late 1967 there were 30,000 RD cadres, and two years later, when the ministry was abolished, 50,000 in 1,400 teams.

The basic element of the program was the fifty-nine-man RD Group that was permanently deployed to a hamlet undergoing pacification. The group was armed and had some security responsibilities, but it also had technical experts whose function was to enhance government presence at the grass roots. A primary mission was to organize the hamlet for defense, including formation of popular forces. The RD Group would organize a hamlet by systematically dividing it into household units of five families with block leaders, then hold monthly meetings in much the same fashion as the various VC-sponsored "liberation associations." Through all this the RD Group studied VCI organization in the hamlet, made a survey of households, and tried to list

VCI members and sympathizers who regularly worked with the Viet Cong. Yet while they fulfilled this intelligence function, the RD cadres had no action role like that of the PATs or CTTs—the Counter-Terror Teams, a name the CIA gave the original PAT initiative once it expanded nationwide. Action remained in the hands of the paramilitary elements or of the national police command, often corrupt and always inefficient. In 1969, when the ministry was abolished and the RD Groups subordinated to local village chiefs, the cadres reverted to being an appendage of the security forces.

In Washington, President Johnson found himself greatly concerned about pacification and all aspects of what he called the "other war" in Vietnam. In this LBJ received able assistance from Robert W. Komer, a member of his National Security Council staff. Johnson put Komer in charge of an interagency group to manage the "other war" in Washington, while its various functions in South Vietnam were consolidated into an Office of Civil Operations (OCO) in Saigon, a unit placed under a deputy ambassador with full authority to make decisions.

Unfortunately, the OCO initiative was stymied from the beginning. Several times since his arrival in Vietnam, General Westmoreland had proposed that pacification functions be consolidated under the U.S. military, arguing that only the military had the manpower to reach down into the villages and do the job well. Ambassador Henry Cabot Lodge had scotched an early version of Westmoreland's approach, and Maxwell Taylor had rejected another. Now William Porter, the OCO chief, found the military in his path at every turn as he tried to get LBJ's "other war" up and running. Despite its evident interest in controlling the function, the U.S. military for the most part continued to give pacification lip service in favor of the war of the big battalions. Had MACV really gotten its hands on pacification in the early days of the war, there is no reason to suppose the result would have been any different.

Robert Komer's solution was to give the military part of what it wanted. Komer reasoned that the way to get MACV on board was to make it directly responsible for pacification. He went on to engineer a new entity linked to the South Vietnamese RD program, an organization approved by LBJ early in 1967. All U.S. pacification functions henceforth would fall under the unit called Civilian Operations and Revolutionary Development Support (CORDS). In turn, CORDS would be a regular staff division of the Military Assistance Command Vietnam, and would exercise operational control over pacification efforts in the field. That included U.S. military advisers assigned to districts and provinces as well as mobile training teams advising regional and popular forces. By late 1967 CORDS controlled almost seven thousand military and one thousand civilian personnel, an increase in military participation of about 40 percent over pre-CORDS levels. In the pacification budget, where in 1966 the military had funded 81 percent of the sum of $555 million committed to pacification support, by 1969 expenditure had risen to $770 million, of which 94 percent came from MACV.

Also crystallizing under CORDS were the elements that would form parts of the program to be called Phoenix. A Saigon-level study of roles and missions in 1966 had recommended initiatives aimed directly at combating the VCI. Assistance to the South Vietnamese police had already created a national interrogation center and provincial equivalents, and in 1967 a joint CIA-Vietnamese Military Security Service interrogation center was formed, as well as a unit to select targets among the VCI. All these went into the CORDS program, as did support for police field operations, formerly handled by the foreign intelligence staff of the Saigon CIA station. All that was required to create Phoenix was to put it all together, and President Johnson had the man for the job—to head CORDS the president appointed Robert Komer.

■ Ebullient, abrasive, and gracious by turns, Komer, who quickly acquired the sobriquet "Blowtorch Bob," irritated military commander Westmoreland but won his respect and support. It did not hurt that Komer had a special relationship with President Johnson, though Westmoreland soon put a stop to the back-channel communications that LBJ seemed to expect from his pacification chief. A longtime observer of the "other war," Komer had been a CIA officer before his White House days and was well versed in the array of pacification options, including the anti-VCI initiative.

One novelty that Komer brought to CORDS helped lead to others, particularly the anti-VCI campaign. That was the computer. Komer provided CORDS with something then very new—a substantial data-processing capability and an analytical component. At the microscopic level of Vietnamese villages, the RD Groups had been assembling a mass of data for what would become the National Identification and Registration Program, aimed at compiling a dossier on everyone over fifteen years of age. With data processing CORDS could store the information and compare dossiers with reports from informants, captured documents, and the like, to compile a picture of the Viet Cong infrastructure. Arrangements for this aspect were made in Saigon between Evan J. Parker, a CORDS official detailed from the CIA, and an army colonel. This became the Intelligence Coordination and Exploitation (ICEX) program.

Information from ICEX flowed down to pacification advisers in the provinces and districts, where American–South Vietnamese committees met to determine the disposition of individual cases or dossiers. There were a number of methods of "neutralizing" the VCI in the field. Members could be induced to defect under the *Chieu Hoi*, or Open Arms, program; suspects could be resettled to cut them off from contact with the infrastructure; or, if there was sufficient evidence, they could be arrested. Underground VCI members could be arrested or wiped out in raids by security forces, efforts that had different names in various provinces. In Quang Ngai, *Phung Hoang* was the name—Vietnamese for Phoenix, the bird who rises from the ashes bearing news of peace. Phoenix, a psychological warfare symbol intended to suggest that the Saigon government was all-present, became the program title in December 1967 when Komer received approval to extend the neutralization campaign across all South Vietnam. Thereafter young Americans arriving in the "Nam" to serve as pacification advisers went first to the Saigon headquarters of the 525th Military Intelligence Battalion for orientation on ICEX and other matters before being sent on to their posts, where some of them were assigned as Phoenix advisers. CORDS in fact requested an additional increment of four hundred officers specifically for Phoenix. In late 1968 Phoenix was officially enshrined as one of the eight points of the 1969 pacification campaign plan.

With charges of murder, torture, and arbitrary detention, in later years Phoenix became one of the most controversial aspects of the Vietnam War effort. It was not intended as such, however, but as more or less of a precision instrument to strike directly at the Viet Cong infrastructure. That would have been a difficult goal in any circumstance, and was especially complicated in that U.S. intelligence was unable even to agree on the size of the VCI. Various military and civilian agencies had estimates of 34,000 or 70,000, even up to 225,000, for the number of active Viet Cong and sympathizers. A given village with four or five hamlets would typically have a party secretary and deputy presiding over an executive committee that supervised sections for finance, frontline supply, security, military affairs, information, social welfare and public health, troop proselytizing (propaganda), and civilian proselytizing. These in turn would coordinate the "liberation associations" and other front groups, gather intelligence, collect taxes, and conduct terrorism and other activities designed to reduce South Vietnamese government effectiveness. Moreover, there were levels of the VCI—their cells were tightly organized and quite security conscious. Some of the most damaging VCI elements, such as agent networks, were not tied in with the local village structure at all. Significant officials operated underground and were always guarded, while the local VCI usually had good penetration of local South Vietnamese security forces.

The difficulty of the anti-VCI task and the lack of agreement among U.S. agencies on the severity of the problem is amply reflected in National Security Study Memorandum (NSSM) 1, an interagency analysis ordered at the outset of the Nixon administration. In response to NSSM-1 questions, the State Department reported that 15,700 VC political cadres had been neutralized during 1968—conservatively, some 16 to 20 percent of a VCI estimated at 30,000 to 100,000. State then reported that before August 1968 neutralization reports had not been screened to eliminate numbers of loyal South Vietnamese taken by mistake, which might reduce the raw number to about 14,500 or to a "working figure" of about 10 percent. Significantly, "only a minimal number of middle- or senior-ranking officials were affected," and the overall impact had been serious in only a handful of provinces. "The Phoenix program," reported State, "however important to a successful anti-infrastructure effort, has certain inherent weaknesses. It does not collect intelligence but merely collates and analyzes information made available . . . from the intelligence community." State reported little cooperation from the South Vietnamese from the program's inception in December 1967 until Nguyen Van Thieu's presidential decree of July 1968, but at least Vietnamese province chiefs were now on notice that their performance would be measured by Phoenix results.

The Saigon embassy agreed with most of this description of problems, but insisted that many of those killed in the 1968 Tet fighting could have been VCI. It quantified neutralizations as 2,255 killed, 11,291 captured, and 2,230 defected, among whom only 2,050 were district-level VC or above. The embassy complained that most who were neutralized did not remain so but "simply vanish into the system of detention and interrogation facilities with no record of their final disposition," while more than half of those tried and sentenced were released within a year. The national police, one of the principal anti-VCI arms, "still devotes very little emphasis to the VCI in its training program." Nevertheless, the embassy observed, VCI concern about Phoenix had been reflected in alerts to subordinate units, attempts to eliminate Phoenix personnel, and anti-Phoenix propaganda that "has bordered on the hysterical."

By contrast, the Pentagon believed the neutralization figures. In reporting the distribution of the VCI as 29.9 percent in I Corps, 33.3 percent in II Corps, 12.6 percent in III Corps, and 24.2 percent in IV Corps, the Pentagon also credited the Saigon area with great inroads against the VCI. The military believed that "progress against the Viet Cong infrastructure has been satisfactory." What remained necessary was to emphasize quality rather than quantity by "providing greater incentives for the identification and capture of high ranking or key personnel."

Some success stories did come from III Corps, as had to be the case for an effort that necessarily compiled a different history in every one of South Vietnam's 240 districts. One such story is that of Lieutenant John L. Cook, Phoenix adviser in Di An district of Bien Hoa Province, just across the Dong Nai River from that city and the major U.S. air base. Cook worked Di An from 1968 to 1970, being extended beyond the usual tour allowed an American officer at the insistence of his Vietnamese district chief. Cook found local relations between the national police and Vietnamese military intelligence to be rather strained, which was not unusual, but he was able to rely on Popular Forces troops and the Provincial Reconnaissance Unit (PRU), specialized strike units set up to support Phoenix, when operations were necessary. A big break came when a disaffected VC, passed over for promotion, rallied and betrayed his VC village chief. Another break came when a jilted girlfriend turned up with good information on the whereabouts of the long-sought district party secretary. Phoenix in Di An became so successful that it was one of the first districts selected for Vietnamization when U.S. advisers were withdrawn and the Vietnamese replaced the program with one they called F-6.

Hau Nghia was another success, a triumph of intelligence collation and analysis sparked by Captain Tim Miller. This American adviser found the Vietnamese lackadaisical about assembling and cross-referencing the Phoenix dossiers (again not unusual), and took over the task himself. He compiled such good information on Trang Bang district that he knew exactly who he had in the fall of 1971 when a VC village secretary rallied after ordering the summary execution for rape of a Vietnamese who turned out to be the nephew of a high party official. The VC was able to name no less than twenty-eight other cadres who were then apprehended, treated well, and induced to name yet more VCI members. Under Miller's direction the infrastructure was systematically rolled up, and VC documents began to refer to "white" villages, places where there was no VCI.

Miller also collaborated with another army intelligence specialist, Captain Stuart A. Herrington, who worked Duc Hue district of Hau Nghia Province in 1971–1972. Here once more the initial break was through a VC rallier, in this case deputy commander of a local VC company. Although the man was later killed by VC security men, other defectors followed whom Herrington and Miller were able to utilize in Duc Hoa, Bao Trai, and other districts of the province. Phoenix was so successful in Hau Nghia that the VC ultimately mounted a road-mining operation that killed the Vietnamese province chief and almost got his American senior adviser as well. The program was also set back, though not crippled, by the 1972 main force fighting, including the siege of An Loc, during which large forces of both sides rolled back and forth through Hau Nghia. The historian Eric M. Bergerud, author of the best account of pacification in Hau Nghia, concludes that the Viet Cong were effectively defeated there. Conditions in Hau Nghia distinguished it from the average South Vietnamese province, starting with its exceptional good fortune in being assigned a succession of the best pacification advisers and running through to its proximity to Saigon, which led to Hau Nghia's being given a higher priority than many other places. The very nearness of Saigon made it easier to bring to bear various types of resources in Hau Nghia. Finally, the losses incurred by the VC as a result of their own decisions to make attacks during the period of Tet in both 1968 and 1969 were key factors in crippling the infrastructure in Hau Nghia province.

The common denominator among pacification success stories was the quality and dynamism of the advisers and their Vietnamese counterparts. The III Corps deputy for CORDS, former army colonel John Paul Vann, who became a Vietnam legend in his own time, would have been the first to recognize this. But all this put a premium on individual initiative and on belief in the efficacity of Phoenix, which could not be guaranteed. In his first months Captain Herrington felt obstructed by a province senior adviser who had little use for Phoenix. Later in his tour Lieutenant Cook had similar trouble with a district senior adviser. Bob Komer considered it an achievement when he persuaded Washington to create, at State's Foreign Service Institute, a year-long pacification course that was supposed to turn out experts, far preferable to a short orientation in Saigon. Yet the senior adviser who created such difficulty for Lieutenant Cook was a product of the Washington course. Other graduates did better. Again it came down to individuals.

Komer sadly concluded in his end-of-mission report, "To date, *Phung Hoang* has been a small, poorly managed, and largely ineffective effort."

In Vietnam especially, formal structure was often seen as the way to institutionalize progress and make it less dependent on the vagaries of individuals, and Phoenix did have a structure. William Colby, the CIA officer who was Komer's deputy and eventual successor at CORDS, did as much as anyone to create the structure, formalized in Thieu's July 1968 directive that Colby helped draft. It provided for a Central Phoenix Committee under the minister of interior, with regional and province committees under it, and a Phoenix Division in the national police command. The working elements were forty-four Province Intelligence and Operations Coordinating Centers (PIOCCs) which supervised identically named units at the district (DIOCC) and village (VIOCC) levels and the Provincial Reconnaissance Units (PRUs).

In its operation, Phoenix worked on the basis of a preventive detention system. Suspects were graded "A," "B," or "C" depending on the strength of evidence, under criteria developed by CORDS legal officer Gage McAfee on Colby's staff. Suspects could be held at a Provincial Interrogation Center for forty-six days, then to be released or sent for trial either to a military field court or, as was most often the case, to the Province Security Committee.

This sounded good on paper, but the opportunities for manipulation of the system were many. For example, trial before the Province Security Committee was not considered a legal proceeding, and there was no appeal. The suspect had no right to see his dossier, no right to counsel, and could not even confront accusers or testify in his own defense. Further, under the so-called "An Tri" law, suspects could be imprisoned for two years (and the sentences could be renewed) with no evidence required, simply for being considered "dangerous to national defense and public security." Even for a real conviction, only three pieces of "evidence" were required. Where security committees in some provinces construed the "three pieces" rule fairly strictly, others were more lax. There were also repeated rumors that suspects could bribe their way out of the Province Security Committee proceedings.

Certainly not everyone apprehended under Phoenix went to prison. One report holds that some 250,000 persons passed through the system each year, while in congressional testimony Colby specified that between 1968 and 1971 a total of 28,978 were captured, 17,717 rallied, and 20,587 killed—87.6 percent of the latter in combat action and only about 12 percent by police or security forces. The CORDS chief estimated that perhaps 5,000 of the Phoenix killed could have been innocent victims, though the figure might be higher. South Vietnamese government figures showed more than 40,000 killed. As for prisoners, official tabulations showed that South Vietnamese jails had space to hold slightly more than 50,000 (International Red Cross studies not released until after the war showed a capacity for more than 70,000). According to Vietnam War critics, these jails were populated by more than 200,000 prisoners.

These results did not come all at once. Phoenix was hitting its stride only in 1969 when 19,534 suspects were neutralized, including 6,187 killed. The activity was sustained by a nationwide structure advised by 600 to 800 Americans, among them a number of CIA specialists variously estimated at 25 to 40 or up to 100. The action arm of PRUs, direct descendants of the CIA's earlier People's Action Teams and paid at four times the rate of the South Vietnamese army, numbered between 1,700 and 4,400. National police strength stood at 94,000 at the end of 1968, rising to over 120,000 by 1972.

The Achilles heel of Phoenix was always its intelligence. Neither the police nor Vietnamese military intelligence, wary of each other, would share their best information. Information passed along by CIA or the American military often did not find its way into the files unless the American advisers themselves, like Tim Miller, did the work. At the DIOCCs the files were poorly maintained, as foreign service officer Wayne L. Cooper found in eighteen months as a Phoenix adviser in the Mekong Delta—wheat and chaff mixed together, no cross-reference by alias, family location, or other useful designation, no intelligence collection plan, little direction for agents, wanted lists and mug shots so poor as to be useless. What intelligence there was could be no better than the agents, who could report rivals, enemies, anything they wanted. Many, though no doubt not all, agents proved conscientious, but there are reports that some collected protection money *not* to report people. In Saigon, Americans of the 525th Military Intelligence Battalion reportedly nicknamed the Quang Ngai agent network "Ali Baba and his Forty Thieves" for the quality of the information they provided. In many places in Vietnam, Phoenix was reduced to targeting people on the basis of very little information at all.

Producing further information from prisoners was an additional problem. Strong-arm methods and torture were endemic in Vietnam, and the Phoenix Provincial Interrogation Centers were no exception. Americans were not supposed to cooperate in this and, under orders Colby issued in 1969, were supposed to report instances when they occurred. But there were not enough Americans to be everywhere all the time, and they had their own jobs to do, including getting along with Vietnamese security officials. The best information came voluntarily from ralliers; smart Vietnamese, as in Bien Hoa, treated prisoners well, but that was by no means the universal approach.

Problems became acute when limited intelligence was combined with quotas—Phoenix was assigned to supply a certain number of bodies, warm or cold but bodies nonetheless. Any lingering doubts about the existence of such a quota system for Phoenix was resolved in 1992 with the declassification of cables from Ambassador Ellsworth Bunker to Washington discussing the quota system and its actual numbers. Komer defended the practice of quotas as a management tool with analogies to factories. He wanted realistic quotas and argued for them but could not prevent Nguyen Van Thieu from setting very high goals. Phoenix quotas plus poor intelligence added up to innocent victims along with the VCI bodies. For American advisers the result was considerable moral conflict. At least one CIA officer reportedly went wild in pursuit of results and had to be transferred out of Vietnam. At the other extreme, Colby's 1969 directive on torture and assassinations was prompted by another American officer, assigned to CORDS, who concluded that Phoenix was immoral and requested transfer. Also in 1969, before they reached Vietnam two young army lieutenants, Francis T. Reitemeyer and Michael J. Cohn, undergoing intelligence training for Phoenix at Fort Holabird, decided to become conscientious objectors when told they would have to fill a kill quota of fifty VCI per month. The two men received honorable discharges from the army. Even in Di An, one of the successful Phoenix districts, Lieutenant Cook objected to quotas when he learned of them.

At a higher level, the level of a military region, MR-3, the area that included Saigon, Hau Nghia, Bien Hoa, and many of the other success stories mentioned here, the experience of CIA police intelligence specialist Orrin DeForest confirms these cautionary comments. DeForest arrived at the end of 1968 to work with Tim Page, Stuart Herrington, and others from the vantage of the MR-3 CIA base, located at Bien Hoa. He found the dossiers a complete mess, lacking sources for allegations, notes on the credibility of witnesses or charges, cross-references—in short, everything that might have distinguished the intelligence files from a mass of unsubstantiated rumor. With commendable energy DeForest turned the situation around, but it was years before the MR-3 files could be considered authoritative, and that said nothing for the dependability of the VCI neutralization lists maintained by other provinces and regions.

Action by Westmoreland's successor, MACV commander General Creighton Abrams, also suggests relatively low confidence in the efficacy of the Phoenix program. Abrams ordered MACV to phase out the use of military personnel as advisers on Phoenix. The American military cadre had peaked at 704 in 1970 and fell both as a result of Abram's antipathy and of Vietnamization. By 1972 there were just 125 U.S. military people with Phoenix. Civilians other than CIA officers peaked at 20 in 1969 and were down to 1 in 1972. The CIA has never provided figures for its participation in Phoenix, but the number 100 has appeared in authoritative treatments of the subject. Unlike Abrams and the military, the CIA's Colby was and remains a Phoenix enthusiast, probably not least because he succeeded Komer as chief of CORDS. In his Vietnam account *Lost Victory* and in public talks, Colby makes much of the fact that he was able to drive through Quang Tin Province on the back of a motorbike at night in 1970.

But the implication that Phoenix—or, on a wider level, pacification in general—was a success, does not follow automatically. The pacification status of South Vietnamese villages was being tracked by CORDS computers using something called the Hamlet Evaluation Survey (HES). This was a sort of report card on local conditions done at village, district, and province levels by both American advisers and South Vietnamese officials. Originally developed for Robert McNamara, who wanted some kind of quantitative measure for pacification control, HES at first included more than ninety criteria for everything from village security to agricultural cooperatives. By these criteria the provinces were showing almost total control by Saigon, according to the HES data, long before Tet—which, if HES were correct, ought to have been impossible for the Viet Cong to pull off. After Tet, in which pacification suffered a clear setback, Komer went to Nguyen Van Thieu with a proposal for a so-called Accelerated Pacification Campaign, which the South Vietnamese approved. It turns out that the accelerated campaign involved eliminating from the HES criteria every category that had to do with quality of life. Among the items eliminated were six of eleven major categories (including eradication of illiteracy, disease, land reform, and so on). Among the categories that were left, thirty-three of fifty-three specific tasks were also eliminated (including listing officials accused of corruption, assisting families returning to the village, reconciling differences among individuals, even setting up intelligence nets to monitor South Vietnamese government activities). It was not long before the HES data, using the revised criteria, showed over 90 percent "control" of the villages by the Saigon government. The question is, how much *loyalty* did control buy? How many hearts and minds were won?

These discussions of pacification also assume that anything gained came as a direct result of American or South Vietnamese initiatives, whether from Phoenix or other, less sinister programs. This ignores the degree to which the Viet Cong themselves lost the hearts and minds of villagers through their tax collections, involuntary recruitment of men and women, assassinations, and other exactments. The account Le Ly Hayslip has written of growing up in a South Vietnamese village which at first was united against the foreign (American) invader and local collaborators, then at length soured on the dogmatic Viet Cong, is telling in this regard. But loss of loyalty to the VC was not the same as giving one's heart to Saigon, especially since Saigon saw the war situation as enabling it to discontinue the programs that benefited villagers.

Despite propaganda from both sides in the war, villagers could see that neither side was especially amenable to their needs. Villagers could also see that the old war of Viet Cong guerrillas was increasingly being supplanted by the new war of regular forces in conventional combat. Under the circumstances, the incentives for Vietnamese villagers were increasingly to take no side in the war. Colby could drive at night because the villagers preferred to stay out of the fighting, not because Saigon had pacified South Vietnam.

The quotas and potential for innocent victims made Phoenix politically controversial in the United States. The South Vietnamese pursued it on their own after the January 1973 Paris accords, giving Phoenix the new name F-6. A Redevelopment and Relocation Program replaced CORDS in the U.S. mission team as the American contribution to pacification, but the anti-VCI campaign became a largely South Vietnamese enterprise. In 1973, particularly as a result of his role in Phoenix, Colby had difficulties when he was being considered for confirmation as director of the CIA.

Despite intelligence mishaps and innocent victims, Phoenix did have an impact on the Viet Cong infrastructure. "White" villages became a reality for the Viet Cong. In interviews for his extensive series of documentary films and book on Vietnam, the journalist Stanley Karnow found a number of Viet Cong officials and North Vietnamese army officers who affirmed the effects of Phoenix. General Tran Do, then deputy military commander, called the program "extremely destructive," while Nguyen Co Thach, later foreign minister, reported that Phoenix "wiped out many of our bases." Others agreed that the program had been dangerous and had cost the lives of thousands of cadres.

Was Phoenix therefore a success?

Unfortunately, Karnow's interviews do not settle the matter. There are a number of reasons to continue to question the effectiveness of Phoenix, concrete military and counterinsurgency reasons. The antiwar protesters were right that Phoenix constituted a massive human rights violation on a national scale, but that can be regarded as a separate issue and just one more reason to question Phoenix. The best arguments are practical and military.

First, in its own terms Phoenix was a campaign to eliminate the Viet Cong infrastructure. In defending the program from charges of assassination, Colby was careful to specify that 87 percent of fatalities occurred in conventional combat situations. To put this in a different light, if conventional means sufficed in 87 percent of cases, just what was Phoenix accomplishing? A later study of army counterinsurgency finds that only about 20 percent of neutralizations could be credited to forces assigned to Phoenix, while the annual share accounted for by Regional and Popular forces ranged from 39 to 50 percent. If the argument is that Phoenix was merely to provide better intelligence on the VCI, what need was there for kill quotas and all that went with them? In the context of a simple intelligence program, one needs to ask how much could have been gained by improvements in intelligence sharing, collation, and analysis without the rest of Phoenix.

Second, as became evident in the final fall of South Vietnam, Phoenix affected very little of the adversary's high-level penetration of the Saigon government and army. It was also much less effective against the senior levels of the VC leadership, those that really counted. That this was apparent from a very early date is evident from the Pentagon's concern in NSSM-1 to provide incentives for neutralization of higher officials. The Pentagon's own figures demonstrate Phoenix's failure in this regard: of the 1968 neutralizations reported in NSSM-1, some 12.9 percent were classed as district-level or higher officials. The corresponding figure for neutralizations in 1970–1971 is only 3 percent. Such success as did occur against the VCI was not unmitigated, because it actually simplified Hanoi's political control over the Viet Cong at the point—in sight of the end of the tunnel—when VC and North Vietnamese objectives might have begun to diverge.

Third, the fact that Phoenix *was* politically controversial in the United States further reduced U.S. freedom of action in pursuing the war, while the moral conflict raised additional questions for Americans still fighting on the ground.

Fourth, for Saigon, combating the VCI became a convenient alternative to political reform.

Fifth, Phoenix achieved such success as it did against the VCI at precisely that moment in the war when the North Vietnamese were able to prosecute the conflict at the conventional level. The same results might have proved decisive ten years earlier, but ten years earlier neither the South Vietnamese nor the Americans had the sophistication for the job.

Finally, for what it accomplished Phoenix contributed to the general security situation in the Vietnamese countryside, in much the same way as did close territorial occupation by military units or militia. General security was an enabling condition, something necessary to permit pacification to work, not a substitute for it. To be successful one needed to evaporate the sea around the Viet Cong fish, to gain the loyalty of South Vietnamese people through a whole range of programs. Thus Phoenix was a success and yet it was not. In the final analysis, Phoenix by itself could not win the war.

If the North Vietnamese were to be beaten, and if Americans and South Vietnamese had already lost the chance of doing it at the village level, much would depend on Hanoi's access to the south. For years the North Vietnamese had been using their Ho Chi Minh Trail through Laos, and for years the Americans had been trying to stop them. Some even believed the Vietnam War had started there, in the upland wilds of Laos. As for who started it, no one ever agreed.

Little World, Big War

In the sleepy days before the troubles came, those who knew thought of Laos as a kind of never-never land. Many saw Laos as the "Land of a Million Elephants"; one writer called it the "Little World." Even after the Franco-Vietnamese War and the political upheavals that afflicted Laos beginning at that time, there continued to be something mysterious about that landlocked country, and some notion of smallness in the concept of its place in the grand scheme of things. Yet the huge American war in Vietnam was to a considerable degree sparked by the Laotian troubles. This sense of contradiction seems to have become embedded in the whole American relationship with Laos during the Indochina war. The United States supported a neutralist government in Laos while paying, training, and advising troops who wanted to oust that government, then forged an alliance with neutralist troops who had fought the American-backed forces. In Laos the U.S. insisted it was in compliance with an international neutralization agreement while fighting a war. When U.S. participation in that war could no longer be denied, Washington attempted to claim its role was peripheral when in fact it was central. North Vietnam also intervened in Laos while asserting its respect for Laotian neutrality, claiming there were no Vietnamese forces in the country even as Hanoi built and operated the extensive road and trail network through the Laotian panhandle that became the lifeline of Hanoi's forces in South Vietnam. That too is part of the contradiction of Laos.

One more contradictory aspect of the conflict in the land of a million elephants is that in spite of its great importance in the Indochina war, the Laotian experience remains the most poorly chronicled facet of the war. Perhaps this follows from the strenuous efforts to deny

THE HIDDEN HISTORY OF THE VIETNAM WAR

there was a Laotian war, or later to minimize it. The work of American local allies, whether lowland Lao, upland tribal groups, or foreign actors such as South Vietnamese and Thai, have barely been recorded. Americans also played a still unheralded role. This is a peek at the Laos story.

■ Far from a sideshow to Vietnam, in a certain sense the Vietnam War began in Laos. Although North Vietnam's creation of the Ho Chi Minh Trail is usually dated to May 1959, in December 1958 a patrol of the Laotian army (the *Forces Armées du Royaume,* or FAR) shot it out with North Vietnamese troops at a point close to one of the key mountain passes that became parts of the trail. While this was the first clear sign of North Vietnamese involvement, the Laotian political situation had already deteriorated to the point of civil war. Under the 1954 Geneva agreement that ended the Franco-Vietnamese War, Laos was supposed to become neutral, with power shared between conservative royalists, other nationalists, and the Communist Neo Lao Hak Xat, or "Pathet Lao." The FAR was to integrate into its ranks Pathet Lao troops, and the government was to include Pathet Lao cabinet ministers.

Neutrality was a difficult formula to meet in reality. Negotiations dragged on for years over how the Pathet Lao army would be incorporated into the royalist forces, with continual disputes over how many officers would be accepted and at what ranks. In May 1958 elections the Pathet Lao startled everyone when they won a majority of the twenty-one seats in the national assembly that were up for balloting, even while receiving only a third of the votes. Soon thereafter the United States halted all foreign aid to the country, forcing out a cabinet that included two Pathet Lao ministers. When the royal army tried to use force to "integrate" (disarm) two Pathet Lao battalions in the spring of 1959, the Communist troops melted away, fleeing their barracks and beginning active resistance to FAR forces. Thus commenced a hot little war in Laos at a time when only the most tentative guerrilla activity had yet occurred in South Vietnam.

Much as it had done in South Vietnam by throwing in its lot with Ngo Dinh Diem at an early date, in Laos too the United States chose sides early on. In the neutralist kingdom that was harder to do, for none of the factions seemed attractive to President Eisenhower or Secretary of State Dulles. Nevertheless, anyone who opposed the Pathet Lao was acceptable to some degree. With its accent on opposition, almost by definition U.S. policy worked against the possibility of a neu-

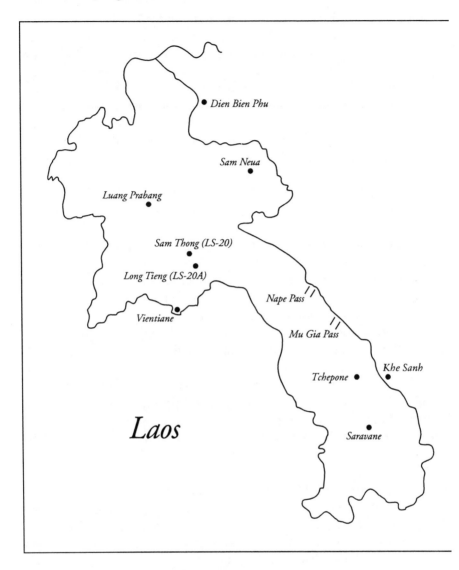

tral Laos. American leaders compounded the effect of this policy by supporting the creation of a new faction, the Committee for the Defense of National Interests (CDNI), an anti-Communist movement with close ties to Laotian military officers. Formed in June 1958 with help from the CIA, the CDNI became the nucleus of a pro–United States political party in Laos.

Laotian neutralist leader Prince Souvanna Phouma initially backed formation of the CDNI, apparently not realizing its potential to disrupt his own political movement, the Rally of the Lao People *(Rassem-blement du Peuple Laotien)*, the majority party in the national assembly. When the U.S. withheld aid payments shortly after the 1958 elections, ostensibly in a dispute over devaluation of the Laotian currency, Souvanna was forced to resign and was succeeded by a cabinet that included CDNI members, a novel development given that that party had not existed at the time of the elections and thus had no elected members. At the same time Pathet Lao officials were expelled from the government. The net result made a mockery of supposed Laotian democracy.

Then came the 1958 shooting incident with the North Vietnamese. The cabinet at Vientiane, the Laotian administrative capital (to distinguish it from the seat of King Sisavang Vong's authority, which was Luang Prabang to the northwest), used the incident to justify assuming emergency powers in early 1959. That spring the Pathet Lao military integration into the FAR miscarried, in effect beginning the Laotian war. The first armed attacks were recorded in Sam Neua province, an area largely dominated by the Pathet Lao, in July 1959.

Americans were in all this action from the beginning. Foreign aid proved a useful lever in influencing Laotian politics. Before the 1958 elections in particular, aid was reprogramed to maximize political impact—using less than 10 percent of that year's aid allocation, the U.S. financed ninety high-visibility rural development projects in selected districts. The civic action programs conducted in South Vietnam (and earlier in the Philippines) by Edward Lansdale were the model for this so-called Operation Booster Shot, coordinated in Laos by Rufus Phillips, who had worked for Lansdale in Vietnam. The high point in terms of drama was the airlift of two parachute-rigged bulldozers from Ashiya, Japan, to points over northern Laos, where they were dropped into remote mountain zones. In all, seventy-two aircraft flights delivered eleven hundred tons of supplies and equipment during Booster Shot. People still debate whether Lansdale really belonged to the CIA, but Phillips surely did.

A formal military aid program was also featured in the American effort from an early date. Because the French kept responsibility for training under the Geneva agreement, the unit the U.S. created in December 1955 was called the Programs Evaluation Office (PEO). It began with just six persons assigned but had twenty within the year and expanded after that. The PEO assisted Royal Laotian armed forces with planning and sent small training teams to the Lao military regions. Hiring Thai interpreters to accompany the PEO teams and translate Lao marked the beginning of a constantly growing role for Thailand in Laos. Meanwhile, the French military mission, increasingly ignored, bided its time—as it turned out, French military presence in Laos outlasted American, being ordered out of the country only toward the end of 1975.

In 1959 the Americans broadened the military advice and training they were not supposed to be giving with Project White Star. This was a covert mission with PEO cover under which 107 U.S. army Special Forces men in civilian clothes worked in teams with FAR units. The Green Berets were from the Seventh Special Forces Group at Fort Bragg, and they were flown in from Bangkok aboard Air America planes. Given that the United States had repeatedly sanctioned increases in FAR strength, raising military aid programs to match, the White Star mission proved crucial to the success of U.S. policy in Laos. The project eventually peaked at 433 men shortly before a 1962 peace agreement. A year earlier, two of the four Green Berets in one White Star team became the first Americans killed in action in Laos when the FAR unit they accompanied was overrun by Pathet Lao; two other men were captured, of whom one died in captivity.

Air America became the third element in the constellation of U.S. capabilities arrayed to support war in Laos. An ostensibly private airline whose true function was to provide CIA an aerial arm, Air America was a "proprietary" in Agency parlance since the CIA controlled it with a hidden hand. Originally formed as Civil Air Transport during the Chinese civil war, in that earlier incarnation Air America furnished the French vital support in their Laotian campaign of 1953 and at Dien Bien Phu in 1954. Reincorporated in Delaware in 1959 as Air America, the company had planes of its own and could also fly aircraft quietly lent to it by the U.S. government. If anyone at this late date still doubts that Air America was a CIA proprietary, it should be noted that Air America artifacts, including a pilot's hat and a baseball cap, are on display in the museum inside CIA headquarters.

Finally, air power in general became central to the war in Laos. Flying artillery that appeared at the behest of American advisers or forward air controllers, air provided the hard edge that cut through the Pathet Lao when all else failed. Air power became increasingly important to the Laotian war as forces increased and their equipment became more sophisticated.

■ Early on, the considered opinion of the United States intelligence community, expressed in Special National Intelligence Estimate

(SNIE) 68-2-59, was that "the communist resumption of guerrilla warfare in Laos was primarily a reaction to a stronger anticommunist posture by the Laotian government and to recent U.S. initiatives in Laos. We consider that it was undertaken mainly to protect the communist apparatus in Laos and to improve communist prospects." The SNIE also found no evidence of North Vietnamese troops with the Pathet Lao at that time (September 1959), and reasoned that Hanoi would rely upon covert rather than overt aid even if foreign forces intervened in Laos. The intelligence components of the army, navy, and State Department all dissented to the CIA's further conclusion that North Vietnamese or Chinese troops might invade in strength if they became convinced that U.S. combat forces were about to enter Laos. The dissenting experts objected to the assessment of better-than-even odds of such an invasion as *overstating* Hanoi's and Beijing's willingness to use major military force against the U.S. These basic views, including the dissenting ones, held through most of the Laotian war.

Laotian politics meanwhile sharpened differences to a point of no return. Pathet Lao former ministers, especially Prince Souphanouvong, cousin of neutralist Souvanna Phouma and a top Pathet Lao leader, were imprisoned when forced out of the government. King Sisavang Vong died in October 1959, to be replaced by Savang Vatthana, who was induced to stand aside while anti-Communists strangled neutralist government. Election rules for an April 1960 election were manipulated in such a way as to prevent any repetition of the Pathet Lao performance in the previous election—this time the Communists were not permitted even to *run* candidates in fifty of the fifty-nine national assembly districts up for election. The CIA also set loose its political-action experts to assist approved candidates. A suitably conservative body of delegates emerged that was closely aligned with the CDNI and rightist military strongman General Phoumi Nosavan who, ironically, during an earlier time of Lao independence efforts against the French, had been a top aide to Souphanouvong.

In a prime illustration of the hardly believable character of Lao politics, a month after the 1960 elections Prince Souphanouvong and all his Pathet Lao comrades imprisoned in Vientiane were able to escape. They did this not by breaking out of jail but by talking the guards into converting to their side!

Laos crossed another watershed in August 1960 when Captain Kong Le used his elite Second Parachute Battalion for a coup d état in Vientiane, overthrowing the right-wing government and then inducing

Souvanna Phouma to return with a new neutralist cabinet. Soon afterward General Phoumi began to assemble his forces in the Laotian panhandle to march on Vientiane, while the U.S. PEO established its deputy chief with a detachment to provide Phoumi direct support.

These events made critical the loyalty of forces in Laotian Military Region II, the area between the panhandle and Vientiane which included the Plain of Jars (so called for its burial sites) as well as tribal settlements. One of the FAR battalion commanders in this region, Lieutenant Colonel Vang Pao, was of the Hmong tribe as were most of the men in his unit. Vang Pao was first and foremost a Hmong, an upland small society of perhaps as many as a half-million souls. When he first met Stuart Methven, the CIA officer who replaced Rufus Phillips in August 1959, Vang Pao's request had been not for money or food but for an anvil to work metal. This kind of thinking impressed Methven, a member of the first class trained at the CIA's secret Virginia facility called Camp Peary. Vang Pao's Hmong lived in a key part of Laos, where the Pathet Lao had their headquarters and main center of operations, where the Pathet Lao's troops had first escaped from "integration" into the FAR, and indeed where Kong Le moved his own neutralist troops to oppose the advance of Phoumi Nosavan. Such aspects were most impressive to the CIA's chief of station in Laos, Gordon L. Jorgensen, and his Washington superiors. The die was cast for war.

By this time Air America was lifting roughly a thousand tons of assorted supplies a month into Laos, mostly from Bangkok to Phoumi's base at Savannakhet. There was enough capacity in the system for a side effort to supply Hmong. President Eisenhower was concerned as well, sending senior officials on a fact-finding tour of Laos in October 1960 and telling John Kennedy during the presidential transition that Laos would be his most critical foreign policy problem. The interest and capability existed for a Hmong program, which the Vientiane CIA station soon cleared with CIA-Bangkok and with the Laotian government. Toward the end of 1960 Stuart Methven introduced Vang Pao to CIA paramilitary expert William Lair and to other Hmong headmen. The presence of a FAR officer at the negotiations served the dual purpose of protecting the CIA with the Laotian government and enabling Agency officials later to claim (as did Douglas Blaufarb in his account of the Laotian operation) that the Hmong agreement was with Phoumi Nosavan. In any case, CIA weapons from Okinawa began to flow to the Hmong, who organized small units at many places in Military Region II. A Joint Chiefs of Staff report dated December 30 makes clear that as of that date Laotian army plans for an attack against the Kong Le–Pathet Lao troops on the Plain of Jars already were providing for the participation of Hmong forces.

The question of Vietnamese intervention in Laos continues to be a point of confusion. In October 1960 PEO chief General John Heintges had been unable to confirm North Vietnamese in Laos. At the end of December, columns were observed in the country coming from the Dien Bien Phu area of Vietnam, but their nationality could not be ascertained. On January 2, 1961, Allen Dulles of the CIA told Eisenhower that Vietnamese were intervening alongside the Pathet Lao, but Secretary of State Christian Herter promptly corrected Dulles—as of that time "nothing has been confirmed concerning this." North Vietnam did in fact enter Laos about this time, but the record establishes that, at best, the CIA intervention was simultaneous with Hanoi's, while it may actually have preceded it.

Air intervention was a further subject of consideration at this time. Evidently at Kong Le's instigation, the Souvanna Phouma government asked Russia to send supplies to the neutralists, and the Soviets responded with a large-scale airlift into the Plain of Jars, including North Vietnamese artillery and mortar batteries. Eisenhower wanted to use B-26 bombers from Thailand to crater the runway and end the airlift, but the only crews available were Americans and so the effort was scotched. The U.S. did give Laos T-6 fighter-bombers, very useful to Phoumi, and shortly thereafter also provided U.S. air force mechanics to repair the Lao planes (at the start 90 Americans were assigned to the Lao air force, which then had total personnel of only 430).

By January 12, 1961, Vang Pao already had 4,300 Hmong troops in the field (2,800 in organized units and 1,500 guerrillas) with another 2,300 FAR soldiers in a drive against the Plain of Jars. Another 500 Hmong were fighting in the vicinity of the Pathet Lao base at Sam Neua. The royal government eventually retook the ground it wanted, but the Pathet Lao reacted by attacking Hmong villages in the highlands. By mid-1961 Vang Pao and many Hmong were being forced out of ancestral villages to trek the periphery of the Plain of Jars to new homes. Vang Pao selected a location after aerial surveys with U.S. officials, including CIA officers and AID workers. A town called Long Tieng, eventually to become the second largest settlement in Laos (40,000 inhabitants) would be created at an airstrip called Lima Site (LS) 20A. A summer 1961 survey of paramilitary activity in Southeast Asia done for President Kennedy put Hmong armed strength at 9,000 men. At the time there were 9 CIA case officers assigned to meet their needs, 3 more Americans handling the administrative side from Vientiane, 9 White Star army specialists, and 99 Thai translators or communicators with thirteen Hmong bases or units.

The Lima Site system became fundamental to the entire war in northern Laos. Lima Site was simply a name for an airfield, each given a number; many were improved airstrips left from the French colonial era. The Lima Site system was set up by Major Harry C. Aderholt, air force unconventional warfare detachment commander, who was an expert on both covert air transport and ground support. Aderholt flew Vang Pao on many of the aerial surveys conducted before the selection of Long Tieng, and he used the flights to chart airstrips all over northern Laos. Instead of using exotic Lao place names, Americans and many others began simply to refer to places by their LS numbers. Thus Long Tieng became LS-20A, though it was typically called "Sky" or "20-Alternate" or just "Alternate." In this a bit of CIA subterfuge was involved, for Sam Thong, the main Hmong refugee aid center, was also numbered LS-20. For military or Air America pilots it made little difference, since the two Lima Sites were separated by nothing more than a mountain ridge and minutes' flying time. For visiting officials or reporters, those minutes made a world of difference, for Sam Thong was a medical and education center while Long Tieng became a fighting base. People who went to LS-20 expecting to see the Laotian war up close were doomed to disappointment.

This play on the numbers of Lima Sites was part and parcel of the whole Laotian experience. It has become fashionable to assert that the "secret war" in Laos was only a fiction—that American media or political opponents of the war called Laos a "secret" war to make it somehow seem dirty and vile. In fact, Laos *was* a true secret war and stayed so right through 1970, when Richard Nixon offered presidential assurances that "no Americans" were in combat in Laos, and journalists managed to travel overland to Long Tieng. During all that time the U.S. government did everything it could to preserve the secret. Money for combat and logistics support drew on accounts for Thailand and South Vietnam, as well as that for Laotian foreign aid. A typical subterfuge was that Agency for International Development (AID) budgets for 1966 and 1967 included the purchase of armored vehicles for the Laotian army. Refugee assistance was also an AID function, and because Vang Pao's army was fighting rather than growing food, Hmong villages whose men were in the field qualified for AID help, as did the fighters themselves, in effect meaning that AID supplied a portion of the Hmong war effort.

Vang Pao's fighting force was explicitly called the *armée clandestine*, the secret army. Its CIA advisers had orders not to go into the field with the Hmong precisely so that Americans would not be seen with the fighters. Similarly, Americans working in Laos (except for embassy and AID personnel) were quartered in Thailand so that it could truthfully be said that no Americans were "in" Laos. Official Americans also had standing orders to avoid talking to others, especially reporters. Actual combat operations were planned only very generally at the embassy in Vientiane, and for the most part were controlled from a secret facility at Ubon, Thailand. The major Air America base was also in Thailand, at Udorn. Air force planes of the First Special Operations Wing, which had the largest share of the support role for the secret warriors, also were based in Thailand. In short, there was a serious effort to avoid disclosure of Laotian operations—the secret war was not a figment of anyone's imagination.

■ Far from the steadily worsening picture that Eisenhower painted, after an initial bout of crisis activity in which marines were sent to Thailand and navy aircraft carriers deployed in the South China Sea, Laos receded as an emergency for President Kennedy. The military situation did not improve, but neither did it worsen, making for a stability of sorts. The relatively relaxed atmosphere is suggested by the recollections of Roswell Gilpatric, deputy to Secretary of Defense McNamara, who reports that the Pentagon did not even consider itself a primary player on Laos policy until sometime in 1962. Before that there would be calls for negotiations from Laotian politicians, Cambodian leaders, and even from the Southeast Asia Treaty Organization, not to say old allies like the British. In March 1961 the sides declared a cease-fire, and in May a diplomatic conference opened at Geneva. Talks continued for more than a year, with the impasse broken in the spring of 1962 and a new Geneva agreement for the neutralization of Laos signed on July 23. Coming full circle, the United States now recognized the Souvanna Phouma government and soon began supplying it military aid.

The 1962 Geneva accord set new ground rules for Laos. Americans from the PEO, and White Star advisers, left the country. The CIA was supposed to abandon its Hmong program as well, but because many doubted that North Vietnam would carry out its side of the bargain, the *armée clandestine* was kept in place, if anything even more secretly, as a form of insurance. In place of the larger American and Thai contingent with the Hmong, just two CIA officers, Anthony Poshepny and Vint Lawrence, were to remain with the Hmong, with strict instructions to stay out of sight. Not coincidentally, Air America received the royal Lao government contract to fly supplies to the uplands; those supplies continued to come from AID. Vang Pao's armed strength was put at 11,000 men. Where before the war ignorance of the Hmong was such that their total numbers were estimated at no more than 50,000, at the time of the 1962 accord there were more than 125,000 Hmong refugees in the new settlements. Their future was accurately predicted by the CIA in a September 1962 special estimate: "Despite Souvanna's assurances that minorities would receive better treatment in the future, it is unlikely that this will come to pass. The principal sufferers will be the [Hmong] and the Khas who have successfully maintained armed bases within [Pathet Lao] territory. The [Pathet Lao] will continue to attack the [Hmong] in particular, refusing to recognize them as part of the FAR."

True to prediction, the North Vietnamese did not pull out of Laos either. Intelligence estimates of Hanoi's strength in Laos at the time of the 1962 agreement stood at about five thousand with the Pathet Lao plus an equal number backing the Kong Le neutralist forces. Only forty North Vietnamese were counted leaving the country by International Control Commission observers. Like the CIA and Hmong, however, the Pathet Lao lay low for some months, not breaking the cease-fire until early 1963. By then both sides were preparing for a new round of warfare.

The *armée clandestine* used the 1962 stand down for a large reorganization. Until then Vang Pao had relied upon small village-based units from a self-defense militia called, in French, *auto-defense de choc*. These, plus a larger semiregular force built around FAR battalions of Military Region II that Vang Pao had originally commanded, provided his main strength. In 1962 began a wider selection of Hmong for larger formations to be called Special Guerrilla Units, or SGUs, which ranged between a company and a battalion in size. Within a year or so the SGUs amounted to ten thousand men out of total Hmong strength of thirty thousand. The Hmong reorganization plan likely led to the first-ever CIA briefing to Congress on the Laotian secret war, in 1962, eventually to be followed by twenty-seven more such briefings over a thirteen-year period. In the argument over whether Laos was a "secret" war, it is clear that Congress helped keep the secret for at least seven years.

During this period a revised support system for the Hmong was also put in place. A small air force unit was installed at the embassy in Vientiane, beginning with three officers and a few men, to schedule, monitor, and provide maps and intelligence for contract air services. This entity, Project 404, eventually helped the U.S. ambassador to Laos in coordinating combat air support missions. Bird Air also supplemented Air America at this time, and both were later joined by Continental Air Services. In 1964, when the air force deployed Detachment 6 of the First Air Commando Wing to Udorn, forward air controllers (radio call name "Raven") were added to the system. In 1963 a new deputy chief of the Joint U.S. Military Advisory Group Thailand began to work solely on military programs for Laos. President Kennedy in July 1963 made important decisions increasing the U.S. covert effort in Laos in anticipation of the Pathet Lao resuming the struggle.

Although there had been numerous incidents of conflict during 1963, including some that spring attributed to the Vang Pao forces, fighting resumed in earnest in the 1964 dry season, when Pathet Lao and North Vietnamese forces mounted an offensive against the Plain of Jars. By then the topsy-turvy nature of Lao politics was reflected in the fact that the U.S. was allied not only with Vang Pao but with former Pathet Lao ally Kong Le and with the Souvanna Phouma government, while maintaining more of an arm's-length relationship with former military allies and CDNI politicians. By 1965 Phoumi Nosavan was forced to flee the country. Later Kong Le also went into exile, and in 1968 his own neutralist army was reintegrated into the FAR.

Meanwhile the Laotian war assumed the character it retained to the end. The dry seasons brought Pathet Lao–North Vietnamese offensives, more often than not successful, usually against the Plain of Jars or some of Vang Pao's Lima Sites. In the rainy seasons Vang Pao counterattacked, and sometimes the FAR did so as well. The long war was punctuated by battles at intervals, as well as military coup attempts in Vientiane (although Souvanna successfully held power through the end). Some of the major engagements were those of Nam Tha, Muong Soui, operation Triangle, Sam Neua, Lima Site 85, Skyline Ridge, Sam Thong, and Long Tieng itself. Vang Pao left Laos only in May 1975, after many long years of war. By then the Hmong were exhausted, used up in the fighting, during the last part of which Thai mercenaries made up a large share of Vang Pao's SGUs. The withdrawal of American air support after the January 1973 Paris peace agreement probably sealed the fate of the *armée clandestine;* but it was simply a proximate cause, for by then the removal of Thai support, the reduction in the scale of available supply, and the continuing indifference of the Vientiane government all helped to destroy the Hmong army.

A final feature of the Laotian war that must be mentioned is drugs. The major cash crop of the Hmong was poppies, processed to make opium or heroin. The Hmong did not use their own product much save for medicinal purposes, but the drug traffic over the years helped to sustain a succession of powers and characters from the French to the Viet Minh, certain Laotian and South Vietnamese generals, and, many charge, the CIA and Vang Pao. The inspector general of the Central Intelligence Agency officially investigated the drug traffic in Laos in the summer of 1972 and found no evidence that any CIA senior officer or the Agency as a whole had ever approved of drug running as a matter of policy. Air America had rules against carrying contraband, but there was no way to prevent individual initiatives by pilots and crews, or Hmong. Laotian traffickers also had the ability to use private air carriers, and some even owned transport aircraft. This said, however, there is also no record that beyond simple rule-making the CIA made a concerted effort to eliminate the drug traffic, which was simultaneously corrupting South Vietnam and the American soldiers who were fighting for that land.

Some former secret warriors, such as one-time CIA station chief Theodore Shackley, have held up Laos as the model for an ideal war, a "third option" to be used against guerrilla movements. This sort of claim demands deeper analysis than it has received. For one thing, the very low estimates advanced for the cost of putting each soldier in the field (just a few dollars per man) appear based on just the cost of weapons. Training, upkeep, maintenance, and monies paid to foreign nationals, such as the Thai, that is, funds from all accounts other than what the CIA alone spent (just in Laos), are not visibly accounted for. In addition, CIA funds themselves were extended by manipulating Laotian and other Far Eastern currency markets, activity that may not always be possible or desirable. A 1974 congressional estimate put real spending for the Laotian secret war at $5 billion, an amount that must still understate the full total of State Department, AID, and Pentagon expenditures for the Laotian war, which was by no means so cheap as sometimes imagined.

Nor was the secret war inexpensive for the Hmong, whose entire society was uprooted and way of life destroyed. Thousands of survivors followed Vang Pao into exile, many of them fortunately permitted to emigrate to the United States, so that more than a hundred thousand Hmong reside in America today. Their brothers and sisters still in Laos, or in Thai refugee camps, continue to suffer. This kind of "cost" of a covert action program should not be passed over lightly.

The toll in American lives is also greater than usually realized. Only 8 fatalities in Laos are acknowledged by the CIA, but this number represents only Agency officers, not contract employees. Between 1970 and 1973 alone, Air America lost 17 Americans and an equal number of local employees in combat or in plane crashes. In addition, in 1969 a State Department release acknowledged the death in Laos of 25 more contractor personnel plus one dependent. The Department of Defense lists 400 combat deaths and 556 missing in action in Laos, and a portion of the 58 battle deaths until recently kept secret and not put on the wall of the Vietnam Memorial also occurred in Laos. Although the data are still too partial to permit a clear comparison, if stated as a proportion of the size of the overall U.S. "deployment," American casualties in Laos may actually match or exceed those in Vietnam— about 500 over the length of the war against a force at a given time of about 1,000 in Laos; compared with 58,000 against 550,000 in South Vietnam). This is a sobering thought.

Exotic, unusual as it was, Laos occupied a particular geographic relationship to Indochina as a whole. Given the political differences that existed in the country, conflict was inevitable, but American efforts to encourage anticommunism as against neutralism in the earliest years contributed significantly to the causes of war. Had the U.S. wholeheartedly supported neutralism and helped a neutral Laos resist encroachments from North Vietnam, it might have been possible to prevent Hanoi's creation of the Ho Chi Minh Trail to the south. Washington's call was different, just as was its call later to *accept* the neutralism of Souvanna Phouma. The latter strategy, again a political judgment, is what rendered impossible the military notion of cutting the Ho Chi Minh Trail by manning a blocking position across the Laotian panhandle. The particular way the United States conducted itself in Laos had a real and lasting impact on the Vietnam War.

Having failed to remove Laos as part of the problem, Americans watched with growing concern as North Vietnamese troops and supplies moved down through the Laotian panhandle while other supplies came by sea and landed at Cambodian seaports on the Gulf of Siam. Soon there were extensive Viet Cong and North Vietnamese bases in Cambodia, a haven for VC and NVA troops whenever they were hard-pressed in the war. Soon there were advocates among American policymakers for an offensive into Cambodia, until then neutral in the Vietnam conflict, to clean out the North Vietnamese base areas. In 1970 Richard Nixon agreed to that operation.

23

Widening the War: Cambodia 1970

As the president delivered his televised speech from the Oval Office—another of those ritual benchmarks of the Vietnam War—the artillery preparation was already rising to a crescendo and air strikes were going in as American troops mounted their tanks and helicopters to invade Cambodia. President Nixon sat behind his desk in the White House, gesturing at a map on an easel behind him. The young GIs following his orders were beginning to move out. South Vietnamese troops were already in motion. The invasion of Cambodia was on.

The Cambodian operation ignited a firestorm of antiwar opposition, including massive demonstrations, campus shutdowns, and killings at Kent State and Jackson State universities. In "the Nam," the invasion was unusual for its border crossing and the size of the operation. In many accounts of this period, the chicaneries of Washington decision-making on Cambodia and the political opposition to the action have overshadowed the military activity. Here our focus will be on the military campaign—what happened and what it accomplished.

Cambodia was about base areas, the "sanctuaries" that North Vietnamese and Viet Cong troops had used for years to rest, train, and supply their forces. Sixteen of these base areas were scattered along the border from the Gulf of Thailand to Laos, most of them long in place. With their tiny armed forces, and intent on maintaining their neutrality, the Cambodians over the years had permitted the establishment of the base areas and had turned a blind eye to activities of the North Vietnamese Army and Viet Cong. Some base areas handled NVA supplies coming down the Ho Chi Minh Trail through Laos, others utilized materiel shipped by sea to Sihanoukville (Kompong Som) on the Gulf of Thailand. In tacit exchange for Cambodian forebearance, the

NVA and VC raised no hand against the government in Phnom Penh, bought rice with American dollars in the Cambodian market—up to 100,000 tons a year, made some use of Cambodian shipping and trucking firms, and confined their bases to a narrow strip along the border only a few miles wide.

The question of NVA and VC supply through Cambodian ports had been controversial within the U.S. command for some time. Since the seizure of a North Vietnamese steel-hulled ship in December 1966, Military Assistance Command Vietnam had been arguing that the seaborne supply line should be cut by blockade or action against the base areas. But intelligence was unable to agree on the extent of this supply or its importance. Data was sparse and judged unreliable. Reports agreed that Cambodian military and commercial firms were involved in the traffic. In response to queries from President Nixon's staff, MACV claimed in early 1969 that Sihanoukville had been the primary port of entry for fourteen thousand tons of military supplies from October 1967 through September 1968, and that Cambodian sources delivered ten thousand tons of this materiel to the base areas. MACV cited 236 reports documenting supplies from Cambodia to South Vietnam, of which only fifteen attributed the observed flow to the Ho Chi Minh Trail. The Central Intelligence Agency agreed there was a flow through Cambodia, but its National Intelligence Estimate in 1968 put the level at only two thousand tons. Pacific Command intelligence essentially accepted the CIA estimate. The State Department argued that "what reliable evidence is available does not suggest that the operation is of the magnitude MACV describes." The view at the Pentagon was that "the methodology of the studies and the information upon which they are based are not reliable enough to make a meaningful estimate at this time."

At the Office of Current Intelligence within CIA, analyst Paul Walsh conducted one of these studies. Walsh had made his reputation with logistics studies, and this one was quite sophisticated. Intercepted radio traffic established merchant vessel itineraries. Taking the ships' time in port, multiplied by off-loading capacity, and subtracting known nonmilitary tonnage, Walsh arrived at a figure of something like six thousand tons from 1967 to early 1970. By then MACV's claims were up to about eighteen thousand.

Nixon responded to the drumbeat of MACV requests to do something about the Cambodia base areas, at first secretly with B-52 bombings begun in the spring of 1969. In early 1970 he allowed MACV to provide logistic support for a series of small cross-border raids launched by the Army of the Republic of Vietnam (ARVN). That March the Cambodian government of Prince Norodom Sihanouk was suddenly overthrown in a coup by his prime minister, General Lon Nol. The coup led to requests for U.S. military aid. Sihanouk formed an alliance with the NVA/VC and the Communist Khmer Rouge to fight Lon Nol. Literally the French words for "Cambodian Reds," Khmer Rouge was the generic term applied to a Communist movement that had undergone many changes of name since its leaders began to be politically active about 1950, and which had crystallized during the period 1960–1964. The Khmer Rouge maintained a loose alliance with the North Vietnamese and Viet Cong, though there was no integrated military command. The continuing ARVN cross-border raids also irritated the NVA and VC, who began to leave their base areas and move deeper into Cambodia to engage Lon Nol forces.

Many from the ARVN and MACV regarded the Lon Nol coup as an opportunity to act against the base areas, with the NVA/VC intervention providing the rationale. ARVN stepped up its raids, beginning to mount multibattalion forays, including armor. Looking ahead to a secret meeting with the North Vietnamese in Paris on April 4, at the end of March the U.S. asked Vietnamese president Nguyen Van Thieu to halt the border raids, which in fact resumed the day following the talks. Thieu then ordered General Do Cao Tri, commander of his III Corps, to conduct a major raid into the "Angel's Wing" area of Cambodia's Svay Rieng Province. This three-day operation involving roughly seven thousand troops, almost a division in size, was executed by the ARVN Twenty-fifth Division and began on April 14. The left flank of the ARVN concentration was screened by the Third Brigade of Major General Edward Bautz Jr.'s Twenty-fifth Infantry Division.

Meanwhile, on March 27 MACV initiated planning for a multi-division incursion into Cambodia. Two weeks later the MACV commander, General Creighton Abrams, met with General Cao Van Vien, chief of the ARVN Joint General Staff (JGS) and confidentially raised the subject of an attack into the Cambodian base areas. Vien immediately reported the discussion to Thieu, who issued verbal orders which JGS passed to III Corps to begin planning. On April 14 JGS directed III Corps to coordinate its planning, then focused on Svay Rieng, with Lieutenant General Michael S. Davison's U.S. II Field Force. Do Cao Tri restricted knowledge of the operation within III Corps and allowed only a small planning staff to work on it. Brigadier General Dennis P. McAuliffe, deputy senior adviser to III Corps, provided liaison with the Americans. The Vietnamese plans were completed on April 27.

Only after this process was in motion was the invasion option broached with U.S. authorities. Visiting Hawaii on April 17 (April 18, Saigon date), President Nixon received a threat briefing from Pacific commander Admiral John S. McCain III that so impressed him he asked McCain to fly to California and repeat it for national security adviser Henry Kissinger. Within a few days Washington was actively considering the invasion option.

Abrams, who was asking Washington on April 18 to be allowed to use tactical air strikes in Cambodia, in addition to the secret B-52 bombing, soon got notice that bigger things might be in the works. On the morning of the 22nd Abrams received a cable from army chief of staff General William C. Westmoreland that "the present concern of higher authority may be conducive to relaxation of some of the constraints under which we have been operating. If this happens we should be prepared to take advantage of the opportunity." Abrams came back with an eight-point suggested program that included continuing ARVN cross-border operations, use of American artillery and tactical air support in Cambodia, riverine operations on the Mekong, and combined U.S./ARVN operations against the Svay Rieng base areas.

Abrams was then brought into White House decision-making as Nixon and Kissinger opened up a back channel to MACV for the general to advise on measures to be taken. In a regular message from the Joint Chiefs of Staff, on April 23 MACV was ordered to send up plans for the ARVN cross-border operation. But the next day, on the back channel, Abrams received word to complete plans for a combined U.S./ARVN incursion into the "Fish Hook" region of Svay Rieng, which contained NVA/VC base areas 352 and 353, one of them thought to host the Central Office for South Vietnam (COSVN), the main NVA/VC headquarters for the south. On April 25, in his regular channel again, Abrams proposed a unilateral U.S. attack on the "Fish Hook" to JCS chairman General Earle Wheeler, but Wheeler allowed that he felt authorization for this would be unlikely and told MACV to stick to the combined attack option. It was the combined attack that Nixon approved, and Wheeler passed the final authorization to Abrams on April 29, twenty-four hours after allowing U.S. support for the associated ARVN attack into the "Parrot's Beak" section that contained base areas 367 and 706.

At lower levels American forces in Vietnam were not at first privy to the maneuvers of command. Suddenly, on April 26, II Field Force sent orders to Major General Elvy B. Roberts, commanding the First

Cavalry Division (Airmobile), to draft the operations plan, coordinate II FF actions, and be prepared to execute the incursion on seventy-two hours notice. The Cav, the "First Team," responded with alacrity and prepared the plan in little more than a day. Since it had previously been operating to screen Saigon, the division's major difficulty was redeploying to assembly areas within the short time allowed.

ARVN, meanwhile, pushed ahead with its Parrot's Beak attack, christened Toan Thang (Total Victory) 42. Do Cao Tri's troops had assembled by April 28 and crossed their line of departure the next evening. First into Cambodia was a U.S. Mike Force battalion with thirty Special Forces troopers. They were followed by three task forces of ARVN armored cavalry and rangers, units organic to the Fifth and Twenty-fifth divisions and III Corps, amounting to about eight thousand men with seventy U.S. advisers. Some hoped that General Tri's offensive would provide a diversion assisting the combined U.S./ARVN attack into the Fish Hook. The II Field Force command augmented each of the ARVN task forces with a mixed battery of 105 mm howitzers, while six batteries of medium and heavy artillery provided general fire support, coordinated by a forward element of the Twenty-third Artillery Group at Go Dau Ha, where III Corps had placed its tactical headquarters.

The combined incursion the Americans designated operation Rock Crusher. For this the Cav assembled a task force under Brigadier General Robert M. Shoemaker, assistant division commander for maneuver. Task Force Shoemaker included the Third Brigade (Colonel Robert C. Kingston) of the division, with the First and Second battalions, Seventh Cavalry, and the Second Battalion, Fifth Cavalry, augmented by the Second Battalion, Thirty-fourth Armor, the Second Battalion, Forty-seventh Infantry (Mechanized), the Eleventh Armored Cavalry Regiment (Colonel Donn A. Starry), and the Third Brigade of the ARVN Airborne Division. Screening the right flank of this disposition were the Ninth Regiment of the ARVN Fifth Division and the ARVN First Armored Cavalry Squadron. During elaboration of the final plans, the division was directed to be prepared to execute on forty-eight hours' notice, which would have been on April 30, but there was a final one-day postponement.

Massive support was laid on for the initial advance, with the bulk of fire support planning done between April 27 and 29, followed by detailed coordination with air assets. Artillery units assumed their positions beginning April 29. Forces included thirty-six 105 mm howitzers, forty-eight 155 mm howitzers, four 8-inch howitzers, and six

175 mm guns. A 390-minute barrage began at 6 a.m. on May 1, delivering 2,436 rounds. Just before the artillery cut in, six serials of B-52 bombers dropped their ordnance on identified hard targets while, as the barrage continued, forty-eight tactical air strikes completed the support ensemble.

Since the intent of Rock Crusher was to capture COSVN and the base area, obstructing any retreat was an important element of the operation. This was to be accomplished by heliborne insertion of the ARVN Third Airborne Brigade behind the enemy positions. As the artillery opened up, at first concentrating on the proposed Landing Zones (LZs), Lieutenant Colonel Clark A. Burnett's First Squadron, Ninth Cavalry sent scout helicopters over the area. At 6:30 a.m. a specially equipped C-130 aircraft dropped a Commando Vault fifteen-thousand-pound bomb that detonated seven feet off the ground to clear LZ East; fifteen minutes later the experience was repeated at LZ Center. At 8:10 a.m. the ARVN Third Airborne Battalion made its combat assault into LZ East. The ARVN Fifth Airborne Battalion, lifted by forty-two ships and covered by twenty-two Cobra gunships, reached LZ Center by 10:15 a.m. while the Ninth Airborne landed at LZ West. NVA troops were seen fleeing and some were engaged by the Ninth Airborne and by Ninth Cavalry helicopters.

To the south of the Fish Hook, Company C of the Second Battalion, Forty-seventh Infantry (Mechanized) crossed the border at 9:45 a.m., closely followed by Second Battalion, Thirty-fourth Armor, and the Second and Third Squadrons of the Eleventh Armored Cavalry. The Second Squadron (Lieutenant Colonel Grail L. Brookshire) received fire right on the border from elements of two enemy battalions. From their command vehicles with the lead tank platoon, Brookshire and Colonel Starry directed artillery and tactical air that immediately suppressed the fire. The Eleventh Cavalry crossed the border at 10 a.m. All four mechanized units moved north throughout the day, securing LZs to be used that afternoon by the Third Brigade, Twenty-fifth Division. They met little opposition until late that afternoon, when a company of the Eleventh came under fire by an estimated battalion as it entered a clearing six kilometers inside Cambodia. Starry ordered Lieutenant Colonel Bobby F. Griffin to hit the NVA in the flank with his Third Squadron. The enemy broke and fled at 4:45 p.m.; two troopers of the Eleventh were the only American fatalities on the first day of Rock Crusher. In the final heliborne assault that day, two companies of the Second Battalion, Seventh Cavalry moved into the northern part of the Task Force Shoemaker area. Support that day was rounded out with another 3,024 artillery rounds plus 137 tactical air strikes.

While the combined forces entered the Fish Hook, ARVN continued its Toan Thang 42 operation around Parrot's Beak. Do Cao Tri's three task forces wheeled south as about ten thousand troops of the ARVN IV Corps, forming a second pincer, attacked to the north. On May 1 III Corps forces entered Svay Rieng town. Three days later the pincers met after engaging elements of the NVA Ninth Division. IV Corps forces then began to reposition themselves for an offensive to clear the banks of the Mekong River. III Corps cleared Route 1 to Svay Rieng and considered it secure by May 11. Do Cao Tri's armored elements conducted further attacks to the north and west into Prey Veng and the Chup plantation and continued active through the end of June. At least two units, the Third Mike Force and ARVN Thirty-first Ranger Battalion, incurred such heavy losses that they had to be replaced as early as May 1.

In the Rock Crusher area on May 2 the Second Squadron, Eleventh Armored Cavalry linked up with the ARVN airborne to complete the encirclement of the Fish Hook. The Second Battalion, Forty-seventh Infantry meanwhile cut Route 7 near Memot and assumed a blocking position on the task force's left flank. One after another, General Shoemaker committed the battalions of the First Cavalry Division assigned to him. Already the ARVN and American troops had begun finding large stockpiles of NVA/VC equipment and supplies, plus camp areas, and their discoveries increased as the days passed.

Despite all the finds, however, there was no COSVN. As late as May 3, in a briefing given to U.S. congressional staff members, MACV officers remained confident the NVA/VC headquarters would be overrun and even described what they thought it might look like. But six days later the subject had dropped out of MACV briefings. A Vietnamese account of the Cambodian incursion observes that the NVA and VC probably expected follow-up operations after the mid-April III Corps attack into the Angel's Wing. Artillery movements and the sudden demand for Cambodia maps before Rock Crusher were also inevitable indicators of the coming offensive. Colonel Starry believes that "the enemy definitely knew of the attack." But the Viet Cong and North Vietnamese definitely had not gotten their warning in the last few days before the attack. Documents captured farther to the north later in May and dated in *March* spoke of a U.S./South Vietnamese intention to attack the sanctuaries. In addition, an authoritative account by the former minister of justice in the VC's Provisional Revolutionary

Government describes in detail the movement of COSVN and associated VC leadership to Kratie in the Cambodian interior, a movement made in March only days after the overthrow of Sihanouk. In the Fish Hook there was no COSVN to capture.

While the big headquarters was gone, Rock Crusher did capture assorted base camps of the enemy Fifth and Seventh divisions. On the afternoon of May 3 the Eleventh Armored Cavalry was ordered to advance forty kilometers to the north and take the town of Snuol. Colonel Starry selected Route 7 as his axis of advance, and by early afternoon on May 4 his lead elements had broken out of the jungle and were atop the ridgeline next to the road. Brookshire's Second Squadron led the advance and reached speeds up to forty miles an hour. Soon the regiment was strung out behind its spearhead. In midafternoon the forward elements encountered a blown bridge but were able to proceed after placing an armored vehicle bridge across the stream. When a second blown bridge obstructed the advance, the regiment commander ordered a halt for the night, enabling the full Second and Third squadrons to catch up to the lead elements. After placing another vehicle bridge, the Eleventh Cavalry moved out the next morning, only to be halted again at a third site that would have required a large bridge. A heavy lift helicopter (CH-54) with an M4T6 bridge was requested, but little progress had been made by noon. Starry, anxious to regain his momentum, set out on foot with a bridging vehicle to find a place where the temporary vehicle bridge could be used. After several tries the stream was bridged, and the Eleventh Cavalry resumed its advance by 1 p.m. The two squadrons met resistance at Snuol, brought up artillery, and attempted to surround the town, unsuccessfully, though they captured it on the first assault.

On May 4, as the armored cavalry headed for Snuol, scout helicopters of the Ninth Cavalry sighted a large base camp. Company C, First Battalion, Fifth Cavalry entered this complex on May 5, and it turned out to be the biggest single supply find of the war. Soon dubbed "The City," the base yielded many tons of ammunition and supplies as well as 1,282 individual and 202 crew-served weapons, and required weeks to search and remove the captured materiel. Searchers found 182 storage bunkers, 18 mess halls, a training area, and a small animal farm. The need to destroy such structures, bridging, and other tasks in the invasion soon generated a substantial requirement for engineering support that was met by battalions organic to the divisions and to the Eleventh Cavalry, as well as by the Seventy-ninth Engineer Group, which fielded the Thirty-first and 588th Combat Engineer battalions plus the Sixty-second, Ninety-second, and 554th Construction Engineer battalions.

Reports of the big supply cache and base finds flowed into Washington from the first day of the offensive. On May 1 (May 2, Saigon date) Richard Nixon went to the National Military Command Center at the Pentagon for an early briefing on results. At the meeting the president suddenly directed that the offensive be expanded to hit all possible base areas, not just those in the Parrot's Beak and Fish Hook. These orders were quickly repeated to MACV which, in conjunction with the Vietnamese, planned additional operations in both the III Corps (II Field Force) and II Corps (I Field Force) areas. Thieu also dispatched orders to his IV Corps commander to plan an operation that would clear the Mekong up to Phnom Penh and evacuate Vietnamese residents in Cambodia. Planning was quickly put in motion and largely completed by May 5.

For the Cav in the Rock Crusher zone, expansion meant an additional attack against Base Area 351 north of Phuoc Long province. To supervise the enlarged sector, General Roberts assumed direct command of all Cav forces in Cambodia on May 5, with Task Force Shoemaker deactivated. The next day Colonel Carter W. Clarke air assaulted two battalions of his Second Brigade into LZs northeast of Bu Dop. On the morning of the 7th, elements of Lieutenant Colonel Francis A. Ianni's Second Battalion, Twelfth Cavalry, discovered another large NVA/VC camp, this one quickly dubbed "Rock Island East." Estimates were that it would take many hundreds of hours of flying time to remove all the captured materiel, so engineers opened up an access road from the border. Even so, it took nine days to clear out Rock Island East. The Second Brigade's last remaining battalion helilifted to an LZ north of Ba Gia Map on May 11. A day later the Fifth Battalion, Twelfth Infantry of the 199th Light Infantry Brigade reinforced the Cav and replaced Fifth Battalion, Seventh Cavalry at Fire Support Base Brown, only to face an NVA counterattack the very next night.

Other operations were going forward in the III Corps sector. One, conducted entirely by ARVN, was Toan Thang 46, a May 6 attack by its Ninth Regiment against Base Area 350. A unilateral U.S. operation was launched the same day by the reinforced Third Brigade, Twenty-fifth Division, striking west of Tay Ninh province into Base Area 354. With four battalions plus the Sixty-fifth Engineers, this effort received helicopter support from the 3/17 Cavalry.

After cooperating with Do Cao Tri in the initial phases of the first ARVN incursion, IV Corps redeployed its forces for the Mekong operation, Cuu Long. Five armored cavalry squadrons, the Fourth Ranger Group, the Ninth Division, and portions of the Twenty-first Division formed strong armor-infantry columns on both banks of the river. On the Mekong itself was Task Force 211, a Vietnamese navy riverine force including the First Vietnamese Marine Brigade. The Vietnamese had U.S. marine advisers, helicopter support from the American Cougar Task Force, and a complement of forty U.S. navy river patrol boats. A joint U.S. navy/Vietnamese navy staff was aboard the *USS Benewah* anchored at Tan Chau. The American craft first came under fire only two miles inside the Cambodian border, even before the formal start of Cuu Long on May 9, but the opposition was swiftly neutralized. As the forces moved upriver more boats were added until they comprised fully one hundred craft, though the American boats stayed within 21.7 miles of the border to conform with a limit of 30 kilometers for the American incursion, first announced by President Nixon at a meeting with congressmen. The Vietnamese, leaving behind their advisers at the 21.7-mile point, proceeded upriver. Along the way they relieved a besieged Cambodian army regional headquarters at Kompong Cham. In continuing operations the boats evacuated seventy thousand Vietnamese refugees and established a riverine base in Cambodia at Neak Luong.

Operations in II Corps posed a special problem for the commander of U.S. I Field Force, Lieutenant General Arthur S. Collins, Jr. American forces had almost completed their withdrawal from the Central Highlands in preparation for repatriation, so that Major General Glenn D. Walker's Fourth Division was operating in Binh Dinh Province near the coast. Collins ordered Walker to move forces back into the interior for Binh Tay, a series of assaults planned for Base Areas 701, 702, and 740, west and southwest of Pleiku. Walker managed to get his First Brigade, reinforced by an additional battalion, into place by the start of the operation on May 6, but his Second Brigade was only arriving in its assembly areas by that time. The initial operations involved the Americans plus elements of the ARVN Twenty-second Division moving on Base Area 702. Again there was some success in uncovering supply caches and only intermittent contact with the enemy. The Americans had withdrawn by May 25, but ARVN operations continued through June, reinforced by a large fraction of their Twenty-third Division. Considerable air force transport activity supported the operations with deliveries to the fields at Plei Djereng, for

Fourth Division, and Duc Co, for the Vietnamese. In late June air transport again proved vital in evacuating Cambodian troops and refugees from the isolated outposts of Ba Kev and Buong Long, moving more than 3,100 Cambodians to Phnom Penh in forty-five sorties, the last of them taking off under small-arms fire. Such fire also inflicted a notable loss on U.S. engineers when a helicopter was shot down while surveying Route 509 about ten miles southwest of Pleiku. Aboard were Major General John A. B. Dillard, the senior army engineer in Vietnam, with a number of engineer command officers.

In addition to their combat engineering in Cambodia and their work in the base camps, engineers did much to make the air logistics support possible, contributing more than fifty thousand man-hours to airfield improvements. In turn, the air logistics made possible the extensive use of heliborne tactics in Cambodia. With the road net, limited as it was, largely taken up by combat movements and removal of NVA/VC supplies, there was little spare capacity to move aviation fuel to the front. This was especially critical for operations of the First Cavalry Division, which air assaulted its last available battalion into Cambodia on June 5. Air transport successively supplied fields at Katum, Tonle Cham, Loc Ninh, Bu Dop, Bu Gia Map, O Rang, and Song Be, not to mention the fields in the II Corps zone. In May, deliveries to First Cavalry alone by air exceeded 3.7 million gallons plus 300 tons of munitions daily. Road movement of petroleum was 6 million gallons, but most of that went to the less advanced bases of Quan Loi, Tay Ninh, and Phuoc Vinh. In two months starting April 30, the 834th Air Division transported 75,000 passengers and 49,600 tons of cargo to twenty-two border airstrips.

In these later phases of the Cambodian campaign, MACV was working against a time limit, for at a press conference in Washington on May 8 (May 9, Saigon date) Nixon had announced that all U.S. troops would be out of Cambodia by June 30. The forces found what supplies they could and engaged the enemy where they could, but there was a limit to what could be done in the time available. The last American troops in fact left Cambodia on June 29.

After the withdrawal Nixon issued a white paper to demonstrate the success of the Cambodian incursion. The invasion had cost $2 billion. It captured 2,156 real or suspected enemy troops; 2,509 crew-served weapons; 22,892 small arms; 15 million rounds of small-arms ammunition; 143,000 rocket, mortar, or recoilless rifle rounds; 199,552 antiaircraft rounds; assorted mines, grenades, and explosives; 7,250 tons of rice; 55 tons of medical supplies; and 435 vehicles, including a Mercedes and a Porsche. Claimed enemy killed were 11,285. Admitted ARVN casualties included 799 battle deaths and 3,410 wounded. Admitted U.S. losses were 339 killed in action and 1,501 wounded, plus 45 aircraft downed.

There is reason to believe that the actual cost of Cambodia was higher than stated. For one thing, a Vietnamese account gives a slightly different picture, listing 1,525 American wounded (this account also lists enemy killed at 11,369 and captured or rallied at 2,328, along with ARVN wounded at 3,009). The white paper said nothing about Americans missing in action or prisoners, though later records list 28 MIAs in Cambodia and another 47 killed there whose bodies were never recovered. No doubt these losses did not all occur in 1970, but a significant portion of them did. The Vietnamese account lists 13 American and 35 ARVN missing in action. Nor is there anything in the white paper about nonbattle deaths. In addition, a recent history of the First Cavalry Division (Airmobile) concludes that its official losses in Cambodia were understated, and this is likely true for other participating units as well.

The direct dollar costs attributed to the operation were also affected by equipment losses. The white paper listed only aircraft, not helicopters, tanks, APCs, or guns. American forces were in fact working under orders that all their major equipment, even if damaged beyond repair, was to be evacuated to South Vietnam. Breakdowns and losses actually forced the withdrawal of Second Battalion, Thirty-fourth Armor just five days into the offensive. The real extent of major equipment losses remains unknown due to accounting tricks, but it would certainly increase the dollar cost of the Cambodian operation.

Finally, the extent to which Cambodia truly set back the North Vietnamese is impossible to determine. In Washington and Saigon, various claims were bandied about during and after the operation. These included estimates of three to four months' delay in NVA activities—or six to eight months, a year, two years. There were no major NVA offensives after Cambodia during 1970, but documents captured during the operation indicated that the North Vietnamese had no intention to conduct any offensives that year. Assertions that the number of weapons captured would have equipped a large number of NVA combat battalions are misleading. The stocks of small arms, for example, were mostly of types no longer used in the field; the North Vietnamese had no reason to expend energy and resources to move them back to North Vietnam. Hanoi's base network and general supply levels were certainly disrupted, but these were probably the first features of the NVA system to recover.

As for assertions that the Cambodian invasion reduced U.S. casualty rates in the months that followed, the data are ambiguous because over the same period American forces were spending less and less time in the field themselves. Only one major U.S. offensive followed in the year after Rock Crusher. Troop levels were constantly falling. Fewer troops and less time in danger inevitably translated into lower casualties, and this "effect" would have been apparent whether or not there had been an invasion of Cambodia.

The truth is, no one really knows how effective the Cambodian invasion was. The one real fact is that the conflict subsequently engulfed Cambodia. The Vietnam War became the Indochina war.

Whatever the impact of Cambodia, the Americans and South Vietnamese felt compelled to conduct a similar offensive foray into southern Laos in the spring of 1971. There the improvements in ARVN effectiveness and morale, the supposed product of Vietnamization, were put to the test. The result came as a surprise, both to MACV and to Washington.

24   Laos 1971: No Plug in the Funnel

It was a splendid project on paper," says Henry Kissinger in retrospect. The helicopters would fly in from the east, deposit instant firebases in the rugged Laotian hills, while a big armored force pushed up the road to join them. The thrust would destroy key North Vietnamese base areas along the Ho Chi Minh Trail. After this raid in the grand style, carried out by South Vietnamese forces, the invaders would hang on through the dry season to dispute North Vietnamese Army passage down the trail. Kissinger was national security adviser in Richard Nixon's White House when the National Security Council considered the Laotian invasion and Nixon approved it. The chief drawback of the Laotian plan, Kissinger now concedes, "was that it in no way accorded with Vietnamese realities."

In accordance with the dictum that defeat is an orphan, Kissinger admits being a major proponent of a dry-season offensive but adroitly distances himself from responsibility for the decision. Nixon did it, according to Kissinger. According to Nixon, he would do it again—"the operation was a military success." Not many would agree with this assessment by their former president. Undersecretary of State U. Alexis Johnson recalls Laos as "ill-conceived from the start." Former Vietnam intelligence chief General Phillip B. Davidson calls Laos the "raid too far." Colonel Do Ngoc Nhan, senior ARVN officer and deputy chief of the South Vietnamese central training command, judges the invasion as "further evidence of our erroneous evaluation of the enemy capability." Kissinger defensively argues that the Laotian invasion did not meet all his hopes but was not a complete failure.

However one may evaluate its results, the Laotian invasion of February and March 1971 proved a watershed of the Vietnam War: it was the last major offensive operation involving American troops. The Americans, in operation Dewey Canyon II, prepared the ground for ARVN soldiers to make the actual invasion. The Vietnamese, who code-named their side of the effort Lam Son 719, were crossing watersheds of their own—the operation was the largest ever conducted by the ARVN, the first to be wholly controlled by South Vietnamese commanders. How they performed became an important benchmark for the Vietnam War. Since 1969 the South Vietnamese, under Nixon's "Vietnamization" program, had been taking over the war; Laos would show their mettle.

On February 8 many of the ARVN soldiers were jaunty as they entered Laos. Four to six weeks later the ARVN units reeled as they were driven back into South Vietnam. This is the story of what happened.

■ The United States had a problem in the summer of 1970 that the top leadership, Military Assistance Command Vietnam, quietly discussed with Washington. After the Cambodian invasion, in which many NVA supply bases had been overrun and NVA troops dispersed into the interior of Cambodia, there seemed little to threaten the southern part of South Vietnam save the Viet Cong infrastructure. The large-unit war had clearly shifted to the northern provinces. The ARVN, however, could not redeploy its forces to the north to match the shift because they were territorially recruited and based, inflexible except for the elite general reserve units. As the Pentagon systems analysts put it, there was a "battalion deficit" in the northern provinces with a surplus in the south. The problem could not be solved by varying the rate of U.S. withdrawals from South Vietnam because MACV had already pulled its troops out of the south, while additional withdrawals in the north would only magnify the deficit. MACV estimated that the ARVN was already short eight battalions in the north.

In the White House, Kissinger's thinking was that an allied dry-season offensive into the NVA base areas would retard the enemy buildup, thus preserving Vietnamization, reducing the battalion deficit, and increasing Hanoi's incentives to negotiate an end to the war. Kissinger thought Cambodia the best target for the offensive because a renewed operation there "was almost certain to succeed." The problem with the notion of a second Cambodian invasion was that it did nothing to solve the major threat to the northern provinces or the battalion deficit. On November 4, 1970, Nixon asked State, CIA, and the Pentagon for an intensive survey of the full range of options.

A review of inspired leaks, press reports, and official statements clearly shows that the Laos invasion option was a straw in the wind. Secretary of Defense Melvin R. Laird had declared on more than one occasion in 1970 that he had the authority to order operations into Laos, and actually had admitted one small operation that had occurred. In mid-November both U.S. and South Vietnamese officers told reporters they expected attacks come spring in the DMZ region, while other reporters were specifically informed of an estimate that Hanoi had doubled its rate of infiltration down the Ho Chi Minh Trail. The implication was left that counteraction was possible and, in late December senior sources in Saigon were quoted in the *New York Times* as expecting that 1971 would be even "more crucial" than the year of Cambodia. In Washington Admiral Thomas H. Moorer, now chairman of the Joint Chiefs of Staff, capped the point by telling an interviewer that one possible course of action might be a South Vietnamese attack into southern Laos. "Any action against those lines of supply," Moorer asserted, "would be effective because they are vulnerable to interdiction."

Decisions on the secret level paralleled the straws in the wind. The president on November 28 confirmed his orders for a canvass of the options. There is some question as to how much of the impetus for what followed came directly from Kissinger's NSC staff. At the time of Lam Son 719 the Nixon administration made some effort to depict the offensive as a purely South Vietnamese creation. The only "decision" taken in Washington, supposedly, was to support the Vietnamese. But evidence shows that the United States was active at every stage in the evolution of the Laos invasion plan and decision.

After Kissinger's recommendation, but without accepting his Cambodia option, Nixon ordered deputy national security adviser Alexander M. Haig to Vietnam for an on-the-spot evaluation of the alternatives. Haig went to Saigon from December 11 to 18 and returned with news of a unanimous view favoring a dry-season offensive in Laos. Agreeing with this course were MACV commander General Creighton Abrams, U.S. ambassador Ellsworth Bunker, and South Vietnamese president Nguyen Van Thieu. At MACV General Abrams began planning an actual military operation. All this followed a script set by Nixon who, according to Kissinger, wished to maneuver the Pentagon into advocating the offensive so as to avoid making the White House the focus for all the criticism that would result from the invasion. Before the Haig visit, recalls an aide to Laird, there was no talk of anything in Laos. After the visit Abrams was actively planning. Moreover, a talk between Kissinger and Nixon on December 18, the day of

Haig's return (a conversation recorded by White House chief of staff H. R. Haldeman), shows that on that very day these officials were in agreement on an operating plan to send South Vietnamese troops into Laos for a major attack without direct U.S. support. The Laird aide also observed signs of a back channel for communication between the White House and MACV which could be used to make it appear that the Laos proposals were simply the idea of General Abrams.

The White House back channel to Abrams bypassed the chain of command through the Joint Chiefs even though Admiral Moorer was a Kissinger ally on Laos. Not only did Moorer help stiffen Secretary Laird, but he floated trial balloons with the press, accompanied Laird on a January 1971 Southeast Asia trip, and had private meetings with Kissinger and Nixon, apparently to plan the scripts for larger national security sessions that would include both Secretary Laird and his diplomatic counterpart, Secretary of State William P. Rogers. But direct White House dealings with MACV had been a feature of the preparation for the Cambodian invasion in 1970, and the formula was repeated for Laos.

As for the South Vietnamese government, there was no planning there, not even after the Haig trip, until Abrams issued a MACV directive on January 7, 1971, authorizing joint planning for certain operations. Abrams also called on his ARVN opposite number, General Cao Van Vien, chief of the Vietnamese Joint General Staff (JGS), to suggest that the two armies plan a drive into the Laotian panhandle. A few days later they met again, and Abrams went into more detail using a map—U.S. troops could clear the way to the border in an initial phase, after which ARVN airborne and armored units would make the main effort up Route 9 into Laos. The objective would be to disrupt NVA Base Areas 604 and 611. A smaller simultaneous operation would be mounted in Cambodia, at the Chup rubber plantation near Snuol, as a diversion for the main effort.

General Vien proved a receptive audience. He had long favored isolating the adversary with a combination of pacification plus attacks into North Vietnam above the Demilitarized Zone. A strike at the Laotian panhandle was not quite that, but it was close. Vien immediately reported the Abrams discussions to Nguyen Van Thieu. The South Vietnamese president agreed, then asked how his JGS chief saw the operation. Cao Van Vien's concept was for an airborne strike at Tchepone as a first step, with an armor and infantry column west along Route 9. The JGS chief wanted to open up a forward airfield at Tchepone and then have the paratroops reverse their steps and attack *east* along the road to link up with the mechanized column. Vien asked his J-3 operations section to identify suitable drop zones and landing zones in the Tchepone sector. Later in the planning process, evidently feeling he had to conform to the MACV concept, General Vien dropped the Tchepone landings without even discussing it with Creighton Abrams. Lam Son 719 would be a more conventional leapfrogging operation with the airborne and mechanized forces advancing in tandem with each other.

MACV and Alexander Haig stood foursquare behind the Laotian scheme. They developed a slick briefing advocating the offensive. Kissinger sat through it so many times he dreaded the briefing, which Nixon insisted on staging for others, and at which the president behaved as though he were reacting to the news for the first time. Secretary of Defense Laird was the critical convert for Nixon, who wanted to deflect the political fallout of the Laotian invasion. On December 23, having already recruited Admiral Moorer, he had Haig describe his trip for Laird. The defense secretary was planning a visit to Saigon, and the president explicitly asked him to evaluate the proposals for the dry-season offensive while he was there. In Vietnam with Moorer from January 11 to 15, Laird learned the gospel from Abrams. For his own reasons Laird elected to advocate the dry-season offensive too. Only the State Department remained outside the circle of consensus.

Planning continued among a small group in Washington and Saigon while Laird made this trip. At the Oval Office on January 18 it was Laird's turn to describe his recommendations. This time William P. Rogers and CIA director Richard Helms sat among the listeners. At the meeting before Christmas the president had told them he would order American air and logistics support for an ARVN offensive; now Laird was presenting a concrete recommendation. According to Kissinger, Rogers went along with the proposal, concerned only about the level of American casualties. Richard Helms uncharacteristically raised the most serious objections: similar offensives had been proposed frequently in the past, Helms argued, and always rejected as too difficult. In retrospect, Kissinger admits, "we allowed ourselves to be carried away by the daring conception." He also complains that the clearest success of Vietnamization seems to have been transferring to ARVN the Americans' facility for clever briefing.

The man who should have been asked appears nowhere in these deliberations. General William C. Westmoreland, army chief of staff, was Abrams's predecessor at MACV. Westmoreland knew more than anyone in the army when it came to invasions of Laos, or at least planning them. A number of such plans had been crafted during his time at MACV. One in late 1966, named Full Cry, had called for a corps-sized offensive of three U.S. and one Vietnamese divisions; a scaled-down plan, Fire Break, followed a couple of months later. After that came the multiphase York plans that had a cross-border component. Still later, in early 1968 General Bruce Palmer, Westmoreland's deputy, presided over El Paso I and II, plans for either two American and a Vietnamese division, or for one reinforced division. Most of these plans envisioned the same thrust forward to Tchepone as featured in Lam Son.

Kissinger claims that only later did he learn that Westmoreland had believed in 1968 that two corps of American troops would be neces- sary for a Tchepone attack. Although a member of the JCS, West- moreland gave no such advice to the White House in 1971, Kissinger says. Westmoreland, meanwhile, has told former colleague Phillip Davidson that he was never consulted about planning the Laotian in- vasion and was informed of it only once it was under way. Yet one rea- son for Nixon's Laotian fiasco, Kissinger adverts, was the apparent unanimity of his advisers, supposedly misleading the president in judg- ing feasibility. If Helms was discounted and Westmoreland not con- sulted, perhaps the administration was actively seeking the unanimity Kissinger retrospectively deplores.

Nixon, his security assistant believes, acted boldly in ordering the invasion, but then at every planning session watered down the opera- tion to preserve consensus among his advisers. This conveyed hesita- tion to those down the chain of command and eventually consumed the plan. As for the advisers, unanimity disappeared as soon as Kissinger began daily meetings of his Washington Special Action Group (WSAG) on January 19. The secretary of state wavered. Under- secretary U. Alexis Johnson raised matters that might indefinitely stall implementation without actually opposing the Lam Son plan. One of these devices, which Kissinger calls a "strange argument," was to insist that Laotian prime minister Souvanna Phouma agree in advance to the intervention. Far from "strange," American ambassadors had been getting Souvanna's consent for their actions since the earliest recon- naissance flights of the tacit war in that country.

Alexis Johnson was indeed opposed to the Laotian adventure. As he put it, Lam Son "required an unproven group of soldiers to strike at an objective that the enemy would defend stoutly in a region where it had superior logistics." Failure could make "the bankruptcy of hasty

Vietnamization" painfully evident. Unable to sway the WSAG members, Johnson remained an isolated voice in the wilderness.

Confounding everyone further, ARVN and JGS did what they could to make Undersecretary Johnson's arguments even more telling. The command structure, already large by Vietnamese standards, added a layer of complexity when Thieu and General Vien decided to involve more formations and give more commanders a piece of the action. The ARVN First Infantry Division would not only be augmented by rangers, armor, and armored calvary units, but the airborne division would assault in support, and the Vietnamese marine division would move to Khe Sanh in reserve. The entire corps-sized disposition was to be supplied by air or up the overgrown single-lane Route 9.

At first JGS' J-3 section did most of the ARVN planning for Lam Son, under its director Colonel Tran Dinh Tho. In mid-January Tho and his MACV counterpart flew to Da Nang and briefed the U.S. XXIV Corps commander, General James W. Sutherland, Jr., and ARVN I Corps commander General Hoang Xuan Lam. Sutherland and Lam then met privately and formed a joint planning group. The only Vietnamese members from the I Corps staff were its intelligence and operations officers. Joint planning guidance emerged in the form of a directive on January 17. Four days later generals Lam and Sutherland detailed their basic plan in a full-dress meeting at MACV headquarters. All set for action, Abrams ordered the 101st Airborne Division (Airmobile) and the Da Nang Support Command to be prepared to provide combat support for a period of ninety days. Final operations plans were completed on February 3 and were accepted by General Lam after a briefing that day. The speed of this planning was later cited by Vietnamese authorities as one of the problems with Lam Son 719.

■ Henry Kissinger meanwhile pushed for a final decision in Washington. The security adviser met with the head of the JCS on January 25 to review the situation before Admiral Moorer's meeting with Nixon the next day. Kissinger was aware of increasingly boisterous objections from Secretary Rogers, and now raised several concerns, "perhaps too late." Afterward Kissinger wrote a memo for the president listing a number of pertinent questions that Nixon could put to Moorer, but the president only touched on the issues on the 26th. On January 27 followed a meeting of NSC principals. There Rogers argued forcefully against the Laotian invasion: there were just too many risks; the NVA already knew of the offensive and would be ready, making battle certain; the outcome risked all the gains of Vietnamization. The turmoil, Rogers warned, could also end the rule of Souvanna Phouma, the most effective Laotian leader. Except for the last point, Kissinger recounts, Rogers was right on target. "Unfortunately, Nixon simply did not believe that his secretary of state knew what he was talking about." Nixon went ahead with the Lam Son plan.

In South Vietnam began Phase I of the Laos invasion—the MACV part, approved by Nixon on January 18 and called Dewey Canyon II by the U.S. command. This featured the First Brigade, Fifth Infantry Division (Mechanized) under Brigadier General John G. Hill, Jr., which swept up to the Laotian border and reoccupied Khe Sanh, abandoned since the summer of 1968, in the wake of its lengthy siege. Hill had a large brigade of five battalions including armor (First Battalion, Seventy-seventh Armor), mechanized (First Battalion, Eleventh Infantry plus First Battalion, Sixty-first Infantry) and airmobile (Third Squadron, Fifth Cavalry, and Third Battalion, 187th Airborne Infantry) troops. The brigade had also been reinforced with an engineer group (Forty-fifth) of two battalions (Fourteenth and Twenty-seventh) to work on Route 9 and open a parallel track so as to permit two-way continuous traffic. On January 30 the first column up Route 9 was led by a big bulldozer from the Fourteenth Engineers. For the first days of Dewey Canyon II, Major General Thomas M. Tarpley of the 101st Division also had operational control (OPCON) of the Eleventh Brigade, Twenty-third Division.

The American phase of the operation proceeded swiftly to its conclusion. On January 31 several battalions air assaulted into Khe Sanh, soon to be met on the ground. Within hours survey parties were evaluating the 3,900-foot airstrip of the old combat base. Engineers went to work immediately to restore the runway to handle C-130 traffic. One of the first major setbacks in Lam Son 719 came when it became apparent that reconstructing the Khe Sanh field was going to take much longer than anticipated.

Up to a point it should have been possible to turn back from the Laotian invasion. But it was Richard Nixon's determination to stick to it. He overrode the objections of State and brought in advisers like Spiro T. Agnew, John Connally, and John Mitchell, who knew little about Vietnam but could be trusted to back the president's judgment. On February 2 came a final round of talk on the concrete question of whether the U.S. should provide air power to support a Laotian panhandle invasion. The bureaucracy's positions were the same. Kissinger's staff had prepared a five-page paper summarizing the pros and cons of the option. Nixon professed to have lingering doubts, which he repeated late that night, after a concert at the White House with singer Beverly Sills, in a further talk with Kissinger. Nevertheless, the next morning the president signed the draft national security decision memorandum authorizing U.S. participation in Laos.

What Nixon feared was domestic political upheaval, not the NVA—he proceeded despite Rogers's argument that the North Vietnamese knew about Lam Son. Kissinger too relates more than once that "surprise had been lost." Late in the offensive it was learned there had been a leak directly out of General Lam's ARVN I Corps headquarters—a staff captain and his wife had passed plans to the North Vietnamese. Still, evaluations by the U.S. XXIV Corps expected that Lam Son would be lightly opposed, the NVA tank threat minimal. Two days of air operations were thought sufficient to soften up the target. The NVA was considered able to build up to two divisions of defenders within two weeks.

True NVA strength, however, was considerably larger than the three regiments and eight "binh tram" supply units first estimated. Hanoi mustered twenty antiaircraft battalions with 170 to 200 guns, altogether about seven thousand NVA, ten thousand supply troops, and five thousand Pathet Lao. As many as eight regiments of reinforcements were located nearby and, as agent reports had indicated in January, the NVA troops had been placed on alert.

A further problem for the ARVN offensive was the weather, which turned out too poor to mount the aerial preparations the Americans had planned for February 6 and 7. At 7 a.m. on the 8th, Lam Son jumped off.

The Americans most immediately affected were the helicopter crews of the 101st Aviation Group augmented by the 223rd Aviation Battalion. The 101st, 158th, and 159th aviation battalions air assaulted the ARVNs into several landing zones north and south of Route 9 while the armor moved up the road. The NVA waited a day to be sure, then their 70B Front ordered up reinforcements for the defensive battle. In the United States the press and antiwar movement were singularly unimpressed with the claim that Lam Son was a purely Vietnamese operation. Americans knew that without the army and marine helicopters, the marine and air force fixed-wing aircraft, and the massive B-52 strikes, the ARVN would never have entered Laos.

Even so, the Vietnamese had a hard time in Laos. They pushed up Route 9 to A Luoi, about halfway to Tchepone, then halted while the NVA launched increasingly fierce counterattacks on the road and flanking firebases. In Washington, Kissinger kept hearing excuses for the lack of progress. He asserts that Pentagon staffs furnished him a new date of arrival at Tchepone no less than six times. In Saigon, Abrams too was concerned. On February 14 he told Cao Van Vien that ARVN units should occupy Tchepone as soon as possible. Then the two generals went north to Dong Ha for meetings with generals Lam and Sutherland and their staffs. Two and a half hours of discussions at ARVN I Corps forward headquarters brought only Vietnamese agreement to seize more firebases south of the Xepon River over the next three to five days. After several days of advance, the ARVN forward movement halted at A Luoi.

The Americans did not know, according to Kissinger, that on February 12 Vietnamese president Nguyen Van Thieu had issued secret instructions to his generals to stop once the army had suffered three thousand casualties. But what they did not know did not keep the U.S. from acting in support of Lam Son. Two reinforced battalions of the 108th Artillery Group fired 208,962 rounds into Laos from positions along the border and at Khe Sanh. The gunships of the Fourth Battalion, Seventy-seventh Aerial Field Artillery, 101st Airborne Division, flew direct support missions for ARVN unrestricted by national boundaries. Almost 24,000 of the 34,000 U.S. gunship sorties during Lam Son were on ARVN support missions. So were 12,000 of the Army's 18,000 air cavalry sorties, 34,000 of 51,000 trooplifts, and 19,000 of 59,000 logistics sorties. Marine helicopters flew about 2,000 gunship and 3,000 lift sorties, while their fixed-wing air accounted for 950 sorties and 2,600 tons of ordnance. Navy air support sorties numbered 1,900. The bulk of tactical air support was from the air force, which contributed 9,114 sorties for more than 14,000 tons of ordnance delivered. Sorties flown inside Laos amounted to a daily average of more than one hundred, with a peak of 277 air force sorties on March 8. Navy and marine tactical air sorties provided another 63 sorties a day on the average.

American air supply was vital to the ARVN offensive. Quang Tri airfield became the advance base for a task force of the 834th Air Division which began work with twenty-eight cargo sorties on January 30. As part of the ARVN buildup for Lam Son, the air force brought up 9,250 troops and 1,700 tons of supplies. Various difficulties prevented the old Khe Sanh airstrip from going into operation until February 12, but a smaller assault airstrip opened nearby on February 4. Planned performance levels were attained the first time on February 19, when forty sorties brought in 350 tons. Thereafter an average of thirty-six C-130s delivered their loads to Khe Sanh each day. In early March the average rose to fifty-four daily, but the big airstrip went out of action again on March 6, part of the strip collapsing under the strain of constant use. The field was repaired, only to be used in the ARVN withdrawal at the end of March, when eighty-two withdrawal flights originated from Khe Sanh. The field then shut down on April Fool's Day.

Within Laos the Americans found conditions dangerous for aircraft of all kinds. A marine detachment at Khe Sanh did a good job controlling the air traffic in tandem with a series of aerial battle command centers, but the real threat was the NVA. Air crews found themselves flying in dense antiaircraft, against radar-directed gunfire in addition to small arms. Fixed-wing aircraft stayed pretty high, but still seven planes were lost (only five admitted by the U.S. government) along with four pilots. Another C-130 was destroyed by rocket fire on the ground at Da Nang.

It was the low-altitude helicopter crews who took the most risks. American choppers far outperformed South Vietnamese, though the latter did lift 8,000 troops into Laos and evacuate 3,500 patients. The losses said it all: the Vietnamese air force sustained 7 destroyed helicopters during the campaign. The U.S. government admitted losing 82 ships (only those actually downed inside Laos) from army chopper battalions, but said nothing about 26 choppers down inside South Vietnam, or of 10 army and marine choppers lost due to accident or mishap. A more recent official account cites army data to MACV showing the loss of 118 choppers inside Laos and another 22 in Vietnam, all to hostile fire. More than 600 choppers sustained damage from fire during the campaign. The 101st Airborne and other support forces suffered some 91 killed, 464 wounded, and 28 missing in action. By contrast, losses among the ground troops in Dewey Canyon II amounted to slightly more than 100 killed, 697 wounded, and 10 missing. Laos was clearly as dangerous an environment for chopper crews in their brief instants of exposure as was full-time exposure in a pitched battle situation for the ground troops. As a monograph on the development of the Vietnamese air force put it, "The difficulty of conducting airmobile operations in a high threat environment without excessive losses was apparent."

As a sop to the public relations people, on March 6 ARVN made a final thrust with an airmobile assault from 120 helicopters at landing zones near Tchepone. But no airfield opened there to take supplies, and no more than scouting parties went into the town. Within days the

Vietnamese soldiers began to pull back, their high-water mark passed. NVA armor and infantry attacks grew in intensity, to the point that a number of firebases, manned by whole battalions, disappeared under attack. The ARVN lost more than nine thousand casualties out of a peak strength of about seventeen thousand. This included more than seventeen hundred killed and almost a thousand missing. In the last days ARVN soldiers, desperate to escape Laos, clung to the skids of choppers leaving without them. That image, pictured in the press, was what the world saw of the ARVN in Laos. Before the end of March all the remaining ARVN troops were back inside South Vietnam.

Vietnamese soldiers abandoned the firebase at A Luoi on March 19. The next day, covering ARVN, came the peak American air effort—270 fixed-wing sorties and 1,388 by gunships, combined with 11 B-52 strikes. It was not enough to turn the tide of battle, as the ARVN continued to make for relative safety across the border. In the end it was not even true that American advisers took no part in the ground fighting—at a critical moment a key commander of the Vietnamese marine division disappeared from his command post and had to be coaxed back by his U.S. marine senior adviser, who in the meanwhile had also been obliged to make tactical decisions for the Vietnamese division.

On the ultimate questions of the success of Lam Son 719 in disrupting NVA supply down the Ho Chi Minh Trail, the claims made for Laos are noticeably thinner than those for the Cambodian invasion the preceding year. Grasping at straws, the ARVN announced the capture of such items as 4 generators, 3 water pumps, and 22 field radios. Americans verified only 20,000 of the claimed 170,000 tons of captured ammunition, while the ARVN verified only 422 of the more than 2,000 vehicles reported destroyed by the U.S. air force. The U.S. verified 88 of the 106 to 110 tanks claimed by the ARVN. American and Vietnamese forces admitted losses of 71 tanks, 163 other combat vehicles, 278 trucks, 100 artillery guns, and 31 bulldozers.

In retrospect, Nixon quoted Kissinger, who said at the end of March, "If I had known before it started that it was going to come out exactly the way it did, I would still have gone ahead with it."

Richard Nixon was no disinterested bystander, but he judged Laos a military success and only a psychological failure. Henry Kissinger rather wishes he had remembered the cautionary advice that German chancellor Konrad Adenauer had given him during the Kennedy years—not to believe everything he was told by generals. Alexander Haig made another visit to Vietnam in late March to find the Vietnamese generals opposed to reinforcing Lam Son 719. Few of them would argue that the operation had been a brilliant success. In a sense, as Kissinger had cabled U.S. ambassador Ellsworth Bunker at the height of the crisis, Nguyen Van Thieu had used up his last crack at massive support from the United States. There would be one more large American sally when great force was used to turn aside the North Vietnamese, but the next time it would be Hanoi, not Saigon, that triggered the events. The occasion came a year later, in the spring of 1972, when North Vietnam launched a huge conventional offensive across the Demilitarized Zone and elsewhere in the south.

One More Option to Try: The Mining of Haiphong Harbor

A central element of United States strategy throughout the Vietnam War was to isolate the adversary in South Vietnam from his sources of supplies and materiel in the north. Any number of paths were followed in the effort to reach this goal through the long years of the war. Special Forces camps along South Vietnamese borders, maritime patrols off the coast, irregular forces operations in Laos, and the massive bombing of Laos and North Vietnam were some of the techniques harnessed in service to this strategy.

One option, however, was saved until the very last phase of the war. Repeatedly considered, each time this option was rejected—until 1972 when President Nixon ordered its execution: the mining of North Vietnamese ports and waterways.

■ By 1972 the American situation in South Vietnam was far different from what it had been in the years of the big battles. Under the "Vietnamization" program the U.S. was systematically withdrawing forces from the country and transferring its military role to the South Vietnamese. Military Assistance Command Vietnam was a pale shadow of what it had been just four years before. General Creighton Abrams, MACV commander, could count his field battalions with less than the fingers on two hands. Total manpower stood at no more than sixty thousand. Abrams had already shifted from large-unit operations, and he conformed his tactics with the withdrawals by reducing the tempo of activity, until American troops stood down and ceased to conduct offensive forays at all. Most of Abrams's residual force he assigned security or support missions.

The Vietnamese had taken over the war now. All those old jokes about the Army of the Republic of Vietnam had better not be true because it was up to them now. ARVN was bigger than it had ever been, and better armed, but so were the Viet Cong and the North Vietnamese Army, who now had tanks and long-range artillery in profusion. The ARVN had performed indifferently in Laos in 1971, the first corps-sized operation it had ever mounted, and only its second multi-division effort. ARVN officers argued that their logistics difficulties and command inexperience crippled the Laos offensive. Both the South Vietnamese and Americans put out hopeful press releases on the amount of enemy supplies destroyed and the degree to which this had set back the NVA. Laos was yet another exercise in isolation of the battlefield.

What the North Vietnamese would do after Laos became the major strategic uncertainty of the war. At peace talks in Paris, plenary sessions went nowhere while secret meetings between Henry Kissinger and the North Vietnamese were stalled. The NVA had incentive to remain quiescent—every month they waited, MACV shrunk and the U.S. commitment diminished. On the other hand, every month ARVN grew stronger. The NVA remained concentrated in its sanctuaries in Cambodia, Laos, and north of the Demilitarized Zone. The uncertainty about NVA intentions cast a pall over each of the progress reports issued from Washington; American public opinion solidified in favor of further withdrawals from Vietnam.

During the summer of 1971 South Vietnamese president Nguyen Van Thieu flatly predicted an NVA offensive in 1972. Opinions differed. Defense Secretary Melvin Laird told a House committee in February 1972 that the NVA lacked both personnel and logistic support—"they cannot conduct a large-scale military operation for a substantial period of time." Admiral Thomas Moorer told the same hearing that the NVA had the capability, if they chose to accept the casualties, to generate a "high point" type guerrilla offensive during Tet, or at the time of President Nixon's projected visit to the People's Republic of China. Moorer was confident the ARVN could handle any large-scale attack the NVA could mount. Laird felt ARVN might lose a few battles but would win most of them.

About three weeks before Congress heard this advice, on February 3, 1972, Hanoi published a speech by Truong Chinh, an influential central committee member, to the Third Congress of the Vietnam Fatherland Front. In a significant public statement of Hanoi's intentions, Chinh declared that the NVA and VC must do "much more" to "wipe out" ARVN and U.S. troops, "chiefly strategic mobile forces," and to "foil" Vietnamization.

The NVA unleashed their major offensive on March 30, following publication of the Chinh speech by only two months. In what has come to be known as the Easter offensive, the NVA plastered the ARVN Third Division with 13,500 shells overnight, then attacked the arc of firebases that protected the DMZ. A formation only a few months old, the Third Division disintegrated under pressure. The ARVN 147th Marine Brigade was also partially overrun. North Vietnamese assaults soon threatened all of Quang Tri Province. A week later the NVA initiated attacks around Loc Ninh and, a week after that, in the Central Highlands. Fighting spread to all of South Vietnam.

■ Creighton Abrams stood his ground in the face of the Easter offensive. He reported laconically on the ARVN's early disasters, then their relative success in holding on to An Loc and Kontum. Abrams refused to request reinforcements; Washington nonetheless ordered substantial deployments of naval and air forces, doubling the air support available to MACV in some categories. Abrams kept his cool throughout April. An Loc remained under siege. On May 1 the NVA captured Quang Tri City, completing their conquest of that province. The next day Abrams reported to Washington that the threat to Hue seemed to be lifting; if Kontum held through the next few days, it might be all right. The monsoon season was due within the month; the NVA, Abrams no doubt felt, could not sustain their momentum much longer.

General Abrams thought all he needed was local air plus strikes in the north.

Washington gave much more than he asked.

■ In 1972 Richard Nixon was anticipating the crowning apex of his career: an opening to the People's Republic of China, with the first visit by a U.S. president; a summit conference in Moscow; an arms-control agreement with the Soviets; and, not least, election to a second term. It was to be a world-class performance, a superplay by a political virtuoso. The Easter offensive threatened Nixon's scenario. His response might lead to cancellation of the summit, failure to conclude an arms-control treaty. Alternatively, defeat in South Vietnam would likely lead to loss of the election.

Nixon's predilection was for a harsh response. From the beginning of the Easter offensive it was regarded as an emergency of the first order in Washington. As such it was handled by Kissinger's Washington Special Action Group (WSAG). Kissinger framed the policy response to the Easter offensive, personally conducted the secret negotiations with Hanoi, and simultaneously managed the National Security Council staff with jurisdiction over all defense and foreign policy matters. Kissinger's job was to give substance to the president's declarations of intent.

Daily meetings of WSAG began as the ARVN Third Division crumbled along the DMZ. Within the Pentagon there were other, purely military meetings. On April 4 Admiral Moorer told his colleagues on the Joint Chiefs of Staff that Nixon had pronounced the NVA offensive an "invasion" of the south. The president wanted all resources on station and other available forces prepared to move forward. The director of the Joint Staff, air force General John Vogt, told a session of the JCS operations deputies three days later that Nixon was "determined to give the North Vietnamese a bloody nose in this action." Nixon told General Vogt that, if need be, he would use every aircraft carrier in both fleets and all United States tactical air power.

The military took immediate measures to implement Nixon's instructions. On April 3 the aircraft carrier *Kitty Hawk* joined *Hancock* and *Coral Sea* on Yankee Station. On the 8th *Constellation* augmented them while *Midway*, in the eastern Pacific, and *Saratoga*, in the Atlantic, were ordered to steam to the South China Sea. Tactical aircraft reinforcement took place under a program called Constant Guard while B-52 deployments carried the designation Bullet Shot. In the first two weeks of the Easter offensive American combat air assets increased by about 300 aircraft. There was an equal increment over the following month. Deployed B-52 bombers reached 115 within two weeks. Combined American and South Vietnamese combat aircraft ultimately totaled more than 1,400, including 185 B-52s.

How these forces were to be used was the major consideration for WSAG and the NSC. An options paper was prepared on April 6 by newly promoted Major General Alexander Haig, Kissinger's deputy on the NSC staff. Haig's paper included a list of possible bombing attacks on targets throughout North Vietnam, over a spectrum of increasing intensity. It also included an option for the mining of all North Vietnamese ports. Admiral Moorer added to the sense of crisis that day, through his luncheon address to the Overseas Writers Association. The admiral maintained that the new factor in the Vietnam War was the presence of NVA armor inside South Vietnam. On April 8 Nixon's chief of staff, H. R. Haldeman, ordered the president's speechwriters to draft an address to sound the "invasion" theme. The next day Kissinger reminded Soviet ambassador Anatoli Dobrynin of periodic U.S. warnings that it might take "drastic measures to end the war once and for all." The occasion for such a decision, Kissinger implied, could now be at hand.

■ Mining the north's waterways was another of those Vietnam options that were frequently discussed but had yet to be tried. Haig broke no new ground in inserting mining as an option in his April 6 paper. The possibility had been in the briefing books since 1964, when mining Haiphong began to appear in Pentagon planning memoranda. In his tour during that period as Commander, Pacific Fleet, Admiral Moorer himself had initiated preparation of a contingency plan for mining.

The mining option nevertheless remained but one item on the menu of choices before the president. The issues always had been whether it could work, and whether it would bring in the Chinese or the Russians. Robert McNamara, when he was secretary of defense, told a Senate committee in January 1967 that no agreement existed with China, formal or tacit, that prevented the U.S. from blockading Haiphong. Rather, blockade was questionable on international legal grounds while McNamara doubted it would work anyway.

Walt Rostow had put the basic case to President Lyndon Johnson in a memorandum on May 6, 1967. As part of a broader analysis of bombing alternatives, Kissinger's predecessor came down against the option of "closing the top of the funnel" at that time. Rostow pointed out that North Vietnamese import capacity stood at about 17,200 tons per day, yet, even with increased requirements due to food shortages and bombing, it was importing only 5,700 tons per day. Rostow believed that with "a concerted and determined effort" capacity might be reduced to below the level of requirements, but this result was no more than "possible." He felt his assessment was supported by the intelligence community.

Rostow too warned of the dangers of Soviet or Chinese responses. "I myself," wrote Rostow, "do not believe the Soviet Union would go to war with us over Vietnam unless we sought to occupy North Vietnam." There *was* a risk, however, and as for Peking, "irrationality cannot be ruled out." Overall Rostow estimated that "the outcome is less likely to be a general war than more likely." Such a course, Rostow believed, would have to be "pursued with great determination and against a background of highly mobilized U.S. strength," and he did not recommend it. President Johnson, unwilling to mobilize United States forces, went no further with the option. McNamara reiterated his own conclusions in his valedictory appearance before the Senate Appropriations Committee.

Mining was again raised in the aftermath of Tet. In a March 13, 1968, report, the CIA's Office of National Estimates predicted that "the Soviets are likely to stop short of precipitating a major confrontation with the U.S." That conclusion notwithstanding, however, the estimate also warned that "the mining of Haiphong would offer a clear challenge to the Soviet Union. Moreover, in the course of this operation or the bombing of the Haiphong docks there would be considerable likelihood of damage or destruction of a Soviet ship and killing Soviet personnel. Therefore, of all actions other than invasion of North Vietnam, mining would be most likely to cause the Soviets to consider serious acts of retaliation against the U.S. Such acts would be most likely to be effective in areas outside Southeast Asia. If the mining proved effective the pressures on Moscow to take some counteraction might grow."

Similar concern was expressed by Clark Clifford, McNamara's successor at the Pentagon. If a Russian ship were damaged or sunk in Haiphong, Clifford told a Senate hearing in May 1968, "I don't believe that would be good for the United States." Appearing again, before the Senate Appropriations Committee on September 17, Clifford remarked that "we all understand what the situation is" as far as Haiphong was concerned: "If you mine Haiphong, (a) the Soviet freighter comes in there and hits a mine and goes down, and President Johnson is concerned he has a bigger war on his hands then; and (b) even if we mined the harbor of Haiphong and made it more difficult for them to get the material into North Vietnam, they could still get it in."

The Nixon administration revived the Haiphong option in 1969. In a planning project codenamed Duck Hook, the Joint Chiefs of Staff suggested a concept for mining North Vietnamese ports plus destroying twenty-nine military and economic targets by bombing. There is some evidence that the CINCPAC contingency plan was updated at this time, plus reports that navy frogmen were inserted into Haiphong estuary to survey the Cua Cam River channel for mining, having been instructed to leave behind evidence of their presence.

Ignorant of U.S. contingency plans, the North Vietnamese continued to rely on Haiphong for 85 percent of their import tonnage, including almost all fuel and oil. The port had a daily unloading capacity of 6,500 tons, using 10 dockside berths, a number of 12-ton load cranes, and dozens of smaller ones. At the height of Rolling Thunder in 1967, when the docks themselves were not being attacked (although related facilities were), Haiphong was handling 47 ships a week. By 1972 the city's population had risen to 500,000, and the North Vietnamese had adopted an ambitious plan to expand the port's capacity by 50 percent. North Vietnam would have saved its investment had it known what was in store.

■ From the start of the Easter offensive, Richard Nixon wanted to use force, emphasizing naval and air power. The main obstacle was diplomatic—China and Russia and how they would respond, made even more delicate by the first blossom of the opening to China and the imminence of the Moscow summit. Nixon determined to risk both initiatives on a throw of the dice in Vietnam.

On April 11 the United States canceled a scheduled plenary session of Vietnam peace talks in Paris. From the 15th to the 17th the Hanoi and Haiphong areas were hit by massive B-52 and fighter-bomber attacks in an operation called Freedom Porch Bravo. Nixon quotes himself exulting to Haldeman, "Well, we really left them our calling card this weekend!"

North Vietnam then canceled a secret negotiating session that had been arranged with Kissinger, but offered to resume such meetings if the United States returned to the plenary talks. Kissinger was preparing for a quiet visit to Moscow to arrange certain affairs for the summit (scheduled for late May), and he had intended to drop by Paris for the meeting with North Vietnamese envoy Le Duc Tho. That plan was scotched by Freedom Porch Bravo, though later a secret meeting was set for May 2.

Nixon was also tough with Kissinger in his instructions for the Moscow presummit talks, for which the national security adviser departed on April 20. Nixon instructed Kissinger to insist on discussing Vietnam first, then castigate the Russians for North Vietnamese activity. Only then could SALT be discussed. In Moscow, Kissinger raised the subject, at which Soviet leader Leonid Brezhnev agreed that events in Vietnam "dampened the atmosphere somewhat." But Brezhnev was careful to say he did not mean the prospects for a U.S.-USSR summit were impaired. Kissinger interpreted the exchange as signifying that the Soviets had only limited concern over Vietnam issues.

The United States also used a private channel to send a diplomatic signal to China, with whom there were no diplomatic relations at that time. An NSC staff officer who was a special assistant to Kissinger went to New York to present an "oral note" to the Chinese representative at the UN on April 3. In what is recalled as the sharpest language yet used in a message to Peking, Kissinger advanced his view of the American stake in Vietnam. The Chinese reply over the private channel hinted at little more than rhetorical support for North Vietnam. This too was interpreted as an indication of limited Chinese concern.

By the end of April there was a belief in the Nixon administration that diplomacy had succeeded in "detaching" the USSR and China from their alliance with North Vietnam. This perception is what led Nixon to order the mining of Haiphong harbor. At that point, for Nixon, it became a matter of following his inclinations to approve the plan presented to him.

■ The Joint Chiefs of Staff thought they had such a plan, or at least the chairman did. Admiral Moorer remembered the CINCPAC contingency plan and discussed mining with Haig early on when that NSC staffer was canvassing the bureaucracy for alternatives. Other navy officers were also well aware of the mining option. The Chief of Naval Operations, Admiral Elmo R. Zumwalt, the current CINCPAC, Admiral John S. McCain, and Pacific Fleet commander Admiral "Chick" Clarey engaged Moorer in discussions of the options almost daily. Moorer had been fleet commander himself in 1964, during one of the earlier iterations of the mining plan, which he had actually brought to the point of implementation (U.S. naval forces had been at six hours' readiness to execute the mining). In 1972 Moorer and the other admirals all preferred mining to blockade because it was tactically simple, less risky for engaged forces, and, according to Zumwalt, "politically more decisive." Talks advanced quickly enough that by April 23 Admiral McCain felt able to ask Washington in a cable for authority to mine Haiphong. The recommendation was seconded in a letter to Moorer from Rear Admiral Kenneth L. Veth, former naval commander in Vietnam. Haig, whom Nixon had sent to South Vietnam on another of his consultative missions, also weighed in to favor the mining option. He advised the president to take strong action and let the Russians themselves call off the summit, if they dared.

Meanwhile, Nixon stuck to his own aggressive position. Secretary Laird reported to the JCS on April 24 that the president was insisting on massive strikes and complaining that General Abrams was not requesting more support. "I sent them," Laird quoted the president as saying, referring to the aircraft carriers en route from the Atlantic and eastern Pacific, "no one else asks for them." Two days later Nixon went on nationwide television to announce another MACV drawdown but inserted his "invasion" rhetoric into the speech.

On the afternoon of April 30 Nixon made a political appearance at a barbeque on John Connally's Picosa Ranch in Floresville, Texas. "The North Vietnamese are taking a very great risk," Nixon declared in answer to a question, "if they continue their offensive in the south. I will just leave it there, and they can make their own choice."

After his return to Washington that night, Nixon drafted a long memo to Kissinger. He saw the military planners as the problem—they were too reticent in offering new options. He had no desire for more of "the dreary 'milk runs' which characterized the Johnson administration's bombing." Nixon dictated, "I have determined that we should go for broke . . . we must *punish* the enemy. . . . Now that I have made this very tough watershed decision I intend to stop at nothing to bring the enemy to his knees." The president intended to cancel the summit if the Vietnam situation did not improve. Regardless of the outcome of the Kissinger–Le Duc Tho secret meeting scheduled for May 2, Nixon ordered a subsequent three-day B-52 attack on the Hanoi-Haiphong area.

On May 1 the NVA captured Quang Tri City. The situation in the Central Highlands also looked bad with Kontum and Pleiku threatened. Then the Kissinger–Tho meeting turned out to be an exchange of invective.

On May 1 in Washington, Alexander Haig discussed the mining and blockade alternatives with CNO Zumwalt, who strongly supported mining. Haig agreed. On May 2 a CINCPAC cable prodded Washington for a decision. Admiral McCain argued that if mining seemed unacceptable, the U.S. should consider blockade. Haig went to the president that day, according to Nixon's diary, and "emphasized that even more important than how Vietnam comes out is for us to handle these matters in a way that I can survive in office." Out of these concerns came a secret political program that spent thousands of dollars in campaign money to produce a supposedly spontaneous outpouring of public support. Expenditures authorized by Jeb Stuart Magruder, an official of Nixon's Committee to Re-Elect the President (CREEP), included at least $8,400 (mostly in $100 bills, according to press reports) used for telegrams and telephone calls to the White House, where on May 10, after the mining had been executed, presidential press secretary Ronald L. Ziegler was conveniently able to declare that public opinion measured by telegrams and phone calls was running five- or six-to-one in favor of the Nixon policy. Similarly, when Washington, D.C., television station WTTG sponsored a mail-in poll on the mining of Haiphong, its results were muddled by deliberate political action. The former chief of CREEP's mailroom reported a year later that campaign workers were sent out to buy more than a thousand copies of the newspaper with WTTG's coupon ballot in it, while CREEP sent an additional couple of thousand postcards. Similarly, an advertisement that appeared in the *New York Times* of May 17, which allegedly represented the opinions of "Middle Americans," was quietly financed by more than $4,000 in CREEP money. A review of these expenditures of political campaign funds made by the General Accounting Office in 1973 concluded they were deceptive and probably illegal.

Such reticence as existed in the Pentagon was due more to Secretary Laird than to the military. From an early date Laird had become worried about the impact on long-term readiness and on the budget of the surge in air and naval forces in Southeast Asia. Admiral Moorer retorted to Laird at a May 3 meeting, "The name of the game *now* is what we do *right now*!" Late the next afternoon, Thursday May 4, Moorer called Zumwalt into his office and asked him to draft an operational plan for mining.

This planning was quietly done in the CNO's shop without telling other JCS members. Admiral Zumwalt was happy to break out of administrative routine and called up a chart of North Vietnamese waters and his ruler and dividers. Zumwalt had five captains, close OPNAV associates, to help him. The whole plan was finished in four hours, by midnight the 4th. It was easy. There was only one 150-yard-wide channel leading to Haiphong; all the attack squadrons were equipped for mine-laying, and most pilots were trained for it; and the *Coral Sea*, the ship designated to execute, already had a stock of aerial mines aboard.

Meanwhile, Nixon was going through the motions of making a decision that had already been made. Upon his return from Paris, Kissinger went immediately to the presidential yacht *Sequoia* to meet with Nixon, Haig, and John Connally. This was followed by a White House meeting among Nixon, Kissinger, and Haldeman. When the national security adviser expressed doubts about the Moscow summit, Nixon sent Kissinger and Haldeman back to Connally. That Texas politician strongly favored mining and opposed canceling the summit, convincing Nixon at least. On the afternoon of May 4 Kissinger phoned Moorer to ask his opinion of mining or blockade, and the JCS chairman argued strongly for mining. At the end of work that afternoon, Haig assembled a number of NSC staffers to tell them he was "98 percent certain" Nixon would order mining.

The president now scheduled a meeting of the National Security Council for May 8 and left for Camp David on the afternoon of the 5th. Over the weekend he told family members his intentions and worked on his speech.

At the Pentagon on the morning of the 5th, Zumwalt presented the mining plan to Moorer. The JCS chairman liked it and told the CNO he would raise mining as a contingency matter in a scheduled JCS executive session. Zumwalt was told he had better pretend to be "surprised as hell" when Moorer brought it up. The scenario played to their satisfaction, and at 4:10 p.m. Zumwalt phoned Admiral Clarey at Pearl Harbor for a long discussion of the mining and possible Soviet reactions.

A similar pro forma meeting of NSC staffers—Kissinger calls it a "debate"—took place at the White House at noon on the 6th. The staffers were briefed on the plan, and only one of them argued strongly against it. That staffer, Winston Lord, was nonetheless supremely loyal, and spent the day following his defeat in this debate helping one of Nixon's speechwriters refine the mining address. Other NSC staffers bore the brunt of coordination planning because Nixon wished to have no interagency activity before the NSC meeting scheduled for May 8.

Early on Sunday morning, the 7th, Kissinger brought the State Department into the circle, phoning Undersecretary of State U. Alexis Johnson. Kissinger told him Secretary William P. Rogers would have to be recalled from his presummit consultations with European leaders for the NSC meeting. Kissinger briefed Johnson on the plan for mining plus bombing to close the top of the funnel. Johnson's initial reaction was that efforts to interdict supply lines had never worked—he felt it had been proved repeatedly in Korea and Vietnam. Kissinger made noises about himself opposing the operation, which by now had acquired the code-name Pocket Money.

The big NSC meeting began at 9 a.m. on the 8th and ran three hours and twenty minutes. "The NSC meeting," recalls Johnson, "was obviously a charade to front for the decision already made." Laird opposed the mining. CIA director Richard Helms argued that the estimates had not changed, that Hanoi would simply change its methods of moving supplies. Rogers said he would be for Pocket Money if it worked. Nixon went on to further talks with Kissinger and Connally at the Old Executive Office Building, from where he gave the final order at 2 p.m., the last moment he could order this action and have it coincide with the timing of his nationwide speech. Nixon also sent a letter to President Thieu informing the South Vietnamese of the mining and of Nixon's speech, which would say that Pocket Money was "fully coordinated" with Saigon even though this was the first they had ever heard of it. "It is important," Nixon wrote, "that these measures . . . be seen as having been taken in consultation with you and in conjunction with your own efforts."

■   The man in charge of Pocket Money was Vice-Admiral William P. Mack, Commander Seventh Fleet. An information copy of a CJCS-CINCPAC message on the morning of May 8 (May 7 in Washington) told him that Moorer wanted preparations for mining. Mack alerted Task Force 77, whose Carrier Division 3 would conduct the operation. The execute order reached CINCPAC at about 2:40 a.m. on the 9th, but at that moment McCain was in an airplane and did not receive the action message. Pacific Fleet commander Clarey thereupon queried McCain and CINCPAC took notice and passed on the order.

Carrier Division 3 was ready for Pocket Money. The *Coral Sea*'s aircraft took care of Haiphong, laying a first string of just six to eight mines between 9:00 and 9:04 a.m. against antiaircraft fire. Planes from two other carriers mined Hon Gai, Cam Pha, Thanh Hoa, Vinh, Quang Khe, and Dong Hoi as well. The navy used an existing Seventh Fleet plan to determine tactical employment. Forward of the carrier task force was a radar picket line, called Positive Identification Radar Advisory Zone (PIRAZ) in Vietnam. This consisted of the missile cruisers *Chicago*, code-named Red Crown, and *Long Beach* and the missile destroyer *Sterret*. Their radars indeed detected North Vietnamese MIGs launching to intercept the *Coral Sea* aircraft, and *Long Beach* knocked down the leading interceptor with a TALOS surface-to-air missile. The others turned away, and radar illumination was sufficient to scare off the MIGs through the rest of the day, although a Navy Fighter Squadron 96 crew from the *Constellation* also shot down another MIG-17 farther to the south.

Simultaneously in Washington Nixon delivered his speech. "There's only one way to stop the killing," Nixon intoned. "That is to keep the weapons of war out of the hands of the international outlaws of North Vietnam."

Meanwhile, in the Gulf of Tonkin a surface bombardment group under Rear Admiral William H. Rogers headed north to hit Haiphong with gunfire. Rogers had the cruisers *Providence*, *Oklahoma City*, and *Newport News*, which had just joined from the Atlantic, and the destroyers *Buchanan* and *Hanson*. The ships went to thirty knots for the final run in and opened fire at about 4 a.m. on the 10th, after straightening on line ahead, slowing to eighteen knots, and cutting within two hundred yards of the outermost channel buoys. The merchant ships in Haiphong and the port itself were lit up. Recalled one participant, "It looked like L.A." *Providence* (Captain Kenneth G. Haynes) alone fired off forty rounds at a barracks complex, coastal defenses, and a fuel storage point.

Combat operations in Pocket Money went off without a hitch. The only major tragedy was a helicopter crash in the gulf that claimed the lives of Rear Admiral Rembrandt C. Robinson (Commander Cruiser-Destroyer Flotilla 11) and his chief of staff and operations officer. Robinson, coincidentally, had last served as Joint Chiefs of Staff liaison to Henry Kissinger at the National Security Council.

The only significant snafu occurred in Washington. There the problem was whether the mining would be taken as a blockade (illegal without a formal declaration of war). To fend off diplomatic protests from seafaring nations, Nixon decreed delayed-action timing for the mines so that Soviet and other merchant vessels could clear Haiphong before they went active. In Nixon's speech, and in Laird's and Kissinger's press conferences, the administration used the phrase "three daylight periods" as the duration of the interval. Diplomatic messages to other nations therefore contained "72 hours" in specifying the duration of the grace period, but an aide to Moorer who was asked to check this with the Pentagon found that that was only a JCS estimate of the *average* delay. Some mines could be expected to go active as quickly as fifty-eight hours after deployment. The State Department resorted to fast footwork to revise all its diplomatic notes.

Few merchant ships took advantage of the grace period. When the mines went in, Haiphong berthed thirty-seven vessels: sixteen Soviet, five Chinese, three Polish, two Cuban, one East German, five Somalian, and four British ships registered in Hong Kong. Of these only two Soviet tankers, two Soviet freighters, and one British ship cleared harbor. North Vietnam could not know that the initial mine field contained only thirty-six mines. The remaining ships were closed up in Haiphong for three hundred days—until the United States itself swept the mine fields in 1973 after the Paris agreement.

■ In what may have been a signal that Hanoi would not desist, the NVA launched a large-scale attack on An Loc about a week after the mining. In what definitely was a response in kind, North Vietnamese frogmen of the NVA 126th Naval Sapper Unit placed limpet mines on the munitions ship *Jefferson City Victory*, damaging her in Da Nang harbor on May 23. Then the monsoon closed in, with major flooding along the central Vietnamese coast that year. The NVA never went much south of Quang Tri; they did not develop their offensive against Hue, Kontum, or Pleiku, and were content to lay siege to An Loc.

Did Pocket Money halt the North Vietnamese offensive? Because of the monsoon we may never know. It *is* known that in July the Swedish embassy in Hanoi received a consignment of tonic water sent by sea, and about the same time the British mission received some curtains it had had shipped that way. Asked by an interviewer about the possibility of successfully interdicting NVA supply, Admiral McCain said in October 1972, "I don't know any way that this could be completely stopped in a country with such rough terrain." Undersecretary of State Johnson, for one, concluded that Pocket Money had failed. Johnson writes, "As I expected, the entire blockade and air campaign never had the slightest effect on the NVA offensive in the south." Reporter Robert Shaplen thought the interdiction campaign might have reduced the flow of aid to Hanoi by as much as 60 percent, but even he concluded that "North Vietnam is plainly not paralyzed." Shaplen visited North Vietnam that summer. He found a plentiful supply of seafood at the Hanoi restaurants.

26   Profile: George Carver (II)

On Saturday, May 6, two days before the president's climactic Haiphong mining decision, another meeting took place at the White House. Henry Kissinger recalls it as a session among his staff experts to make sure they had reviewed all the possibilities, but one man present did not work for Henry. That man was George A. Carver, Jr., and he worked for Richard Helms, chief of the Central Intelligence Agency. Carver officially represented the intelligence viewpoint in these talks about mining.

According to Kissinger, at the Haiphong mining meeting Carver reiterated the CIA analysis previously propounded by Helms: that North Vietnam would be able to use overland shipping routes to substitute for the capacity it lost through the mining of Haiphong. But according to journalist Tad Szulc, who wrote a major study of the foreign policy of the Nixon administration, Carver had abandoned the CIA's position to argue that the Agency would support the mining because it could result in considerable pressure on Hanoi's leadership. Because some of the relevant CIA reports have been declassified, we can conclude that Kissinger's recitation of what George Carver said is probably closer to the mark than Szulc's. But why should there have been two such widely varying perceptions of George Carver's and the CIA's view?

Perhaps this is not so surprising. Something similar appears to have happened in the dispute between the CIA and military intelligence over the VC/NVA order of battle. As the director's Special Assistant for Vietnam Affairs (SAVA), Carver was also at the center of that fracas. As we have seen earlier, Carver encouraged investigation by his analyst Samuel Adams, then went along with a suggestion by the military to resolve the discrepancy in their respective intelligence viewpoints by shuffling papers. When the particulars of the dispute became a subject of a trial during the 1980s, Carver testified that he had originally admired Sam Adams's enthusiasm and initiative but had come to see him as intolerant. Be that as it may, George Carver's seven-year-long tour as SAVA, an extraordinary tenure even by CIA standards, through Democratic and Republican administrations, could scarcely have been achieved without a certain intellectual legerdemain.

Perhaps Carver had learned his lesson in the little bureaucratic war that had taken place over the 1963 National Intelligence Estimate (NIE) on South Vietnam (see Chapter 4), the first draft of which he had written. Or there may have been other forces at work as well. Certainly the doubts expressed in the NIE differed by a great margin from the tone of a true believer that Carver assumed in the two articles he published in the journal *Foreign Affairs* in 1965 and 1966. Writing as a sparsely identified observer of international relations, with no relationship to the Central Intelligence Agency stated or even hinted, these Carver articles are worth mention as capsule summaries of the official views of the United States government at the times they appeared.

Carver's 1965 *Foreign Affairs* article was titled "The Real Revolution in South Vietnam." It had the virtue of recognizing South Vietnamese Buddhism as a valid, nationalizing political force, and in fact saw the politicization of Buddhism and the political activism of the ARVN generals as two sides of the same coin, a social revolution under way in South Vietnam. On the other hand, ignoring (purposefully?) the national appeal for unification, independence, and freedom from foreign dominance that fueled the Viet Cong and the Viet Minh before them, Carver saw Vietnamese politics as complicated by the "lack" of "any unifying traditional symbols." As for Hanoi and the Viet Cong, they were pictured as dedicated to the eradication of the extended family and of private property, alleged objectives sure to incur the ire of liberal Western readers.

A year later, in April 1966, *Foreign Affairs* carried a second Carver article titled "The Faceless Viet Cong." Here Carver focused on the theme of communism, making the Vietnam War simply the third act of "a continuous political drama" in which the Indochinese Communist party (of the 1930s) was attempting to usurp Vietnamese nationalism and subvert it to its own ends. Such an argument had a certain plausibility for Americans who knew little of Vietnam, but in fact Carver had sidestepped the key question, which was the degree to which Communist cadres represented the mainstream of Vietnamese nationalism and not some perversion of it. Ho Chi Minh was not a hero to only a few Vietnamese, nor was his stature due merely to propaganda from Hanoi. Carver's article *was* right to link the National Liberation Front directly to Hanoi's leadership. Yet in painting black hats on the North Vietnamese, Carver relied to an extent on a source that would come back to haunt him: Hoang Van Chi's book *From Colonialism to Communism*, which the CIA official endorsed as meriting "the careful attention of anyone interested in Vietnamese affairs." It would later be revealed that this book, by a disaffected former Viet Minh, had been secretly financed by the CIA and published under a covert CIA program.

The man willing to propound messages such as these was the CIA officer whom director Richard Helms sent forth to inform Congress on Agency activities in Vietnam. His marching orders were to answer the questions asked—not those which ought to have been asked—and to say so when he felt he could not talk about something. This kind of approach added to misinformation and confusion, which was advantageous in the short run as the Johnson and Nixon administrations maneuvered on Capitol Hill, but which in the long run did grave damage to the CIA and U.S. intelligence generally in the 1970s when its credibility collapsed in the face of a series of vile revelations and haunting allegations.

One example is that wonderful "secret war," Laos, where the CIA's perfidy ultimately soured relations between Congress and the Agency. As SAVA, George Carver was present at the creation of some of that antipathy. Later Carver apparently told Thomas Powers, biographer of Richard Helms, that he had briefed Senator Stuart Symington on the CIA's Laos program in September 1966. Symington later (in 1969) played a key role in revealing the "secret war," leading several CIA officers to deplore the senator as someone who had told them they were doing great only to betray them later. Not so visible in this is the intertwining of intelligence and politics beyond the control of both Senator Symington and his CIA critics. First, the Agency had been telling individual senators on Symington's own committee about Laos for *four years*, yet Symington himself, a powerful member of Armed Services, was informed only when he was about to make an extensive trip to Laos and Thailand to survey the effectiveness of the air war. It was not possible for Symington to do the Laos-Thailand circuit without stumbling into the CIA's operation, so it was better he be told about it in Washington first. It must have rankled Symington that he had been kept ignorant this way. Second, like his Senate peers, Symington in fact kept quiet about Laos for two and a half years thereafter. Third,

Symington, *in 1968* (that is to say, a year in advance) informed Lyndon Johnson that he intended to speak up if the president did not reverse course on Vietnam. The senator clearly saw his role as blowing the whistle on the executive branch's supposed indifference to American political opinion. The CIA in Laos just happened to be the proximate congressional target, but since Helms had directed George Carver to play coy in the first place, he could hardly object once the Agency became caught in its own web of obfuscation.

Like later CIA congressional relations staffs, who would quibble over the range of activities subject to oversight, or argue the scope of operations to be included, the SAVA was good at splitting hairs. George Carver, Sr., had been chairman of an English department at a school in China, and his son liked nothing better than to quibble, even when it was over the usage or particular implication of a word or phrase. George, Jr., after all, was author of an academic treatise he called "Aesthetics and the Problem of Meaning." At the *Westmoreland v CBS* trial, when Carver was called on statements in 1968 cables and memos from SAVA, the former CIA potentate breezily dismissed the extravagance as poetic license. For example, Carver described the Tet offensive in a CIA document as mere "recent urban excitement." What place such poetry ought to have in intelligence reporting he did not explain. A senior colleague told Thomas Powers, about the SAVA, that "Carver can do more, with less evidence, than any other man I've ever known." Almost the identical words were once used by Russell Jack Smith, CIA's deputy director for intelligence during this period, in describing silver-tongued Arthur Lundahl, the prince of CIA aerial photo interpreters. In Lundahl's case one could be certain that what the briefer added to the simple photograph was based on encyclopedic knowledge of pictures taken earlier, or photos of similar things taken elsewhere. With Carver one could not be so sure.

The CIA's assessments mattered in Washington. They were important to Lyndon Johnson, who had a great appetite for intelligence opinion. The CIA's opinions were vital for Robert McNamara, who used them to argue that the bombing of North Vietnam was not the panacea some in the military were saying. George Carver's SAVA was responsible for a couple of the intelligence memoranda denigrating bombing effectiveness that McNamara relied upon. Perhaps it was seeing this play in progress, one cannot be sure, but SAVA soon became the object of a campaign by White House national security adviser Walt W. Rostow to encourage a more optimistic view of Vietnam. According to David Halberstam, who interviewed many of the key players on Vietnam, "In savvy Washington circles it was said that there were two CIAs: a George Carver CIA, which was the CIA at the top, generally optimistic in its reporting to Rostow; and the rest of the CIA, which was far more pessimistic."

Given these tendencies, Walt Rostow and his boss, President Johnson, were all the more stunned with what happened when George Carver briefed a group of senior advisers whom LBJ had called together for a policy review after Tet. Carver had inevitably been affected by the offensive—he had been in his office with State Department official Phillip Habib when word came that the embassy in Saigon was under attack. He had already been sitting on the explosive issue of the order of battle numbers, and in a session a few days later with McNamara, the defense secretary effectively reopened the debate by pointing out that many of the Viet Cong units identified in combat intelligence as participating in the Tet attacks were not even listed in the order of battle. Nine days later, on February 13, Carver cabled Saigon to inform CIA station chief John L. Hart that the order of battle issue would be reopened.

McNamara was in the audience in late March when Carver came to brief Johnson's "Wise Men" advisory group. As nearly as can be determined, for no records of the Carver briefing have been declassified, the SAVA relied principally upon a paper by one of his top analysts, George Allen, which straightforwardly asserted that while Tet had not been a military success for the Viet Cong or Hanoi, it had been a clear political and psychological victory. LBJ was outraged when he heard his Wise Men express pessimistic views and ordered Carver and others who had met with the group to repeat their briefings. The president was annoyed, but George Allen was out of a job—he was sent to England for a year to cool his heels as an exchange student at the British military staff college.

An acute observer of bureaucratic behavior, George Carver did not fail to appreciate the import of the Wise Men episode. When the extent of NVA supply through Cambodian ports became an important intelligence issue, SAVA kept his head down. Carver professed to know nothing in advance about the 1970 invasion of Cambodia. Asked to assemble a position paper on the Phoenix program in 1971, Carver took the easy path of advising against the CIA giving its files to the South Vietnamese police or turning over its agents to their control. In 1975, with just a few weeks left before the fall of Saigon to North Vietnamese troops, CIA analyst Frank Snepp was astonished when he was shown a draft paper Carver had written as one of a group of visiting experts: the paper asserted that a couple of successes could galvanize ARVN and that more U.S. aid could save South Vietnam.

Where was the dispassionate, fearless intelligence that might, once and for all, have dispelled the fog in Washington's streets and minds? There was wisdom at the CIA, but much of it never got past the doors of Langley, and there was plenty of ignorance too. John Hart, former Saigon station chief, admitted in 1982 that his analysts had not even had a dependable figure for *the population of South Vietnam*! The number they used was picked out of the air after some talk among the analysts. Since a lot of other data—from the percentage of people under Saigon control to formulas for aid money to the South Vietnamese—all depended on the population number, plenty of things were skewed by this lack of a single fact. In this most quantified of conflicts, half the data was fictitious.

These gaps in knowledge were crucial because the data were used as "facts" and relied upon to buttress decisions on war strategy. Problems in the data could not be overcome because *the system was not self-correcting*. As the episode of Carver and the Wise Men illustrated so graphically, presidents were wont to shoot the messenger of bad tidings. Much as they complained about poor data in the system—and the policymakers were aware of this problem—they did not truly wish to hear the bad news, nor were they willing to go along with the broad reforms that would have been necessary to rectify the system. Meanwhile, individuals up and down the chain of command saw their futures bound up in reporting the "right" data to their superiors. Once the data fed the next strategic decision, the circle was complete.

Is it any wonder the Vietnam War was lost?

In a way the troops saw more clearly than everyone else. The "grunts" in the field, the men doing the fighting and being killed, who saw the mines and booby traps, even the guns their generals insisted could not be there because the people wielding those weapons or placing those traps were not represented on the NVA order of battle—the grunts saw what was real, and their growing qualms effectively stopped the war. More and more soldiers rejected the insanity of the system by tuning out, by becoming less and less willing to take on missions, by questioning their orders, not merely carrying them out. "GI resistance" became a reality during the Nixon years. As much as anything else, that meant that the war had to be brought to an end. Typically, however, before that point was reached, the Nixon administration tried to shoot the messengers, supposing that its problems would go away if only the antiwar movement could be eliminated. As a result the Vietnam War led to a war at home, a war *directly against Americans*, especially those Vietnam veterans who came home to oppose the war. This particular Nixon campaign came to a head in Miami and Gainesville, Florida, in 1972 and 1973.

The Veterans' Antiwar Movement Under Siege: Miami and Gainesville

This is a story of desperate circumstance, of courage under fire, one that contains the very elements we associate with classic accounts of heroism. For too long veterans have thought about Vietnam as if the story stopped at the water's edge. There was "the Nam" and "the World." As if the weeks, months, and years spent trying to build new lives after Nam were not part of the story, or indeed, as if America was a great void while the war went on over there. Ultimately it is impossible to bring closure to the story of the Vietnam War, to Americans' understanding of what happened to them and around them, without confronting the myths that have grown up surrounding the image of a monolithic antiwar movement. When one breaks the old molds, the first thing discovered is that Vietnam veterans played key roles in the antiwar movement just as they did in the war itself. Most everyone has heard of the largest such veterans' group, Vietnam Veterans Against the War (VVAW), particularly its April 1971 action in Washington, where almost a thousand veterans met to hold an intensely emotional demonstration on the steps of the U.S. Capitol. This story is about what happened later on.

■ The Nixon administration apparently felt especially threatened by the existence of an organization made up primarily of veterans and opposing the Vietnam War. Attorney General John Mitchell gave instructions to Robert C. Mardian, then director of the Internal Security Division at the Justice Department, to take the offensive against the antiwar movement. With the national attention VVAW received from its Dewey Canyon III demonstration in 1971, the general instructions were applied specifically to that organization. Mardian ordered the chief of his special litigations section, Guy L. Goodwin, to develop an investigation of VVAW. The veterans' movement again made news in December 1971 when members simultaneously occupied the Statue of Liberty, the Betsy Ross House in Philadelphia, the Lincoln Memorial in Washington, and the South Vietnamese consulate in San Francisco, plus a veterans' hospital ward in California. Federal Bureau of Investigation documents declassified in the late 1980s and 1990s make clear that the U.S. government had detailed knowledge of the demonstrations, including accounts of meetings held for planning and itineraries. Despite the material excised from these documents, one can readily infer from the type and quality of the information that the sources must have included not only informers infiltrated into the organization but also wiretaps and home break-ins.

By early 1972 the veterans were well aware that VVAW had been targeted by the Justice Department. Talk about informers became an undercurrent whenever VVAW vets gathered, but with 1972 a presidential election year and Richard Nixon running for a second term, the antiwar veterans determined to throw their full weight into the balance. Plans were made to attend the Democratic and Republican conventions, both held in Miami Beach that year. Final arrangements followed a southern regional meeting in Gainesville, at the home of Scott Camil, the VVAW coordinator for Florida. At the end of the late-May weekend of meetings, one of the participants, Arkansas-Oklahoma regional coordinator William L. Lemmer, confessed that he *himself* was an FBI informer. Over the following weeks Lemmer talked to local VVAW friends and others who accumulated between eight and fourteen hours of tape recordings in which he described his odyssey toward the FBI's orbit.

According to Lemmer and lawyer Frank Donner, who assembled the best account of Lemmer from Arkansas friends and his increasingly estranged wife, the former paratrooper (173rd Airborne Brigade, in Vietnam from February 1969 to February 1970) was afraid, and that fear drove him into the arms of the FBI. Lemmer thought he had been under surveillance by U.S. army intelligence agents from the fall of 1970, when he lay in an army hospital in Japan recovering from a severe attack of bronchial asthma. Lemmer's fears were not all that far-fetched, for it was during 1970 that the army admitted that since 1965 it had been conducting surveillance of suspected antiwar elements, both in uniform and among the American public. A special staff called CONUS Intel, for Continental United States Intelligence, had even been formed to coordinate action against the antiwar movement. Despite his fears, Lemmer volunteered for a second Vietnam tour, begun in the summer of 1970, but he was soon reassigned to Fort Benning due to further asthma attacks. Lemmer first began informing at Benning, according to later trial testimony, for he got permission to leave the post and attend the Dewey Canyon III demonstration in Washington in exchange for reporting to military intelligence on the events that occurred. Lemmer in fact appeared before a congressional hearing, presenting a petition protesting conditions at Fort Benning signed by 112 other soldiers from his unit.

Soon after Lemmer left the army he acquired growing importance in VVAW, becoming an acting regional coordinator in early 1972, partly on the strength of his being able to afford the trips (by that time the bills were being picked up by the FBI) to periodic meetings among the regional representatives. When arrested and held for five days as a result of an April 1972 demonstration at Tinker Air Force Base, Lemmer had been working under FBI control for about six months. En route to Gainesville he reportedly told a woman riding with them to Orlando that she should not attend the Miami conventions because there was going to be rioting, and that the VVAW leadership would be arrested and taken out of circulation.

Shortly after Lemmer attended the regional VVAW convocation at Gainesville he disappeared from sight; later it became known he was being sequestered under the federal witness protection program. Justice Department official Guy Goodwin supervised while a grand jury convened at Tallahassee to investigate allegations that VVAW had planned—at the May meetings—to disrupt the Republican convention that summer. Most of the VVAW's national and regional leaders, along with a number of Florida members, were subpoenaed to testify. Thus the Vietnam Veterans Against the War were under intense pressure just as the 1972 political season began.

■ Far from the image of the Vietnam veteran scorned by the American people, Vietnam vets were lionized at the Democratic convention in 1972, the most decidedly antiwar group ever to coalesce within a mainstream political party. In particular, Vietnam Veterans Against the War received official convention representation, was permitted to speak before the Democratic Platform Committee, and was even given free food for those attendees who were camping out in Miami Beach's Flamingo Park, courtesy of the Democratic party and Kentucky Fried Chicken. On July 13, the final day of the convention, the federal grand jury in Tallahassee handed down a six-count indictment based essentially upon the regional coordinators' discussions at Gainesville in May. The indictment accused seven VVAW members of conspiracy to disrupt the Republican convention (which would not take place until August) by creating "fire teams" of members who would attack Miami police stations, cars, and stores with automatic weapons, incendiary devices, slingshots (using specially prepared "fried" marbles), wrist rockets, and crossbows. Hearing of the indictment, the Democratic convention passed a resolution condemning the Nixon administration for a political prosecution and demanding it cease and desist.

With the Republican convention now fast approaching, the Vietnam Veterans Against the War were in a quandary. The organization already stood accused of plotting against the convention; certainly those named in the indictment were now powerless. The national leadership also was forced to stand aside so as not to be seen as abetting the alleged plot, with the exception of national office member Barry Romo, who was in Florida for months negotiating with local authorities for parade permits and camping permits, and making other arrangements. Local VVAW chapters and even individual members had to pick up the slack, but the result turned out better than anyone could have anticipated. Chicago VVAW members Bart Savage and Greg Petzel got the idea for a series of motorcades, in effect convoys, from different parts of the country, to meet in Florida and head for Miami Beach. They not only produced a plan but a full itinerary for three convoys that would leave from San Francisco, Milwaukee, and Boston, all to converge at Fort Pierce, just north of Miami. The plan soon acquired a name—the Last Patrol.

When August came, the antiwar veterans were ready. The convoy from Milwaukee was led by John Lindquist, who knew exactly what he was doing, having served as radioman in the lead vehicles of eighty-eight Third Marine Division truck convoys delivering supplies near the Demilitarized Zone in Vietnam. His Midwest convoy left Milwaukee with fifteen cars and picked up more along the way, starting with the Chicago contingent and vets from St. Louis and Kansas City. Before the end of the first day the convoy had forty vehicles. The East Coast Last Patrol had thirty cars by the time it reached Maryland. These two finally joined up as scheduled, and the united convoy, Lindquist still leading, was more than a mile long. The West Coast convoy, slowed by police who stopped it in Arizona and Texas, lagged behind the others and came in later. In all there were 105 vehicles.

As the Last Patrol neared Miami Beach, the hostility of the authorities became more evident. In one instance a Florida state trooper, at the highway ramp next to his barracks, pulled Lindquist over, determined to give him a ticket for driving too slowly. Lindquist, who had learned in the marines the importance of maintaining a steady rate of progress, had been traveling at exactly fifty miles per hour. Instructed to head into the state police parking lot, the Last Patrol followed him. Soon VVAW vehicles filled the police barracks, extended along the shoulders back to the ramp, and then down the ramp and back onto the highway. The police shift supervisor bawled out the trooper who had stopped the convoy and ordered him to get the cars out of there. That was when Lindquist discovered his walkie-talkie was no longer working and he could not talk to the rear vehicles to get them moving. Meanwhile, near the end of the convoy as it was pulled over, VVAW members saw "contraband" of several kinds go flying out the windows of cars ahead of them as they pulled over to face the police. Gambling that the situation was not that serious, some vets retrieved what they could.

As during the Democratic convention, the campsite set aside for demonstrators at the Republican convention was a walled enclosure in Flamingo Park. The Last Patrol veterans pulled up to discover a strange scene—members of the American Nazi party, mounting a demonstration of their own, had taken over the stage and podium at the park and were haranguing the crowd. While there were only a couple of dozen or so of the Nazis (by veterans' estimates), and perhaps 3,500 or so assorted antiwar activists already in Flamingo Park, no one seemed to be able to do anything about the Nazis. Camp organizers approached VVAW members begging them to get the American Nazi party people off the stage. When Del Rosario of the VVAW national office mounted the stage to ask the Nazis to vacate, someone, evidently a bodyguard for the speaker, picked up a chair and hit Rosario with it from behind. Outraged, the VVAW vets then surrounded the stage and pulled the offenders off one by one, passing them from hand to hand to the edge of the park where a really big veteran named Fred Rosenthal literally threw them out into the street, some by the scruff of their necks. The Nazi speaker reportedly went straight up *over* the wall, suffering injuries when he landed on the other side.

This incident with the Nazis made the Last Patrol veterans the darlings of Miami Beach, if not of the Republicans. Suddenly a Jewish alderman, who had most vociferously opposed VVAW at every turn during the weeks leading up to the convention, was asking veterans if they had enough portable toilets, if they needed electricity, anything at all. When the veterans refused to camp inside the walled enclosure, which they considered not secure and which was becoming packed with less-disciplined antiwar demonstrators, it suddenly became all right for the veterans to move to a new site two hundred meters south. Jewish residents materialized with baskets of food and bottles of wine, feeding the VVAW that first night as they set up camp. Finally, relations were cemented with the Miami Beach police, who cooperated amicably with the VVAW for the duration of the Last Patrol. When the Nazis later tried to return, with more cars and bodies, they were turned back by Miami Beach residents—little old ladies with garden hoses and men with shovels. When they heard the story, veterans felt proud to have given an example.

The next day, August 21, began the real business of the antiwar demonstrations. With their focus on the military and the war, VVAW were the only activists to hold a demonstration outside the local high school where the administration had stationed a contingent of the Florida National Guard plus selected specialists from the Eighty-second Airborne Division, in place to reinforce convention security. The Florida Guard's later report on its activities in Miami Beach commented favorably on VVAW's conduct and discipline.

Discipline was manifestly evident when the veterans, who had between twelve hundred and fifteen hundred members in Miami Beach for the event, marched past the convention hall and the Fontainebleau Hotel, site of Republican party headquarters. Save for a few whispered instructions passed among vets doing march security, the demonstration was entirely silent—and haunting. When the press asked about the march, a VVAW source replied simply, "There's nothing left to say."

The antiwar veterans' actions in Miami Beach scarcely resembled the accusations in the federal indictment. In fact, the veterans had a general agenda which, with a convention schedule, was used to make specific plans that were finalized more or less on the spot. Many VVAW actions were carried out the same way as these had been, for example, in Dewey Canyon III, which had also involved on-the-spot voting over whether the veterans ought to take certain actions. The central assumption behind the federal indictment—that there was a "VVAW plan"—has been denied by several key participants, by VVAW national and regional officials, and by Gainesville defendants. As for the idea of using slingshots, it was true that Scott Camil had acquired some slingshots (five dozen—not very many among fifteen hundred demonstrators), but they were never intended for anything other than self-defense. As national officer Barry Romo put it, "Do you think these combat vets just back from Vietnam were stupid enough to think they could attack riot police with slingshots?"

The strongest action by the VVAW at Miami involved nothing more than wire-cutters and motor oil. Scouting the convention site, veterans saw that the Republicans were bringing people in buses that went around the back of the building, through a gate, and up a ramp. A garage door was raised to admit the buses, then lowered when they had passed. Some California veterans got the idea of immobilizing buses on the ramp. On the evening of Richard Nixon's acceptance of the nomination, August 23, a squad of VVAW activists used wire-cutters to clip through the chain-link fence, then spread four quarts of motor oil on the steep ramp. Then they returned to the main body of demonstrators in front of the convention hall. The next bus to come along promptly stalled. As other buses lined up behind it the entire entry system collapsed.

The delegates on their buses perforce had to confront the demonstrators. Many rolled down their windows and shouted at the state troopers to "get" the veterans. Several VVAW members heard shouts of "Gas 'em!" The troopers deployed and began to use teargas. Then a remarkable thing happened—the wind changed direction and blew the gas back toward the convention hall. The buses with open windows were soon filled with gas. Worse, the hall had opened its garage door in expectation of buses entering, and the gas wafted inside. Spiro Agnew stopped briefly in the middle of his introductory speech, tears in his eyes. Richard Nixon himself writes, "My eyes burned from the lingering sting of tear gas as I entered the hall."

In the convention audience were four VVAW members, three of them in wheelchairs, who had received tickets from California representative Pete McCloskey and were helped by several pro-McCloskey girls who also wished to protest the Vietnam War. When they raised signs these were ripped from their hands and torn up; when they shouted, Republicans tried outshouting them and security guards ejected them from the premises. Nevertheless Bobby Mueller, Bill Wieman, Mark Clevinger, and Ron Kovic felt they had been effective. So hostile was the atmosphere that Kovic, in his wheelchair, was spat upon, but at another point he was interviewed for more than two minutes on network television and was able to get his point across.

Meanwhile, the antiwar veterans were aware that arraignment of their seven accused (and one codefendant) was scheduled for Gainesville, where the case had been transferred, the very next day. The VVAW crew broke camp even as the demonstration was beginning downtown, and left as soon as the troopers began their rampage. In the early moments, when the authorities were lashing out indiscriminately, many veterans were able to shelter in hotel lobbies, storefronts, and even homes, all opened to them by Jewish Miamians grateful to the veterans for their treatment of the Nazis a few days before.

Veterans were counseled to drive together in groups of cars, stay together, leave with full gas tanks, and travel as far as they could before stopping. With this advice they avoided the state troopers, who staked out the highways leading north to harass demonstrators but only began to do so the next morning. The conglomeration of other activists bore the brunt of the troopers' repression, both in Miami and on the roads out of the city, including the compound at Flamingo Park. There the enclosure turned into a trap, with police along the walls lobbing gas canisters into the enclosure. By then the veterans were gone.

Several hundred veterans drove through rain all night, a good eight hours, to reach Gainesville the next morning. Again they mounted a powerful demonstration, not so much in numbers but in symbolism. Marching through driving rain—one participant remarked that it rained so hard it reminded him of the monsoon—they walked silently once more, and with their hands on their heads in the manner of prisoners of war. Reaching the courthouse plaza, they linked arms to surround the building and then began to whistle "When Johnny Comes Marching Home." Then they marched silently away again. "It even spooked me," recalled VVAW member Annie Daily. "You can imagine how those FBI guys felt."

■ After the Miami convention there was almost a year of legal maneuvering before the Gainesville Eight, as they came to be called, went to trial. During all that time the government continued its campaign of intimidation against the VVAW. In New Orleans, which for a time had only three men in its VVAW chapter, all three were government informants. Two of three in Jacksonville were informants and stole materials from the third. In Miami, FBI and Dade County police broke into members' homes and planted drugs, later to recruit the individual under threat of a drug arrest. Other Dade County police joined the VVAW organization and became its most militant members, constantly advocating violent tactics. The individuals involved were later to be produced as witnesses at the Gainesville trial. Scott Camil's lawyer had her office burglarized and his case file stolen. In New York other members' apartments were also burglarized and their files rifled. Harassment reached such heights of pettiness that at the national office the bathroom was seeded with an itching powder that contaminated the skin and clothes of anyone who sat on the toilet seat.

A wider, Watergate context was supplied by the U.S. Senate investigation of the Nixon administration's unsavory activities. An individual previously used as an informer to infiltrate another antiwar group testified to the Senate that he had been ordered by H. Howard Hunt, Republican intelligence chieftain (and former CIA officer), to penetrate VVAW. Another individual declared that Hunt had offered him a large salary to do the same but that he had rejected it. One political-cum-intelligence operation that Hunt did pull off, the harassment of Daniel Ellsberg, included not only a break-in into his psychiatrist's office but an out-and-out beating from a group of thugs as he emerged from a speaking engagement. Later it transpired that one of those arrested for the assault, a Miami Cuban named Pablo Manuel Fernandez, had been a police informant too, and was specifically sent to Scott Camil to try to elicit an overt act of conspiracy, offering access to weapons of types ranging from rifles to 81 mm and 60 mm mortars. The antiwar veteran had had no interest. When VVAW lawyers tried to question senior Justice Department officials in the matter of political motivation for the actions taken against VVAW, federal district judge Winston E. Arnow disallowed seven of the eight proposed subpoenas. Only former Attorney General John Mitchell came before the court to make a bland statement, after which the judge refused to permit more than thirty questions posed by the lawyers. It was a harbinger of what was to come.

In the Gainesville case, the Justice Department prosecutor, at the time of the original indictments in 1972, had appeared in court and sworn that a whole series of individuals had no connection with the government. One of these persons, Emerson L. Poe, a good friend of Scott Camil and his successor as Florida coordinator, was later produced at the trial as an FBI informer. Poe had participated in legal and strategic preparations for the defense until just weeks before. Other informers who turned up at the trial included a roommate of defendant Alton Foss, and another former VVAW national officer, Carl Becker, not to mention the now notorious Bill Lemmer. Not only had government informants advocated strenuous actions and offered access to weapons, but when VVAW put together a preconvention newsletter that discussed the Miami demonstrations, the FBI made the copies to be sent to the VVAW membership. Readers of George Orwell should see something familiar here.

On the first day of the Gainesville trial, as the defendants and their lawyers conferred in the room set aside for their use, one, Peter P. Mahoney, thought he heard noise coming from behind the screen of the ventilation vent. Looking up, he thought he saw movement. U.S. marshals were summoned to open the utility closet that adjoined the defense conference room. Inside they discovered FBI agents Carl Ekblad and Robert Romann with a briefcase full of electronic equipment. The array included a telephone receiving device, alligator clips, earphones, an "output transmitter," an amplifier, and a battery pack. The FBI agents asserted they were simply checking phone lines. "These gentlemen have been perfectly candid and honest" said Judge Arnow, accusing defense lawyers of "making mountains out of molehills." In mid-August, halfway through the trial, the jury forewoman sent the judge a note reporting that three-quarters of the jurors believed their own home phones were being tapped.

Prosecutorial misconduct continued rife throughout the Gainesville trial. Guy Goodwin was seen coaching witness Lemmer in the hallway; other witnesses admitted under cross-examination that they too had been coached. One witness, still under oath and in cross-examination at the end of a day of testimony, was specifically ordered to have no contact with federal authorities. He left the building, got into his car, and drove to Ocala where he went into the federal building. The prosecution repeatedly delayed or did not supply documentary material pertaining to its own witnesses, for example producing the records of Lemmer's talks with his FBI control, agent Richard O'Connell, only at the very end of the trial, as the case was about to go to the jury.

Judge Winston Arnow engaged in arbitrary actions of his own. In addition to getting the FBI off the hook for being caught in the act, he was virtually unresponsive to the defense's pretrial motions. Arnow rejected numerous defense objections to trial procedures and at one point told defense lawyers he would no longer *hear* objections; only written submissions would be entertained. When cross-examiners wished to press William Lemmer on whether provocation had figured in his relationship with the FBI, Arnow sent the jury out of the room, in effect making the matter of provocation irrelevant. He made similar choices with other lines of questioning and other witnesses. When Judge Arnow got tense he would break the pencils he was constantly playing with on the bench—observers reckoned he must have gone through a good hundred pencils during the trial. One of VVAW's more creative support demonstrations occurred when members brought pencils with them and filled the gallery, then began playing with the things.

As had happened in 1972, VVAW mounted demonstrations to benefit its defendants in the August 1973 Gainesville trial. The defendants, Scott Camil, Peter Mahoney, Alton C. Foss, John W. Kniffin, William J. Patterson, Donald P. Perdue, Stanley K. Michelson, and John K. Briggs, were subject to a gag order imposed by Judge Arnow, which made more silent demonstrations a logical tactic. The FBI bugging incident provoked a march with the slogan "FBI/Out of the Closet!/Into the Street!" The gagged defendants also poked fun at Guy Goodwin, who favored bow ties, by coming to court one day wearing the loudest bow ties they could find. About 175 VVAW members came from all over the country for efforts which, given the relatively small numbers in hand, focused on outreach. After four days of daily marches, guerrilla theater, and picketing of an A&P store in support of the United Farm Workers, on August 4 a full-scale rally was held at Santa Fe Community College which attracted more than nine hundred Gainesville citizens in addition to the antiwar veterans. Afterward most of the support group packed up and moved out, many of the New York contingent, for example, boarding an old school bus the chapter had found and reconditioned after buying it from a church in Kansas.

The Gainesville Eight faced the remainder of their trial with only local allies. But this proved less daunting than it could have been because the government's case grew continually weaker. Testimony that Camil had M-14 rifles in his closet evaporated when the witness, who claimed to be a former air force weapons instructor, could not tell the difference between an M-14 and the handle-grip M-16, or indeed between a real M-16 and the toy rifles Camil kept for VVAW demonstrations. Allegations that the veterans intended to hide slingshots in their pants legs or in underwear became ridiculous once the slingshots were actually demonstrated—they featured two six-inch bars at right angles to each other. Talk of "fried" marbles or steel pellets looked silly when FBI ballistics tests showed that at short range they could not even penetrate the skin of a rabbit (the ASPCA filed a protest with the FBI about the use of rabbits in these tests). Talk of bombs was discredited by the FBI's own explosives expert as well as by an expert witness for the defense. Judge Arnow again refused to dismiss the indictment after the prosecution rested its case.

Defendants and their lawyers, with some trepidation, felt sufficiently confident to put on little defense, calling but a single witness—the explosives expert. When the jury took the case, after a month-long prosecution, it was only three and a half hours before forewoman Lois

Hensel emerged to deliver a verdict of not guilty on all counts. One juror remarked, "They had nothing on those boys."

Although the Justice Department looked pathetic at the close of the Gainesville trial, in important ways they had attained at least some of their objectives in harassing VVAW. At a critical moment the administration diverted the effort of a key antiwar organization to defending itself. Despite VVAW's good fortune in gaining legal assistance from the Centre for Constitutional Rights plus Florida and Texas lawyers, the organization had spent $275,000 (a huge sum for a voluntary group like VVAW in the early 1970s) that could have gone toward its primary purposes. Events also decimated the ranks of Southern members who, according to former senior members, were fewer and farther apart (thus more vulnerable) than their Western and Northern brethren, and were now terrified of government informers. "Some people think the only war we had to fight was over there," reflected a New York veteran. "Actually the war we fought here was a lot tougher."

28   Victory as an Illusion

Even now, years after the Vietnam War, when its outcome is clear to see, some observers still pine for the lost victory. If only *this* had been different, or *that* done better, victory would have been ours. A number of these ideal solutions are proposed by witnesses to Vietnam who were themselves participants in the war. But memory fades, and the proponents of one or another of these latter-day solutions do not recall the way solutions were advanced then, every day, with equal confidence and self-assurance. The men who led the war, the "best and the brightest" in David Halberstam's phrase, had every opportunity to fulfill Lyndon Johnson's dream and "nail the 'coonskin to the wall." The war nevertheless ended in 1975, with Hanoi's troops marching into Saigon and ARVN's generals fleeing on American helicopters.

Given the way Vietnam ended there is no reason to suppose that the perfect strategies now advanced would have succeeded any better than those that were actually employed. In fact, *because* of the way the war ended, claims of a perfect strategy should be subject to special scrutiny. The burden of proof must be on claimants to show that a postulated strategy would necessarily have led to victory. Instead many Americans have uncritically accepted assertions that instant "decisive" intervention, or a bombing campaign of maximum violence, or a perfected Phoenix program would have been ideal solutions. We have evaluated a number of these strategies here and found them wanting. These are *prima facie* criticisms to be sure, but the apparent flaws in the victory strategies show that the claims made today do not differ in substance from the kinds of arguments used for strategy proposals while the Vietnam War was still going on.

Let us walk away from the confining strictures of military strategies for a moment and think of the quest for victory in Vietnam as an intellectual problem. Doing this we can set criteria that a proposed strategy should have to meet, an exercise that ought to clarify the whole matter. First, any victory strategy had to utilize what was there, what was available in South Vietnam, and since the national identity and the aspirations of Vietnamese favored the other side, any potential strategy had an extra obstacle to overcome. Moreover, since the institutions of South Vietnam were of such recent creation, they were of limited strength and subject to manipulation (as in the military coups of the 1960s or the Buddhist Struggle Movement) in ways inimical to our hypothetical strategy.

Second, a winning strategy had to utilize the military and intelligence methods and forces of the time, or, at the margin, those conceivable at the time. Since Americans' preliminary definition of the problem (counterinsurgency against a "foreign" adversary) was imperfect, a process of triangulation had to occur before the strategy could fit the problem. A number of perceptive analysts have examined American military doctrines of the time and come away with the impression that we did not understand, or wholeheartedly commit ourselves to, the kinds of activity that might have addressed the problem in Vietnam. Under those circumstances, no winning strategy was possible.

Part of the triangulation of strategy and force that had to occur was a match between the degree of American commitment and the capacity of South Vietnam to absorb and utilize the forces dispatched. We have shown that in fact the deployment to Vietnam occurred at about the fastest rate possible given inherent limitations of port and transport infrastructure. Therefore there is very little room in our hypothetical winning strategy for varying rates of force commitment to Vietnam. Proponents of these kinds of solutions have simply not looked at both sides of the equation.

Third, the triangulation that had to be made between problem and strategy would inevitably occur against an evolving threat. The clock was running, not only as North Vietnam and the Viet Cong improved their infrastructure and military striking power, but also domestically. American politics permitted only a certain length of time for the perfect solution to be found, after which reversal of political support would occur. This is the real meaning of Tet, and the problem is by no means confined to the Vietnam War. The way the perception of what was accomplished in the 1991 Gulf War reversed itself, and the way the politics of the Somalia intervention evolved in a fashion similar to Vietnam shows that this problem is now endemic in American politics.

Moreover, it can be argued that the rate at which events develop is accelerating. As for Vietnam, the political argument is not simply retrospective, for the French had fallen victim before us to the same kind of trap.

Fourth, the winning strategy had to be found in the face of a system generating false information for the top decision-makers, a system that was not operating to correct itself. The problem of false information compounds the other criteria for a winning strategy—it means that more *time* is needed to do a triangulation, it means that *uncertainty* remains when observers tentatively think they have a fit between problem and strategy. Equally troubling, since false information was characteristic in Vietnam and cannot be fixed retrospectively, any proposed winning strategy had to be one that would have succeeded in spite of the false information in the system.

Fifth, a proposed strategy cannot telescope history. That is, a winning strategy cannot rely upon elements of a situation or forces which did not exist at the time it had to be implemented. For example, Richard Nixon could mine Haiphong in 1972 because of diplomatic and other developments which had already reduced the intensity of the cold war and the probability of Russian or Chinese intervention. Mining Haiphong in 1966 would have thrown down a gauntlet to the Russians and the Chinese. Hypothetical strategies that telescope history like this really depend on after-the-fact observations for their effectiveness (that is, the Russians did not intervene when we mined Haiphong in 1972, so we would have stopped Hanoi if only we had mined in 1966). Such post hoc arguments for strategy are not admissible.

Sixth, a winning strategy had to have been effective against the real adversary in Vietnam, not the one we thought existed. This is the problem with proposed pacification solutions implemented at a time Hanoi had moved on to conventional warfare, or of war-fighting solutions attempted while the opponent continued to concentrate on guerrilla warfare. Mismatch between strategy and threat was a continual obstacle to American success in South Vietnam, one obviously exacerbated by false information in the system.

Given these criteria, a winning strategy for Vietnam seems unattainable. As a matter of logic and theoretical tests the problem is hard enough; as a matter of flesh and blood and men following a jungle track, many "perfect strategies" seem so facile as to be laughable. The truth is that American military force was seductive, seemingly omnipotent, against an opponent who appeared fragile. Victory became a vision; there had to be a formula for success, simply because we were so strong and they so weak. Visions of victory led Americans to Khe Sanh, to Phoenix, to Cambodia and Laos, to Haiphong harbor. But all that time the clock was running, as the visions led us on. In the end, Americans set off three World War IIs' worth of explosives on the land of Indochina without making the vision concrete.

Victory was an illusion.

Given the constraints that were operating in Vietnam, the limitations in American understanding, and the falsified data in the system, it simply was not possible to perform a proper triangulation, to fit strategy to problem within the amount of time available to the United States to find a solution. Claims for perfect strategies are all based on unlimited opportunity and time to analyze the problem.

Victory is still an illusion.

There is wisdom too in knowing when to stop. In the strategy of poker, the most skillful element lies in understanding when to hold your cards, when to bluff, when to fold your hand and walk away. American strategists have drawn about as much as possible from pursuit of the illusion of victory in Vietnam, but there is vast unexplored territory in identifying points at which the U.S. might have stopped. It seems clear that in the post–cold war world, strategies for holding out amid uncertainty without damaging escalation; for defusing local crises by bluff and maneuver; for disengaging from crises by walking away—these are concepts that could be of enormous value in our nation's future. Progress on such novel strategic concepts, using Vietnam's fertile ground for research, seems a good deal more useful than further debate over the illusion of victory in the past. Beyond matters of strategy, at the national level it is time for closure; America should move beyond real or imagined disputes over the Vietnam War.

Many have already done this on an individual, personal level. People like Thich Nhat Hanh and Tim Brown have found, in peace and comradeship, valid results from the Vietnam War. Their victories are not illusions.

A Note on Sources

1. THE FIRST AMERICAN PRISONERS

Numerous general histories exist of the origins and course of the Vietnam conflict. Among the more accessible is Stanley Karnow's *Vietnam: A History* (New York, 1983). On the American role, a seminal work is George McTurnin Kahin and John Lewis, *The United States in Vietnam* (New York, 1967). A more recent reconstruction of the period under consideration in this chapter, one based on the declassified documentary record, is Lloyd Gardner's *Approaching Vietnam* (New York, 1988). There are many significant French-language accounts of the battle of Dien Bien Phu. Perhaps the classic account available in English is that by Bernard B. Fall, *Hell in a Very Small Place* (New York, 1967). American military activity connected with Dien Bien Phu is best seen in the present book and in my previous *The Sky Would Fall: Operation Vulture, the U.S. Bombing Mission in Indochina, 1954* (New York, 1983). The present account of the American detachments in Vietnam, "Little America," and the first prisoners is entirely reconstructed from formerly classified records, contemporary periodicals, and my own interviews.

2. PROFILE: WAITING IN THE WINGS

In my opinion, the best recent biography of Lyndon Johnson is that by Robert Dallek, *Lone Star Rising: Lyndon Johnson and His Times, 1908–1960* (New York, 1991). The closest perspective on LBJ for this particular period is George Reedy's *Lyndon B. Johnson: A Memoir* (New York, 1982). Reedy was among LBJ's key political advisers at the time of Dien Bien Phu, and his memoranda of this period reflect the bulk of political advice Johnson received about the crisis. The recent biographer referred to in the text is Robert A. Caro, who has so far completed two of a projected three-volume Johnson biography: *The Years of Lyndon Johnson: The Path to Power* (New York, 1982), and *Means of Ascent* (New York, 1990). The Johnson quote about Korea and war with Russia, and that from the May 6, 1954, speech are from Dallek. All other quotes are from Johnson's senatorial papers, housed at the Lyndon Baines Johnson Presidential Library, Austin, Texas. On John F. Kennedy, see Richard Reeves, *President Kennedy: Profile of Power* (New York, 1993). On Richard Nixon, see his *RN: The Memoirs of Richard Nixon* (New York, 1978). Also useful for this period is the first volume of Stephen E. Ambrose's three-volume biography, *Nixon: The Education of a Politician 1913–1962* (New York, 1987). A further interesting perspective is Fawn M. Brodie's *Richard Nixon: The Shaping of His Character* (New York, 1981).

3. CONFUCIANS AND QUAGMIRES

Bernard Fall is quoted from his book *The Two Vietnams: A Political and Military Analysis*, 2nd rev. ed., (New York, 1967). On Ngo Dinh Diem, see Sirdar Ikbal ali Shah, *Vietnam* (London, 1960). Also see the admiring Anthony T. Bouscaren, *The*

Last of the Mandarins: Diem of Vietnam (Pittsburgh, 1965), dated now but at the time the best biography of Diem. A more recent defense of Diem appears in Ellen J. Hammer, *A Death in November: America in Vietnam, 1963* (New York, 1987). An overview of the military aid program appears in the official history, which carries the series title *United States Army in Vietnam*. The relevant volume is Ronald H. Spector's *Advice and Support: The Early Years, 1941–1960* (Washington, D.C., 1983). Ambassador Frederick Nolting is quoted from his *From Trust to Tragedy: The Political Memoirs of Frederick Nolting, Kennedy's Ambassador to Diem's Vietnam* (Westport, Conn., 1988). John Mecklin is quoted from his *Mission in Torment: An Intimate Account of the U.S. Role in Vietnam* (Garden City, N.Y., 1965). On U.S. policy in general, see the exhaustive *The U.S. Government and the Vietnam War* series by William C. Gibbons (Princeton) currently in its fourth volume. For the Kennedy period, see Roger Hilsman, *To Move a Nation: The Politics of Foreign Policy in the Kennedy Administration* (Garden City, N.Y., 1967).

The thesis that John Kennedy intended a total withdrawal from Vietnam is advanced most directly by John M. Newman, *JFK and Vietnam: Deception, Intrigue, and the Struggle for Power* (New York, 1992). See also William J. Rust, *Kennedy in Vietnam: American Vietnam Policy 1960–1963* (New York, 1985). Classic journalistic accounts include Denis Warner, *The Last Confucian: Vietnam, Southeast Asia and the West* (New York, 1963); Malcolm W. Browne, *The New Face of War* (Indianapolis, 1965); and David Halberstam, *The Making of a Quagmire* (New York, 1965).

Many official documents from this period appear in the Department of State series *Foreign Relations of the United States* which, as of this writing, is in print through 1964 on the subject of Vietnam. Comments on Kennedy's National Security Council and other meetings mentioned here are taken from the original documents in the John F. Kennedy Papers, John F. Kennedy Presidential Library, Boston, Massachusetts.

4. PROFILE: GEORGE CARVER (I)
Material on George Carver is from my biographical collection plus interviews.

5. THE COVERT WAR
As yet there are no specific studies of the covert war, though one is expected from former intelligence specialist Sedgwick Tourison. Nevertheless, this subject is touched upon in many sources. See, for example, *The Vietnam Experience: War in the Shadows*, edited by Samuel Lipsman (Boston, 1988). Edward Lansdale's role cannot be gleaned from his own memoir, which stops in the Diem period, but see Cecil Curry's *The Unquiet American* (Boston, 1988). Curry's title is a play on that of Graham Greene's novel *The Quiet American* (New York, 1955), which features Lansdale, as does another fictionalized treatment, *The Ugly American*, by Eugene Burdick and William J. Lederer (New York, 1958). A CIA view of this period is furnished by William E. Colby in his two books, *Honorable Men* (with Peter Forbath, New York, 1978) and *Lost Victory* (with James McCargar, Chicago, 1989). Colby is quoted from the second of these works. A fictionalized account of Special Forces activities, which sparked public interest, helping to create the conditions that led to the popularity of Barry Sadler's song "The Ballad of the Green Berets," is Robin Moore's *The Green Berets* (New York, 1965). Lansdale's 1961 report and

McGeorge Bundy's comment to President Kennedy are quoted from the original documents which reside in the Kennedy presidential papers. Quotes from NSAMs, Joint Chiefs of Staff memoranda, Ambassador Lodge, Admiral Sharp, John McCone, and General Taylor are all from documents in the Lyndon Johnson papers.

6. SIX MYSTERIES OF THE TONKIN GULF

The basic source here, as well as for some details on 34-A operations given in the preceding chapter, is Volume 2 of the official history series *The United States Navy and the Vietnam Conflict: From Military Assistance to Combat, 1959–1965* (Washington, D.C., 1986), by Edward J. Marolda and Oscar P. Fitzgerald. Marolda and Edwin E. Moise debated events at length after each presented papers in 1987 (William B. Cogar, ed., *New Interpretations of Naval History: Selected Papers from the Eighth Naval History Symposium* (Annapolis, 1989). Original documents on the subject are drawn from the LBJ Library. Older but of continuing value are two contemporary studies: *Tonkin Gulf* by Eugene Windchy (Garden City, N.Y., 1971), which centers on events aboard the ships, and *The President's War* by Anthony Austin (New York, 1971). An eyewitness account by one of the aircraft pilots is *In Love And War* by Jim and Sybil Stockdale (New York, 1985). Interviews are the source for claims of unusual radio traffic, while daily diary notes kept to back up Lyndon Johnson's schedule identified the president's meetings with the chief of naval operations during 1964.

7. PROFILE: GENERALS AND POLITICS IN SOUTH VIETNAM

The author's biographical collection is the most important source for this chapter. The mention of Richard Critchfield is a reference to his book *The Long Charade: Political Subversion in the Vietnam War* (New York, 1968). Data on regional backgrounds of ARVN recruits (other than the generals) is drawn from Robert S. White, "Anthropometric Survey of the Armed Forces of the Republic of Vietnam" (U.S. Army: Natick Laboratories, October 1964). The 1969 study quoted is National Security Study Memorandum NSSM-1, "Vietnam," reprinted in *Congressional Record*, May 10 and 11, 1972. Nguyen Cao Ky is quoted from his memoir *Twenty Years and Twenty Days* (New York, 1976).

8. SPECIAL WARFARE IN THE CENTRAL HIGHLANDS

Material in this chapter comes from three broad sets of sources. First are the accounts of Special Forces actions in Vietnam, starting with the same ones listed in *Chapter 5*. Material on the Special Forces role with the Montagnards can also be found in general histories of this force, including Shelby L. Stanton's *Green Berets at War* (Novato, Calif., 1985); Charles M. Simpson's *Inside the Green Berets* (Novato, Calif., 1983); and Colonel Francis J. Kelly's *Vietnam Studies: U.S. Army Special Forces, 1961–1971* (Washington, D.C., 1973). Green Beret accounts specific to the CIDG program include L. H. "Bucky" Burruss, *Mike Force* (New York, 1989), and James C. Donahue's *No Greater Love: A Day with the Mobile Guerrilla Force in Vietnam* (New York, 1989). Intelligence memoirs, particularly those of Bill Colby and Peer de Silva, were also useful. The Medal of Honor story of Roger H. C. Donlon was told to Warren Rogers and published as *Outpost of Freedom* (New York, 1965). A second group of materials are those specifically on montagnards, primarily articles. An excellent source on the revolts is Howard Sochurek's "American Special Forces in Action in Vietnam" (*National Geo-*

graphic, vol. 127, no. 1, January 1965). Sochurek returned to the subject in "Viet Nam's Montagnards: Caught in the Jaws of a War" (*National Geographic*, vol. 133, no. 4, April 1968). Bernard Fall's overview is in his "The Montagnards" (*New Republic*, October 17, 1964). Anthropologist Gerald C. Hickey produced voluminous reports and books before, during, and after the war, and all of his works are worth consulting, especially *The Highland People of South Vietnam* (1967) and his two-volume account *Sons of the Mountains* and *Free in the Forest* (1982). A well-conceived short account is by Charles A. Joiner, "Administration and Political Warfare in the Highlands," reprinted in Wesley R. Fishel, ed., *Vietnam: Anatomy of a Conflict* (Itasca, Ill., 1968). Detailed studies of every tribe are in Department of the Army Pamphlet 550-105, *Ethnographic Study Series: Minority Groups in the Republic of Vietnam* (United States Army, 1966). A third broad group of sources includes declassified documents and interviews. All quotes in the chapter are from declassified documents.

9. BULLETS, BOMBS, AND BUDDHISTS

Despite the importance of the subject, relatively little has been published on the Buddhists and Vietnamese politics, with the notable exception of a variety of materials appearing in accounts of the 1963 coup that toppled Ngo Dinh Diem. The Catholic-Buddhist competition is the subject of Piero Gheddo's *The Cross and the Bo Tree* (New York, 1970). South Vietnamese politics in general are the focus of *Vietnam: The Unheard Voices* (Ithaca, 1969) by Don Luce, a senior IVS volunteer, and John Sommer. General political material also appears in compilations of news reporting from Vietnam, such as Keesing's Research Report 5, *South Vietnam: A Political History, 1954–1970* (New York, 1970). A broad prize-winning account is *Fire in the Lake* (Boston, 1972) by Frances FitzGerald. See also Robert Shaplen's *The Road from War: Vietnam 1965–1971* (New York, 1971). The Vietnamese military perspective appears in Major General Nguyen Duy Hinh and Brigadier General Tran Dinh Tho, *Indochina Monographs: The South Vietnamese Society* (Washington, D.C., 1980). On the specific political impact of Buddhism, a highly useful paper is John Alosi's "The Role of Religious Groups in the Quest for Popular Government in South Vietnam, 1963–1971," presented at the conference "Remembering Tet" at Salisury State University (Maryland), November 20, 1992. The Alosi paper may appear in a forthcoming collection of conference papers. Cao Ngoc Phuong's activities are detailed in the memoir written under her Buddhist name Chan Khong, *Learning True Love* (Berkeley, Calif., 1993). The best contemporary Buddhist source is Thich Nhat Hanh's *Vietnam: Lotus in a Sea of Fire* (New York, 1967). All the intelligence reports quoted here are declassified documents, some drawn from John F. Kennedy's papers, others from Lyndon Johnson's. Quotes from LBJ's meetings at the White House are from declassified meeting notes taken by Jack Valenti, at the LBJ Library. Comments by William P. Bundy and Walt W. Rostow are from Ted Gittinger, ed., *The Johnson Years: A Vietnam Roundtable* (Austin, Tex., 1993). General Lewis W. Walt's quote is from his memoir *Strange War, Strange Strategy* (New York, 1970). Madame Nhu's comments are quoted in Stanley Karnow's *Vietnam* and by Roger Hilsman in his memoir *To Move a Nation*. Malcolm Browne reports advice to him in *The New Face of War*. Mac Bundy's reaction to meeting with Buddhist representatives is noted by National Security Council staff member Chester Cooper in his *The Lost Crusade: America in Vietnam* (New York, 1970).

10. PROFILE: BUDDHIST IN A SEA OF FIRE

The main source here is Thich Nhat Hanh himself, in person, in his religious talks, in periodicals reporting on his visits to the United States, and in Nhat Hanh's writings, beginning with *Lotus in a Sea of Fire*. The reverend's later religious writings also occasionally contain useful autobiographical comments, including *Being Peace* (Berkeley, Calif., 1987) and *Peace Is Every Step* (New York, 1991). Chan Khong's memoir also contains recollections of Thich Nhat Hanh.

11. PARAMETERS OF VICTORY

Colonel Summers's *On Strategy: A Critical Analysis of the Vietnam War*, was first published by the Army War College (1981) in a simple green-covered edition. It was then republished by Presidio Press (Novato, Calif.) in 1982 and rereleased on the occasion of the Persian Gulf War in 1991, suggesting quite directly the construction that has been placed on the work's original arguments. Data on the exact pace of the military deployment to South Vietnam is available from Commander in Chief Pacific and Commander U.S. Military Assistance Command Vietnam, *Report on the War in Vietnam (as of 30 June 1968)* (Washington, D.C., no date [1969])—cited hereafter as Sharp and Westmoreland. My analysis assumes that a "brigade" contains three battalions, and a "division" three brigades. Data on the engineering task of creating a South Vietnamese port system is from Major General Robert L. Ploger, *Vietnam Studies: U.S. Army Engineers, 1965–1970* (Washington, D.C., 1974). See also Lieutenant General Joseph M. Heiser, *Vietnam Studies: Logistic Support* (Washington, D.C., 1974), and Lieutenant General Dong Van Khuyen, *RVNAF Logistics* (Washington, D.C., 1980). Some material on these matters appears in *The Pentagon Papers: The Defense Department History of United States Decisionmaking in Vietnam* (Senator Mike Gravel edition, Boston, 1971). Large quantities of data on these matters, in particular on shipping to Vietnam, is contained in the records of President Johnson's National Security Council staff, primarily in the Komer-Leonhart File of the National Security File in the LBJ Library. Additional documents on the subject appear in the papers prepared for President Johnson's 1966 Guam summit with South Vietnamese leaders. Ambassador Bunker's cable, quoted here, is from the LBJ Papers.

12. WHITE WING TO PERSHING: THE FAILURE OF LARGE-UNIT WAR

The experiences of the First Cavalry Division (Airmobile) are among the best-documented aspects of America's Vietnam War. A good unit history is Shelby L. Stanton's *Anatomy of a Division* (Novato, Calif., 1987). The Ia Drang battle, though not directly the subject of this chapter, is featured in the fine history *We Were Soldiers Once . . . and Young* by General Harold G. Moore and Joseph L. Galloway (New York, 1992), and an earlier account by J. D. Coleman, *Pleiku* (New York, 1988), as well as in S. L. A. Marshall's *Battles in the Monsoon* (New York, 1966). Marshall's account spills over into the Binh Dinh events of 1966, as do those of most individuals recounting their own experiences during this time. A quintessential personal account is Robert Mason's *Chickenhawk* (New York, 1983). See also Kenneth D. Mertel's *Year of the Horse: Vietnam* (New York, 1990), and Robert W. Sisk's *Wings for the Valiant* (New York, 1991). Oral histories of "Cav" veterans throughout the period are in two volumes by Matthew Brennan, *Headhunters* (New York, 1987) and *Hunter-Killer Squadron* (Novato, Calif., 1990). An official account of the Cav's Vietnam War is General John J. Tolson's *Vietnam Studies: Airmobility, 1961–1971* (Washington, D.C., 1973). The Marine side of operations in Binh Dinh is covered by Jack Shulimson's official history, *U.S. Marines in Vietnam: An Expanding War, 1966* (Washington, D.C., 1982). Succeeding annual volumes of the marine history contain data on later years. Casualty data is from Sharp and Westmoreland, *Report on the War in Vietnam*. Interviews and other personal accounts also contributed to the story told here.

Explicit treatments of the operational concepts involved in large-unit war include Guenther Lewy, *America in Vietnam* (New York, 1978); Larry Cable, *Unholy Grail: The U.S. and the Wars in Vietnam, 1965–1968* (London, 1991); and James W. Gibson, *The Perfect War: The War We Couldn't Lose and Didn't Win* (New York, 1988). A number of statistical measures of how American large-unit operations were unable to establish predominance, as well as much else, are displayed in Thomas C. Thayer's *War Without Fronts: The American Experience in Vietnam* (Boulder, Colo., 1985). Discussions by authorities of how the Pentagon established that in fact the Viet Cong and the North Vietnamese Army were selecting which battles to fight and which to avoid appear in the *Pentagon Papers* and in Alain C. Enthoven and K. Wayne Smith, *How Much Is Enough* (New York, 1971).

13. WAR OF NUMBERS: WESTMORELAND CASE REPRISE

The issues in litigation in the *Westmoreland v. CBS* case arose from Columbia Broadcasting System's documentary report *The Uncounted Enemy: A Vietnam Deception*, produced by George Crile and reported by Mike Wallace. A biography of the general is Samuel Zaffiri's *Westmoreland* (New York, 1994). The account by CIA officer Sam Adams is his *War of Numbers: An Intelligence Memoir* (South Royalton, Vt., 1994). Adams originally went public with his charges in the article "Vietnam Coverup: Playing War with Numbers," published in *Harper's*, May 1975. The allegations became the subject of congressional hearings through the fall and winter of 1975; see U.S. Congress (94/1) House Select Committee on Intelligence, *Hearings: U.S. Intelligence Agencies and Activities: The Performance of the Intelligence Community*, Parts 2 and 5 (Washington, D.C., 1975). The Wheeler cable is quoted from Sam Adams's book, Westy's "light at the end of the tunnel" speech from the *New York Times*, November 22, 1967. General Phillip Davidson's account is in his *Secrets of the Vietnam War* (Novato, Calif., 1990). The Carver cable is quoted from Adams's *War of Numbers*, as is Ludwell Montague of the CIA Board of National Estimates. The MACV briefing is quoted from the original document in the LBJ Papers, as is the comment in a memo by William P. Bundy. The best overall account of the legal case and Westmoreland suit is in Bob Brewin and Sydney Shaw, *Vietnam on Trial: Westmoreland vs CBS* (New York, 1987).

14. WHAT SURPRISE? WHOSE PREDICTION? INTELLIGENCE AT TET

General Graham is quoted from the same 1975 congressional hearings that considered Sam Adams's "war of numbers" charges. Phillip Davidson recounts his Tet in *Vietnam at War: The History 1946–1975* (Novato, Calif., 1988). Westmoreland's speech is quoted from the *New York Times*, November 22, 1967. Don Oberdorfer's "Psychological Strategy Committee" identification is given in his book *Tet!* (Garden City, N.Y., 1971). Westmoreland's press conference is quoted from his papers, housed at the LBJ Library. The NVA B-3 Front Directive is quoted from a translation in the LBJ Papers, as is the Vien notebook. Herbert Y. Schandler's account is *The Unmaking of a President: Lyndon Johnson and Vietnam* (Princeton, 1977). The CIA analysis of late November is reprinted in Walt W. Rostow's book *The Diffusion of Power, 1957–1972* (New York, 1972). All Westmoreland cables and MACV J-2 reports cited are quoted from the original documents in the LBJ papers, and the Daniel Graham account in 1982 is from an oral history he gave to LBJ Library interviewers. General Weyand is quoted by Graham in the same place. A useful study of Hanoi's intentions is that by Ronnie E. Ford, "Tet Revisited: The Strategy of the Communist Vietnamese" (*Intelligence and National Security*, vol. 9, no. 2, April 1994). A full-length treatment of the subject is in James J. Wirtz, *The Tet Offensive: Intelligence Failure in War* (Ithaca, 1991). For a dissenting view, see Thomas L. Cubbage's review of the Wirtz book in *Conflict Quarterly* (vol. 13, no. 3, Summer 1993). See also Cubbage's paper "Intelligence and the Tet Offensive: The South Vietnamese View of the Threat" in *The Vietnam War as History*, edited by Elizabeth J. Errington and B. J. C. McKerchner (New York, 1990). A South Vietnamese commentator approaches the subject directly in Hoang Ngoc Lung's *Indochina Monographs on Intelligence* (U.S. Army Center for Military History, 1982), and *The General Offensives of 1968–69 (Ibid.,* 1981). A more recent statement of my own view is contained in "The Warning That Left Something to Chance: Intelligence at Tet," in the *Journal of American-East Asian Relations* (vol. 2, no. 2, Summer 1993). For a personal view of a MACV intelligence officer describing how the American command center at Tan Son Nhut was physically taken by surprise the night of Tet, and how it responded, see Bruce E. Jones, *War Without Windows* (New York, 1987).

15. TET!

The best overall account of the Tet offensive is in Don Oberdorfer's *Tet!* which also includes a fine study of the assault on the Saigon embassy. Additional details are provided by Peter Braestrup in his *The Big Story* (Boulder, Colo., 1977), which charges the press with responsibility for the adverse political impact of Tet in the U.S. Westmoreland's account can be read in his memoir *A Soldier Reports* (Garden City, N.Y., 1976). See also Davidson, *Vietnam at War*, and Hoang Ngoc Lung *The General Offensives of 1968–69*. The South Vietnamese Joint General Staff published a town-by-town account of the fighting in *The Viet Cong Tet Offensive*, edited by Pham Van Son and Le Van Duong (Saigon, 1968). A personal account of the defense of the MACV headquarters is in Jones, *War Without Windows*. The Army historical pamphlet series *Vietnam Studies* was also used in this chapter, as were interviews. Ambassador Bunker's cable is quoted from the original document in the LBJ papers.

16. RED TIDE AT NIGHT

A full-length account of the battle for Hue is Keith W. Nolan's *Battle for Hue: Tet 1968* (Novato, Calif., 1983). Most of the sources cited in the last chapter also contain material on this subject. Especially useful material can be found in the series of daily memoranda to President Johnson written by General Earle Wheeler on the basis of his telephone conversations with General Westmoreland. The MACV staff's notes of Westmoreland's phone conversations within Vietnam also have relevant data. Both sources are located at the LBJ Library, the first in the Johnson papers (NSC Histories series), the latter in the Westmoreland papers (Fonecon series). The intelligence report is quoted from the original document in the LBJ papers (Vietnam Country File, folders of "CDEC Bulletins"). The Westmoreland cable is quoted from the document in the Johnson NSC Histories. The *MACV Command History: 1968, vol. I* (U.S. Army Center for Military History) contains a summary of the battle. Articles with additional information include Michael D. Harkins, "Storming the Citadel," *Vietnam* Magazine (vol. 2, no. 5, February 1990); Richard S. Sweet, "Blocking the NVA Retreat" (*Ibid.*, vol. 5, no. 5, January 1993); and David Novak with Marian Faye Novak, "Back to Hue," *Naval History* (vol. 7, no. 3, September–October 1993). North Vietnamese accounts can be found in Nguyen Khan Vien, ed., *Hue: Past and Present* (Hanoi, 1973); and H. Linh's "The Battle of Hue," in Vien, ed., *Face to Face with U.S. Armed Forces, II* (Hanoi, no date [c. 1977]).

17. NO DAMNED DINBINPHOO! KHE SANH AND THE U.S. HIGH COMMAND

I believe I do not exaggerate in saying that the best single source on the battle of Khe Sanh is Ray W. Stubbe's and my book, *Valley of Decision: The Siege of Khe Sanh* (Boston, 1991). See also Robert Pisor, *The End of the Line* (New York, 1982), and David B. Stockwell, *Tanks in the Wire* (New York, 1990). The Marine Corps has an official monograph on the battle in Moyers S. Shore, *The Battle for Khe Sanh* (Washington, D.C., 1969). For air operations, see Bernard C. Nalty, *Airpower and the Fight for Khe Sanh*. Fine first-person accounts include Richard D. Camp, Jr., with Eric Hammel, *Lima-6* (New York, 1989), and Ernest Spencer's *Welcome to Vietnam Macho Man* (1987). A collection of oral histories on the subject is Eric Hammel's *Khe Sanh: Siege Above the Clouds* (New York, 1989). A journalist's fine account is Michael Herr's *Dispatches* (New York, 1977). Westmoreland is quoted from his memoir *A Soldier Reports*. The *Report on the War in Vietnam* from Admiral Sharp and General Westmoreland is also quoted. All Rostow memos and MACV cables are quoted from the original documents in the LBJ papers, as is the JCS memorandum of February 29, 1968, and the Wheeler memorandum of February 3, the various Maxwell Taylor missives to President Johnson, and the CIA report of March 13. One Taylor quote is from his memoir *Swords and Plowshares* (New York, 1972).

18. PROFILE: TIM BROWN'S VIETNAM

Material in this chapter comes essentially from interviews. An account of the battle for Ngok Tavak is in Hardy Z. Bogue, "The Fall of Ngok Tavak," *Vietnam* Magazine (vol. 5, no. 2, August 1992). The best account yet published on the battle of Kham Duc appears in Ronald Spector's book *After Tet: The Bloodiest Year in Vietnam* (New York, 1993).

19. VICTORY THROUGH AIR POWER

The air force has yet to release its official volumes on the air campaigns in North Vietnam and Laos after 1968, while at last news the navy had yet to finish compiling its companion volume covering Rolling Thunder. Critics of the campaign start with Admiral U.S. Grant Sharp, who is quoted here from his memoir *Strategy for Defeat—Vietnam in Retrospect* (San Rafael, Calif., 1978). The Joint Chiefs of Staff are quoted from a memorandum in the Lyndon Johnson papers. Department of Defense goals for the campaign from John McNaughton are quoted from the *New York Times* edition of the *Pentagon Papers* (New York, 1971). The important review of the bombing by Mark Clodfelter is in his *The Limits of Airpower* (New York, 1989). The perspective of a key American air commander is General William W. Momyer's *Airpower in Three Wars* (Washington, D.C., 1978). Momyer has also provided a useful analysis of the South Vietnamese air force in *The Vietnamese Air Force, 1951–1975* (USAF Southeast Asia Monograph no. 4, 1975). The best contemporary compilation on the subject is Raphael Littauer and Norman Uphoff, eds., *The Air War in Indochina*, rev. ed. (Boston, 1972). A retrospective case study is James C. Thompson's *Rolling Thunder: Understanding Policy and Program Failure* (Chapel Hill, 1980). Finally, an overview of the later period is provided by John Morrocco, ed., *The Vietnam Experience: Rain of Fire: Air War, 1969–1973* (Boston, 1984). A vision of the air war that is part memoir and part analysis is Earl H. Tilford, Jr.'s *Setup: What the Air Force Did in Vietnam and Why* (Maxwell Air Force Base, 1991), a book which has since been republished by Texas A&M Press.

20. SPOOKS IN THE ETHER

Except for brief mentions in any number of works, there is almost no literature on communications intelligence in the Vietnam War. Despite the importance of the method and the contributions of communications intelligence, almost all material on the subject remains classified. This chapter is chiefly based on an initial tranche of material obtained under the Freedom of Information Act. Less detailed but still informative material can be found in the official history by John D. Bergen, *The U.S. Army in Vietnam: Military Communications: A Test for Technology* (Washington, D.C., 1986). The Vietnamese side is represented by Le Dinh Y et al., *Essential Matters: A History of the Cryptographic Branch of the People's Army of Vietnam, 1945–1975* (Hanoi, 1990, translated and edited by David W. Gaddy; translation published by the Center for Cryptologic History, National Security Agency, 1994). Articles on aspects of the subject include Don E. Gordon, "Private Minnock's Private War" (*International Journal of Intelligence and Counterintelligence*, vol. 4, no. 2, no date [fall 1990]); and William E. LeGro, "The Enemy's Jungle Cover Was No Match for the Finding Capabilities of the Army's Radio Research Units," *Vietnam* Magazine (vol. 3, no. 1, June 1990). The CIA officer quoted on Tet is Sam Adams from his *War of Numbers*. Some items in this chapter are also drawn from interviews.

21. PHOENIX: THE WAR AGAINST THE VIET CONG APPARAT

Material on pacification in general, and Phoenix in particular, has proliferated since the war, in which pacification was held to be a central element of strategy. For views from the top, see the works of William E. Colby previously cited, as well as Robert W. Komer, *Bureaucracy at War: U.S. Performance in the Vietnam Conflict* (Boulder, Colo., 1986). An official account of the period up to 1968 is in Thomas W. Scoville, *Reorganizing for Pacification Support* (Washington, D.C.,

1982). A fine study of the role of individuals in the pacification program is Neil Sheehan's *A Bright Shining Lie: John Paul Vann and America in Vietnam* (New York, 1988). For a CIA view see Orrin DeForest and David Chanoff, *Slow Burn: The Rise and Bitter Fall of American Intelligence in Vietnam* (New York, 1990). Several memoirs by American pacification advisers also inform this chapter. These include Thomas Carhart, *The Offering* (New York, 1987); John L. Cook, *The Advisor* (Philadelphia, 1973); and Stuart A. Herrington, *Silence Was a Weapon: The Vietnam War in the Villages* (Novato, Calif., 1982). William R. Corson recounts his novel pacification tactics in *The Betrayal* (New York, 1968). The Marine Corps has an official monograph on its Combined Action Program, and there is additional data in the annual volumes of its official history. A classic study of pacification at the province level is Jeffrey Race's *War Comes to Long An* (Berkeley, Calif., 1972). A history of security conditions in an adjoining province is Eric M. Bergerud's *The Dynamics of Defeat: The Vietnam War in Hau Nghia Province* (Boulder, Colo., 1991). A similar history of conditions in a village near Hue is in James W. Trullinger, *Village at War: An Account of Conflict in Vietnam* (Stanford, Calif., 1980). Sources on the maladaptation of the American military for pacification include Larry E. Cable, *Conflict of Myths: The Development of American Counterinsurgency Doctrine and the Vietnam War* (New York, 1986), and Andrew F. Krepinevich, Jr., *The Army and Vietnam* (Baltimore, 1986). In recent years some books have focused specifically on the Phoenix program, including Dale Andradé, *Ashes to Ashes: The Phoenix Program and the Vietnam War* (Lexington, Mass., 1990), and Douglas Valentine, *The Phoenix Program* (New York, 1990). Each of these latter studies has the virtue of the other's defect: the Valentine book uses few documentary sources but seems to have interviewed most of the key players involved in Phoenix (note that some former officials disavow their quoted comments), while the Andradé volume is replete with documentary sources but relies upon them to such an extent that the reader has to remind himself how self-serving were many of the reports written in Vietnam. Respective conclusions remind one of John F. Kennedy's questioning of two American officials early in the war as to whether they had visited the same country. A significant Vietnamese view from the villages themselves is Le Ly Haislip with Jay Wurts, *When Heaven and Earth Changed Places* (Garden City, N.Y., 1989). For what it is worth, the documentary record has recently been enriched to a great degree by the opening at the LBJ Library of the Komer-Leonhart series of the National Security File in Johnson's papers, which specifically centers on pacification issues. National Security Study Memorandum No. 1 is quoted from the original text, leaked and reprinted in the *Congressional Record*, May 10 and 11, 1972. North Vietnamese officers and officials are quoted in Stanley Karnow, *Vietnam: A History*.

22. LITTLE WORLD, BIG WAR

The title here is a play on Oden Meeker's *The Little World of Laos* (New York, 1959). An excellent scholarly treatment of the conflict is Timothy N. Castle, *At War in the Shadow of Vietnam: U.S. Military Aid to the Royal Lao Government, 1955–1975* (New York, 1993). Older standard sources include Arthur J. Dommen, *Conflict in Laos* (New York, 1964, 1971); Hugh Toye, *Laos: Buffer State or Battleground* (New York, 1971); Nina S. Adams and Alfred W. McCoy, eds., *Laos: War and Revolution* (New York, 1970); and Charles A. Stevenson, *The End of*

Nowhere: American Policy Toward Laos Since 1954 (Boston, 1972). On the early period, see Bernard B. Fall, *Anatomy of a Crisis: The Laotian Crisis of 1960–1961* (Garden City, N.Y., 1969). On the Pathet Lao, see Paul F. Langer and Joseph J. Zasloff, *North Vietnam and the Pathet Lao* (Cambridge, Mass., 1970), and Joseph J. Zasloff, *The Pathet Lao: Leadership and Organization* (Lexington, Mass., 1973). Views of a former U.S. ambassador are in William H. Sullivan, *Obbligato: Notes on a Foreign Service Center* (New York, 1984). For CIA perspectives, see the writings of former station chiefs; Douglas S. Blaufarb, *The Counterinsurgency Era* (New York, 1977), and Theodore Shackley, *The Third Option* (New York, 1981). For a biography of Shackley, see David Corn, *Blond Ghost: Ted Shackley and the CIA's Crusades* (New York, 1994). On the upland tribes in general, see Peter Kunstadter, ed., *Southeast Asian Tribes, Minorities and Nations* (Princeton, 1967), and the U.S. Army area handbooks on Laos (editions of 1965 and 1972) and on Minority Groups of North Vietnam (1972). For a Hmong voice, see Jane Hamilton-Merritt, *Tragic Mountains: The Hmong, the Americans, and the Secret Wars for Laos, 1942–1972* (Bloomington, Ind., 1993). For the role of the CIA proprietary Air America, see Christopher Robbins, *Air America* (New York, 1979), and William M. Leary, *Perilous Missions: Civil Air Transport and CIA Covert Operations in Asia* (University, Ala., 1984). Robbins also has an account of American forward air controllers working with the Hmong, *The Ravens: The Men Who Flew in America's Secret War in Laos* (New York, 1987). On the experiences of the Lao people under U.S. bombing, see Fred Branfman, *Voices from the Plain of Jars* (New York, 1972). For the bombing itself, consult Jacob Van Staaveren, *The United States Air Force in Southeast Asia: Interdiction in Southern Laos 1960–1968* (Washington, D.C., 1993). A no-holds-barred look at the difficulties of search and rescue is in Earl H. Tilford's *Search and Rescue in Southeast Asia 1961–1975* (Washington, D.C., 1980). A "perfect strategy" that involved sealing off the Laotian panhandle is offered by Norman B. Hannah in *The Key to Failure: Laos and the Vietnam War* (Lanham, Md., 1987). The 1959 SNIE is quoted from the original document, obtained under the Freedom of Information Act; the 1962 SNIE is also quoted from the original, located at the John F. Kennedy Presidential Library. Secretary of State Herter is quoted from General Andrew Goodpaster's record of the meeting located in the Staff Secretary subseries of the White House Office collection at the Dwight D. Eisenhower Presidential Library. Richard Nixon's assurance is from the president's official statement on the war in Laos, printed in the *New York Times*, March 7, 1970. A perspective on the Laotian armed forces is offered in General Oudone Sananikone's *The Royal Lao Army and United States Army Advice and Support* (Washington, D.C., 1980).

23. WIDENING THE WAR: CAMBODIA 1970

Quotes on the intelligence dispute over North Vietnamese use of Cambodian ports are taken from NSSM-1. A published source that covers this debate in some detail is Thomas Powers, *The Man Who Kept the Secrets: Richard Helms and the CIA* (New York, 1979). An Army Indochina Monograph covers the invasion itself: General Tran Dinh Tho's *The Cambodian Incursion* (Washington, D.C., 1979). For American accounts, see J. D. Coleman, *Incursion* (New York, 1991); Shelby Stanton, *Anatomy of a Division*; and General Donn A. Starry, *Vietnam Studies: Mounted Combat in Vietnam* (Washington, D.C., 1978). Sihanouk's account is in

My War with the CIA: The Memoirs of Prince Norodom Sihanouk as Told to Wil-fred Burchett (New York, 1973). General Westmoreland's cable is quoted from William Shawcross, *Sideshow: Kissinger, Nixon and the Destruction of Cambodia* (New York, 1979). Some material in this chapter also came from interviews. Shawcross goes on to cover subsequent events up to the fall of Cambodia; a Cambodian military view of the same period can be found in General Sak Sutsakhan's *The Khmer Republic at War and the Final Collapse* (Washington, D.C., 1980). There is a substantial literature on the Khmer Rouge and their depredations in Cambodia during and after the war.

24. LAOS 1971: NO PLUG IN THE FUNNEL

The most accessible source on the operation into Laos is Keith W. Nolan's *Into Laos: The Story of Dewey Canyon II/Lam Son 719* (Novato, Calif., 1986). A Vietnamese view is General Nguyen Duy Hinh's *Lam Son 719* (Washington, D.C., 1979). Neither work covers the origins of the invasion especially well; it is reconstructed here from documents in the Nixon Library Project of the National Archives as well as a variety of memoirs. Henry Kissinger quotes are from his *White House Years* (Boston, 1979). Richard Nixon's diary is quoted from his *RN: The Memoirs of Richard Nixon*, vol. 1. U. Alexis Johnson is quoted from his memoir with Jef O. McAlister, *The Right Hand of Power* (Englewood Cliffs, N.J., 1984). Admiral Thomas Moorer is quoted in the *New York Times*, December 27, 1970. Opinions on the effect of the invasion are drawn from Kissinger; from Phillip Davidson's *Vietnam at War*; from Colonel Do Ngoc Nhan's "Initiative in the Vietnam War" (*Military Review*, August 1972); and from Richard Nixon's later book *No More Vietnams* (New York, 1985). The opinion quoted concerning helicopter operations is General William Momyer's in his *The Vietnamese Air Force, 1951–1975*. Statistics on various equipment claimed captured is drawn from *Vietnam Bulletin*, a biweekly publication of the Republic of Vietnam Embassy in Washington, D.C.

25. ONE MORE OPTION TO TRY: THE MINING OF HAIPHONG HARBOR

There are few general sources on the North Vietnamese offensive of 1972. The two best known cover only portions of the fighting in I Corps. These are Colonel George H. Turley's *The Easter Offensive: The Last American Advisors in Vietnam, 1972* (Novato, Calif., 1985), and John G. Miller, *The Bridge at Dong Ha* (Annapolis, 1985). No monograph exists on the mining of Haiphong, though naval historian Edward Marolda has written a study of the sweeping of those mines after the Paris Peace Agreement of January 1973. My account has been constructed from a variety of sources, including CIA reports, translations from the North Vietnamese press by the Joint Publications Research Service, periodical coverage, and congressional hearings. Melvin Laird's statement of February 1972 is from testimony before the House Armed Services Committee (92nd Congress, 2nd session, on the Fiscal Year 1973 budget). General John Vogt, as well as a later comment to Laird by Admiral Moorer, are from Admiral Elmo R. Zumwalt, Jr., *On Watch* (New York, 1976). Kissinger is quoted from his *White House Years*. Walt Rostow's memorandum of May 6, 1967, is at the LBJ Library. Clark Clifford's statements are from his appearances before the Senate Armed Services Committee (90th Congress, 2nd session, on the Fiscal Year 1969 budget, respectively from parts 4 and 5); the Robert McNamara quote is from testimony before the Senate Appropriations Committee (90th Congress, 1st session, Fiscal Year 1968). Laird's news conference statement is from a text printed in the *New York Times*, May 11, 1972, and Nixon's declaration at the Connally Ranch is from the same source on May 1. The Nixon note to Kissinger is quoted from *RN: The Memoirs of Richard Nixon*. Alex Johnson's comment on the NSC meeting is from his memoir *The Right Hand of Power*. Nixon's letter to Nguyen Van Thieu is reprinted in Nguyen Tien Hung and Jerrold L. Schechter, *The Palace File* (New York, 1986). Richard Nixon's speech on the mining is quoted from the *New York Times*, May 9, 1972. The sailor's comment off the North Vietnamese coast is quoted in Donald Kirk's "Banging Holes in the Land," *New York Times Sunday Magazine*, June 4, 1972. Menus in Hanoi restaurants are described by Robert Shaplen, "Letter from Hanoi," *New Yorker*, August 12, 1972.

26. PROFILE: GEORGE CARVER (II)

Kissinger's rendition of George Carver's view is in *White House Years*; Tad Szulc's is in his *The Illusion of Peace: Foreign Policy in the Nixon Years* (New York, 1978). Carver's own articles are "The Real Revolution in South Viet Nam" (*Foreign Affairs*, April 1965), and "The Faceless Viet Cong" (*Foreign Affairs*, April 1966). Hoang Van Chi's book is *From Colonialism to Communism* (New York, 1964). Carver's interview with Thomas Powers is used by that author in his *The Man Who Kept the Secrets*, as were later cited comments about Carver from CIA colleagues. David Halberstam is quoted from *The Best and the Brightest*. Frank Snepp recounts the 1975 episode in his book *Decent Interval* (New York, 1977).

27. THE VETERANS' ANTIWAR MOVEMENT UNDER SIEGE: MIAMI AND GAINESVILLE

This chapter is largely constructed from interviews. The Vietnam Veterans Against the War are mentioned in virtually every account of the antiwar movement but seldom receive detailed treatment, and most of what there is stops with the Dewey Canyon III demonstration, which received considerable attention. The two histories that offer the most coverage are Charles DeBenedetti (assisted by Charles Chatfield), *An American Ordeal: The Antiwar Movement of the Vietnam Era* (Syracuse, N.Y., 1990), and Tom Wells, *The War Within: America's Battle over Vietnam* (Berkeley, Calif., 1994). The organization of antiwar veterans is of some interest to Gloria Emerson in her *Winners and Losers* (New York, 1976), and a subject of special interest to Robert Jay Lifton in *Home from the War: Learning from Vietnam Veterans* (Boston, 1973), though the latter does not deal with the VVAW actions at issue in this chapter. On the Lemmer case, a published source is Frank Donner's "Confessions of an FBI Informer," *Atlantic*, December 1972. John Kifner of the *New York Times* also wrote on Lemmer (August 14, 1972) and provided that paper with substantial coverage of the Gainesville trial itself. The veteran's comment during VVAW's silent march in Miami is taken from the *Washington Post*, August 22, 1973. Richard Nixon is quoted from his memoir *RN*. All other quotes are from interviews.

Index

Vietnamese and Laotian personal names consist of three elements, the family name being the first. Names in this index are alphabetized by family name—thus, for example, Ngo Dinh Diem. Many individuals frequently referred to are cross-indexed for convenience.

A NOTE ON THE AUTHOR

John Prados was born in New York City and studied history and international relations at Columbia University,
where he earned a Ph.D. in political science. There he
worked with nuclear expert Warner R. Schilling and international theorist William T. R. Fox, the man who
coined the term "superpower." Since the 1970s Mr. Prados has been a designer of combat models and a leading
historian of national security affairs, intelligence operations, and international security concerns. He is the in-
ventor of more than two dozen board strategy games and
author of many articles. *The Hidden History of the Vietnam War* is his eighth book. His earlier books on Vietnam include *Valley of Decision: The Siege of Khe Sanh*
(with Ray W. Stubbe), named a notable book by the U.S.
Naval Institute, and *The Sky Would Fall: The Secret U.S.
Bombing Mission to Vietnam, 1954*. Several of Mr. Prados's books and games have been awarded prizes by professional associations. He lives in Washington, D.C.